The history of the earthly Jesus

is the story of the eternal Word

brought into the fallen world

and put at its mercy (Mark 14:41).

In the same way, God's investment

in the words of Scripture

means that in the short term,

in their own journey into the world,

the divine words are subject to a

similar submission to and separation

from their heavenly speaker,

and a similar surrender to sinful speakers,

hearers and readers. . . .

In delivering [the Bible] to the world,

God makes his words vulnerable,

for a time, to abuse.

Telford Work,
Living and Active: Scripture in the Economy of Salvation

Manfred T. Brauch

ABUSING SCRIPTURE

THE CONSEQUENCES OF
MISREADING THE BIBLE

IVP Academic

An imprint of InterVarsity Press
Downers Grove, Illinois

InterVarsity Press
P.O. Box 1400, Downers Grove, IL 60515-1426
World Wide Web: www.ivpress.com
E-mail: email@ivpress.com

InterVarsity Press ® *is the book-publishing division of InterVarsity Christian Fellowship/USA* ®, *a student movement active on campus at hundreds of universities, colleges and schools of nursing in the United States of America, and a member movement of the International Fellowship of Evangelical Students. For information about local and regional activities, write Public Relations Dept., InterVarsity Christian Fellowship/USA, 6400 Schroeder Rd., P.O. Box 7895, Madison, WI 53707-7895, or visit the IVCF website at <www.intervarsity.org>.*

Scripture quotations, unless otherwise noted, are from the New Revised Standard Version of the Bible, *copyright 1989 by the Division of Christian Education of the National Council of the Churches of Christ in the USA. Used by permission. All rights reserved.*

Design: Cindy Kiple

Images: John Lund/Tiffany Schoepp/Getty Images

ISBN 978-0-8308-2579-0

Printed in the United States of America ∞

Library of Congress Cataloging-in-Publication Data

Brauch, Manfred T.
  Abusing Scripture: the consequences of misreading the Bible /
  Manfred Theophil Brauch.
      p. cm.
  Includes bibliographical references (p.   ).
  ISBN 978-0-8308-2579-0 (pbk.: alk. paper)
  1. Bible—Hermeneutics. 2. Bible—Use. I. Title.
  BS476.B589 2009
  220.601—dc22

                                                                                                2008054475

P	21	20	19	18	17	16	15	14	13	12	11	10	9	8	7	6	5	4	3	2
Y	27	26	25	24	23	22	21	20	19	18	17	16	15	14	13	12	11	10	09		

For Gregory, Tonya and Christopher,

whose serious and honest questions about the Christian faith

have always challenged me to be a trustworthy and honest interpreter

of the meaning and message of Scripture, the foundation of our faith.

CONTENTS

PREFACE

We live in a world characterized by abuse: in personal lives marked by substance abuse; in marriages and families distorted by physical and emotional abuse; within human social structures where prejudice, bigotry, and ethnic and racial strife reign; in cultural realities such as over-under power structures in gender relationships and in the diminution of the sanctity of human life; in international conflicts marked by violence and oppression; in economic exploitation grounded in greed and quest for power, resulting in injustice, inequity, and the impoverishment of the lower economic classes.

Christians believe that there is another reality, another story, in and through which our broken, abuse-ridden human story is addressed—with the goal of liberation from its bondage to decay, sin, death, distortion and alienation. We believe that we have been given—by divine inspiration—a record of that other story in Scripture. We affirm it as the Word of God, because we are convinced—together with Jesus and his earliest disciples and the vast majority of the Christian church throughout the past two thousand years—that God has acted and spoken redemptively:

through the creation of a covenant community in which God's steadfast love and faithfulness was at work, shaping a people to be a light to the nations; through God's servants the prophets, calling Israel and the nations—in the midst of their brokenness—back to God's ways of righteousness, justice and peace; through the revolutionary life of Jesus and his challenging, countercultural teaching about the in-breaking of the reign of God's transforming love, his redemptive death on the cross and his victorious resurrection; through the Spirit-empowered community of Jesus' disciples, an emerging new humanity intended to be God's alternative to the brokenness of human life and society, called to embody the values and character of God's kingly reign in human affairs.

This story of God's liberating and redemptive acting and speaking—which we call gospel, the evangel, the good news—this story that has transformed countless distorted human stories, that has been told and lived by transformed individuals and communities for over two thousand years, is increasingly under siege in our time. It is actively opposed in the academy; it is marginalized and ignored in secular political agendas, policies and programs; it is selectively used in support of political ideologies on the left and the right; it is caricatured and misrepresented in the media; and it is trivialized and mocked in the arts. As a result, this abused world—which our redemptive, liberating story seeks to address and transform—sinks ever more into its abuse.

Why? Why is "the greatest story ever told" increasingly falling on deaf ears, particularly in the northern and western hemispheres? Many and diverse causes lie at the root of this state of affairs. Chief among them has been the worldview of scientific naturalism and its rejection of the transcendent, a worldview that has become increasingly pervasive and dominant in the past two centuries. More recently, postmodernism has made its contribution. Its rejection of any notion of absolutes and its contention that there is no such thing as a metastory (such as a Christian worldview) that informs all microstories means that the great variety of cultural values and belief systems all have equal standing. But much of the blame for the diminution of the Christian voice in contemporary society must be placed at the feet of the Christian community itself, which throughout its history has frequently told the story badly, lived it brokenly and distorted it terribly.

This reality is expressed in such events as the medieval crusades, where cross and sword marched hand in hand, followed by centuries of pogroms by Christian communities (especially against the Jewish people), the witch hunts and inquisitions and torture chambers, the persecution and execution of Anabaptist leaders by other reformers in Switzerland, the often-brutal colonization and forced Christianization of native populations, the continuing divisions within the worldwide Christian movement, the often mean-spirited and acrimonious doctrinal and ethical battles within Christian communions, and the very public sexual and financial scandals involving Christian leaders and organizations.

All these and more are evidence of brokenness within our ranks, and they are contributing factors to reasons why the good news falls on deaf ears in our time. But at the core of these broken realities within Christian faith and life there lies a fundamental problem, which I identify as "the abuse of Scripture." It consists of interpreting and applying biblical texts in ways that distort their meaning and message, thereby undermining the veracity and vitality of Christian witness and presence in the world, and thus contributing to the distorted reality of abuse within it.

It is the burden of this book to articulate this intimate relationship between the abuse of the Bible and abuse in the church and in the world, to point beyond it toward a better way, and to challenge all those who affirm the inspiration and authority of Scripture to increasingly participate in this better way.

Manfred T. Brauch
Easter 2008

ACKNOWLEDGMENTS

I wish to express deep gratitude:

To Marjean, for her faithful and effective partnership with me in the work of the gospel, expressed in her love and care for her patients in the practice of medicine; for her steadfast encouragement and support in my work in theological education; and for her patience and long-suffering during my lengthy absences in the study for research and writing.

To Christian friends at Carey Baptist College in Auckland and throughout New Zealand, whose generosity and gracious hospitality provided the opportunity to first explore the theme of the abuse of Scripture, and who enthusiastically encouraged me to keep at it.

To Randy Frame, my longtime colleague at Palmer Theological Seminary, who persuaded me to undertake this project and gave both stimulating and invaluable counsel regarding the content and direction of this study.

To Joel Scandrett, my editor at InterVarsity Press, for clear and steady guidance, invaluable advice, astute critical observations, and necessary cautions when my passions unduly overpowered considered judgment. And, above all, for his gracious encouragement and enthusiastic affirmation of my work.

To the members of the Academy of St. John at Mt. Pleasant Presbyterian Church, who allowed me to test out on them some of the ideas in this book during its formative stages. They received them enthusiastically and gave helpful feedback.

And to the many students that I've had in over three decades, whom I've had the privilege of leading into the pages of Scripture and whose challenging questions during their journey through Scripture often caused me to see Scripture more clearly and to interpret it more faithfully.

INTRODUCTION

I have a deep concern. It is about the integrity and viability of our Christian witness in today's world, a witness that is frequently undermined and distorted by the abuse of Scripture. By "Scripture abuse" I mean interpreting and applying the Bible in questionable or irresponsible ways. For example, when we interpret a text without proper regard for its literary or historical context in order to justify a particular theological position, or when we apply Scripture to a current political issue in a way that it was never intended to be applied, we abuse Scripture.

I very deliberately chose the term *abuse* to point to the serious nature of misreading the Bible. I am well aware that the word *abuse* conjures up the terrible images of children burned, beaten and neglected, or of women battered, verbally demolished and psychologically scarred. In light of these images, my use of the word is an intentional decision to drive home the point that abuse—in the sense of "doing violence to"—is precisely what happens when Scripture is misinterpreted and misused: violence is done to its message and meaning. Victims of physical abuse are often beaten so severely that their true identities are unrecognizable, or they are scarred so deeply in their psyches or spirits that their true selves cannot emerge. Similarly, this is what happens when we misinterpret and misapply Scripture. The meaning and message of Scripture becomes obscured, its authentic nature cannot easily be recognized, it is not allowed to speak its deepest truths, and its voice is muted, throttled or silenced.

Abuse can be both intentional and unintentional. Much of what I identify throughout this study as the abusive reading and application of Scripture is not the result of deliberate, intentional abuse for the purpose of manipulation or control. These unintentional abuses are often the result of letting our backgrounds, preconceptions, or biases influence and control the way we read and apply Scripture. The analogy of abuse in human relationships is instructive here. The abuser in a parent-child relationship, or in a spousal relationship, can often be totally oblivious to the fact that he or she is committing abuse. This is especially true in cases of excessive preoccupation with work (or even ministry!) that can result in the abuse of neglect; or through the learned patterns of communication from one's family of origin, a child or a spouse may be put down, marginalized or demeaned; or abuse may occur when, through (superior) rational argumentation, the feelings and emotions of the other are unwittingly silenced, their voices not heard and their gifts ignored. However, whether in relationships or in the reading and application of the Bible, abuse is abuse, whether inflicted intentionally or unintentionally.

I am particularly concerned about the abuse of Scripture within the tradition of the Christian faith that upholds the Bible as the unique Word of God and affirms its divine inspiration and authority. This tradition, which is generally identified as evangelical and of which I consider myself a part, transcends denominational and confessional boundaries. It seeks to honor the text of Scripture, claiming it as the irreducible foundation of the faith "once for all entrusted to the saints" (Jude 3). Nevertheless, on a regular basis, in our interpretation and application of the Bible, we grievously abuse Scripture; we do violence to its message and meaning.

Why am I focusing primary attention on the abuse of Scripture within this tradition? Because I believe that such a commitment to Scripture's inspiration and authority calls us to a much higher level of accountability with regard to trustworthy interpretation than a view of Scripture that does not affirm its divine inspiration and authority in the same way or to the same extent. Thus when the content of Scripture is seen to primarily be inspired human thinking and believing, or the collected faith traditions of particular faith communities, all kinds of interpretations of the biblical texts become possible and can be legitimized as consistent with such understandings of the Bible.

A good example is the use of a Marxist understanding of social constructs and economic realities as a grid through which to interpret biblical texts in some liberation theologies. Similarly, a radical feminist perspective can legitimize its rejection of the Bible's understanding of the distorted Creator-creature relationship and God's redemptive, atoning work in Christ because it sees the Bible as reflecting ancient cultural concerns about appeasing angry gods through sacrificial offerings. If Scripture is not affirmed as the divinely inspired revelation of the human condition as "lost" and in need of "salvation," then those aspects of the biblical story can easily be set aside. In some liberal traditions of Christian faith, parts of Scripture are primarily understood as providing inspired human insight about God and life. They can therefore be mined for lofty, general ethical principles (such as "tolerance," "inclusion," "love") while ignoring or relativizing biblical teachings about sexual morality or the sanctity of marriage.

From the perspective of historic, orthodox, evangelical views of Scripture, such readings and uses of Scripture are clearly abusive; they distort the Bible's meaning; they do violence to its message. While from their presuppositions about the Bible these interpretations can be legitimized, they can also be critically engaged and challenged.[1]

Those who affirm the Bible as the Word of God, inspired and authoritative for Christian faith, life and presence in the world, must be true to those convictions when interpreting and applying the Word. The apostle Paul wrote that we are "servants of Christ and stewards of God's mysteries" (1 Cor 4:1). He then went on to say that "it is required of stewards that they be found trustworthy" (1 Cor 4:2). Paul was certain that "God's mysteries" had been fully disclosed in the life, death and resurrection of Jesus Christ (1 Cor 2:1;

---

[1]See, e.g., N. T. Wright, *The Last Word: Scripture and the Authority of God—Getting Beyond the Bible Wars* (San Francisco: HarperSanFrancisco, 2005), who responds to misreadings of the Bible on both the left and the right (especially pp. 106-13). Other recent examples of critical engagements with abusive interpretations on the liberal end of the theological spectrum are Timothy P. Jones, *Misquoting Truth: A Guide to the Fallacies of Barth Ehrman's Misquoting Jesus* (Downers Grove, Ill.: Inter Varsity Press, 2007); and Luke T. Johnson's *The Real Jesus: The Misguided Quest for the Historical Jesus and the Truth of the Traditional Gospels* (San Francisco: HarperSanFrancisco, 1996).

Eph 3:1-10). For us, by extension, "trustworthy stewardship" of this revealed mystery in Jesus Christ (2 Cor 4:5-6) certainly includes Scripture—that vehicle in and through which God's redemptive and transforming purpose for the world has been transmitted to us.

On the basis of commitment to trustworthiness in stewarding the whole truth of God's mysteries—beginning with the creation accounts of the Old Testament and climaxing in the vision of a redeemed creation in the book of Revelation—we must refuse, with Paul, "to practice cunning or to falsify God's word" and instead give allegiance to "the open statement of the truth" (2 Cor 4:2). This stance and commitment with regard to the interpretation and application of Scripture must characterize Christian presence and witness.

The tragedy, however, is that many who most passionately and stridently proclaim allegiance to the Bible and love for the inspired, authoritative Word of God often interpret and apply Scripture in ways that are abusive, thus distorting its meaning and message. Consequently, instead of releasing the transforming power from God and the treasure of God's Word into the world in and through the earthen vessels of our presence and witness (2 Cor 4:7), we contribute to brokenness and abusiveness in our world. How do we do that? A few examples should suffice to illustrate the serious problem of Scripture abuse.

1. We affirm that the Bible is the vehicle of the gospel, the good news of God's redemptive love. And then we use it as an instrument of bitter warfare, both within our own circles and against outsiders: we condemn, judge, malign, demean and reject. What does this say about the validity of the central message of Jesus—loving not only brothers and sisters but also neighbors and adversaries?

2. We announce that the Bible speaks the truth from God about human life and relationships, but then we undermine our commitment to that truth by using all kinds of biblical proof texts—often out of context and not in keeping with their original meaning or intent—in an effort to "prove" to those with whom we disagree that we are "on the Lord's side" and they are of the devil (or at least very wrong!). Is this attitude and practice compatible with the spirit and teaching of the Jesus of the Gospels?

3. We use biblical texts selectively to build arguments for particular theo-

logical doctrines or biblical teachings, while conveniently ignoring biblical texts that stand in tension with our views. Or we employ sophisticated (and often deceptive!) "exegetical gymnastics" to eliminate tensions between and among diverse texts, or we reinterpret texts that are inconvenient and do not support our dearly held convictions or doctrines. What does this say about integrity in the work of interpretation?

4. We invest tremendous energy and time on matters that our Lord told us were not to be our primary concern (such as timetables of the end times) and spend too little time and energy on matters that both God's prophets and our Lord, as well as his earliest followers, placed very high on their agendas—such as a passion for justice, peacemaking, concern for the poor and righteousness in human affairs. Does this not undermine our claim that the *whole* Bible is our authority?

5. In the midst of the confusing and distorting voices about human sexuality in our time, we champion Scripture's call to holy living and morality, grounded in creational intention and covenant commitment. And so we must. But at the same time we often blithely set aside or ignore the cancers eating away at the communal life and witness of our churches—such as strife, bitterness, gossip, backbiting, greed, divisiveness—all named in New Testament texts as incompatible with kingdom values (1 Cor 6:9-11; Eph 4:25-32; 5:3-5). Are we then not guilty of distorting the Bible's claim on *all areas* of human life and community?

These are examples of abuses that undermine the integrity of our Christian witness. They raise serious questions about our claim to be bearers of the truth from God. They marginalize the potential significance and impact of our proclamation of the gospel, relegating it to the backwaters of our culture's increasingly secular and neopagan mainstream.[2]

AVOIDING SCRIPTURE ABUSE

How can such abuses of Scripture and its message—both in our interpretation and application—be avoided? How can we be more trustworthy stewards of the treasure of Scripture, "rightly explaining the word of truth" (2 Tim 2:15)?

---

[2]For a contemporary analysis of negative perceptions of the Christian faith and of Christians, based on extensive research by the Barna Research Group, see David Kinnaman and Gabe Lyons, *Unchristian: What a New Generation Really Thinks About Christianity . . . and Why It Matters* (Grand Rapids: Baker Books, 2007).

My response to these questions begins with an analogy from the field of behavioral sciences, specifically from the perspective of family systems theory. Dysfunctional and abusive patterns in marital and family relationships must be identified, recognized and acknowledged before corrective intervention can begin the process of healing. In the same way, abusive interpretation and application of Scripture must be identified and acknowledged before corrective intervention can alter it. In other words, we need to be self-critical, honest and clear. We need to call a proverbial spade a spade by acknowledging the many ways in which Scripture is abused among us—wittingly or unwittingly, intentionally or unintentionally. Thus in each chapter we will focus our attention on a specific way that Scripture is commonly abused and discuss a variety of examples to illustrate each particular form of abuse. This identification and acknowledgment will be accompanied by affirmation of and reflection on guidelines and principles of interpretation—broadly recognized in Christian scholarship and biblical hermeneutics—that must be observed in our reading, study and application of God's Word. Only close and consistent attention to those guiding perspectives and principles, and their use in our study of biblical texts, will mitigate the abuse of Scripture.

As indicated in the book's title, my central concern is the reality that the abuse of Scripture, in both interpretation and application, has consequences. Some abuses of Scripture have consequences that are relatively benign. They may affect doctrinal nuances, or various Christian understandings of the end times, or relatively inconsequential theological positions, or formal-structural aspects of ecclesiastical life that are perhaps important to us "insiders" but do not, in any way, threaten essential doctrines or impact and undermine the veracity of Christian witness and presence in the world. However, there are other abuses of Scripture that have serious negative consequences, both for the health and vitality of congregational life and for the way the Christian message is heard and experienced by outsiders. These are the primary focus of this book.

In light of the central concern and primary focus articulated above, there are three matters—among several dozen that are addressed throughout this study—that emerge repeatedly, in multiple chapters, as illustrations of various kinds of abusive interpretation of biblical material. They are (1) the use and justification of force and violence in human affairs; (2) the relationship between men and women in home, church and society; and (3) the concern for justice and the sanctity of life in all areas of human relationships, institutions and culture.

There are several reasons for this. First, using a particular issue several times to illustrate various ways that Scripture is abused reveals that abusive interpretations of Scriptural texts or ideas are often interrelated and influence each other. Second, I believe that abusive interpretation and application of Scripture in these areas has had, and continues to have, very serious negative consequences for the viability of Christian witness and presence in our world. Third, abusive readings and applications of biblical material in these areas continue to shape Christians and Christian communities who, often unknowingly and unintentionally, contribute to: (a) the fallen human tendency to opt for the use of force and violence in human relationships and in national and international affairs; (b) the tragic abuse and brokenness in male-female relationships; and (c) the all-too-pervasive attitudes and actions that perpetuate injustice and the demonization of "the other" in human and social relationships and institutions. And fourth, I believe that these three broken and distorted areas of corporate human life are core areas of "the dominion of darkness" in our world, which the reign of God (kingdom of God) in Jesus' life and ministry confronts and which the followers of Jesus, individually and collectively, are called to engage and transform.

However, as important as these foci are for Christian life, presence and mission in our world, their repeated appearance throughout our study is primarily illustrative and should not distract from the issue that they, and the several dozen other examples, illustrate. Namely, that the misreading of Scripture within and by the Christian community not only calls into question the credibility of Christian proclamation and presence but contributes to the brokenness of human life.

1

THE NATURE OF SCRIPTURE

Before we plunge into the task of identifying how Scripture is abused, we must first address a fundamental issue. Namely, what is the nature of Scripture? How do we understand or define its inspiration and authority? Answers to these questions are extremely important, for they provide the assumptions and presuppositions that guide one's approach to Scripture and greatly influence the process of interpretation.

Not all Christians answer these questions in the same way. Even among those who clearly affirm the inspiration of the Bible and hold it to be the authoritative Word of God for Christian faith and life (whether or not they identify themselves as evangelicals), these questions have been answered in a variety of ways.[1] For the purpose of this book, and in fairness to the reader, I will briefly articulate my understanding of the nature of Scripture—seen as the result of divine inspiration and human reception—that is broadly affirmed within the historic orthodox and evangelical Christian traditions.

---

[1]I. Howard Marshall, *Biblical Inspiration* (Grand Rapids: Eerdmans, 1982), pp. 31-73, provides a helpful summary and critical discussion of the broad range of views on biblical inspiration and the consequent understandings of the nature of the Bible.

That understanding of the nature of Scripture is grounded in two foundational assumptions. The first—which is at its core an article of faith—is the
affirmation that those who wrote the various parts of the Bible over the course
of many centuries were inspired by God. They were guided by God's Spirit
in their understanding of God and God's redemptive work in the world in
and through the history of Israel, which culminated in the life, death and
resurrection of Jesus, and the witness of his earliest followers. The second
assumption—which is grounded in the actual data of Scripture—acknowledges the concrete historical reality of the writers as participants in the process, and it affirms both the recipients' specific humanity and their coopera-
tion as instruments of divine inspiration as being important dimensions of
the nature and character of Scripture.

An early and articulate exponent of this view of biblical inspiration and the
nature of the Bible is J. I. Packer, who speaks of the mysterious intersection of
the divine and human dimension of Scripture as "concursive."[2] On the human
level is the very specific, historical activity of the biblical writers, who used
written sources, collected information, interviewed witnesses, recorded prophetic visions and messages, derived moral lessons and wisdom from observation of both human and animal life, composed letters, reflected on the meaning of revelatory events, put in writing the oral traditions passed down for
decades or centuries about the history and faith traditions of their faith communities, and bore witness to what they had seen and heard.[3] On the level of
divine inspiration, "we can assert that the Spirit, who moved on the face of the
waters at Creation (Gen 1:2), was active in the whole process so that the Bible
can be regarded as both the words of men and the Word of God."[4] Connected
with this understanding of the process involved in the writing of Scripture is
the conviction that, because of the presence and guidance of the Spirit, the
result is "infallible."[5] This means that the Bible, despite the limitation of the

---

[2]James I. Packer, *Fundamentalism and the Word of God* (London: Inter-Varsity Fellowship, 1958);
and *God Has Spoken* (London: Hodder and Stoughton, 1985).

[3]See Ecclesiastes 5:18; 6:1-2; 7:15; 9:1; Luke 1:1-4; John 1:1-4; and Acts 15:1 for examples of biblical
texts that reflect such activity.

[4]Marshall, *Biblical Inspiration*, p. 42. Acts 15 specifically speaks of this "concursive action" as a
basis for the deliberations and decisions of the so-called "Jerusalem Council," communicated to
the Christian community at Antioch: "For it has seemed good to the Holy Spirit and to us" (Acts
15:28).

[5]See Marshall, *Biblical Inspiration*, p. 53, for a brief discussion of the term *infallible* in connection
with the purpose of God in the composition of the Scriptures.

human writers—which includes the possibility of misunderstanding, mishearing, or only partially hearing and understanding the revelatory speaking and acting of God—is trustworthy and perfectly sufficient for the redemptive, life-and-world-transforming purpose for which God inspired it.

I believe that this understanding of inspiration and the nature of Scripture, which affirms the dual reality of both the divine and the human dimensions, is most consistent with the Bible's own explicit affirmations, its diverse content and essential character. As such, it provides a solid foundation for the trustworthy stewardship of the treasure of Scripture.

It is common among Christians who affirm the inspiration of the Bible to file charges against one another. Some call their view of Scripture "high"—meaning that it is true, correct, orthodox—and describe the view of others as being "low"—meaning faulty, inadequate, wrong. An interesting exchange illustrates this. After giving several lectures at an American seminary, the noted Swiss theologian Karl Barth was asked: "How would your theology differ if you had a higher view of the Bible?" Without hesitation Barth replied: "Sir, there is no view of the Bible which is higher than the one which I hold!"

I contend that the *highest view of Scripture* is that which is most faithful to the *intention* of Scripture and takes with utmost seriousness the fact that God's final, ultimate form of revelation is the *incarnation*—Jesus Christ, the Word made flesh (Jn 1:1, 14). Any view of Scripture that seeks to be trustworthy must hold in the highest regard these twin pillars—of *intention* and *incarnation*.

I approach the question of the Bible's essential nature and authority as an *exegete*, concerned specifically with understanding the *phenomenon of Scripture* (what Scripture really is). As an exegete, I am convinced that the text of Scripture should receive priority in any attempt to understand the nature of the Bible and its authority. To state it another way, our understanding of Scripture must be based on its own stated purposes and intentions *(inductively)*, rather than on the basis of certain theological assumptions and presuppositions that impose a particular view of Scripture from the outside *(deductively)*.

INTENTION AND INCARNATION: KEYS TO THE NATURE OF DIVINE INSPIRATION AND THE NATURE OF THE BIBLE

Clearly, divine inspiration must be assumed as that reality that gives to the Bible its authoritative character. The concept of inspiration is derived primarily from the use of the Greek word *theopneustos* (literally "God-breathed" in 2 Tim 3:15-16 NIV) in connection with the terms *sacred writings* and *Scripture*.[6] Though the word *theopneustos* is used only here in the New Testament,[7] the intimate relationship between the speaking and acting of God, on the one hand, and the content of both the Jewish Scriptures and the emerging New Testament documents, on the other hand, is broadly affirmed in the Bible.[8] In New Testament references to the Old Testament, formulas such as "God says" or "the Holy Spirit says" are common (e.g., Acts 1:16; 2 Cor 6:16). God and Scripture were so intimately linked that "what Scripture says" and "what God says" could at times be equated (Rom 9:17; Gal 3:8). Jesus' use of the Old Testament and his attitude toward it strongly confirms this sense of Scripture's divine origin and content (e.g., Mt 5:17-18; Jn 10:35).[9] It is also clear from the New Testament that the teaching of Jesus and the witness of his followers were understood to be continuous with the inspiration and authority of the Old Testament (e.g., Jn 12:49; 1 Cor 2:13; 1 Thess 2:13; Heb 3:7).

There is no doubt that the biblical writers were aware of, and claimed, divine inspiration. But what is the *intention* of this inspiration? What is the divine purpose for this inspiration? In answering this question, we must resist the temptation to determine in advance what the nature and inspiration of the Bible *must* be. This was the concern of Old Testament scholar and former president of Fuller Theological Seminary, David Hubbard, when he wrote: "How can we let the Bible be what it is?"[10] Noted New Testament scholar Hermann Ridderbos put the matter this way: "Scripture has in many respects a character other than that which a theoretical concept of inspiration or infallibility—*detached from its purpose and empirical reality*— would like to demand. One must be careful when reasoning about what is,

---

[6]That the text refers to the Old Testament is clear from the Greek word for "sacred writings" (2 Tim 3:15, *hiera grammata*); the term commonly applied to the Jewish Scripture by Greek-speaking Jews.

[7]The use of this term reflects the way first-century Judaism viewed its Scripture. Cf. J. N. D. Kelly, *A Commentary on the Pastoral Epistles* (New York: Harper and Row, 1964), p. 203.

[8]See Wayne Grudem, "Scripture's Self-Attestation and the Problem of Formulating a Doctrine of Scripture," in *Scripture and Truth*, ed. D. A. Carson and John D. Woodbridge (Grand Rapids: Zondervan, 1983), pp. 19-59.

[9]See the very clear and balanced discussion in Leon Morris, *I Believe in Revelation* (Grand Rapids: Eerdmans, 1976), chap 3.

[10]David Hubbard, "The Current Tensions: Is There a Way Out?" in *Biblical Authority*, ed. Jack B. Rogers (Dallas: Word, 1977), p. 151.

and what is not, possible under inspiration by God."[11] Commitment to the Bible's authority demands that we take its own statements with utmost seriousness. When we do so, we find that the Bible's authority—its character as the Word of God—is related to its *intention*. The question "inspired for what end?" is extremely important here.

The classical passage about divine inspiration in 2 Timothy 3 defines inspiration in terms of "instruct[ion] . . . for salvation" (2 Tim 3:15). This scope of inspiration is further explicated as "for teaching, for reproof, for correction, and for training in righteousness" (2 Tim 3:16) so that we might be "equipped for every good work" (2 Tim 3:17). This passage teaches that God's inspiration in and through Scripture provides for us the knowledge and guidance that is intended to bring about salvation and the renewal of life and the world, through faith in Jesus Christ. The biblical writings are "for our instruction, so that by steadfastness and by the encouragement of the scriptures we might have hope" (Rom 15:4). This redemptive purpose of inspired Scripture is also the point of John 20:31, where the evangelist states that his account of Jesus' life, of his teachings and of his deeds was "written so that you may come to believe . . . and that through believing you may have life."

The account of Philip's encounter with the Ethiopian (Acts 8) is also very instructive. The understanding and interpretation of the passage from Isaiah (53:7-8)—which the Ethiopian has been reading—has one purpose: "starting with this scripture, he [Philip] proclaimed to him the good news about Jesus" (Acts 8:35). That is the "what for," the purpose. Jesus never recommended the Bible as a book of divinely given facts about things in general (such as science, history, psychology, anthropology, cosmology). Rather, he pointed to the Old Testament writings and said: "it is they that testify on my behalf" (Jn 5:39). This is the basis for my insistence throughout this study (but especially in chapters 6-8) on a Christocentric hermeneutic.

The Scriptures exist by divine providence and inspiration so that Jesus and his good news can be proclaimed. And this ought to be our primary concern with the Bible. For if the study of Scripture is isolated from this explicit purpose, the attempts (often very ingenious) to deal with problems and tensions

---

[11]Hermann Ridderbos, *Studies in Scripture and Its Authority* (Grand Rapids: Eerdmans, 1978), p. 28, italics mine. Cf. E. Harrison, "The Phenomena of Scripture," in *Revelation and the Bible,* ed. Carl F. H. Henry (Grand Rapids: Baker, 1958), p. 239: "We may have our own ideas about how God should have inspired the Word, but it is more profitable to learn, if we can, how he has actually inspired it."

in the Bible tend to close it rather than open it; they tend to block the way to meaningful understanding rather than paving the way.

In addition to the critical matter of the Bible's *intention,* we must consider the nature of the biblical documents in light of the paradigm of the *incarnation,* the enfleshment of God's Word through human words, culture and history.

"Divine inspiration," Ridderbos contends, "does not necessarily mean that those who spoke and wrote under inspiration were temporarily stripped of their limitations in knowledge, memory, language and capability of expressing themselves, as specific human beings in a certain period of history."[12] The presence of this "human factor" in Scripture has been acknowledged throughout the church's history.[13] From the early church fathers, such as Athanasius and Augustine, to the Reformers and beyond, the reality of God's accommodation to human weakness and limitation in the actual writing of the Scriptures has been affirmed. The condescension of a nurse or a schoolmaster to the limitations of children has been used as an analogy. God stoops down to us into the human character of Scripture so that we might hear and understand, and become whole.[14]

But what is the nature and extent of this accommodation to limited human reality? In the attempt to answer this question, the analogy to the incarnation has been an important consideration. We must recover the truth contained in this analogy, for it is still the most fruitful path toward understanding the mysterious—and sometimes perplexing and frustrating—dual nature of Scripture: God's Word in human vocabulary, and human vocabulary bathed in the Word of God.[15]

As God humbled himself in Christ, and "the Word became flesh and lived among us" (Jn 1:14), so Scripture, as the "word written," participates in this

---

[12]Ridderbos, *Studies,* p. 25. See also Raymond E. Brown, *101 Questions and Answers on the Bible* (New York: Paulist, 1990), p. 50. "Writing is a human activity; and divine inspiration respects the conventions of that activity."

[13]For a thorough discussion, see Jack B. Rogers and Donald K. McKim, *Authority and Interpretation* (New York: Harper and Row, 1979).

[14]See Telford Work's discussion of the analogy of the word in the church fathers Athanasius and Augustine in *Living and Active: Scripture in the Economy of Salvation* (Grand Rapids: Eerdmans, 2002), pp. 33-66.

[15]Cf. James Smart's proposal that the inspiration of Scripture should be understood in analogy to the inspiration of Jesus. His contention is that just as the full reality of the Spirit in Jesus did not dissolve his humanity, so the full inspiration of Scripture does not eliminate its humanity. James Smart, *The Inspiration of Scripture* (Philadelphia: Westminster Press, 1961), pp. 160-68.

enfleshed nature. Bernard Ramm, one of the most influential evangelical theologians of the last century, put it this way: "Just as the Son of God emptied himself and lowered himself to our estate, so revelation comes to us in a humbled, lower form."[16] If there is to be integrity in the use of this incarnational model for an adequate understanding of the dual reality of Scripture, the mystery of Jesus' complete humanity and divinity, in unabridged union, must be consistently applied.

Throughout the New Testament, Jesus is seen as the one who, in his being, is completely one with God. In his person, his words, his deeds and the events of his life, God himself was revealed (e.g., Jn 14:9; 20:28; Col 1:15, 19; Heb 1:1-3). The witness of the New Testament affirms just as strongly that this complete oneness of Jesus with God was realized without the dissolution of his thoroughly human nature. He was born not only through the agency of the Holy Spirit, but also of Mary. He was a helpless infant within the limitations of human life. He grew "in wisdom and in years, and in divine and human favor" (Lk 2:52). So complete is his humanity that his relationship with God is maintained, nurtured and empowered in a life of prayer. He was made like us "in every respect": he was tempted as we are, learned obedience, and was perfected in his humanity through suffering (Heb 2:10, 14, 17-18; 4:15; 5:8). His ability to discern what was in people's hearts and minds (e.g., Mt 12:25; Mk 2:8) stands side by side with the affirmation of limited knowledge (Mk 13:32).

For the authors of the New Testament, there was no contradiction in asserting both the divinity and humanity of Jesus' words, deeds and being. The only qualification regarding his complete identity with us in our humanity—namely that he was without sin (Heb 4:15)—does not mitigate his fully human essence. For sin is not an essential, ontological aspect of authentic humanity created in the image of God. It is rather an intrusion (Gen 3) into that which is essentially human. Thus, full accommodation to human limitation in the incarnation does not demand sinfulness. What *is* an essential part of "creatureliness" is "fleshness," which in the Hebraic frame of reference denotes weakness and limitation. And it is this fleshness that is affirmed of Jesus.[17]

---

[16]Bernard Ramm, *Special Revelation and the Word of God* (Grand Rapids: Eerdmans, 1961), p. 33.

[17]For a very perceptive and balanced discussion of the presence of both divine knowledge and human limitation in Jesus, see Raymond E. Brown, *Jesus, God and Man* (New York: Macmillan, 1967).

This paradigm of the incarnation provides clues to God's way of self-disclosure, to God's way of revelation, which often stands in tension with what we might wish the nature of the biblical revelation to be. That is, we may wish that God's revelation in Christ had come to us without ambiguity, but God's ways are often not our ways, and we dare not dictate our terms to God. The New Testament documents are clear about the fact that the limiting reality of the Word made flesh created numerous problems for Jesus' contemporaries. It led to serious misunderstandings about his person and purpose and caused outright rejection and enmity: "Can anything good come out of Nazareth?" (Jn 1:46). "We know that God has spoken to Moses, but as for this man . . ." (Jn 9:29). "We know where this man is from; but when the Messiah comes, no one will know where he is from" (Jn 7:27).

The eternal, divine *Logos* (Word) was present in the human nature of Jesus, but many who encountered him—including, at times, his disciples—failed to discern the divine reality. Even at the point where the transcendent power of God broke through human limitations, such as in Jesus' demon exorcisms, there were those who did not see divine power at work. Rather, they attributed Jesus' actions to the work of the prince of evil (Lk 11:14-23).

Yet the limiting human reality that created this ambiguity did not invalidate the presence of the divine reality. The earthen vessel of the incarnation did not abrogate the presence of the glory of God (Jn 1:14). The truth of God in the words and deeds of Jesus was not tainted by falsehood or error just because it came to expression through the limitation and weakness of human enfleshment.

God's way of revelation in the incarnation calls for faith: to see in and through and beyond the limiting human expression to the heart of God. "We walk by faith," said Paul, "not by sight" (2 Cor 5:7). Faith accepts the limiting human expression of God's revelation in Jesus *as God's way,* and in that acceptance, it finds the truth. Unbelief sees only the human form and misses the truth of God revealed therein. If, as the orthodox creeds (such as the Nicene Creed from A.D. 325 and the Chalcedonian Creed from A.D. 451) affirm, on the basis of the biblical data, that the completely divine and human dimensions are inextricably and mysteriously present in the incarnation, the presence of this mysterious duality should not be denied to Scripture, which as the written Word of God, derives its final authority from Jesus Christ, the enfleshed and living Word of God. Since all Scripture points either forward (Old Testament) or backward (New Testament) to the incarnate Logos, it is surely legitimate, if not imperative, that all of Scripture be understood in light of this ultimate divine self-revelation.[18]

Thus the human dimension of Scripture would seem to be precisely God's way of "incarnating" the truth expressed in the event of the incarnation. As with the living Word, so also in the written Word the human dimension can be a stumbling block. It can be used, in the context of critical dissection and analysis, as a reason for rejecting "the faith that was once for all entrusted to the saints" (Jude 3). But in faith, the human dimension of Scripture can be affirmed as that vehicle whereby God in grace approaches us.

This juxtaposition of the human and the divine in both the incarnation of the living Word and in the written Word is ultimately a paradox and mystery. Yet I believe that the Gospel of Luke provides us with a perspective for cautiously and haltingly entering that mystery. Luke presents Jesus as conceived by the Spirit and endowed with the Spirit at his baptism. He is the one who, "full of the Spirit," is "led by the Spirit" into the wilderness (Lk 4:1). He inaugurates his ministry "in the power of the Spirit" (Lk 4:14) and is anointed by the Spirit to proclaim "good news" (Lk 4:18; cf. also Mt 12:28, where Jesus' demon exorcism activity is attributed to the power of God's Spirit). What this emphasis in Luke seems to indicate is that the presence of the Spirit in Jesus' person and ministry empowers the divine reality, namely the eternal Word within the confines and limitations of Jesus' human reality, so that Jesus' words and deeds can be heard and experienced as expressions of God's word and deed. The Spirit, at work in the Incarnate One, guarantees that the eternal Word speaks through the human words of Jesus. In Jesus' words and deeds, God speaks and acts.

Such an understanding of the *incarnation* has important implications for the nature of the Bible. It is fully human, with all that this implies regarding the presence of limitation, and it is fully divine, with all that this implies about its inspiration and authority. Our hearing and believing of the divine authority, in and through the fully human character of Scripture, is made

---

[18]See the lucid discussion of the grounding of biblical authority ultimately in the incarnation in N. T. Wright, *The Last Word: Scripture and the Authority of God—Getting Beyond the Bible Wars* (San Francisco: HarperOne, 2005); and Peter Enns, *Inspiration and Incarnation: Evangelicals and the Problem of the Old Testament* (Grand Rapids: Baker Academic, 2005).

possible by the Spirit. Perhaps this is what Luther was pointing to when he stated:

> Holy Scripture possesses no external glory, attracts no attention, lacks all beauty and adornment. . . . Yet faith comes from this divine Word, through its inner power without any external loveliness. . . . It is only the internal working of the Holy Spirit that causes us to place our trust in this Word of God, which is without form or comeliness.[19]

This understanding of the nature of the Bible and its inspiration provides the framework within which our analysis of Scripture abuse and our discussion of corrective approaches and attitudes takes place. Much of the abuse of Scripture is the result of not taking the *intention* of Scripture—both the intention of God's inspiring action and the intention of the particular authors of the biblical documents—with full seriousness. A second reason behind the abusive interpretation and application of Scripture is a disregard for, or a diminution of, its *incarnational* character. For when the historical, cultural and situational contexts of particular biblical texts are not given their proper due—or when their redemptive intention is not adequately considered—the trustworthy reading and understanding of the biblical word is seriously compromised.

These two pillars of *intention* and *incarnation* are also the backbone of responsible, trustworthy interpretation of the Bible. The various principles and perspectives for correcting Scripture abuse to be discussed throughout this book reflect these insights about the nature of Scripture and seek to assist students of Scripture in the critical task of avoiding its abuse.

---

[19]Cited by Jack B. Rogers, "The Church Doctrine of Biblical Authority," *Biblical Authority* (Dallas: Word Publishers, 1977), p. 25.

2

THE ABUSE OF THE WHOLE GOSPEL

As servants of Christ and as trustworthy stewards of the treasure of Scripture, we are called to be bearers—in word and deed—of the "Whole Gospel for the Whole World."[1] We are obligated to hear and apply the comprehensive, whole Word of God to all aspects of life in this world.

The tragedy of not hearing and living the whole gospel—in both personal and corporate Christian faith and life—is that it presents a truncated gospel to the world. A truncated gospel is a caricature of the real thing. It is, at best, incomplete and, at worst, inauthentic. Consequently, the transforming power of the whole gospel is blunted, and the larger culture is deprived of the potential impact of Christian witness and presence—energized and informed by a holistic biblical message and comprehensive biblical worldview.[2]

---

[1]This is the motto of the Eastern Baptist (now Palmer) Theological Seminary, where I served for twenty-six years. In 1925, the founders of the school—in deliberate reaction against both a drift to the theological left and a fundamentalistic narrowness on the right—sought to establish a seminary that was committed to "the whole gospel," thereby rejecting the one-sided emphases of both the liberals and the fundamentalists. (See appendix A for a brief historical sketch of this fragmentation of the whole gospel within American Protestantism.)

[2]A recent study (2003) by the Barna Research group shows that a comprehensive biblical worldview, one that shapes our attitudes, beliefs, values and opinions, significantly influences the way we are

THE GOSPEL OF PERSONAL SALVATION OR THE SOCIAL GOSPEL

From the beginning to the end of the biblical story, we are faced with two truths: (1) that human life, in both its individual/personal and corporate/social dimensions, is out of joint and distorted; humanity lives in rebellion against God and in opposition to the purposes of God; and (2) that the wholeness of human life, as intended by God, in both its personal and social dimensions is possible only when persons and human communities live in life-giving, life-sustaining and life-transforming relationship with God.

The early chapters of Genesis (Gen 3—11) set the stage. Human beings, represented in and by Adam and Eve, grasp at equality with God, seek to transcend creational boundaries, and reject dependence on their Creator (Gen 3:1-13). That rejection of the Creator-creature relationship led to a cursed, broken, distorted human existence characterized by (1) conflict between the human creation and the rest of the created order (Gen 3:14-15; cf. Is 24:4-6); (2) the experience of sorrow, agony and distress[3] in the fulfillment of the complementary vocations of giving and sustaining life (Gen 3:16-19); (3) distortion of the redemptive, complementary relationship of man and woman, which leads to wholeness (depicted in Gen 1:26—2:25),[4] into a cursed hierarchy of superior and inferior (Gen 3:16); (4) enmity and hatred within human community (Gen 4:1—6:6); and (5) human arrogance vis-à-vis God, leading to the total fragmentation of human community and symbolized in

---

present in our culture. The study also "suggests that a large share of the nation's moral and spiritual challenges is directly attributable to the absence of a biblical worldview." The research indicates that even among devoutly religious people, very few have such a biblical worldview. Among those who identify themselves as born-again Christians, only 9 percent have such a comprehensive perspective on life. Reported in The Road to Emmaus website, "A Biblical Worldview Has a Radical Effect on a Person's Life" (December 1, 2003) <www.theroadtoemmaus.org/RdLb/11Phl/WrldV/WvwEffctBarna.htm>. It is my contention that a significant factor contributing to this lack of a holistic biblical perspective on Christian life and the world is the abuse of Scripture and, in this case, the abuse of the whole gospel.

[3]The Hebrew word 'iṣṣābôn, normally translated as "pain" (in Gen 3:16) and "toil" (in Gen 3:17), can refer to either physical pain and stress or to emotional pain and stress (agony, sorrow, despair, emotional trauma). It is very possible that Genesis 3:16-17 refers to emotional pain, rather than the traditionally understood physical pain of the woman giving birth or the man's physical pain in hard labor. In the ancient Near East, infant mortality was extremely high, so childbearing was always attended by the possibility of the child's death. Likewise, in agrarian life, crops were always threatened by pests, storms, hail or floods, so the production of food was always attended by the possibility of its destruction. Therefore, one result of Adam and Eve's rejection of creaturely boundaries may be that—in their complementary vocations of giving and sustaining life—they experience sorrow.

[4]See chapter three for a discussion of the nature of the male-female relationship in God's created design.

the confusion of tongues (Gen 11:1-9). This biblical picture of the thorough distortion of human life is concisely summarized in Genesis 6:5, 11:

> The LORD saw that the wickedness of humankind was great in the earth, and that every inclination of the thoughts of their hearts was only evil continually. . . . Now the earth was corrupt in God's sight, and the earth was filled with violence.

The psalmist utters the same conviction. The Lord, he says,

> looks down from heaven on humankind
>> to see if there are any . . . who seek after God.
> They have all gone astray, they are all alike perverse;
>> there is no one who does good,
>>> no, not one. (Ps 14:2-3)

While this is an assessment of the global human condition, Israel's prophets discern the same reality among God's covenant people. God "expected justice," says Isaiah, "but saw bloodshed"; he looked for "righteousness, but heard a cry!" (Is 5:7). Amos's judgment is even harsher: "Ah, you that turn justice to wormwood, and bring righteousness to the ground!" (Amos 5:7).[5]

The New Testament's analysis of the human condition is in full agreement with that of the Old Testament, and even intensifies it. Human life is marked by lostness (Lk 15), darkness (Jn 1:5), enmity (Rom 5:10), separation (Eph 2:15-17), ungodliness (Rom 1:18) and alienation from the life of God (Eph 4:17-18). The New Testament's most comprehensive term for the human reality defined by these representative characteristics is *hamartia* ("sin"), which means literally "missing the mark" of God's intention for human life. The most thorough and penetrating biblical analysis of this human situation is Paul's discussion in Romans 1:18—3:23, in which he depicts the downward spiraling of personal and communal life, resulting from the rejection of the Creator, the giver and sustainer of authentic life (Rom 1:18-23). He concludes with the climactic statement that "all have sinned and fall short of the glory of God" (Rom 3:23).

This picture of the pervasive brokenness of human life and community is

---

[5]This assessment is pervasive in the prophetic literature of the Old Testament (See, e.g., Is 10:1-2; 59:1-15; Ezek 34; Jer 5:1-3; 22:13-17; Amos 2:4-8; 5:10-12; Mic 3:1-3, 9-11), as well as in the historical literature about the united kingdom (1-2 Sam) and the kingdoms of Judah and Israel (1-2 Kings). The repeated refrain regarding many rulers is this: "He did what was evil in the sight of the LORD, as his ancestors had done" (2 Kings 15:9). "Justice," in the Old Testament, always has to do with right relationships, characterized by truth, fairness, goodness, compassion, equity and love.

the stage setting for the incarnation: the coming of God's Light to dispel the world's darkness (Jn 1:1-5; 8:12; 9:15); of God's Savior to seek humans in their lostness (Lk 15:11-32);[6] of God's truth to liberate humans from the shackles of falsehood (Jn 8:31-32; 14:6; 18:37); of God's atonement in Christ to cleanse us from our sinfulness (Mt 1:21; Jn 1:29; Rom 3:23-26; 5:8); of God's reconciling love in Christ to overcome our enmity (Rom 5:10; 2 Cor 5:17-21); and of God's resurrection power in Christ to overcome our death-dominated existence and, ultimately, to overcome death itself (Rom 6:3-11; 1 Cor 15). These affirmations, representative of many more throughout the New Testament, constitute the evangel, the good news, the gospel. The gospel is the announcement that, in the event of Christ, God has acted to redeem human life—in its personal-relational totality—from its bondage to sin and death, and to restore persons to life-giving and life-sustaining relationship with God: "in Christ God was reconciling the world to himself" (2 Cor 5:19).

This good news—that restored relationship with God is the ground for authentic life—is already anticipated in the Old Testament. In the midst of Israel's checkered history of faithfulness and faithlessness, the people of Israel are repeatedly invited to "seek the Lord," with the promise that "you will find him if you search after him with all your heart and soul" (Deut 4:29).[7] To seek the Lord—to live life in his presence—is to really live (Amos 5:4-6; Is 55:3). To seek the Lord is to find him, to encounter his mercy, to receive forgiveness (Is 55:6-7).[8]

This Old Testament theme of seeking God and finding life in relationship with him is concisely summarized in the word of Jesus who, as the one who stands in a relationship of oneness with God (Mt 11:27; cf. Jn 5:26), says: "Come to me, all you that are weary and are carrying heavy burdens, and I

---

[6]The so-called parable of the prodigal son might better be called the parable of the two lost sons. The setting of the parable (Lk 15:1-2) shows clearly that the younger son represents all those defined in Judaism as "lost," as "sinners," while the elder brother represents the Pharisees and scribes, sitting in judgment of "sinners." It may be said that the elder brother is as lost as his younger brother, perhaps more so since he does not recognize his lostness. His relationships with both his father and his younger brother are distorted.

[7]See also 1 Chron 16:10-11; 28:9; 2 Chron 7:14; 15:2; Ps 14:2-3; 105:3-4; 119:2; Jer 29:13.

[8]Cf. Jeremiah 31:34, where "knowing God" is the result of God's redemptive forgiveness. This prophetic call to "know God" (Hos 2:20; 4:1; 6:3) is virtually synonymous with the invitation to seek and find God and live. To "know God" is not the same as "to know about God" (in the sense of knowing truths about God). It is rather to stand in personal, experiential relationship with God. The Hebrew word yāda' ("know") is also used for the intimacy of sexual union (e.g., "Now the man knew his wife Eve, and she conceived" [Gen 4:1]).

will give you rest" (Mt 11:28). The same truth is stated incisively in John 10:10, "I came that they may have life, and have it abundantly." This affirmation builds on the Old Testament and at the same time goes decisively beyond it. For the good news is precisely this: In Jesus Christ, God comes "to seek out and to save the lost" (Lk 19:10) and to bring broken, alienated, sinful people back into relationship with God (Rom 5:6-10; 2 Cor 5:18).

It is this gospel, central to historic Christian teaching for two millennia, that has been the passionate focus and concern of the evangelical movement within Protestantism, particularly during the past century. Its major focus— through evangelistic work, international mission outreach, and congregational worship, fellowship, discipleship training and education—has been to invite people to respond in faith to God's grace (Eph 2:8), to enter new life through spiritual rebirth (Jn 3:3-10; 1 Pet 1:3, 23), to confess Jesus Christ as Savior and Lord (Lk 2:11; Jn 4:42; Acts 13:23; Rom 10:9; 2 Pet 2:20), and to follow Christ into a lifetime of being transformed into the image of Christ through personal discipleship (2 Cor 3:17-18; Eph 4:22—5:11).

This biblical teaching, presented above in very condensed form, is what has often been referred to as "The Personal Gospel" or "The Gospel of Personal Salvation." The primary purpose of the proclamation of this essential dimension of biblical teaching has been the "saving of souls," both in the here and now and for eternal life beyond death.

Side by side with this dimension of the biblical revelation of God's redemptive purpose and action is a related dimension, which has to do with God's concern for the larger arena of human life in community, in social groupings, in political and cultural structures. In the biblical view of human life, authentic personhood is primarily relational rather than individualistic. There is a sense of corporate solidarity and belonging vis-à-vis our modern (particularly Western) concept of personal autonomy and individualism.[9] This truth comes to clear expression in Jesus' response to the question: "Teacher, which commandment in the law is the greatest?" (Mt 22:36). Jesus responds by combining two commandments from the Old Testament. He cites what, in Israelite tradition, was known as the *Šĕmaʿ*[10] (Deut 6:4-5):

---

[9]The Old Testament scholar H. Wheeler Robinson demonstrates this in his *Corporate Personality in Ancient Israel* (Philadelphia: Fortress, 1973).

[10]It was called the *Šĕma* because of the first word in the Hebrew of Deuteronomy 6:4, *šĕmaʿ*, meaning "hear."

"You shall love the LORD your God with all your heart, and with all your soul, and with all your might," and then affirms that "a second is like it: 'You shall love your neighbor as yourself' " (Mt 22:39, citing Lev 19:18). Two complementary relationships are here in view: relationship with God and relationship with "the other." The "vertical" divine-human relationship has consequences for the "horizontal" human-human relationships. They are like two sides of the same coin, inseparably linked. Consequently, authentic piety (loving God, being rightly related to God) must find concrete expression in the larger areas of human community (loving the neighbor, the other, even the enemy; Lk 10:29-37; Mt 5:44). This dual perspective is pervasive throughout the Bible.

The prophet Micah places the divine call "to walk humbly with your God" side by side with the requirement "to do justice, and to love kindness" (Mic 6:8). Likewise, Jeremiah's word from the Lord is that "to know me" is "to do justice and righteousness" and to regard "the cause of the poor and needy" (Jer 22:15-16). Since God "in his holy habitation" is "father of orphans and protector of widows" (Ps 68:5),[11] can those created in the image of God do anything less?

This is precisely what Psalm 72 affirms—spoken most likely at the coronation of one of Israel's kings. The psalmist calls on God to grant the king his justice and righteousness (Ps 72:1) so that he will rule in righteousness (Ps 72:2), defend the cause of the poor with justice (Ps 72:2, 4), and deliver the needy from oppression (Ps 72:4, 12).

Because God's people and their leaders—redeemed by the Lord from Egyptian political bondage and oppression—violated his will for justice and wholeness of life by not embodying that divine calling within the economic and social structures of the nation, their prophets repeatedly denounced their shallow, empty piety. Particularly potent are the prophets Isaiah and Amos on this matter. In a lengthy critique of Judah by "the word of the Lord," Isaiah points the divine finger of judgment at the tremendous gap between worship, on the one hand, and political, social and economic corruption, on the other hand (Is 1:11-15). At the heart of this judgment is the word of the Lord: "I cannot endure solemn assemblies with iniquity" (Is 1:13). Therefore, "learn

---

[11]In ancient Near Eastern society (including Israel), widows and orphans were the most weak, vulnerable members of the social order. Thus, repeatedly, they are the objects of God's special concern.

to do good, seek justice, rescue the oppressed, defend the orphan, plead for the widow" (Is 1:17).[12] Rather than holding a fast day to demonstrate humility before the Lord, while at the same time oppressing their workers (Is 58:3, 5), God's people are called to "fast" in a radically different way:

> Is not this the fast I choose:
>> to loose the bonds of injustice,
>> to undo the thongs of the yoke,
> to let the oppressed go free,
>> and to break every yoke?
>
> Is it not to share your bread with the hungry,
>> and bring the homeless poor into your house? (Is 58:6-7)

Amos, in his prophetic word addressed to Israel, likewise exposes the hypocrisy of a formal piety that is corrupted by social and economic injustice:

> They lay themselves down beside every altar
>> on garments taken in pledge;
> and in the house of their God they drink
>> wine bought with fines they imposed. (Amos 2:8)

While claiming to be the redeemed people of God,

> they sell the righteous for silver,
>> and the needy for a pair of sandals—
> they who trample the head of the poor into the dust of the earth,
>> and push the afflicted out of the way. (Amos 2:6-7)[13]

Finally, in a powerful word of judgment the Lord denounces Israel's worship (festivals, solemn assemblies, offerings, sacrifices, hymns; Amos 5:21-23) because their social and economic life and practices are characterized by injustice, especially for the poor and needy. He challenges Israel to express their calling as God's people concretely within the social and economic spheres of their community:

> Let justice roll down like waters,
>> and righteousness like an ever-flowing stream. (Amos 5:24)

This theme of the intimate connection—in the lives of the redeemed peo-

---

[12]See also Is 1:21-23; 3:13-15; 5:7, 20-23; 10:1-2; 58:8-10; Jer 5:27-28; 7:5-6; and especially Jer 7:21-26; 8:10-12.
[13]See also Amos 5:10-12.

ple of God—between personal piety (right relationship with God), on the one hand, and the embodiment of God's desire for justice and wholeness of life in community, on the other hand, is also an essential hallmark of the New Testament. Those who have become participants in the reign of God that has broken into history in the life and ministry of Jesus, and who have been set free from the bondage to sin by the redemptive work of Christ on the cross, have been "created in Christ Jesus for good works" (Eph 2:10). These "good works" are neither limited to personal acts of kindness and generosity and compassion, nor to an upright life marked by moral integrity, nor to an advocacy of sexual purity and relational fidelity. As the New Testament shows in unbroken continuity with the prophetic voices of the Old Testament, the good works for which we are created also include words and deeds that incarnate the reign of God in the social and economic areas of life.

In what has come to be called his "inaugural sermon" at the beginning of his messianic mission in his home town of Nazareth (Lk 4:16-21), Jesus cites the prophet Isaiah (Is 61:1-2), claiming that he is anointed by the Spirit of the Lord "to bring good news to the poor . . . to proclaim release to the captives and recovery of sight to the blind, to let the oppressed go free, to proclaim the year of God's favor." Thus Jesus' messianic mission has clear implications for the political, economic and social spheres, decisively so if the references to freedom for the oppressed and "the year of the Lord's favor" are references to the year of Jubilee.[14] The year of Jubilee was intended to be a year of release for debtors and liberty to return from servitude to one's family.[15]

Much in Jesus' ministry echoes this inaugural mission statement. He reaches out to the marginalized: the most vulnerable, such as women, children and the poor (Mt 18:10-14; Mk 10:13-16; Lk 8:1-3, 43-48; 13:10-17; 18:15-18); the socially and religiously ostracized and segregated, such as lepers and Samaritans (Mt 8:2-4; Lk 9:51-56; 10:29-37; 17:11-19; Jn 4); and the unclean and sinners, such as Gentiles and tax collectors (Mt 8:5-13; Lk 5:27-32; 7:36-39; 15; 19:1-10). In the event of the cleansing of the temple (Mt 21:12-13; Mk 11:15-19; Lk 19:45-48; Jn 2:13-17), Jesus challenges sinful

---

[14]The year of Jubilee, described in Leviticus 25, was to be held every fifty years. A Qumran text (11Q Melchizedek) links Leviticus 25 explicitly with Isaiah 61:1. See Craig A. Evans, *Luke*, New International Biblical Commentary (Peabody, Mass.: Hendrickson, 1990), p. 75.

[15]I. Howard Marshall, *Gospel of Luke*, New International Greek Testament Commentary (Grand Rapids: Eerdmans, 1978), p. 184; and David L. Tiede, *Luke*, Augsburg Commentary on the New Testament (Minneapolis: Augsburg, 1988), p. 107.

structures, such as the economic exploitation of poor pilgrims,[16] and the discriminatory racial segregation of Gentiles, by driving the moneychangers and merchants from the outer "court of the Gentiles."[17] He charges the authorities with having turned the temple—intended as "a house of prayer for all the nations" (Mk 11:17, citing Is 56:7)—into a "den of robbers" (citing Jer 7:11). Very much in continuity with the prophets' critique of corruption in Israel's social and economic dealings, Jesus takes the religious leaders to task for the disconnect between their demonstration of piety (tithing, long prayers in public), on the one hand, and neglect of justice and mercy (Mt 23:23), as well as actively defrauding widows of their property (Mk 12:40), on the other hand.

This focus in Jesus' ministry is a central feature of his teaching concerning the kingdom (or better, reign) of God. In his life and teaching, the reign of God has broken into history (Mk 1:15; Lk 17:21) and is doing battle with the reign of evil (Lk 11:20-23), wherever and however that reign manifests itself. Indeed, Jesus' demon exorcisms are signs that the reign of God has invaded the stronghold of Satan: "if it is by the finger[18] of God that I cast out demons, then the kingdom of God has come to you" (Lk 11:20).

In the world of the New Testament—as reflected both in New Testament texts and in extrabiblical literature[19]—evil spirit powers (Satan, the ruler of this world, demons, principalities, powers, elemental spirits, rulers, authorities, spiritual forces of evil in the heavenly places, etc.) were understood to stand behind human authorities, political power, social structures and economic practices, insofar as these were opposed to God and his redemptive purposes.[20] Given this reality, Jesus' life—his teaching and actions—repre-

---

[16]Evans, *Luke*, pp. 291-96. "Passover celebrants were almost surely being overcharged for sacrificial birds and animals, and were perhaps even being cheated when money was exchanged for the shekels needed to buy these animals" (pp. 291-92).

[17]See Craig Keener, *The IVP Bible Background Commentary: New Testament* (Downers Grove, Ill.: InterVarsity Press, 1993), pp. 165-66, for the religious and historical background.

[18]"Finger of God" represents the power of God (see Ex 8:19). Such a meaning is confirmed in the version of this saying in Matthew 12:28, where we read: "It is by the Spirit of God that I cast out demons." Here as elsewhere, this refers to the power of God's Spirit, present and working in Jesus.

[19]See the discussion of this material in Clinton Arnold, *Powers of Darkness: Principalities and Powers in Paul's Letters* (Downers Grove, Ill.: InterVarsity Press, 1992), pp. 19-86.

[20]Several excellent studies are recommended on this complex reality, representing a variety of perspectives on the nature of "the powers" and their relationship to cultural, social, political and economic structures: Heinrich Schlier, *Principalities and Powers in the New Testament* (Freiburg: Herder, 1961); Hendrik Berkhof, *Christ and the Powers*, trans. John H. Yoder (Scottdale, Penn.: Herald Press, 1977); Richard Mouw, *Politics and the Biblical Drama* (Grand Rapids: Eerdmans, 1976); and Arnold, *Powers of Darkness*.

sents a frontal assault on "the ruler of this world" (Jn 12:31) and all the sinful social and political structures and policies that are the instruments of the evil one, which oppress, marginalize and demean human life.

Paul was convinced that the *decisive battle* against the powers was fought and won on the cross of Christ, who there "disarmed the rulers and authorities . . . triumphing over them in it" (Col 2:15).[21] But he was also keenly aware that the war against the reign of evil, in human life and institutions was still very much in process (Eph 6:10-14). He knew that Christ's victory over the powers had to be appropriated in a lifetime of faithful discipleship and presence in the world (Phil 2:12-13). Those "in Christ" were called to embody the reign of God in all areas of life and society, and therefore the "over-under" power structures in racial (Jew/Gentile), social (free/slave) and gender (male/female) relationships needed to be challenged and transformed (Gal 3:27-28).

As Jesus spoke truth to power and acted in ways that challenged their religious and social authority insofar as it embodied the designs of the evil one (Jn 8:44), so Paul challenged Christians to "not be conformed to this world" (Rom 12:2)[22] and to "take no part in the unfruitful works of darkness, but instead expose them" (Eph 5:11).[23]

It is very clear from the above journey through the biblical witness that God's encounter of the world's brokenness—in and through the people of Israel and culminating in the redemptive life, death and resurrection of Jesus—is all-inclusive. God's salvation, the in-breaking of God's kingdom (reign), is directed toward (1) individual persons in their concrete physical, emotional and spiritual totality, and their relational and social interconnectedness, *as well as* (2) the cultural, social, economic, and political contexts and structures that are part of the sinful reality of human life in community. There is no aspect of sinful, distorted human life that lies outside the sphere

---

[21]This Pauline conviction is certainly in continuity with Jesus' affirmation that his and his disciples' demon exorcism, and finally his "glorification" on the cross (Jn 12:31), meant that Satan had been robbed of his enslaving power.

[22]"When Paul spoke of 'this world' in a moral sense, he was thinking of the totality of people, social systems, values and traditions in terms of their opposition to God and his redemptive purposes" (Arnold, *Powers of Darkness*, p. 203).

[23]Ronald J. Sider, *Christ and Violence* (Scottdale, Penn.: Herald Press, 1979), p. 57. Sider contends that Paul's word in Ephesians 3:10—about the church making known the manifest wisdom of God "to the rulers and authorities in the heavenly places"—is a challenge to Christians to confront governing authorities when their policies and programs violate God's purposes.

of God's redemptive work in Christ, including the pollution of the environment and the exploitation of the earth's resources through greed and selfish gain.[24] Neither sinful persons, nor the sinful cultural, social, economic and political structures they have shaped, are exempt from the claims of God's kingdom.

The new humanity created in Christ Jesus (Eph 2:15-22) is called to be the vanguard of this redemptive and transforming work of God. As "God's temple" in whom "God's Spirit dwells" (1 Cor 3:16), this new humanity is intended to be God's option, God's alternative to the fragmentation, the distortion, the brokenness of human life and society. As such, this new humanity in Christ is called both to bear witness to the whole gospel and to embody it in personal and corporate presence and action. There is no room here for the either-or of personal gospel or social gospel, of the "saving of souls" or the transformation of sinful structures, of personal justification or work for justice. The personal gospel and the social gospel are part of a seamless robe, two sides of the same garment. From the perspective of the whole gospel, you cannot have one without the other.

Thus, the modernist-liberal vision, in its primary (and often exclusive) concern about social and structural transformation, is a denial of the whole gospel. It offers a social gospel without a personal Savior; a gospel of political peace without the Prince of Peace; a gospel of bread for the world without the Bread of Life; a gospel of harmony in human relationships without a life-giving and life-transforming relationship with the Holy One of God.

For its part, evangelicalism, in its primary (and often exclusive) concern for personal salvation from bondage to sin, and thus commitment to the evange-

---

[24]Isaiah 24:4-8 connects human sin and the polluted earth (cf. Rom 8:19-21). See Francis A. Schaeffer, *Pollution and the Death of Man: The Christian View of Ecology* (Wheaton, Ill.: Tyndale House, 1970). Schaeffer was one of the earliest evangelical voices addressing Christian responsibility for the environment. One reviewer states that "Schaeffer discusses the Christian approach to the environment and deals with the all-too-common misperception peddled by those Christians who are either ignorant of Biblical truth in this area, or are so insistent on distancing themselves from the pantheistic, bleeding-heart tree-hugging left that they come across as uncaring and abusive" (Benjamin Gardner, "Excellent Analysis of Christianity and the Environment," Amazon.com [May 1, 2002], <www.amazon.com/Pollution-Death-Man-Francis-Schaeffer/dp/0891076867/ref=pd_bbs_sr_1?ie=UTF8&s=books&qid=1221768282&sr=8-1>). Sadly, a recent Barna poll showed "evangelicals as the least concerned segments among more than 50 population groups studied" when it comes to the issue of global warming (The Barna Group webpage, "Born Again Christians Remain Skeptical, Divided About Global Warming," [September 17, 2007] <www.barna.org/FlexPage.aspx?Page=BarnaUpdate&BarnaUpdateID=279>).

listic task of the church, also offers the world a half-gospel. An authentic, biblically grounded and informed witness and presence in the world means commitment to the Savior who both redeems individuals from the ravages of sin and leads them into transforming social concern and action. It means commitment to the Prince of Peace, who both calms the turmoil of the heart and leads us into fruitful work for peace within the often-divided Christian community and within the larger world of human society. It means commitment to the Bread of Life, who both feeds the hunger of the human spirit and inspires us to be there for those who have no bread. It means commitment to Jesus the Justifier, who both justifies us before a holy God and empowers us to challenge injustices and to be doers of justice. It means commitment to Jesus the Reconciler, who both reconciles us to restored relationship with God and calls us to be ambassadors and ministers of reconciliation in the midst of the continuing divisive realities of racial hatred and bigotry in our land and across the human landscape.

A bifurcated gospel—the result of the abuse of the whole gospel in hearing and applying biblical teaching—has severely impaired, limited and distorted Christian witness to, and within, secular culture. As such it is, at its deepest level, an offense against the Lord who seeks, through his people, to make *all things new.*

AVOIDING THE ABUSE OF THE WHOLE GOSPEL

In our study of Scripture, and in the application of the result of that study to our lives and our world, how can we avoid this abuse, this bifurcation of the whole gospel in our proclamation and presence in the world? I offer the following challenges and guidelines to assist in this important task.

1. Just don't do it! If our analysis of the biblical material is valid—namely that God's redemptive work, culminating in Christ, is addressed to and concerned with every dimension of human life in this world—then it is *imperative* that we hold the personal and social dimensions of the gospel together. Then, and only then, are we being "trustworthy stewards" of the biblical revelation. Thus, whenever we are tempted to favor one of these dimensions to the exclusion or diminution of the other, this challenge ("just don't do it!") should ring in our ears.

2. Apply the whole of yourself to the study of Scripture, and the whole result of that study to yourself. This principle for biblical interpretation and its application is attributed to the eighteenth-century German theologian and Greek New Testament scholar Johann Albrecht Bengel. His admonition to his students is particularly relevant for our task of avoiding the abuse of the whole gospel. For when we bring the *totality* of our lives to the biblical Word, we begin to recognize that it speaks to and makes claims on that totality—in its connectedness to the whole web of human life (relationship with others, social institutions, politics, economics, the arts and sciences, etc.). But the *hearing* of the whole of Scripture in relation to the totality of human life must then be followed by the *application* of that whole gospel to ourselves, not only to the personal dimension, but also to the social dimension.

3. If your vocation calls you to focus on one side of the gospel, make space to support the other side. When called particularly to a vocation whose focus is primarily (or exclusively) on either the personal or social dimensions of the gospel (such as sharing the good news of salvation in an evangelistic ministry or building homes with Habitat for Humanity), one ought to make some space in one's life and presence in the world for the advocacy and support of, or participation in, the other dimension of the gospel. Some time ago, Billy Graham was asked if, looking back on a lifetime of inviting people to new life in Christ through his crusades—which have touched the lives of millions around the globe— would he change anything? In his response, he stated that he wished he had said more about the social implications and claims of the gospel. He was uniquely called and gifted to preach the gospel of personal salvation. We can only imagine what even greater impact his powerful proclamation of the gospel would have had, had those millions who came to Christ been challenged more significantly to express their faith in Christ through social engagement.

A powerful example of the refusal to bifurcate the whole gospel at the point of application is the life and ministry of a monastic community in Italy. One half of the members of this community give themselves for six months to a life of prayer, contemplation, study of Scripture, worship and fellowship with one another in order to nurture their personal and communal relationship with Christ. The other half of the community spends those same six months in the villages and towns of the region, engaged in social ministries and acts of compassion. During the next six months, these two groups trade places. See Ron Sider's *Cup of Water, Bread of Life* (Grand Rapids: Zondervan, 1994) for numerous examples of churches and ministries that combine these two dimensions of the gospel in their lives and missions.

3

THE ABUSE OF SELECTIVITY

The foregoing chapter, "The Abuse of the Whole Gospel," is in a certain sense an instance of the abuse of selectivity, and it was originally conceived as an example of this sort of abuse. But on further reflection I became convinced that the bifurcation of the whole gospel into "social gospel" and "personal gospel" represented more than the problem of selectivity in biblical interpretation. It represents a different kind, or order, of selectivity, namely a distortion (abuse) of the *totality* of the biblical witness that addresses the *totality* of human life, seeking the transformation of everything through reconciliation with God and reconciliation within human relationships and human communities. This bifurcation of the gospel is in some profound sense a frontal assault on, and abuse of, the totality of God's reclamation project: the redemption of the entire creation from its bondage to decay (Rom 8:18-21). In the present chapter, we will tackle specific instances of selectivity within the purview of both the personal gospel and the social gospel.

Selectivity in the use of biblical texts—which leads to an unbalanced, and often distorted and misinformed, understanding of the message of the Bible on numerous aspects of Christian life and faith—is a particularly problematic abuse of Scripture. Why? Because it is more subtle than other types of abuses that we will discuss in this book. The selective way of reading and using the Bible is not an outright distortion of the meaning of given texts (such as taking passages or verses out of their textual or historical or cultural contexts). In fact, this abuse of Scripture can easily masquerade under the guise of the phrase "the Bible says," or "the Bible teaches," giving it almost immediate legitimacy. Specific biblical passages under consideration clearly seem to say this or that. And if the text contains a particular instruction of the apostle Paul or Peter, or a divinely given instruction through Moses to the people of God, then that instruction is presented as normative for Christian faith and life: this is what God's Word demands of us or calls us to or teaches us about various aspects of human life. The danger of this abuse of Scripture lies in its ignoring or rejecting (either outright or by omission) other parts or passages of Scripture that support a different teaching, or present an alternative perspective, or advocate an opposing view.

When individual Christians or communities of Christians practice this kind of selectivity in the interpretation and use of Scripture, a one-sided, incomplete or distorted biblical message is the outcome. And since Christians—on the basis of their likes and dislikes, their cultural conditioning, their faith traditions, their life situations and their personal needs—use Scripture selectively in different ways, the total Christian witness in and to the world becomes confusing and perplexing. What do these people who call themselves Christians really believe?

Numerous issues in human life and society in general, and among Christians in particular, are addressed in the Bible by people of diverse perspectives or attitudes, or by people giving specific instructions. We will see that when these diverse perspectives are ignored in favor of a definitive, monovocal teaching, the broad spectrum of biblical guidance on a particular issue becomes muted, and important voices are silenced. At times, tragic consequences are the outcome.

A host of examples could be used to illustrate this way of abusing Scripture, such as: the tension between God's sovereignty and human freedom; the use of force to solve disputes versus the call to be peacemakers; the relationship between God's blessing and faithful, righteous living; obedience to God and obedience to the state; the relationship between men and women in home, church and society; evangelism focused on personal salvation or concern for social justice. Virtually all of these tensions, and more, will be addressed or touched on in connection with the various abuses of Scripture discussed in this book. For the purpose of this chapter, I have chosen three of these topics that I consider to be of critical importance in our time.

SUBMISSION TO GOVERNING AUTHORITY

How are followers of Jesus to relate to the state, to governing authorities, to cultural values and to the rules of the larger societies in which they find themselves? Throughout Christian history, individual believers and groups of Christians have struggled with the tension that often exists between their citizenship in this world and their citizenship in the kingdom of God. How should they respond when the demands of the one conflict with the demands of the other? What are they to do if their understanding of the lordship of Christ and its implications for particular areas of life are diametrically opposed to the dictates of "Caesar" (governing authorities, laws, social norms and cultural values)?

How does the Bible respond to these questions? Or better, what is the Word of God—in and through the variety of biblical voices—that addresses itself to these real dilemmas? A look at a number of biblical texts will reveal two major perspectives on this critical matter.

Paul's instructions in Romans 13 have long been pivotal in this discussion. Writing to Christian believers in Rome who were living in the shadow of Roman imperial power, Paul gives very specific teaching about the nature and purpose of governing authority, as well as instructions about Christian attitudes and actions toward those in authority. In brief, his argument is as follows: Christians should be "subject to the governing authorities." Why? Because "there is no authority except from God, and those authorities that exist have been instituted by God" (Rom 13:1). Since that is the case, "whoever resists authority resists what God has appointed" (Rom 13:2). Paul goes on to explain *why* God has appointed those in authority. Governing authorities, he says, are "God's servant" for the purpose of punishing evil and restraining bad conduct through fear of consequences (Rom 13:4) and for promoting and encouraging good conduct (Rom 13:3). Given that these governing functions are in keeping with God's purposes for human society, Paul concludes that it is therefore appropriate that Christians "pay taxes" and thereby support these activities of the state (Rom 13:6).

A parallel passage, with similar instructions, is found in 1 Peter 2:13-17. Christians are admonished to conduct themselves "honorably among the Gentiles" in order to bring glory to God (1 Pet 2:12). One way in which that "honorable" presence in the world is embodied is through the acceptance of "the authority of every human institution, whether of the emperor as supreme, or of governors" (1 Pet 2:13-14). This is to be done "for the Lord's sake" (1 Pet 2:13), since it is in keeping with the will of God (1 Pet 2:15) that "those who do wrong" are punished by the authorities and "those who do right" are praised (1 Pet 2:14). To drive home his teaching about submitting to governing authorities, the author concludes with this summary admonition: "Honor everyone. Love the family of believers. Fear God. Honor the emperor" (1 Pet 2:17).

These instructions in Romans and 1 Peter to submit to the governing authorities are particularly striking in light of the fact that the Roman Caesars claimed for themselves the status of divinity. "Caesar is Lord" was the confession of Roman citizens. And that claim to divine status and authority was diametrically opposed to the earliest Christian confession, "Jesus Christ is Lord" (Phil 2:11; Rom 10:9; 1 Cor 12:3).[1] How remarkable, then, that Christians are nonetheless instructed to submit to the emperor and his governors throughout the provinces of the Roman Empire. Does not this teaching create a serious conflict of interest? And does not Paul elsewhere express this conflict when he says that, as far as Christians are concerned, there is only "one Lord, Jesus Christ" (1 Cor 8:6), even though "many lords" exist (1 Cor 8:5)?

It is likely that the inspiration or foundation for these admonitions about submission to governing authorities was the teaching of Jesus. In the Gospel texts (Mt 22:17-21; and parallel texts in Mk 12:14-17; Lk 20:22-25), Jesus was asked by his opponents whether or not it was "lawful to pay taxes to the emperor." The paying of taxes to Rome was, of course, a sign of one's allegiance and submission to the emperor (willing or coerced!) that faithful Jews deeply resented and at times resisted.[2] After taking a Roman coin and identifying Caesar's image imprinted on it, Jesus' response to the question was the

---

[1]Gerald F. Hawthorne, *Philippians,* Word Biblical Commentary, vol. 43 (Dallas: Word Books, 1983), p. 93. See also James D. G. Dunn, *Romans 9—16,* Word Biblical Commentary, vol. 38B (Dallas: Word Books, 1988), pp. 607-8.

[2]See Craig S. Keener, *The IVP Bible Background Commentary: New Testament* (Downers Grove, Ill.: InterVarsity Press, 1993), pp. 105-6, for helpful comments regarding the historical background of Jesus' interaction with the Pharisees and Herodians about paying taxes to Caesar.

simple declaration, "Give therefore to the emperor the things that are the emperor's, and to God the things that are God's" (Mt 22:21). Within the Jewish context, this word of Jesus was very clear. The central thrust of Jewish faith, shared by Jesus, was that God has absolute authority and demands ultimate allegiance from his people. At the same time, Jesus affirms that there is a legitimate sphere of human authority, and giving "to the emperor the things that are the emperor's" represents submission to that (derived and limited) authority.

On the basis of this Word of God, in and through the teaching of Jesus and his apostles, many Christians and Christian communities—from the first century to the present—have concluded that the state (governing authorities and rulers of all kinds, including dictators) possess a delegated authority given by God, and therefore, Christians are duty-bound to submit to the dictates of the state and give their allegiance to it.

But is this the whole biblical picture? Are these biblical instructions intended for, and to be obeyed by, all Christians, in all circumstances throughout history?

The truth is that there are voices within the biblical revelation on this issue of submission to governing authorities and laws of the state that stand in significant tension with, and even oppose, what has been understood by many Christians as the clear will of God. Those other voices are pervasively present in both the Old and New Testaments, beginning with the prophetic critique and denunciation of the vast majority of Israel's rulers.

The prophets spoke truth to the leaders in the name and power of Yahweh when Israel's rulers failed to exercise their authority in keeping with God's purposes. Those purposes included doing good, seeking justice, rescuing the oppressed, defending the orphans, pleading for the widows (Is 1:16-17) and defending the rights of the innocent (Is 5:23). That divine calling on the leaders of Israel, says Isaiah, has been rejected by them. Therefore, the Lord "enters into judgment with the elders and princes of his people: It is you who have devoured the vineyard; the spoil of the poor is in your houses. What do you mean by crushing my people, by grinding the face of the poor? says the LORD God of hosts" (Is 3:14-15). They make "iniquitous decrees," "write oppressive statutes" and "turn aside the needy from justice" (Is 10:1-2).

The prophet Hosea joins that voice of divine protest by announcing that "the king of Israel shall be utterly cut off" (Hos 10:15). The divine judgment is this: "You have plowed wickedness, you have reaped injustice, you have eaten the fruit of lies. . . . You have trusted in your power and in the multitude of your warriors" (Hos 10:13). Speaking on behalf of God, the prophet Micah likewise speaks a word of judgment against the "heads of Jacob and rulers of the house of Israel" because they do "not know justice . . . hate the good and love the evil" (Mic 3:1-2). These "shepherds of Israel"—as Ezekiel calls the rulers of the people (Ezek 34:2)—have abandoned their divine mandate (Ezek 34:2-9). Therefore, the Lord God is "against the shepherds" (Ezek 34:10).

The message seems clear. Since God has absolute authority over all of life, rulers possess authority only derivatively. Only when their exercise of that authority is in keeping with God's intention for human life and community are they truly God's servants. The failure of Israel's "shepherds" at precisely this point is exposed by the prophets. Yahweh, they knew, was "Father of orphans and protector of widows" (Ps 68:5).[3] That was the divine model for human rule, which is so powerfully expressed in the coronation prayer of Psalm 72:

> Give the king your justice, O God,
>   and your righteousness to a king's son.
> May he judge your people with righteousness,
>   and your poor with justice.
> May the mountains yield prosperity for the people,
>   and the hills, in righteousness.
> May he defend the cause of the poor of the people,
>   give deliverance to the needy,
>   and crush the oppressor. . . .
>
> For he delivers the needy when they call,
>   the poor and those who have no helper.
> He has pity on the weak and the needy,
>   and saves the lives of the needy. (Ps 72:1-4, 12-13)

The common thread that runs through the prophetic opposition to the rulers of Israel and Judah is their failure (with very few exceptions) to reflect the character of God's kingly reign in *their* kingly reign. Thus they have forfeited their authority as God's agents within human affairs.

---

[3]Widows and orphans are often coupled as a pair. They were, in the context of Israelite society, the most vulnerable social group.

This prophetic theme is clearly the background for those voices in the New Testament that stand in tension with the mandate to be submissive and give virtually unquestioning allegiance to governing powers. The Gospel accounts of Jesus' life and ministry make clear that he did not accept all legal and governing authority, whether religious or temporal, as ultimate dispensers of God's will. Throughout his ministry, he took on the structures that restricted and lessened people's lives—as in his challenges to restrictive sabbath regulations (e.g., Mt 12:3-8; Mk 3:1-6). He upset the cultural and religious status quo—as in his rejection of the "clean-unclean" religious and social categories that demeaned and segregated people (e.g., Mk 2:15-16; 7:14-23). He confronted the powers and the legal and ideological systems they represented—as in his cleansing of the temple and his denunciation of officially sanctioned practices that deprived the poor (Mt 21:12-13; Mk 11:15-18).[4]

Jesus' entire ministry was characterized by bitter conflict with the religious authorities—scribes, Pharisees, Sadducees—who, under the umbrella of Roman imperial power, were responsible for upholding the law in the towns and cities throughout Palestine. His uncompromising utterances against them (e.g., the "woes" in Matthew 23) intensified the conflict until the final crisis in Jerusalem. With the Pharisees, the high priests and the elders of the people in concert, Jesus was executed by the Roman authorities, "ostensibly in the interest of maintaining the Jewish law and Roman order" and to avoid "a tear in the delicately woven fabric of political collaboration."[5]

The seeds that Jesus' words and deeds sowed in the lives of his followers bore fruit in their own response to, and interaction with, the authorities. According to Luke's account of the early church in Acts, Peter and John are brought before the Sanhedrin, the supreme governing council of Judaism (consisting of their rulers, elder, scribes and high priests, Acts 4:5-6), and ordered "not to speak or teach at all in the name of Jesus" (Acts 4:18). Their response to this order is the courageous statement: "Whether it is right in God's sight to listen to you rather than to God, you must judge; for we cannot

---

[4]For a discussion of the political and social implications of Jesus' acts and words, see Howard Yoder, *The Politics of Jesus* (Grand Rapids: Eerdmans, 1972). Mortimer Arias, in *Announcing the Reign of God* (Lima, Ohio: Academic Renewal Press, 2001), pp. 50-51, shows that Jesus' teaching about the in-breaking kingdom of God was a decisive challenge to the carefully constructed power arrangements between Jewish religious authorities and Roman political authorities.

[5]William R. Farmer, *Jesus and the Gospel: Tradition, Scripture, and Canon* (Philadelphia: Fortress, 1982), pp. 42-43.

keep from speaking about what we have seen and heard" (Acts 4:19-20). In response to the apostles' continuing ministry of healing and proclamation (Acts 4:23—5:16), they are arrested again by the temple authorities, put in prison and then tried before the Sanhedrin (Acts 5:17-27). The disciples justify their deliberate refusal to obey the council's "strict orders" (Acts 5:28) with the ringing confession: "We must obey God rather than any human authority" (Acts 5:29).

Later in the story of the early church, Paul and Silas are described by their opponents as those "who have been turning the world upside down" (Acts 17:6) and who "are all acting contrary to the decrees of the emperor, saying that there is another king named Jesus" (Acts 17:7). And in following the example of their Lord and his earliest disciples, countless martyrs in subsequent centuries gave their lives because they resisted the decrees of "Caesar," recognizing them as contrary to God's will.

The book of Revelation gives final voice in the New Testament to the principle that the Christian's ultimate allegiance belongs to God, not the state. Revelation 13 pictures the state—most certainly Rome[6]—as a beast opposed to the purposes of God. And Revelation 18 speaks of the downfall of "Babylon" in which "was found the blood of the prophets and saints" (Rev 18:24)—again clearly a reference to Rome in its opposition to God's purpose, most likely under the ruthless emperor Domitian.[7]

The above survey of the wider biblical perspective—in contrast to the teaching of Romans 13, 1 Peter 2 and Matthew 22 about obedience and submission to governing authorities—clearly reveals that submission to the authority of the state is not the only biblical teaching on that issue.

Where does this dual and very complex biblical teaching leave us? If the "abuse of selectivity" has its way, we simply listen to one part of the biblical chorus and close our ears to the other part. But the problem with such selective listening to the biblical word is that it can lead to tragic historical consequences or to terribly divisive battles within the Christian community—both of which seriously undermine the viability of Christian witness and presence in our world. Many examples from the two-thousand-year history of Chris-

---

[6]Craig S. Keener, *Revelation*, The NIV Application Commentary (Grand Rapids: Zondervan, 2000), pp. 335-42.

[7]Robert H. Mounce, *The Book of Revelation*, New International Commentary on the New Testament, rev. ed. (Grand Rapids: Eerdmans, 1998), pp. 324-25.

tianity could be cited, but a few from not-too-distant history should suffice.

Many Bible-believing Christians in Germany supported and lauded Hitler and his National Socialist Party (and their programs) on the basis of the biblical teaching to submit to the governing authorities. In the campaign to arrest Jews and send them to concentration camps, many Christian leaders and countless rank-and-file churchgoers identified and exposed Jewish people in their neighborhoods to the Gestapo. And a good number of concentration camp guards were faithful churchgoers. As a young teenager growing up in postwar Germany, I asked my parents, who were committed Christians, how it was possible that Christians participated in this tragic extermination of the Jewish people. The answer, in addition to the recognition of deep-seated anti-Semitism in Europe, was that these Christians believed that they were obligated by the teaching of the Bible to obey the dictates of the state. I will never forget my mother telling me that, after one attempt on Hitler's life had failed, many Christians gathered in their churches for prayers of thanksgiving that God had spared the Führer's life. Why, I asked? The answer was that "the Bible taught them that rulers are instituted by God and are to be honored and obeyed."

This mindset of many so-called German Christians is confirmed in numerous studies of the German church during the Nazi era (1930-1945). The German theologians who supported Hitler's rise to power in the early 1930s "saw the fulfillment of the will of the Creator in the German hour and the rise of National Socialism."[8] Indeed, these German Christians sought to have the backing of Hitler himself: "The goal of the faith movement 'German Christians' is an evangelical German state church. The State of Adolf Hitler calls for the church; the church must hear his call."[9] Total and unquestioning obedience to the state on the basis of biblical teaching was a significant theological rationale for the acquiescence of many Christians to the Nazi agenda.

There were of course many other Christians and Christian leaders who, in listening to the other voices within Scripture, concluded that the Nazi agenda was diametrically opposed to God's purposes revealed in Scripture. They

---

[8]James H. Charlesworth, ed., *Jews and Christians: Exploring the Past, Present and Future* (New York: Crossroad, 1990), p. 235.
[9]Ernst Wolf, *Barmen: Church Between Temptation and Grace* (Munich, 1970), p. 50, quoted in *Jews and Christians: Exploring the Past, Present and Future*, ed. James H. Charlesworth (New York: Crossroad, 1990), p. 234.

formed the "Confessing Church" movement, which actively and vocally resisted the demands of the state; many were exiled, imprisoned or executed.

But two brief examples from our more recent national history make clear how even many American Christians, convinced of the divine mandate in the biblical texts under discussion (Rom 13; 1 Pet 2; Mt 22), supported unquestioning obedience to the state.

Until the advent of federal civil rights legislation and its enforcement in the 1960s, there existed in the United States segregation of whites and blacks. There were prohibitions against admitting blacks into public facilities, such as bathrooms and restaurants, that were used by whites; blacks were prevented from voting in elections and from participating in community events; they were restricted to the rear of buses; and many residential districts in inner cities were red-lined by the banking establishment so that minority residents could not get fair mortgage rates and loans—all these and more were enforced on the ground of numerous laws and regulations promulgated by state legislators and local city councils.

Many Christians strongly supported these ordinances and often participated in enforcing them. Are we not obligated, so they argued, to give allegiance to the governing authorities, to obey the dictates of the state? As a student during that era in an evangelical Christian college, I heard this argument repeatedly from fellow students whose thinking and believing had been shaped within this cultural and religious milieu. My wife, who grew up in the South, often questioned the validity and morality of these practices on the basis of her understanding of the gospel. In response, she was regularly reminded by pious church folk that these practices were in keeping with local and state laws and were to be obeyed on the basis of biblical teaching about submission to authorities. So here, as during the National Socialist era in Germany, demeaning and dehumanizing attitudes, practices and actions were embodied in the lives of Christians and in Christian communities, and they were justified on the basis of "clear" biblical mandates.

During the tumultuous Vietnam War years in the 1960s and 1970s, many Christians were confronted with the tension between the dictates, on the one hand, of their consciences and their commitment to the lordship of Christ over all of life, and on the other hand, to the demand of political authority. The concepts of "civil obedience" and "civil disobedience" were significant elements in rigorous discussions in the larger society, as well as within Christian communities. I have vivid memories of these often-heated discussions during my graduate studies and first few years of teaching at a seminary in the Chicago area. The central question in many of these discussions was this: Is it acceptable for Christians to actively oppose the war in Vietnam, to protest against the government's actions, and to refuse to participate in the armed struggle there by draft resistance or evasion? Often, those who believed in such resistance and thus refused to serve in the armed forces were judged as standing against the clear teaching of Scripture, located in texts such as Romans 13, 1 Peter 2 and Matthew 22.

What are we to conclude from this dual, and seemingly contradictory, teaching in the Bible? When we resist the temptation to pick and choose certain texts, thereby ignoring others, but take the whole of the biblical testimony seriously, a coherent, nuanced biblical teaching emerges. Insofar as the state and other governing powers exercise their authority in keeping with God's intention, they act as God's servants for the common good of the governed. In that case, on the basis of a careful reading and interpretation of Romans 13, 1 Peter 2 and Matthew 22, governing authorities deserve our trust, positive support and honor, as well as prayer (1 Tim 2:1-2). However, if the authority of the state runs counter to this divine intention, then that authority cannot be understood as God-given. Indeed, it becomes quite clear from the texts we have surveyed that when governments dispense injustice, support and promote moral decay, trample on the weak and powerless, are corrupt and deceitful, they are being influenced by demonic powers and forces. In such a context, the followers of Jesus are called to stand against, and resist, its demands.

THE RELATIONSHIP BETWEEN MEN AND WOMEN IN HOME, CHURCH AND SOCIETY

The nature of the relationship between men and women in the human community in general and in the Christian community in particular continues to be a matter of considerable debate and concern. In many traditional male-dominated societies and cultures, we continue to witness terrible discrimination against, and often oppression of, women, particularly in radical Islamic cultures. Even in Western society, traditional patriarchal power structures have left their legacies. Studies have shown that the traditional ideology of male dominance has contributed greatly to the tragic abuse of women, both physically and emotionally.[10] Within many sectors of the Christian community worldwide, women are significantly restricted with regard to leadership and particular ministries in the church.[11] Within these same Christian traditions, the correlation between male dominance and domestic violence has become a serious concern.[12]

These realities in our world and within the communities of Jesus' followers confront us with this important question: What is the biblical teaching about the male-female relationship? In seeking to answer this question, we once again enter a situation of some complexity. There are a number of biblical texts that seem to clearly support male hierarchy. At the same time, there is also a wealth of biblical material that opposes such a hierarchical structure. We will begin with those biblical passages that have traditionally been understood to provide the normative, inspired biblical teaching regarding the place and role of women in relationship to men. The consideration of these texts will be followed by a discussion of texts and themes that point in a different direction.

The foundation for the view that men are intended to exercise leadership and authority over women is located in the creation narrative of Genesis 2 and the narrative of the Fall in Genesis 3. According to Genesis 2, man is formed first, out of the dust of the ground (Gen 2:7), and given the mandate to take care of the earth (Gen 2:15). Woman is formed subsequently, "because it is not good that the man should be alone" (Gen 2:18). She is formed out of the man ("bone of my bones / and flesh of my flesh," Gen 2:23) as a "helper," "suitable for him" (Gen 2:18, 20).

A common understanding of this narrative is that by virtue of the chronological sequence of their creation and the designation of the woman as man's "helper," God's creational intention for man is to be the leader and authority figure, and for the woman to be the follower, the assistant, the one who submits to his leadership and authority.

---

[10]Mildred Pagelow, in *Woman-Battering: Victims and Their Experiences* (Thousand Oaks, Calif.: Sage, 1981), develops a theoretical framework for understanding wife battering in which she identifies "traditional ideology" regarding male-female relationships as a major contributor to the abuse of women.

[11]Robert G. Clouse and Bonnidell Clouse, eds., *Women in Ministry: Four Views* (Downers Grove, Ill.: InterVarsity Press, 1989), pp. 4-21. The historian Robert Clouse surveys the various historical, cultural and ecclesial factors and developments in this matter of the role of women in the church. He concludes that "this is one of the most pressing problems facing believers in the closing years of the twentieth century."

[12]James and Phyllis Alsdurf, *Battered into Submission: The Tragedy of Wife Abuse in the Christian Home* (Downers Grove, Ill.: InterVarsity Press, 1998).

This view is supposedly confirmed by the narrative of the Fall in Genesis 3. The demonic temptation to rebel against divinely set boundaries (to "be like God," Gen 3:5) leads to the cursedness of human existence (Gen 3:8-19). A significant dimension of this cursed existence for the woman is that "he [the man] shall rule over you" (Gen 3:16). This word, addressed to the woman by God, was believed by subsequent Jewish and later Christian interpreters to be God's punishment for her transgression, and it was also believed to be the divine command, mandating this hierarchical model for the male-female relationship from that point forward, throughout human history.

This understanding of the divine purpose for the male-female relationship is seen to be corroborated in the authoritative teaching of the New Testament. The most specific echo of Genesis 2—3 with respect to the male-female relationship is found in 1 Timothy 2. There, women are instructed to "learn in silence with full submission" (1 Tim 2:11). Further, women are not permitted to "teach or to have authority" over men (1 Tim 2:12). These instructions are then grounded in an interpretation of the Genesis 3 narrative: "For Adam was formed first, then Eve; and Adam was not deceived, but the woman was deceived and became a transgressor" (1 Tim 2:13-14). The submission of woman to man's authority is here based on Adam's priority in creation, while the prohibition against a woman's teaching and therefore her silence is based on the assertion that Eve was the first to be deceived (Gen 3:4-6).

One or both of these themes—the submission of women to the authority of men and the restrictions imposed on women in the life and ministry of the church—are present in several other New Testament texts. We will briefly consider 1 Peter 3 and the Pauline passages in 1 Corinthians 11, 14; Ephesians 5; Colossians 3; and Titus 2.

The statement in 1 Peter 3:1—"Wives . . . accept the authority of your husbands"—is part of a series of instructions for Christian living designed to show to the larger Gentile world that the followers of Jesus, who are being maligned as evildoers, are in fact honorable people (1 Pet 2:12). The instruction for wives' submission is given for a particular purpose: so that unbelieving husbands may be won over to the faith "by their wives' conduct" (1 Pet 3:1-2). Wives' submission to their husbands is illustrated from an Old Testament narrative: "Sarah obeyed Abraham and called him lord" (1 Pet 3:6; citing the Greek translation [LXX] of Gen 18:12). Just as in 1 Timothy 2:11-14, submission to the man's authority is grounded in an Old Testament text.

So in addition to the fact that, in these New Testament texts, we have apostolic authority behind the specific instructions that are given, the fact that they are justified with appeal to the sacred Scriptures (our Old Testament) is seen as further proof that we have normative teaching in these texts regarding the male-female relationship for Christian life.

Paul's instructions in 1 Corinthians 11 and 14 about the relationship of men and women, and women's participation in the worship life of the church in Corinth, is seen to provide additional biblical material for the hierarchical model. In 1 Corinthians 11:2-11, the problem seems to be proper and acceptable apparel and/or hairstyle for women in worship, while praying and prophesying (1 Cor 11:5-6, 13-15). In light of their freedom in Christ, women in the congregation not only participated with men in worship activities (praying and proclaiming the good news, 1 Cor 11:5, 13), but they apparently also felt free to do so without the customary head covering (or hairstyle, 1 Cor 11:5-6, 13), thus blurring the distinction between the sexes and bringing shame on the men in the congregation (or wives on their husbands).[13] Such behavior was apparently improper (1 Cor 11:13) in the context of the culture. The situation addressed by Paul is that of women heaping shame on the men (or their husbands) in the congregation.[14]

Paul launches his response to this situation by stating that "Christ is the head of every man, and the husband is the head of his wife, and God is the head of Christ" (1 Cor 11:3). He goes on to argue that when a woman "prays or prophesies with her head unveiled" (or uncovered), she "disgraces her head" (1 Cor 11:5). The intimate connection with verse 3 shows that the "head" that a woman disgraces when she does not wear a head-covering is man (or her husband). The word *head* (Greek *kephalē*) is used metaphorically here to designate man (or husband). Man is designated "head" in relationship to woman in some sense. We will discuss the metaphorical meanings of the word *head* in chapter five, where we will look at the abuse of Scripture that results when the original meanings of Greek or Hebrew words or expressions are not carefully considered.

---

[13]The same Greek word *(anēr)* is used for both *man* and *husband*. Likewise, there is one Greek word *(gynē)* for both *woman* and *wife*. Paul seems to be moving back and forth between these meanings. Which meaning he has in mind must be determined from the context and flow of the passage. The NIV opts for man/woman; the NRSV for husband/wife.

[14]See the thorough and lucid discussion of this entire passage in Gordon D. Fee, *The First Epistle to the Corinthians*, New International Commentary on the New Testament (Grand Rapids: Eerdmans, 1978), pp. 491-512.

For the moment, it is clear from the history of the interpretation of this passage that the "head" metaphor—as referring to man in relationship to woman—has largely been understood to identify the man as an authority figure, a leader, chief, boss or ruler. Such a meaning is, of course, one of the common metaphorical meanings of the word *head* in the English language, as in "head of state" or "head of the company." From this way of reading the phrase "man is head of woman" (or "the husband is the head of his wife") the so-called doctrine of headship has been derived, which posits a divinely or-dained authority structure for the male-female relationship.

This interpretation of the meaning of 1 Corinthians 11:3-4 is seen to be advanced in the remainder of Paul's argument. As in 1 Timothy 2:11-14 and 1 Peter 3:1-6, Paul appeals to scriptural authority to buttress his argument. In 1 Corinthians 11:8-9 he refers to the creation narrative of Genesis 2 by stat-ing that "man was not made from woman, but woman from man. Neither was man created for the sake of woman, but woman for the sake of man." Because of this, woman is "man's glory" (1 Cor 11:7 NIV). Her creation, her existence brings glory and honor to the man. But when the women in the congregation are present in worship without a head-covering, they instead heap shame on the men. And since, so it is argued, man is in a position of authority over woman, her disgracing him in public assembly is particularly offensive and represents a refusal to submit to his divinely given authority over her.

Another text used to support an authority structure in the male-female relationship (1 Cor 14:34-35) is particularly problematic. In the passage just considered (1 Cor 11), Paul clearly assumes and affirms the freedom of women to participate in public worship by praying and prophesying.[15] Two chapters later (1 Cor 14) such participation is forbidden: "Women should be silent in the churches. For they are not permitted to speak, but should be subordinate, as the law also says. If there is anything they desire to know, let them ask their husbands at home. For it is shameful for a woman to speak in church."

In faithful biblical interpretation, the outright contradiction between 1 Corinthians 11 and 1 Corinthians 14—regarding the participation of women in public proclamation and prayer—must be addressed, and we will

---

[15]It is clear from Acts 2:14-21, as well as in the Pauline writings, that prophetic speech was the authoritative proclamation of the Word of God to the people of God. It was Spirit-inspired, intel-ligent teaching and proclamation. That is true both of the prophetic word in the Old Testament and prophetic speech in the New Testament, as is unmistakably so in 1 Corinthians 14.

do so in chapters six and seven of this book, where we deal with the abuse of Scripture when various contexts are not adequately considered. For now, it is sufficient to acknowledge that this text, by itself, teaches a restrictive role for women in the church and the home.

Two more texts used in support of the traditional Christian teaching that there is a divinely ordered hierarchy in the male-female relationship are Ephesians 5:22-33 and Colossians 3:18-19. These texts are part of a larger directive about household duties and practices, and they address wives, husbands, children, fathers, slaves and masters. Scholars have long recognized the significant parallels between these letters and are certain that they must have been written at nearly the same time. The instruction in Colossians 3:18 reads: "Wives, be subject to your husbands, as is fitting in the Lord." Since this instruction is almost verbally parallel to Ephesians 5:22 (though without the larger context of Paul's theological and christological reasoning that we find in Ephesians 5, which I discuss thoroughly in chapter six, "The Abuse of Context: Literary and Theological"), we will focus our attention on the extended text in Ephesians.

Without taking the larger context of our text into consideration at this point, the apostolic instruction regarding the wife's relation to her husband seems rather straightforward and unambiguous. Ephesians 5:22 reads: "Wives, be subject to your husbands as you are to the Lord." Many see here a decisive analogy between "the Lord" and "husbands." That is, just as Christian wives are subject to the lordship of Christ, so they are also subject to the "lordship" of their husbands. This understanding of the meaning of the verse determines how the following instructions are heard. Paul gives two reasons for his directive for wifely submission: "For the husband is the head of the wife just as Christ is the head of the church, the body of which he is the Savior" (Eph 5:23). As indicated earlier in our discussion of 1 Corinthians 11, we will investigate, in chapter five of this book, the metaphorical meaning of the Greek word *kephalē* (head) as used by Paul for both the husband and Christ. Those who believe that the Bible teaches a hierarchical male-female relationship[16] understand the Greek word for "head" as designating a figure of authority (as in English usage). Thus wives are to submit to their husbands because husbands are in authority over them.

---

[16]E.g., Susan T. Foh, "The Head of Woman is the Man," in *Women in Ministry: Four Views*, ed. Robert G. Clouse and Bonnidell Clouse (Downers Grove, Ill.: InterVarsity Press, 1989), pp. 69-105.

The second reason Paul gives for the subjection of wives is that, "just as the church is subject to Christ, so also wives ought to be, in everything, to their husbands" (Eph 5:24). Here, the relationship of the church to Christ and the relationship of the wife to the husband are seen as paralleling one another. In both cases, it is held to be an "authority over" relationship.

The final text for brief consideration here is Titus 2:3-5, where the apostle asks Titus to tell the older women in the fellowship to teach the younger women "to love their husbands, to love their children, to be self-controlled, chaste, good managers of the household, kind, being submissive to their husbands." The reason given for this behavior is "so that the word of God may not be discredited." This reason is similar to the concern voiced in 1 Peter 2—3, where the honorable conduct of Christians (slaves, wives and husbands) is enjoined so that the unbelievers may see their honorable deeds and have no cause to malign them as evildoers (1 Pet 2:12). In Titus 2, particular conduct for the young men is also prescribed, so that "any opponent will be put to shame, having nothing evil to say of us" (Tit 2:8). And all Christians are reminded "to be subject to rulers and authorities, to be obedient" (Tit 3:1). In chapter seven ("The Abuse of Context: Historical Situation and Cultural Reality"), these texts will be further considered. But apart from those further explorations and the importance of contextual considerations, Titus 2:5 contains the straightforward instruction that the wife should submit to her husband.

The biblical texts surveyed above are seen by many to teach that, by divine design and continuing intention (confirmed in apostolic teaching), men are called to leadership, to exercise authority, to govern and guide the marriage, the home and the church, while women are called to be subordinate to that leadership and authority and to function in largely supportive ways. But as indicated earlier, there are significant and bountiful "alternative voices" throughout the biblical record that do not support a hierarchical model for the male-female relationship but rather advocate a relationship of equality and complementary partnership.

We saw above how the second creation narrative of Genesis 2 has been understood by many to show that the priority of the man in creation signifies his leadership role, and that the woman's creation from his being, as well as her designation as his "helper," signifies her subordinate and supportive role. That understanding of the meaning of Genesis 2 stands in significant tension with Genesis 1.

The creation of male and female, narrated in Genesis 1:26-27, gives to them, in contrast to the animal kingdom (Gen 1:20-25), a unique identity and task. Their unique identity is the result of their being created in the image and likeness of God. They are designed as God's representatives, as those who "image," or reflect and embody, the character and purposes of God within the context of the entire creation.[17] Their unique task is expressed in Genesis 1:26 (cf. Gen 1:28): "and let them have dominion" over the rest of the created order. These texts are clear in their affirmation that both male and female members of the human race are created equally in the image of God. There is absolutely no difference in their identity. In this cohumanity, they are now given a task: Let them "have dominion" (Gen 1:26, 28). Together, as those who are created to image and reflect the character and purposes of God, they are called to exercise what some biblical scholars and theologians have called the "cultural mandate."[18] Both are given the mandate to exercise responsible dominion and stewardship over, and within, creation. There is no hint here of second-class citizenship for one gender, no indication of "functional inequality" (i.e., the man rules and leads; the woman submits and follows).

This primary theological perspective about male-female equality and complementarity in creation must be taken into account when reading and interpreting the second creation narrative in Genesis 2. While Genesis 1 focuses on humanity in its male-female polarity, created in the image of God, Genesis 2 focuses on the *particularity* of that polarity (one man and one woman) in the intimacy of belonging (Gen 2:23-24). In other words, the affirmations made about the male and female members of humanity in Genesis 1:26-28 must inform the interpretation of the man-woman relationship in Genesis 2.

A central aspect of the biblical theological tradition is the social, relational nature of God. This is seen in the fact that God enters into covenant relationship with humanity, and specifically with a called-out people, namely Israel. Theologians have also seen this in the trinitarian understanding of God

---

[17]In the ancient Near East, it was common for a conquering monarch to leave a statue, an "image" of himself in the conquered territory, as a visible reminder of his continuing sovereignty over it. In creation, God conquers chaos, creates order, and places the human creation within it as God's image, the image of the great heavenly King, to exercise responsible dominion within and over creation.

[18]Mary Stewart Van Leeuwen, *Gender and Grace* (Downers Grove, Ill.: InterVarsity Press, 1990), p. 42.

(Father, Son and Spirit). God exists in a "community of love," and humanity is created in the image of this God, to exist in a "community of love." Therefore, "It is not good that the man should be alone" (Gen 2:18). Contrary to the understanding that Genesis 2 sets down a model of hierarchical leadership on the basis of the man's chronological priority, the only judgment pronounced in the text regarding the man's isolated existence prior to the woman is that it is "not good." The woman is, if anything, pictured as a redemptive instrument in God's design. She complements and completes him. Her creation redeems the man from "aloneness."

This creational picture of equality, mutuality and functional partnership in fulfilling the cultural mandate becomes terribly distorted by the human quest to cross creational boundaries in the Creator-creature relationship in order to become "like God" (Gen 3:5). This quest to be like God, to have absolute knowledge and thus to transcend creaturely limitation, has the opposite result: humanity becomes less than fully human. And that "less than" has disastrous consequences for both man and woman.

In their complementary vocations, as understood in primitive nomadic and agrarian societies—she in her unique function as the life-giver (Gen 3:20) and he in his primary function as provider of food for the nurturing of that life—both will experience sorrow (Gen 3:16-19).[19] Further, their relationship of mutuality and complementary partnership becomes a "power-over" relationship: "He shall rule over you" (Gen 3:16).

This account of the cursedness of human life, including the distorted male-female relationship, has traditionally been understood as a divine imperative, a command, a *prescription* for the nature of that relationship henceforth. Yet the entire story of God's redemptive acting—beginning in Genesis 12:1 with the call of Abraham and concluding with the vision of a new heaven and a new earth (Rev 21—22) in which "nothing accursed will be found there any more" (Rev 22:3)—is the story of God's work of liberating humanity and the entire creation from its *cursed existence* (see Rom 8:19-23). In light of this redemptive activity, the curse of Genesis 3 is to be understood not as *prescriptive* (what *should* be) but as *descriptive*, revealing *what is* the human condition when separated from relationship with God. It is also clear from the sweep of biblical revelation that the people of God are called to participate in, and

---

[19]See my discussion (in chap. 5) of the Hebrew word ʿiṣṣābôn, usually translated as "pain" or "toil."

embody, this liberating, transforming work of God. Israel is called to be a "blessing" and a "light to the nations" (Gen 12:2-3; Is 19:24-25; 42:6). And the new covenant community of Jew and Gentile "in Christ" is intended to be God's alternative, God's option to the brokenness of human society, including the distorted male-female relationship in the here and now.

Old Testament scholars have recognized that central theological concerns in the faith traditions of Israel are often best understood as "over against" the environment, the polytheistic cultural context in which Israel sought to live out its vocation as God's covenant people.[20] The affirmations in Genesis 1—2 about male and female being created in the image of God, and about woman being of the same essence and substance as man ("bone of my bones and flesh of my flesh"), are a critique of the idea—prevalent in the Near East right down into the New Testament period—that women were made from inferior material. That idea about the essential inferiority of women was, of course, also present in ancient Israel, which in many ways was very much a part of the surrounding culture. And therefore the Word of God in the creation narratives, when it was heard in the worship of Israel, was a critique of its culturally inculcated understanding of the male-female relationship. Israel's cultural and social reality, evidenced throughout the Old Testament, was pervasively patriarchal and hierarchical. Here, as in other areas of her life and faith, the light of the creation narratives became muted with regard to male and female as co-image bearers.

During the Intertestamental Period (ca. 300 B.C. to A.D. 100) an ominous note arose in Judaism that widened the division in status and authority between men and women within Jewish patriarchal culture. Based chiefly on the interpretation of the Fall narrative in Genesis 3 and Genesis 6:1-4, women were increasingly seen as (1) chiefly responsible for humanity's fall; (2) more susceptible to temptation than men; and (3) temptresses to sin because of their sexual attractiveness. Numerous texts—from the Jewish intertestamental literature (the Apocrypha and Pseudepigrapha), rabbinic citations, and the writings of leading Jewish thinkers like Philo of Alexandria and Josephus—all too clearly document this reality (see appendix B for a representative sample of this material).

In contrast to this background, the life and ministry of Jesus was nothing

---

[20]See G. Ernest Wright, *The Old Testament Against Its Environment* (London: SCM Press, 1951).

short of revolutionary. Here, as in other areas, Jesus rejected "the tradition of the elders." In his life and ministry, he showed a radically different way for the relations between men and women. Jesus' actions with regard to women, recorded especially in the Gospel of Luke, clearly point away from the inherited tradition. Jesus allowed a woman (a known "sinner") to touch him (making him thereby ritually unclean), and he addressed her in public (Lk 7:36-50). In addition to his twelve male disciples—clearly representing the twelve sons of Jacob in the "new Israel"—Jesus was accompanied by a number of women disciples: Mary Magdalene, Joanna, Susanna "and many others" (Lk 8:1-3). Mary the sister of Martha was taught by Rabbi Jesus and affirmed in her desire to be taught the way of the Lord (Lk 10:38-41). When another "unclean" woman touched him, he addressed her as "daughter," an address of respect (Lk 8:43-48). Again, Jesus healed a crippled woman who by religious definition was "unclean," referring to her with the honorific title "daughter of Abraham" (Lk 13:10-17). He spoke of himself in an analogy as a mother hen, seeking to gather her chicks under her wings (Lk 13:34). A traditional rabbi in Jesus' time would never have done these things!

Luke 23:49, 55 goes on to mention "the women who had followed him from Galilee." These women disciples were the first to be commissioned with the central gospel message, "He . . . has risen" (Lk 24:1-5). The text goes on to name them: "Mary Magdalene, Joanna, Mary the mother of James, and the other women" and relates the fact that they "told this to the apostles" (Lk 24:10). The response of his male disciples was predictable, given their conditioned distrust of women's testimony: "But these words seemed to them an idle tale, and they did not believe them" (Lk 24:11).

In addition to this narrative record from Jesus' ministry, there is his teaching about the subversion of power and authority structures, which represents a frontal assault on male privilege and power. The stage was set in the so-called Magnificat in Luke 1:46-55, which saw in the coming one, Jesus, the fulfillment of the hopes of Israel: "He has brought down the powerful from their thrones / and lifted up the lowly; / he has filled the hungry with good things, / and sent the rich away empty" (Lk 1:52-53). This theme of the reversal of "up-down" categories is embodied in the paradox of Jesus' incarnation: the Lord makes himself a servant, and he calls all other "lords"—including husbands—to imitate him, most particularly in the community of his disciples. The account of the three predictions of Jesus' suffering in the Gospel of Mark

(Mk 8:31-33; 9:30-32; 10:32-34) and the dialogues with the disciples that follow are very graphic examples of this new way. In each case, there is a stark contrast between Jesus' servanthood and the disciples' quest for power, status and authority. In each case, we also find Jesus' rejection of the triumphalistic, messianic power tradition pervasive in Judaism as not being in keeping with God's purposes. (I will discuss these texts more fully in chapter six.)

In the new community that Jesus inaugurated, authentic power is not used to dominate, to control, to exercise authority over others. Rather, it expresses itself in service to others. Jesus' power is not control from above but strength from beneath; it serves and invites; it does not coerce or demand. Jesus' "new way" with respect to women—and his revolutionary challenge regarding the nature and exercise of authentic, divinely modeled power—clearly left its imprint on the practice and proclamation of the earliest Christian communities.

The account of Pentecost in Acts 2:14-18 reveals the conviction that the prophecy of Joel 2:28-32 regarding the outpouring of God's empowering Spirit is being fulfilled: "Your sons and your daughters shall prophesy / . . . upon my slaves, both men and women, / in those days I will pour out my Spirit; / and they shall prophesy" (Acts 2:17-18). These earliest Christians knew that the Spirit of God—who, according to the teaching of the rabbis, had departed from Israel—was now empowering sons and daughters, men and women for authoritative, inspired proclamation of the Word of God to the people of God. We are told in Acts 21:8-9 that Philip the evangelist had four daughters who were engaged in the prophetic work of the gospel, a concrete demonstration of the truth revealed at Pentecost. Moreover, according to Acts 18:18-19, Paul is accompanied in his missionary work and proclamation of the gospel by Priscilla and Aquila. This husband-wife ministry team instructed Apollos, the learned Alexandrian Jew, into a deeper understanding of the way of the Lord (Acts 18:24-26). It is interesting to note that when both Luke and Paul mention this ministry team, they regularly mention Priscilla first, a very unusual order, given standard Jewish practice.

In addition to the record of the early church in Acts, the Pauline epistles further reveal that in the new age inaugurated by Christ, women are set free to participate, along with men, in worship, teaching and proclamation.[21] In his greetings to the church in Rome (Rom 16:1-12), Paul recognizes, and

---

[21]Fee, *First Corinthians*, p. 487.

thereby honors, several women who were clearly in positions of leadership and active ministry in the Pauline churches: Phoebe is called a deacon (Greek *diakonos*), meaning "a minister," or "one who serves"; Prisca is recognized as a person "who work[ed] with me in Christ Jesus"; Mary had "worked very hard among you"; Junia is lauded as "prominent among the apostles" (certainly a leading authority figure); and Persis is named as one "who has worked hard in the Lord." Two other women, Euodia and Syntyche, are mentioned in his letter to the church in Philippi as those who "have struggled beside me in the work of the gospel, together with Clement and the rest of my co-workers" (Phil 4:2-3).

Crowning this story of a new way in the relationship between men and women, and a new understanding of women as gifted by the Spirit for equal partnership with men in the work of Christ, is Paul's powerful word in Galatians 3:27-28, considered by some the ultimate expression of a "charter of freedom" for the new humanity in Christ Jesus:

> As many of you as were baptized into Christ have clothed yourselves with Christ. There is no longer Jew nor Greek, there is no longer slave nor free, there is no longer male nor female, for all of you are one in Christ Jesus.

In this triad of contrasting pairs, Paul is unquestionably writing in reference to, and polemic against, the ancient synagogue prayer, in which God is praised for not having made them (men) either slaves or Gentiles or women. As a student under the great Rabbi Gamaliel, Paul had surely prayed this benediction regularly and proudly! The powerful statement that he makes in Galatians 3:27-28 is that "in Christ Jesus"—that is, in the new, concrete historical community of Jesus' followers, the "body of Christ"—the culturally prescribed and religiously sanctioned "up-down" power categories can no longer be maintained. A new order has been brought into being, in which the old superior-inferior structures of ethnicity (Jew-Greek), social status (slave-free) and gender (male-female) are being overcome. Paul knew that "the present form of this world is passing away" (1 Cor 7:31).

The biblical picture that we have sketched reveals an understanding of the male-female relationship that stands in significant tension with, if not as a serious challenge to, the traditional view of hierarchical authority and submission in the male-female relationship, grounded in an interpretation of particular biblical texts. When these texts are isolated from the larger biblical witness, and the voices from that larger witness are not heard and taken seriously, then Scripture is being abused.

How are we then to understand the texts that limit women's participation in the life and ministries of the church and place them in submissive relationship to men? This question will be addressed in subsequent chapters, where we will look at specific texts in terms of such things as the historical situation that is addressed, the literary context, the cultural setting and the meaning of words.

THE RELATIONSHIP BETWEEN GOD'S BLESSING AND FAITH

It is probable that no other issues affect the lives of Christians more directly than that of health and wealth and their relationship to the will of God. Is it God's intention that believers experience good physical health? Is a Christian promised financial success by virtue of his or her faith in Christ? If a Christian does not experience these "blessings," is he or she outside the will of God? Answers to these questions are, of course, dependent on how one reads and interprets the Bible. If the Bible presents a variety of perspectives on these issues, which particular texts are selected and how are they interpreted?

In the past few decades, a particular way of answering the above questions has become so prominent that a recent issue of *Time* magazine devoted a cover story to what has become known as the "Prosperity Gospel" movement.[22] Also known by such names as the "Health and Wealth Gospel" and "Name It and Claim It," its proponents include Christian authors, megachurch leaders and TV personalities such as Joel Osteen, Kenneth Hagin, T. D. Jakes, Benny Hinn and Kenneth Copeland. In their TV broadcasts, sermons and books,[23] they make particular claims about what the Bible teaches on our subject. Essential aspects of their understanding of biblical teaching may be summarized in these pronouncements: "You can have what you say"; "The reason you have not been healed is that you don't have enough faith"; "We can write our own ticket with God if we decide what we want, believe that it's ours, and confess it"; "He wants you rich and healthy"; "What is the desire of your heart? Name it, claim it by faith, and it's yours! The

---

[22]David Van Biema, "Does God Want You to Be Rich?" *Time*, September 18, 2006, cover story.
[23]Kenneth Copeland, *The Laws of Prosperity* (Newark, Tex.: Copeland Publications, 1980); Kenneth Hagin, *Seven Things You Should Know About Divine Healing* (Tulsa, Okla.: Faith Library Publications, 1979).

heavenly Father has promised it. It's right there in the Bible."[24]

The claim that this message is biblical has been subject to strong criticism. Some have said that it rests, at best, on a simplistic theology and leads to misguided ways of living, and at worst, it is dangerous. Historical theologian Michael Horton of Westminster Theological Seminary states that it is based on "a twisted interpretation of the Bible" and is "a wild and wacky theology."[25] Noted New Testament scholar Gordon Fee speaks of it as a diseased understanding of biblical truth.[26] Has this health-and-wealth gospel emerged because of the abuse of selectivity, and is it, therefore, "a different gospel"[27] in contrast to the authentic gospel (Gal 1:6-7)?

Our purpose here is not to enter into this critical discussion as such, but to survey the biblical texts and their pronouncements relative to this issue. When we do so—as with the other issues addressed in this chapter—we are once again confronted not by a biblical choir singing in unison but by a multivoiced chorale.

What *is* the biblical teaching about health and wealth in relation to faith and obedience to God's will? We will look at three kinds of texts: those that affirm that God's blessing rests on those who put their trust in him and live in faithful obedience to his will; those that provide grounds for the health-and-wealth teaching; and those that stand in tension with that teaching or oppose it.

Across the broad spectrum of the biblical revelation from Genesis to John's Apocalypse, the people of God are given the assurance that the blessing of God will be on those who are properly related to him, who trust their lives to him and live in faithful obedience before him. In Genesis 12:1-3, Abraham is called to leave his home and kin to follow the leading of God. As a consequence, God's blessing would rest on him and his descendants. This promise of the Lord's blessing in response to faithfulness and obedience is reaffirmed for Abraham's descendants through Moses (Deut 30:15-20).

In the worship of Israel, reflected in the Psalms, the truth of the relation-

[24]Watchman Fellowship page, "How the Health and Wealth Gospel Twists Scripture" (2000) <www.watchman.org/reltop/health$.htm>.

[25]Cited by Bill Smith and Carolyn Tuft, "The Prosperity Gospel," *St. Louis Dispatch,* November 18, 2003 <rickross.com/reference/tv_preachers/tv_preachers4.html>.

[26]Gordon D. Fee, *The Disease of the Health and Wealth Gospels* (Vancouver, B.C.: Regent Publishing, 1985).

[27]Dan R. McConnell, *A Different Gospel* (Peabody, Mass.: Hendrickson Publishing, 1995).

ship between God's blessing and faithful obedience is celebrated repeatedly. Blessed are all those whose "delight is in the law of the LORD" (Ps 1:2), who "take refuge in him" (Ps 2:12), and who place their trust in him (Ps 84:12; cf. Prov 16:20). Particular emphasis is placed on the blessed life of those who come into God's presence in worship, who stand in awe before him (Ps 115:13), "who walk, O LORD, in the light of your countenance" (Ps 89:15). Since the Lord is concerned about wholeness of life in community, blessed "are those who observe justice, who do righteousness at all times" (Ps 106:3; cf. Prov 3:33; 10:6). These promises are summed up in the opening verses of Psalm 119:1-2 (NIV):

> Blessed are they whose ways are blameless,
>   who walk according to the law of the LORD.
> Blessed are they who keep his statutes
>   and seek him with all their heart.[28]

The prophets Isaiah and Jeremiah join their voices to this chorus of praise and thanksgiving. Blessed are those who "maintain justice, and do what is right," who keep the sabbath and refrain from doing any evil (Is 56:1-2). Blessed are those "who trust in the LORD," for

> They shall be like a tree planted by water,
>   sending out its roots by the stream.
> It shall not fear when heat comes,
>   and its leaves shall stay green;
> in the year of drought it is not anxious,
>   and it does not cease to bear fruit. (Jer 17:7-8)

This Old Testament conviction about the direct correspondence between the blessing of God and faithful, trusting obedience is echoed in the New Testament. Jesus teaches that "those who hear the word of God and obey it" (Lk 11:28), and those who follow his example by loving and serving each

---

[28]The NIV renders the Hebrew *'ešer* with the traditional "blessed," whereas the NRSV uses, I think unfortunately, the translation "happy" (here, and throughout most of the Old Testament). The Greek translators of the Hebrew Bible rendered the Hebrew *'ešer* with the Greek word *makarios,* the word used throughout the New Testament (e.g., in the Beatitudes of Mt 5:3-11). Both the NIV and the NRSV render *makarios* with "blessed." I believe the English "blessed" is a more adequate rendering of the depth of the biblical *ešer* and *makarios.* See, for example, Robert Gundry, *Matthew: A Commentary on His Literary and Theological Art* (Grand Rapids: Eerdmans, 1982), p. 68: *"Blessed* means *to be congratulated* in a deeply religious sense and with more emphasis on divine approval than on human happiness."

other, are blessed (Jn 13:17). The seeds of these teachings clearly took root in the lives and beliefs of Jesus' followers. In a striking analogy, the author of Hebrews expresses the conviction that God blesses those whose lives bear fruit:

> Ground that drinks up rain falling on it repeatedly, and that produces a crop useful to those for whom it is cultivated, receives a blessing from God. (Heb 6:7)

The apostle Peter calls his fellow Jewish believers to "unity of spirit, sympathy, love for one another, a tender heart, and a humble mind" (1 Pet 3:8), because it is "for this that you were called—that you might inherit a blessing" (1 Pet 3:9). The climax of this centuries-old biblical faith tradition comes in the prophetic word of John to the seven churches in Asia. The heading that stands over the instructions to these churches—given to John by the one who is "the first and the last," Jesus Christ the resurrected one (Rev 1:17-18)—consists of these words:

> Blessed is the one who reads aloud the words of the prophecy, and blessed are those who hear and who keep what is written in it. (Rev 1:3)

But what is the content of this promised blessedness? What does the life blessed by God look like? What are the blessings bestowed on the life of faith and obedience?

The almost-unanimous testimony of God's faithful, especially in the Old Testament, leaves us with little doubt with regard to their answer to these questions. Beginning with the calling of Abraham, a host of specific blessings are cited as evidence of God's favor. According to Genesis 12:2 and Genesis 22:15-18, Abraham's trust in God and his obedience lead to personal fame, a great nation and power over enemies. Abraham's son Isaac is blessed with great wealth and the gift of land (Gen 26:3-5, 12-14).

In Moses' instructions to the people of Israel during the Exodus wanderings and on the verge of entry into the Promised Land of Canaan, the specifics of divine blessing are clearly articulated. Exodus 23:25-26 states that the rejection of idolatry and worship of the Lord leads to God blessing their bread and water, to God removing sickness, miscarriages and childlessness, to God granting long and full life, and to the defeat of enemies. Several of these blessings are repeated, and new ones added, in Moses' word to God's people recorded in Deuteronomy. Heed God's ordinances "by diligently observing them" (Deut 7:12), and God's blessing will be seen in the fruit of your womb and the fruit of your ground, your grain and your wine and your oil, the increase of your cattle and the issue of your flock. . . . You shall be the most blessed of peoples, with neither sterility nor barrenness among you and your livestock. The LORD will turn away from you every illness. (Deut 7:13-15)

These specific blessings, in response to faithful obedience, are reaffirmed in Moses' final words to his people (Deut 28:1-14; 30:8-10): "The LORD will make you abound in prosperity" (Deut 28:11) because he "will again take delight in prospering you" (Deut 30:9).

The psalmists and Israel's wisdom teachers express this same conviction. "Happy are those who fear the LORD, / who greatly delight in his commandments," sings the psalmist (Ps 112:1). Then he goes on to affirm that an evidence of that blessedness is "wealth and riches . . . in their houses" (Ps 112:3; cf. Prov 10:22; 22:4).

In addition to this pervasive Old Testament faith tradition, the advocates of the health-and-wealth teaching point to several New Testament texts for additional support. Jesus' words in John 10:10, that the purpose of his coming was so that we "may have life, and have it abundantly" is interpreted as referring to financial prosperity and health. Such a meaning is also claimed for John's greeting of Gaius (3 Jn 2), particularly in its KJV rendering: "Beloved, I wish above all things that thou mayest prosper and be in health, even as thy soul prospereth."[29] In his encouragement of the Christians in Corinth to be generous in their contributions to the collection for the needy brothers and sisters in Jerusalem, Paul reminded them of Christ's example: "For you know the generous act of our Lord Jesus Christ, that though he was rich, yet for your sakes he became poor, so that by his poverty you might become rich" (2 Cor 8:9). For some advocates of the health-and-wealth gospel, financial prosperity is seen to be one of the benefits of the atonement.[30]

The interpretation that these New Testament texts refer to physical health and financial prosperity is open to serious question—on the basis of hermeneutical principles involving cultural and literary contexts and the meanings of words, which I'll discuss in subsequent chapters. However, the "prosperity"

---

[29]Kenneth Copeland, quoted in Watchman Fellowship page, "How the Health and Wealth Gospel Twists Scripture," (2000) <www.watchman.org/reltop/health$.htm>.

[30]"Word of Faith," Wikipedia (September 13, 2008) <http://en.wikipedia.org/wiki/Word_of_Faith>.

interpretation, together with the Old Testament material surveyed above, provides significant grounds for the idea that the Bible posits a direct correspondence between faithful obedience and specific blessings, such as health and wealth. Yet even as we hear these convictions expressed in one part of the biblical chorus, the voices of other parts of this chorus claim our attention.

In the Old Testament Wisdom literature (Proverbs, Ecclesiastes, Job), which reflects the concrete human experiences of the faithful, [31] there emerge voices of protest that implicitly or explicitly question the traditional belief about the direct connection between faithful obedience and specific divine blessings. In Proverbs 18:11-12, the danger of riches is highlighted with the observation that it can lead to haughtiness and destruction. Rather than seeing poverty as a sign of God's disfavor and wealth as a sign of God's blessing, we hear in Proverbs 22:2 and Job 34:19 that God does not regard the rich more than the poor. Indeed, it is better to be poor and walk in integrity than to be rich and walk in crooked ways (Prov 28:6). Here the accumulation of wealth is uncoupled from faithfulness and God's blessing.

Concerns about the dangers inherent in wealth are forcefully articulated by that astute observer of human life, the preacher of Ecclesiastes. If wealth is a sign of divine blessing (Eccles 6:2), why is it that "the lover of money will not be satisfied with money; nor the lover of wealth, with gain" (Eccles 5:10)? Therefore, the preacher concludes, "sweet is the sleep of laborers, whether they eat little or much; but the surfeit of the rich will not let them sleep" (Eccles 5:12). Contrary to the traditional, pervasive assertion that righteous living is blessed by long life, the preacher observes that "there are righteous people who perish in their righteousness, and there are wicked people who prolong their life in their evil-doing" (Eccles 7:15).

Beyond these tentative voices questioning the popular theology of the tradition, the book of Job as a whole launches a loud protest against the all-too-easy equation: faithful obedience and righteousness go hand in hand with health and prosperity, while adversity is the lot of the wicked. Throughout this book's powerful, deeply profound struggle with the question of the suffering of the righteous, the three "friends" of Job contend for the age-old tradition (Job 20:4-5). They are convinced that there must be unrighteous-

---

[31]See Walter Bruggemann, *In Man We Trust: The Neglected Side of Biblical Faith* (Louisville, Ky.: John Knox, 1972); R. B. Y. Scott, *The Way of Wisdom in the Old Testament* (New York: Macmillan, 1971); Gerhard von Rad, *Wisdom in Israel* (Nashville: Abingdon, 1972).

ness in Job; why else would he undergo his terrible deprivation and suffering? This note is present throughout,[32] but it is most strikingly expressed in Job 22:4-5:

> Is it for your piety that he reproves you
>   and enters into judgment with you?
> Is not your wickedness great?
>   There is no end to your iniquities.

Yet in the midst of his suffering, Job continues to cling to the conviction that his relationship with God is unimpaired, that he is innocent and blameless (Job 9:15, 17, 20-21). In his response to his friends' accusations, he argues that their analysis of his situation is mistaken, that the direct correspondence between faithful obedience and health and wealth flies in the face of reality and truth. For the blessings promised to the faithful (like Job) are in fact enjoyed by the unrighteous (Job 21:8-13, 17-18, 23-24). "Why," he laments, "do the wicked live on, / reach old age, and grow mighty in power?" (Job 21:7). He knows from his own experience that the blameless are not spared suffering (Job 9:21-23).

This truth is confirmed in the divine rebuke of Job's friends, whose comprehension of the ways of God are judged to be wanting (Job 42:7). That is indeed the central message of the book of Job. Health and wealth are not necessarily evidences of faithful obedience or signs of God's blessing. The promise of Job to the faithful is that, as the result of entrusting themselves to God, they will know—in the midst of their suffering, and through their suffering—the grace, love, compassion and healing of their God: "I know that my Redeemer lives" (Job 19:25). Even as he continues to contend against and argue with God, Job is certain that this living God will finally make all things whole and new: "After my skin has been thus destroyed . . . I shall see God" (Job 19:26).

The tentative questioning in the Proverbs, the probing of Ecclesiastes and the outright protest of Job, move front and center when we enter the pages of the New Testament. Indeed, Jesus' teaching intensifies the criticism of that prevalent equation within the faith tradition. A great reversal takes place in which the blessing of God is pronounced on the poor, the hungry, the mourn-

---

[32]See especially Job 4:7-9; 8:3-6, 20; 11:20; 15:17-35; 18:5-21; 20:4-5.

ing, the oppressed and the rejected (Mt 5:3-11; Lk 6:20-22).[33]

That theme, together with significant warnings about the danger of material wealth, continues to echo throughout the New Testament, especially in the Gospel of Luke. In Mary's song and the announcement of Jesus' mission, the poor are the primary objects of the good news, while the rich are sent away empty-handed (Lk 1:53; 4:18-19). According to Luke 12:15-21, "abundance of possessions" can be evidence of greed, as well as poverty in one's relationship with God. "Woes" rather than blessings are pronounced on those who are rich and well-fed and highly regarded (Lk 6:24-26).[34] The story of the rich young ruler (Mt 19:16-30; Mk 10:17-31; Lk 18:18-25) strikingly drives this point home. Given the popular theology about blessings and wealth, he must have seen his wealth as a sign of God's blessing and reward for his righteousness. This was the badge of his identity that he could not relinquish. For weren't his wealth and status evidence of his righteousness?

Finally, the message of Job—that the suffering of the righteous is not evidence of the absence of God's blessing—is pointedly affirmed by Jesus in the Beatitudes (Mt:5:3-11; Lk 6:20-22) and echoed in 1 Peter 3:14, where those who "suffer for doing what is right" are blessed. In the story of Jesus' encounter of the blind man in John 9, the traditional idea that lack of physical wholeness is a result of sin is roundly rejected in Jesus' response to the disciples' question about the connection between sin and lack of health (Jn 9:2-3).

Let us summarize this section of the present chapter. We have looked at three sets of biblical texts: first, texts that declare that those who live before God and with each other in faithful obedience to the will of God stand under God's blessing; second, texts that see specific evidences of God's blessing in such things as material wealth, status within the community, health and a long, full life; third, texts that question or oppose the equation of material and physical wellness with divine blessing and assert that even in the midst of suffering and deprivation, God's blessing rests on the faithful.

This complex, and at points tension-filled and internally contradictory

---

[33]Matthew's parallel to Luke 6:20 uses the phrase "poor in spirit" (Mt 5:3) rather than "poor." While Luke's citation of Jesus' words focuses on material, economic poverty, Matthew emphasizes the spiritual side. " '*Poor in spirit*' refers not to those with a deficit of moral righteousness," but to those who, in their economic poverty, "became wholly dependent on God" (Craig Keener, *A Commentary on the Gospel of Matthew* [Grand Rapids: Eerdmans, 1999], p. 168).

[34]These warnings about the danger of riches are also found in Jesus' explanation of the parable of the sower (Mt 13:22; Mk 4:18; Lk 8:14) and heard in 1 Timothy 6:9-10, 17 and James 1:9-11.

biblical testimony, is easily subject to "the abuse of selectivity." On the one hand, there are those who conclude—on the basis of the "woes" uttered against the rich and the warnings about the dangers of material possessions—that these are intrinsically negative and stand under the judgment of God, while poverty and simplicity of life are almost glorified. The result of this selective reading and use of biblical texts flies in the face of both concrete human reality and the biblical vision. There are countless Christians and non-Christians alike who have become wealthy by hard work, creativity and inventiveness, and who have shared their wealth compassionately and generously—through education, health care, housing, social justice projects, and relief through providing food and clothing. The selective use of biblical texts to demonize wealth as intrinsically evil results in hurtful judgmentalism, casts negative light on genuine philanthropy, and is in conflict with biblical admonitions and encouragement to give generously in proportion to one's possessions in response to human need (2 Cor 8:14).[35]

In the same vein, the selective use of texts regarding the blessedness of the poor can easily lead to the romanticizing of poverty. But those who have experienced it and those who have seen its devastating effects know there is nothing intrinsically good or blessed about poverty.[36] The faithful poor are blessed because they know their lives are in the hands of God, no matter what. And a wealth of biblical material reveals that God is particularly concerned about the poor, and he calls on his people to be instruments in overcoming poverty.[37]

On the other end of the spectrum—regarding the selective use and application of Scripture, relating faithfulness and God's blessing—are the advocates of the health-and-wealth gospel. Biblical texts (especially in the Old

---

[35]See, for example, the sharing of possessions in the early Christian community in Jerusalem (Acts 4:32-35) and the Pauline collection among the churches in Asia Minor and Greece for the relief of the Christians in Jerusalem (Rom 15:25-27; 1 Cor 16:1-4; 2 Cor 8—9; Gal 2:10). A good resource for a comprehensive understanding of this aspect of the biblical vision is Ronald J. Sider, *Just Generosity: A New Vision for Overcoming Poverty in America* (Grand Rapids: Baker Books, 1999).

[36]Perhaps the leading evangelical thinker on the issues of poverty and wealth is Ronald J. Sider, founder and president of Evangelicals for Social Action. See, for example, his *Rich Christians in an Age of Hunger*, rev. ed. (Dallas: Word Publishing, 1997), chap. 1.

[37]E.g., Ps 72:1-4, 12-14; Prov 31:8-9; Is 1:16-17, 21-23; 3:13-15; 10:1-2; 58:3-7; Jer 5:27-28; Ezek 34:4; Amos 2:4-6; 5:10-12. In the Gospels, the in-breaking reign of God in the life and ministry of Jesus is characterized by "good news [for] the poor" (Lk 4:18; 6:20-22). That good news took on flesh and bones in the teaching and practice of Jesus' followers (e.g., Acts 4:32-37; Jas 2:14-17; 1 Jn 3:17-18). See also Sider, *Rich Christians,* chap. 3.

Testament) that enumerate specific blessings for health and material possessions as a reward for faithful obedience are used selectively to promote a view of Christian faith and life that is in significant tension with other major aspects of biblical truth. As such, that view is heretical and has serious consequences. For the promoters and followers of this teaching, it leads to focusing on, and being preoccupied with, gaining status, notoriety, material possessions, financial gain and power. Greed and corruption, in fulfillment of the warnings in the Bible, are frequently the result. And for those in the grip of poverty, deprivation or disease, the prosperity gospel casts negative aspersions on their level of faith and trust in God, and it questions the alignment of their lives with the will and purposes of God.

The experience of a colleague in ministry has brought the tragedy of this abuse of Scripture into bold relief for me. In his youth, a disease robbed him of most of his sight. In faith and trust in God's way for him, he courageously and joyfully lived with this limitation in fruitful and caring ministry. But in recent association with a particular Christian community, he has been increasingly confronted with the suggestion that if he only had more faith, then God would surely restore his sight. That experience has deeply affected him, causing him to question both the integrity and validity of his faith, as well as God's ways with him. This abuse of selectivity can easily manifest itself in the abuse (or distortion) of Christian life and faith.

AVOIDING THE ABUSE OF SELECTIVITY

How can we avoid the abuse of selectivity, and thus prevent its debilitating and distorting consequences, as illustrated by the three issues discussed above? I propose the following guidelines and principles for trustworthy biblical interpretation in this matter.

1. Never be satisfied with only part of a loaf of the "biblical bread." If we affirm all of Scripture as Word of God, as a lamp for our feet and a light for our path (Ps 119:105), as inspired for our "reproof, for correction, and for training in righteousness" (2 Tim 3:16), then being satisfied with a partial loaf will ultimately leave us, at best, spiritually undernourished and immature, and at worst, with a heretical and counterfeit understanding of the faith, resulting in a confused and distorted Christian presence in the world.

2. Seek to hear and understand the **whole** *counsel of God in Scripture on particular issues.* This requires *intentionality* and *persistence* (occupying us for the rest of our lives!). It is all too easy to take shortcuts here, to try to avoid ambiguity and struggle. Whenever we are confronted with the claim that "this is *the* biblical teaching" on a particular issue, our first impulse should be to listen carefully; the second should be to question respectfully and critically. Since we hold the treasure of the biblical revelation in "jars of clay" (2 Cor 4:7), we "know only in part" (1 Cor 13:9), and see God's truth for us "in a mirror dimly" (1 Cor 13:12), so absolutist claims should be subjected to a healthy dose of skepticism, which should lead us to a comprehensive examination of the entire spectrum of biblical voices related to that area of Christian life and faith.

3. When confronted with tensions between biblical affirmations or apparently contradictory voices in Scripture, employ "the forest versus the trees" principle. In biblical interpretation as in all other matters, it is certainly true that the whole is greater than the individual parts. Particular texts need to be understood and interpreted in light of the entire Bible, or the whole of the New Testament, or all of Paul's teaching and practice. Important questions to ask are the following: What is the overarching thrust of the biblical revelation about this particular area of human life *(the forest)* in light of which individual texts *(the trees)* need to be understood? What is the vision of the gospel as a whole *(the forest)* in relation to particular texts *(the trees)?* How are we to understand particular Pauline instructions to particular churches or individuals *(the trees)* in light of the entirety of his teaching and practice *(the forest)?* When these questions are asked and followed by a careful investigation of the *forest,* it becomes apparent at times that particular texts *(trees)* are intended for the specific situation addressed and are not universally applicable.

4. Compare specific biblical texts—that support a particular point of view, doctrine or practice—with the "redemptive movement" within Scripture. The foundation for this principle is the fact that the "redemptive movement" [38] is present within Scripture itself. Jesus rejected the binding authority of the Old Testament's "clean/unclean" categories, declaring "all foods clean" (Mk 7:19),

---

[38]William J. Webb articulates and develops this hermeneutical principle in his *Slaves, Women and Homosexuals: Exploring the Hermeneutics of Cultural Analysis* (Downers Grove, Ill.: InterVarsity Press, 2001). Webb analyzes all the specific biblical texts regarding the three groups of people chosen for the study and asks: How are these texts to be understood in light of the movement, the development and the direction of God's redemptive work as revealed in the whole of Scripture? See also Glen Scorgie, *The Journey Back to Eden: Restoring the Creator's Design for Women and Men* (Grand Rapids: Zondervan, 2005), for an excellent example of the use of a redemptive movement hermeneutic.

and he had fellowship and contact, contrary to the law, with the "unclean" (such as sinners and lepers; Mt 8:1-4; Mk 2:15-16; Lk 7:39; cf. Acts 10). Similarly, Paul spoke of the revelation of God's will in the law as "our disciplinarian until Christ came," but that in Christ "we are no longer subject to a disciplinarian" (Gal 3:24-25).

As seen in our discussion of texts about the relationship between women and men, the human condition of cursedness on this side of the Fall includes the man's rule over the woman (Gen 3:16). This power-over relationship is therefore to be understood as a distortion of God's creative design and intention. While the advocates of the hierarchical model contend that this dimension of humanity's cursed existence is the will of God for the male-female relationship in perpetuity, the application of the redemptive-movement principle reveals that God's redemptive work—which comes to its climax in the event of Christ and the inauguration of the reign of God (kingdom of God)—is about liberating humanity from the bondage of its cursed existence. As we saw, there are New Testament texts that reveal that aspects of this cursed existence have not yet been overcome. But there are also plentiful signs that overcoming this cursedness has begun in Jesus' ministry and teaching, as well as in the teaching and practice of the early church. Thus the redemptive movement within biblical revelation points the followers of Jesus beyond the cursed reality of this power-over relationship and toward the reaffirmation and reactualization of God's created intention.

4

THE ABUSE OF BIBLICAL BALANCE

The abuse of Scripture discussed in this chapter is related to, but significantly different from, the abuse of selectivity dealt with in the previous chapter. As we saw, that abuse is characterized by the use and application of selected biblical texts to support one's position or ideology while ignoring or rejecting biblical voices that clearly oppose one's position, and then going on to reinterpret texts that are in tension with that position—or by reading meanings into texts that were not originally intended.

The "abuse of biblical balance," on the other hand, distorts the overall message and purpose of Scripture by emphasizing certain biblical doctrines, perspectives, teachings, themes or mandates, while ignoring or minimizing the equal, or even greater, importance of complementary ones. This practice of one-sided emphasis results in significant imbalance in Christian faith and life and introduces imbalance into the nature of the Christian presence in, and engagement of, the world.

We will discuss the abuse of biblical balance in terms of several contrasting emphases that continue to characterize Christian thinking and acting in our time: (1) "sins of the flesh" and "other sins"; (2) the quest for correct beliefs and doctrinal certainty without sober restraint and humility; and (3) the passion for truth and ethical enthusiasm.

It should at once be obvious that each side of these three sets of polarities are grounded in the biblical word. Yet emphasis on one side or the other of these contrasting pairs continues to be a significant hallmark of Christian witness and presence. It is a source of both internal conflict within the global church and of a confusing, distorted proclamation and embodiment of the gospel in the world.

THE PRIORITY RANKING OF VARIOUS CATEGORIES OF SIN

An important area where the abuse of imbalance manifests itself is in the interpretation and application of the Bible's teaching about sin and sinning. As discussed in chapter two ("The Abuse of the Whole Gospel"), the fundamental core of the human dilemma, of human sinfulness, is alienation from God and its distorting consequences in all human relationships. Separation from God means that we are out of touch with God's purposes for human life.[1]

This basic human reality—being sinners—manifests itself in a whole variety of specific ways: (1) in wrongdoing, in moral failure. This is the most common and pervasive understanding of sin and the act of sinning. Sexual immorality, deceit, stealing, abuse, murder—these are transgressions against others that violate God's intentions. (2) In distorted, hurtful, demeaning personal and social relationships. These are the consequences of such sins as infidelity, slander, prejudice, racial bigotry, injustice, jealousy and hate. (3) In self-righteousness—often based on a rigorous, legalistic understanding of Christian faith—which manifests itself in boastful pride and judgmental attitudes and actions toward those judged less righteous or unrighteous. (4) In emptiness, meaninglessness, anxiety and despair. This is the reality that Augustine identified in the well-known prayer: "O Lord, you have made us for yourself, and our hearts are restless until they find their rest in you."[2] (5) In being alienated from the rest of God's creation and abusing it. Examples here are such actions as the pollution of the environment for economic gain with no regard for its hurtful consequences for others, or the greedy exploitation of

---

[1]Paul clearly shows, in Romans 1:18-32, how the rejection of God, and therefore allegiance to other "gods" (idolatry), leads to the distortion of human life.

[2]*Confessions* 1.1.1; see also Eph 2:12.

natural resources that rapes the land and despoils it.[3]

The biblical depiction of human life as alienated from God and rebelling against God's purposes is all-inclusive and pervasive. No area of human life is untouched. We are created for life-giving and life-sustaining relationship with God, and for wholeness of life in ourselves and in relationship with others. Wherever and however these characteristics of God-purposed human life are threatened or violated, sin is at work.[4]

Given this comprehensive view of human sinfulness, it is regrettable how, in various Christian faith traditions, we have constructed what may be called "hierarchies of sin." Certain categories of sin have been placed at the top of the list, while others have been relegated to realms of lesser status and importance. Some sins are identified as more harmful than other sins, and consequently they become the focal point of special attention.

For example, in the more conservative, evangelical Christian traditions, there has been a significant preoccupation with what are called "sins of the flesh," especially sexual sins (adultery, promiscuity, homosexual practice), and sins that violate the sanctity of life (such as abortion, end-of-life choices, the use of embryos for genetic research). On the other side of the theological spectrum, in the more liberal Christian traditions, there has been a preoccupation with "structural evil" (such as injustice, economic disparity, racism) and "social sins" (such as prejudice, bigotry, psychological manipulation and abuse).

When either of these preoccupations is present to the neglect or diminution of the other, the abuse of biblical balance is at work. In this abuse, the world's brokenness is addressed and challenged in a haphazard, partial way. The idea is conveyed that certain sins and categories of sin are of minor or lesser importance, deserving little or no attention, while others deserve the full weight of righteous indignation.

Examples from our more recent history illustrate this imbalance rather well. When President Bill Clinton was involved in an adulterous relationship with a White House intern, conservative Christians were quick to condemn him, calling for his impeachment. As one marred by this act of sexual im-

---

[3]Some years ago, the provocative film *Sugarcane Alley* spoke powerfully to this reality.

[4]The most common word for *sin* in the New Testament is *hamartia,* which literally means "missing the mark." It is an image taken from the field of archery, when the arrow misses the target or falls short of it. See Romans 3:23: "all have sinned *(hēmarton)* and fall short of the glory of God."

morality, he was not considered fit to serve as leader of this country. On the other side, liberal Christians tended to minimize this moral transgression, relegating it to the sphere of "consenting adults." From that perspective, the president's sexual infidelity was deemed largely a private, personal matter, to be dealt with between him and his wife, but they considered it ultimately inconsequential in comparison to his policies that sought to address larger global issues, such as economic injustice, equitable health care and the genocidal war in Bosnia.

A second example comes from the time of President George W. Bush. When he led the nation into the war against Iraq, liberal Christians tended to criticize him for flagrant violation of "just-war" principles—the traditional Christian teaching about conditions that must be present for war to be justified, such as for self-defense and as an absolute last resort when all other options have been exhausted.[5] Conservative Christians, on the other hand, tended to support the president's actions on the basis of his overt expressions of personal faith, his commitment to seek God's guidance daily in prayer, and his dependence on that divine guidance in his decision making; they also supported him based on the belief that the war was necessary to protect this nation against terrorism. The moral character of the president—evidenced by the absence of overt sins of the flesh—elevated him in esteem and garnered the loyalty of conservatives. At the same time, tax policies that created more economic inequity, favoring the rich over the poor—and judged as sinful by more liberal Christians—were largely minimized and ignored, or even broadly supported, by conservatives.

What has placed sins of the flesh at the top of the hierarchy of sins within the conservative, evangelical tradition, while social and structural sins are higher on the hierarchy of sins within the liberal tradition? There are multiple factors behind this divide, this abuse of imbalance, that are both theological and historical/cultural. For our purposes, we will seek to understand this divide from the perspective of biblical background and terminology.

According to the Old Testament's theology of creation, the physical world is considered the result of the creative word and work of God (Gen 1—2; Ps

---

[5]"Just-war theory" has its origin in the writings of Saint Augustine in the early fifth century, and it has been widely affirmed within Christendom (see appendix C). There are, however, Christian traditions, such as the Mennonite and Brethren traditions, who reject any justification for war and hold to a pacifist position, largely grounded in Jesus' teaching to love the enemy (Mt 5:43-44; Lk 6:27-28) and his rejection of the use of force (Mt 26:52-53; Lk 22:47-51).

8:3-5; 33:6; Is 45:12; 48:13). That physical creation is called "good" (Gen 1:31). Human beings, who are created in the image of God (Gen 1:26-27) to reflect the character and purposes of God within the total creation, are physical beings animated by the life-giving and sustaining "breath of life" (Gen 2:7 NIV).[6] It is that animating, divine breath that constituted humans as "living beings"[7] as opposed to "dust of the ground" (Gen 2:7). The creative act of God constitutes human beings as animated bodies, not as beings consisting of various aspects or separable parts (such as body, soul and spirit). This unitive understanding of human nature is dominant and pervasive throughout the Old Testament.[8]

That understanding of human nature was not, however, the dominant view in the Mediterranean world of the New Testament period. That thought-world was dominated by the ideas of Greek philosophy. Within that larger thought-world, Plato's dualistic view of the world and human beings was highly influential. He conceived of a two-tiered reality: (1) the *corporeal world* that appears to our senses (observable objects, the material realm), which is in some way defective and filled with error, and (2) the perfect realm of *forms* or *ideas* that are eternal and changeless.

Human beings were thought to participate in this bifurcated structure of reality. They were conceived as being constituted of essentially two parts (or dimensions): mind (or soul) and matter. The mind/soul aspect was viewed positively; through it the eternal forms could be contemplated and discerned. The physical/matter dimension was viewed negatively, as a burden and hindrance to the soul. A wordplay used in Plato's writings illustrates this dualistic view of human nature. The Greek word *sōma* (body) was paired with the word *sēma* (prison or tomb) to express the belief that the physical human body was a tomb, the place where the soul was imprisoned.

This understanding is the basis for the Greek idea of the immortality of the soul.[9] Here, the death of the physical body is seen as a liberating event to

---

[6]The Hebrew word used here for "breath" is *nĕšāmâ*, although *rûaḥ* is the more common word in the Hebrew Bible (e.g., in Gen 1:2; 6:17; 7:15; Ps 33:6) for the breath or spirit of God—through which creation came into being and which animates human life.

[7]The Hebrew term is *nepeš ḥayyâ*. The Authorized Version (KJV) rendered the term "living soul." The word *soul* is here not used to designate a particular aspect of the human being, but rather in the sense of "person" (as in "a mere ten souls lived in this community").

[8]See the allegory of the valley filled with dry bones in Ezekiel 37:1-10 for a graphic illustration of this view.

[9]See the classic study regarding the significant difference between the Greek idea of the immortal-

be celebrated rather than mourned, for the soul is seen to be liberated from its prison. The soul (or spirit/mind) was conceived of as the essential person, the locale of the true individual, while the body (the flesh) was by definition mortal, limited, weak.[10] Since the New Testament was written in Greek and largely addressed a Greek-speaking world, including large sectors of Judaism in the dispersion, it is not surprising that the New Testament writers—in communicating the good news of God's redemptive work in Christ—used ideas and terminology about human nature that would help them express that good news in ways that could be understood. This was particularly true of Paul, the apostle to the Greek-thinking and Greek-speaking Gentiles. Both Greek ideas and Jewish rabbinic thought were his tutors.[11] In addition, it is clear that he was deeply steeped in the thought-world of the Old Testament. Paul often used terminology from Greek thought about human nature, but at significant points he imported meanings into that terminology derived from his Old Testament and rabbinic background, as well as his understanding of God's redemptive work in Christ.[12]

In chapter five, where I'll deal with the abuse that is often committed when biblical terms are understood in ways that are not in keeping with their original meanings in their contexts, we will see that Paul's use of words like *flesh* and *spirit* frequently do not conform to Greek philosophical categories. His use of these terms does not support a dualistic understanding of human nature as consisting of a higher self versus a lower self, or a spiritual nature versus a physical nature. And yet this dualistic understanding of Paul's frequent contrast between living according to the flesh and living according to the Spirit, or being in the flesh and being in the Spirit, became a dominant way of understanding Paul. Christian thinkers and teachers in the early centuries of Christian history were largely trained in Greek philosophy, and thus tended to understand Paul through the lenses

---

ity of the soul and the New Testament teaching about the resurrection of the body: Oscar Cullmann, *Immortality of the Soul or Resurrection of the Dead? The Witness of the New Testament* (London: Epworth, 1958).

[10]While in Platonic thought the body, the physical, was not conceived of as intrinsically evil, in the later Hellenistic period (including the time of the New Testament) the physical was increasingly deemed as evil.

[11]An important study of this double influence is G. H. C. MacGregor and A. C. Purdy, *Jew and Greek: Tutors unto Christ* (New York: Charles Scribner's, 1936).

[12]An excellent study related to this issue is Robert Jewett's *Paul's Anthropological Terms* (Leiden: E. J. Brill, 1971). See also the incisive study by W. D. Stacey, *The Pauline View of Man in Relation to Its Judaic and Hellenistic Background* (London: Macmillan, 1956).

of Greek thought. Christian thinking and believing today is still, in significant areas, influenced by this legacy.

Such a dualistic view of human nature continues to influence much of our thinking about sin. For if the body (the physical dimension of human life) is intrinsically negative, the seat of our sinful human nature, and is especially prone to the distorting claims of sin, then the sins of the flesh are easily singled out as most dangerous to the so-called higher self, the spiritual dimension. Within much of the evangelical tradition, this is precisely the rationale for giving top billing, in a hierarchy of sin, to the sins of the flesh.

An unbalanced concern for certain categories of sin—such as sexual sin—and at the same time a lack of equal concern for other categories of sin—such as social and structural sins—is an abuse of Scripture. Why? Because the Word of God is equally concerned with both the personal and the social dimensions of life, with both what we do with our bodies and what we pursue with our minds, with both the sanctity of life in the womb and the sanctity of the life of individuals and communities threatened by war, violence, oppression, hunger and injustice.[13]

As early as the Ten Commandments (Ex 20:2-17; Deut 5:6-21) we find this balanced, holistic concern about all areas of life marred by sin. The more obvious "sins of the flesh" (murder, adultery, stealing) stand side by side with sins of the mind (dishonor of parents, bearing false witness, desiring what is not ours). All of these distort life as purposed by God, and they make wholeness of life in community impossible. This broadly balanced concern is also present in the legislation of Leviticus 17—26.[14] In these chapters, prohibitions against sins of the flesh, such as incest (Lev 18:6-18; 20:17-18), adultery (Lev 18:20; 20:10), homosexual practice (Lev 18:22; 20:13) and bestiality (Lev 18:23; 20:15-16) stand side by side with ethical obligations about honor of parents (Lev 19:3), care for the poor (Lev 19:9-10), bearing false witness

---

[13]A historic 2004 policy document of the National Association of Evangelicals, "For the Health of the Nation: An Evangelical Call to Civic Responsibility," points the way toward this kind of biblical balance. While championing continuing commitment to the moral issues that have been high on the evangelical agenda (such as sexuality and sanctity of life), the document expresses equal concern about "justice for the poor, care for creation, peace, freedom and racial justice." Cited by Ronald Sider, "The Religious Right Has Lost the Evangelical Center," *Prism: America's Alternative Evangelical Voice* 14, no. 4 (2007): 40.

[14]These chapters contain cultic requirements regarding Israel's worship and sacrifice practices, as well as ethical obligations for the life of the community. They are often called the "Holiness Code" because of the dominant theme in them: Israel is called to holiness because God is holy (Lev 19:2).

(Lev 19:11), defrauding the neighbor (Lev 19:13), harming handicapped persons (Lev 19:14), slandering others (Lev 19:16), hating one's brother (Lev 19:17-18), unfair trading practices (Lev 25:14-17), defrauding with false weights and measures (Lev 19:35), unjust rulings in court (Lev 19:15) and oppression of aliens in their midst (Lev 19:33-34).

The concern of Leviticus 19:33-34, about aliens within the nation of Israel, is particularly challenging in light of the fierce and continuing debate about undocumented immigrants in the United States. Hospitality to strangers was a very important aspect of ancient Near Eastern culture. But the word of the Lord to Israel goes significantly beyond the culturally expected norm: "The alien who resides with you shall be to you as the citizen among you. You shall love the alien as yourself" (Lev 19:34). Should not this injunction receive as much attention as the words about adultery and homosexuality? Unfortunately, that is not the case. Our leaders in the administration and our lawmakers in Congress are paralyzed by powerful and relentless pressure from the "conservative base" among the electorate, who want to keep (certain!) aliens out as much as possible and deport or punish those who are here illegally. Even policy proposals that would allow undocumented alien workers to earn their citizenship over the course of many years have met with strong resistance from the conservative electorate, including the very vocal Religious Right.[15] Thus many Christians who claim the Bible as the Word of God and as authoritative for all of life are often beholden to a national political agenda that needs to be critically examined and questioned from the perspective of the Bible's revelation of God's concern for "the other," the alien.

It is eminently clear that social sins are taken every bit as seriously in Scripture as sins of the flesh (if not more so). This is certainly the case in the prophetic literature. The prophetic critique of Israel and Judah focused on matters of social justice and structural evil; these categories of evil tore at the fabric and strength of the community of God's people and did violence to the divine purpose that Israel, God's servant (Is 44:1-2, 21), should be the instrument of God's glory in the world (Is 49:3) and "a light to the nations" (Is 42:6).

The prophets were particularly potent in addressing the Word of the Lord

---

[15]According to the Bliss Institute at the University of Akron, nearly 50 percent of what is generally considered the Religious Right are evangelicals. See Ronald J. Sider, "Evangelical Voters, Practice What You Preach" (2008) <www.beliefnet.com/story/162/story_16252.html>.

to the huge gap between personal and corporate demonstrations of piety, on the one hand (such as fasting, sacrifices, religious festivals, temple worship and prayer—Is 1:11-17), and the concrete, everyday embodiment of that religiosity in the lives of individuals and in the life of the nation, on the other hand. The failure of that embodiment of piety they primarily addressed to social and structural sins. Yet other categories of sin were also within their purview, such as adultery and other sexual transgressions (e.g., Ezek 22:9-11; Mal 2:13-16). In Ezekiel 18, social and sexual sins are named together in several lists. All of them, and each of them, stand under the signature of death (Ezek 18:4, 13, 18, 24).

When we enter the pages of the New Testament, this same balance prevails. Certain expressions of human sinfulness receive particular attention in certain contexts. All of them are taken with utmost seriousness as violations of God's purposes. All are evidence of distortions in our relationship with God and each other in both intimate relationships and in larger communities.

Much of Jesus' life and ministry, as reflected in the four Gospels, is defined by his controversies and conflict with the religious leadership. While they were very articulate in pointing out the sinners—prostitutes, adulterers, publicans, Samaritans, the ritually unclean[16]—they were at the same time largely blind to their own sinfulness, particularly pride in their own piety, self-righteousness leading to contempt and judgmentalism, and the arrogance that comes from status within the religious community. Because these manifestations of sinfulness are more subtle and insidious, they are frequently the focus of Jesus' attention.[17] He does not minimize the seriousness of those sins that fall in the category of sins of the flesh, like adultery (Jn 8:11) and promiscuity (or prostitution; Lk 7:37). They are, indeed, distortions of God-intended human wholeness. They are aspects of human lostness that need overcoming, and they are evidence of brokenness that needs healing (Mk 2:17; Lk 15:2). Yet the dimension of sin that receives his most incisive attention is in the area of attitude, motivation and thought. His deepest concern is with spiritual

---

[16]Lk 7:36-39; 15:1-2; 18:10-14; 19:7; Jn 4:9; 8:3-11.

[17]Note, for example, the parable of the Pharisee and publican (Lk 18:9-14); the woes pronounced on the Pharisees (Mt 23; Lk 11:42-43); Jesus' sarcastic definition of the religious leaders as "the righteous" who (so they believe) have no need of a physician (Mt 9:9-13; Mk 2:15-17; Lk 5:29-32); and his denunciation of empty external manifestations of piety (Mt 6:1-6; in the Greek text, the word rendered in the NRSV as "piety" is *dikaiosynē*, which might be better translated as "righteousness").

pride, lust, judgmentalism and self-righteousness. The act of adultery is easily
identified and pointed out by his religious opponents (Jn 8:3-4)—it is, after
all, a very specific sin of the flesh—but for Jesus, the very thought of an illicit
sexual encounter is already an act of adultery (Mt 5:27-28). Jesus goes to the
very core of the matter: "For it is from within, from the human heart, that evil
intentions come: fornication, theft, murder, adultery, avarice, wickedness, deceit, licentiousness, envy, slander, pride, folly" (Mk 7:21-22).

What we find in Jesus' teaching then, in addition to his attention to the
dimensions of personal/relational sins of the flesh and social/structural sins,
is a deeper dimension of a biblically balanced and inclusive understanding of
sin. This dimension of attitude, of motivation, is the subtle, invisible ground
from which all other manifestations of our sinfulness emerge. Thus both the
conservative preoccupation with sins of the flesh and liberalism's concern
with social and structural sins must be balanced with one another, and both
of these must be leavened by, and grounded in, this fundamental dimension
that is Jesus' central concern. Such a balanced, multifaceted understanding of
sin is an implicit rejection of our propensity in various Christian traditions to
construct hierarchies of sin. The rest of the New Testament, and particularly
the Pauline literature, further supports this balance and the rejection of a
hierarchical structuring of categories of sin.

In Paul's most comprehensive discussion of human sinfulness (Rom 1:18—
3:23), "sins of the flesh" (such as homosexual practice and adultery) stand side
by side with sins that break relationships and tear society apart (such as cov-
etousness, strife and ruthlessness). The former are distortions of God-
intended male-female sexual intimacy and fidelity. The latter are distortions
of God-intended wholeness in community. Both categories of sin are equally
the consequences of brokenness in the Creator-creature relationship.

Similarly, in the Corinthian correspondence, Paul lists sins that are incompatible with the presence of the reign of God in both individual lives and
in human institutions (1 Cor 6:9-20). Distortions of God-intended sexual
intimacy in marriage are fornication,[18] adultery, prostitution[19] and homo-

---

[18]The Greek word *porneia* (from which is derived the English *pornography*) is the most general word
for sexual immorality, but it is particularly used for sexual promiscuity and prostitution.

[19]The term "male prostitutes" (1 Cor 6:9) is from the Greek *malakoi* (which literally means "soft"),
which was a term commonly used in Hellenistic texts as a pejorative epithet for the passive youth
in a homosexual relationship. In Greek society, young men often sold themselves as "mistresses"
for the sexual pleasure of older men.

sexuality.[20] Then follows a litany of sin's distortions in other areas of personal and social life: theft, greed, drunkenness, reviling and robbery. In 1 Corinthians 5, sexual immorality receives the apostle's scrutiny side by side with spiritual arrogance and boasting.[21] Both are equally destructive to wholeness of life.

The same balanced, comprehensive understanding of sin is present in Galatians, Ephesians, Philippians and Colossians. In Galatians 5:13-15, Paul admonishes his readers not to use their Christian freedom "for self-indulgence,"[22] and then defines that self-indulgence in terms of intense, bitter strife within the Christian community in Galatia ("If . . . you bite and devour one another," Gal 5:15). This admonition is followed by another list of practices that are incompatible with life lived by the power of the Spirit (Gal 5:19-21). He names sins that are specifically connected to the physical appetites: fornication, impurity, drunkenness, carousing. Then he gives a lengthy list of what might be called sins of the heart and mind: licentiousness, idolatry, sorcery, enmity, strife, jealousy, anger, quarrels, dissensions, factions, envy. In Ephesians, he identifies attitudes and practices that "grieve the Holy Spirit of God" (Eph 4:30), such as evil talk (as opposed to "words [that] may give grace to those who hear," Eph 4:29), bitterness, wrath, anger, wrangling, slander and malice. In Ephesians 5 he names things that are incompatible with the kingdom (reign) of God. In this list, greed and obscene, vulgar talk get equal billing with fornication and impurity. In Philippians, where he is addressing conflict within the Christian community, "selfish ambition or conceit" (Phil 2:3) as well as "murmuring and arguing" (Phil 2:14) are named as attitudes and practices that should not characterize people marked by the

---

[20]The English word *sodomites*, which designates homosexual men, is derived from the narrative in Genesis 19 in which the men of Sodom demand sexual intercourse with Lot's visitors. The Greek word translated "sodomites" (NRSV) and "homosexual offenders" (NIV) is *arsenokoitai*. This is a compound word, consisting of *arsēn* (male) and *koitē* (intercourse), not used outside the New Testament prior to its use by Paul. The term is most likely a translation (coined by Paul) of the Hebrew *miškab zākûr* (literally "lying with a male"), derived directly from Leviticus 18:22 and 20:13, and used in rabbinic texts to refer to homosexual intercourse. The Greek translation of the Old Testament, in use in New Testament times, rendered the Hebrew of Leviticus 18:22 and 20:13 with precisely the same words that Paul used (*arsēn* = male and *koitē* = intercourse).

[21]See Gordon D. Fee's discussion of the Corinthians' spiritual pride, which elevated them above concern about what they considered bodily trivialities (like sexual intercourse) in *The First Epistle to the Corinthians*, New International Commentary on the New Testament (Grand Rapids: Eerdmans, 1987), pp. 4-15, 198-99.

[22]The literal translation of the Greek term is "for the flesh." I will discuss Paul's use of this term and its specialized meaning in the next chapter.

mind of Christ (Phil 2:15). Finally, in Colossians 3:5-9, the apostle calls on the believers to "put to death" acts and attitudes that are evidences of sinful brokenness. As throughout Paul's writings, fornication and impurity are named side by side with such vices as evil desire, greed, anger, wrath, malice, slander and abusive language.

The above survey of the broad sweep of the biblical material leads to the inescapable conclusion that trustworthiness in hearing and applying the Bible's teaching requires faithful, consistent attention to this balanced, holistic biblical concern about all areas of personal and social life that are ravaged by the power of sin. I've already stated the conviction that the evangelical community—given its deep commitment to the divine inspiration and authority of Scripture—has a special obligation to be "trustworthy stewards," in word and deed, of this Word of God. Therefore, when we do violence to its balanced and inclusive agenda by lopsided attention to half of the gospel, or to a narrow focus on certain categories of sin, we present to the world a caricature, a distorted understanding of Christian faith.[23] Indeed, our presence within the larger secular culture becomes a caricature. This is clear from the way the secular media uncritically uses the terms "evangelical" and "evangelicals" synonymously with "Religious Right" and "fundamentalists." Then, on the basis of this caricature, evangelicals are summarily dismissed as misguided obscurantist zealots, in league with right-wing political agendas, imbued with a racist and sexist mindset, beholden to American "exceptionalism" ("God bless America") and the arrogance of power.

This caricature—and that is precisely what it is[24]—is, to a great extent, the result of our abuse of biblical balance. Rejecting that abuse, we must speak as loudly and passionately about restraining the use of force in international af-

---

[23]Absence of the Bible's balanced agenda is, of course, also a reality in the liberal traditions of the Christian faith. In these traditions, views of the Bible's inspiration and authority are much less rigorous than in the evangelical tradition. Several representative positions are: (1) the Bible as the result of human mythmaking and speculation about God and the world; (2) the Bible as containing lofty human inspiration and moral wisdom; (3) the Bible as consisting of divinely inspired and revelatory material that needs to be carefully sifted and evaluated via reason and scientific criteria; (4) the Bible as one authority for Christian faith and life, together with experience, reason and tradition. Given these perspectives, the way the Bible is interpreted and applied to life in these traditions does not require the same attention to the Bible's comprehensive, inclusive dimensions as in the traditions that affirm the Bible's divine inspiration and authority.

[24]See the essay by Tom Sine, "Celebrating the Demise of America's Culture Wars," *Prism: America's Alternative Evangelical Voice* 14, no. 4 (2007): 4-5; and idem, "The Times They Are A-Changin,'" *Prism* 14, no. 5 (2007): 4-5.

fairs as about abortion; about responsible care for and stewardship of the earth as about premarital and extramarital sexual abstinence; about poverty and its dehumanizing power as about family values; about the continuing and all-too-pervasive racism in our midst as about ethical concerns regarding stem-cell research; about divisive battles between and within Christian traditions as about the integrity of marriage; about gossip and slander in our churches as about homosexuality; and about self-righteousness and judgmentalism as about adultery. Perhaps then our witness and presence in our culture and our world will be taken more seriously.

THE QUEST FOR CORRECT BELIEF AND THE RESTRAINT OF HUMILITY

A second illustration of the abuse of biblical balance is in the tension between (1) the biblical concern for faithfulness to the truths of God revealed in Scripture and (2) faithful acknowledgment and practice of both the biblical admonition to humility and the recognition of our limited creatureliness. The truths of Scripture—while having their origin in the absoluteness of God's nature and purposes (2 Tim 3:16)—are given to us by divine design in the garb of human languages, historical contexts and cultural realities. Just as the living Word of God, Jesus Christ, came in the limited and limiting form of "fleshness,"[25] so the Word of God in and through Scripture is "incarnational." This incarnational character of the biblical Word corresponds to the fact that we, together with all hearers and readers of the scriptural record for several thousand years, come to the text of Scripture with our linguistic, historical and cultural "trifocals."

We stand before the Incarnate Word, transmitted to us in and through the incarnate biblical text, as limited creatures, people of flesh. Each generation, from Moses' time to the present, has come to the sacred writings with the natural deposit of its own historical context. All bring to the "seeing" of the biblical text the lenses of their own cultural conditioning, historical situation, faith traditions, existential needs and personal/group biases. It is this reality that makes the biblical admonitions to humility in our relationship with God, as well as in our believing and thinking about the truths of God and responding to them, so critically important.

---

[25]Creaturely weakness and limitedness in power, knowledge, etc., is the characteristic meaning of *flesh* in the Bible. See George R. Beasley-Murray, *John*, Word Biblical Commentary, vol. 36 (Waco, Tex.: Word Books, 1987), p. 14.

We are called to trustworthy stewardship of the truths of Scripture.[26] At the same time we are called to engage in this task with creaturely humility. Preoccupation with either of these critically important perspectives, to the minimizing or ignoring of the other, is an abuse of Scripture that has had, and continues to have, serious consequences for the integrity and effectiveness of Christian witness and presence.

The biblical witness, from Genesis to Revelation, affirms that God has spoken and acted, and that both in God's speaking and acting (and in the result), truth about God and us and the world has been revealed. Scripture attests to the fact that knowledge about God (his glory, power, divine nature) has been revealed in and through the creation (Ps 19:1-4; Rom 1:19-20). But beyond these dimensions of God's being, God's revelatory speaking and acting—which reveal truths about God's character, the human condition, God's will for human life and God's redemptive work—are the subject matter of the entire Bible.

The Old Testament is a rich depository of affirmations about the person and character of God. He is "the everlasting God, the Creator of the ends of the earth" (Is 40:28; cf. Ps 90:2). As such, he is also the sovereign Lord of history: "Your kingdom is an everlasting kingdom, and your dominion endures throughout all generations" (Ps 145:13; cf. Ps 103:19; Dan 4:3, 34; 7:14). These confessions are grounded ultimately in the self-revelation of God, the Lord of Israel, as the eternally existing one, the "I AM WHO I AM" (Ex 3:14-15),[27] the "first and the last" (Is 44:6), beside whom "there is no god" (Is 44:6; 45:5, 18, 22; 46:9).

Israel's cultic and legal tradition (especially in Exodus, Leviticus and Deuteronomy) and its liturgical/confessional tradition (particularly in the Psalms and the prophetic literature) fills in this picture of the being of God with an array of affirmations about the character of God and the will of God. Central is the belief in God as the Holy One: "I the LORD your God am holy" (Lev

---

[26]See Jn 17:17-19; Gal 2:5, 14; Col 1:5; 2 Tim 2:15. This focus on the truths of Scripture is the primary concern of David F. Wells, *No Place for Truth, or, Whatever Happened to Evangelical Theology?* (Grand Rapids: Eerdmans, 1993); and Andreas Köstenberger, ed., *Whatever Happened to Truth?* (Wheaton, Ill.: Crossway Books, 2005).

[27]The name of Israel's God, YHWH (pronounced Yahweh), revealed here to Moses and Israel for the first time (see Ex 6:2-3) is here closely related to the verb *hāyâ* ("to be"), used in Exodus 3:14 in the phrase "I AM WHO I AM." Hebrew scholars have noted that the name Yahweh is in a third person form and could mean "he causes to be." As such, the divine name would refer to the action of God in creation and history.

19:2; Ps 99:3, 9). God is separate from, and above, all human defilement, uncleanness, sin and distortion. And because God is holy, God's people are called to holiness of life (Lev 11:44-45; 19:2; 20:26). This truth about the ultimate moral character of God, about his "holy otherness," is further revealed in the nature of God's kingly rule, which is characterized by righteousness and justice. The psalmist proclaims,

> Righteousness and justice are the foundation of your throne. (Ps 89:14)

> Mighty king, lover of justice, you have established equity;
>   you have executed justice and righteousness in Jacob. (Ps 99:4)

This holy, just and righteous God—who calls Israel, and through her the nations, to lives and relationships characterized by holiness, justice and righteousness—is also supremely the God who is "merciful and gracious . . . abounding in steadfast love and faithfulness" (Ps 86:15). There are no terms more frequently used to designate the character of God and his relationship to Israel, and the entire creation, than the terms "steadfast love" and "faithfulness,"[28] often used as a pair.[29] Out of this character of God emerges his redemptive, saving action toward Israel and the world. It is God's steadfast love and faithfulness that delivers, protects and saves.[30]

These truths about God's nature, character and redemptive acting find their most complete historical manifestation—according to the New Testament—in the person and work of Jesus Christ. Just as God's glory is revealed in his steadfast love and faithfulness (Ps 115:1), so the glory of God in the incarnation, the "enfleshment" of the Word of God, is revealed in the life, death and resurrection of the One who is "full of grace and truth" (Jn 1:14, 17). This couplet in John 1:14 is the equivalent of the Old Testament's common "steadfast love and faithfulness," which in the Greek translation of the Old Testament is rendered as *eleos* ("mercy," "grace") and *alētheia* ("truth").[31]

---

[28]"Steadfast love" translates the Hebrew *hesed,* which is used over 180 times. "Faithfulness" translates the related Hebrew words *'ĕmûnâ* and *'ĕmet,* used about thirty-five and sixty-five times, respectively.

[29]The terms "steadfast love" *(hesed)* and "faithfulness" *('ĕmûnâ, 'ĕmet)* appear as couplets over twenty times (e.g., Ex 34:6; 2 Sam 2:6; Ps 40:10-11; 57:3, 10; 89:1-2, 14; Is 16:5; Hos 2:19-20). Note that while the NRSV renders both *'ĕmûnâ* and *'ĕmet* primarily as "faithfulness," the NASB renders *'ĕmet* mostly as "truth." This varying translation reflects the fact that *'ĕmet* carries also the meaning "trustworthiness" and "truthfulness." To be faithful is to be trustworthy, to be truthful in one's expression of fidelity and loyalty.

[30]Ps 40:10; 57:3; 69:13; 85:7-13; cf. Jn 3:16: "God so loved the world."

[31]See Beasley-Murray, *John,* pp. 14-15, who states that *"alētheia,* truth, is a key Johannine term in

The revelation of truth—about God, human life, God's work in Christ and its meaning for human wholeness—is a central feature of the Gospel of John. In Jesus, the truth of God is embodied (Jn 1:14, 17; 14:6). He speaks and bears witness to the truth (Jn 8:32, 40, 45-46; 16:7; 17:17; 18:37). Commitment to the truth of God in the life and ministry of Jesus was a deep, central concern of Jesus' earliest followers in continuity with the teaching of Jesus about the ongoing work, presence and teaching of "the Spirit of truth" in their lives (Jn 15:26; 16:13). So Luke begins his two-volume work (the Gospel of Luke and Acts) by stating that his purpose for writing about the life of Jesus is that the truth about Jesus' person, work and teaching might be made known (Lk 1:4).

The apostle Paul is equally concerned about "the truth of the gospel" (Gal 2:5, 14; cf. Eph 1:13), which is Paul's shorthand for what he considers to be the truthfulness of his teaching and writing about God's redemptive work in the life, death and resurrection of Jesus. Paul understands Christ's sacrificial servant life to be a vehicle of God's truth (Rom 15:8). And that truth for Paul most certainly includes the conviction that in Christ "the fullness of God was pleased to dwell" (Col 1:19; cf. Col 2:9), that "he rescued us from the power of darkness" (Col 1:13), granted us "redemption, the forgiveness of sins" (Col 1:14) through his death on the cross (Col 2:14-15), and was raised from the dead in triumph over the power of sin and death (Rom 10:9; 1 Cor 15). These central truths, and many more that are articulated throughout the New Testament, are certainly in view[32] in the cautionary words of the apostle to Timothy and Titus.[33] In their congregations the "knowledge of the truth" (1 Tim

---

which the Hebrew and Greek concepts of truth come together." Whereas the Hebrew 'ĕmet "represents firmness, stability and of persons['] steadfastness or trustworthiness . . . alētheia denotes that which *really* is; in this Gospel it often represents eternal reality revealed."

[32]See 1 Tim 1:15; 2:5-7; 3:16; 2 Tim 1:8-10; 2:8; 4:1; Tit 3:4-7.

[33]The Pauline authorship of the so-called Pastoral Epistles (to Timothy and Titus), as well as of Ephesians and Colossians, has been called into question by many New Testament scholars. Reasons for this critical assessment are readily available in standard introductions to the New Testament, as well as in the commentaries on these letters. I continue to be unpersuaded by the arguments against Ephesians and Colossians in particular. At the very least, they contain the mature fruit of Paul's theological thought, perhaps gathered together by a Pauline disciple (with Paul's blessing) and written to the churches in Asia Minor. While the case against Pauline authorship of the Pastoral Epistles may be somewhat stronger, it still seems plausible to me that the pastoral context of these young students of Paul called for a kind of pastoral instruction significantly distinct in style and theological vocabulary from the acknowledged Pauline letters. The differences in style and content may, of course, be the result of Paul communicating through a scribe who was quite free in his articulation and formulation of Paul's instructions.

2:4; 2 Tim 2:25; 3:7; Tit 1:1; cf. Heb 10:26), "the word of truth" (2 Tim 2:15; cf. Jas 1:18) and "the truth" (2 Tim 2:18; cf. Jas 5:19) was being threatened by ignorance, neglect, false teaching or rejection.[34]

The biblical affirmations briefly sketched above—about fidelity to the revealed truths from God—have been (and remain) the source of the deep concern for correct doctrine (orthodox teaching) throughout the history of Christianity. Scripture makes truth claims that are the basis for Christian faith, beliefs, doctrines and actions. Truth matters. This is especially so if we are convinced that biblical truth has its origin in God, the source of all truth. "You will know the truth," said Jesus, "and the truth will make you free" (Jn 8:32)—free from the darkness of ignorance; free from false and distorted views about God and human life and the world; free from the power of sin; free from false understandings of the gospel. Because truth matters and has consequences for Christian life and mission in the world, immense and intense emotional, spiritual and intellectual energy has been invested—for nearly two thousand years—in the quest to "get it right"; to correctly understand the *truths* expressed in biblical revelation; to articulate Christian *beliefs* precisely; to formulate *doctrinal* positions clearly and in fidelity to the biblical Word; and to do *apologetics* of the Christian faith passionately and with intellectual rigor.

A few brief definitions of the italicized words in the previous paragraph are in order: The scriptural record is replete with revealed *truth* claims: these are the foundation stones for the superstructure of the Christian faith. *Beliefs* are statements of assent to biblical propositions or truth claims. The so-called Apostles' Creed is an early second- to third-century statement of central Christian beliefs. *Doctrines* are the result of a further step in the church's theological reflection; they are more comprehensive, complex formulations of a belief or a group of beliefs. Thus, while the Apostles' Creed affirms belief in "God, the Father," "Jesus Christ, his only Son," and "the Holy Spirit," the later Nicene Creed (early fourth century) reflects the development of these beliefs into the doctrine of the Trinity, an affirmation of how the relationship between the three persons of the Trinity is to be understood. A defense of the Christian faith against attack, misunderstanding and falsification is known as an *apologetic*. Apologetic work has been a significant thread in Christian

---

[34]See 1 Tim 1:3-7, 19-20; 3:9; 4:1-2, 7; 2 Tim 2:17-18; 3:8; 4:3-4; Tit 1:9-11; 3:9; cf. Jas 3:14; 2 Pet 2:1-2.

believing and thinking ever since Paul's controversy with Peter and the "Judaizers" in the early decades of the Christian movement (see Gal 1:6—2:21). This two-thousand-year-old work of Christian believing and thinking—namely the movement from biblical affirmations, to the articulation of beliefs, to the formulation of doctrine and its defense—has been critical and essential in shaping Christian faith and identity.[35]

Yet this story is, at the same time, also a very tragic story that has repeatedly undermined the integrity of the Christian faith and blunted the authenticity of its witness and its effective presence in the world. In the laudable and necessary quest to "get it right," to "guard the truth," to protect it from heresy and distortion, and to defend it against criticism and attack, the age-old sin of *hubris* has, and continues to, assert itself.[36] The fundamental manifestation of this hubris is depicted in the Fall narrative in Genesis 3:5—"You will be like God, knowing good and evil."[37] It is the assertion of moral autonomy, the quest to transcend the boundaries of creaturely limitation, to have absolute knowledge, and thus absolute certainty. This quest, in the process of the formation of Christian doctrine, has been particularly at home in the Greek-Western intellectual tradition, where ambiguity, paradox and cognitive dissonance are to be avoided at all cost.

It is the presence of the sin of hubris in the Christian's pursuit of truth that has marred and scarred the Christian story. From the early post-Apostolic period right into the present, the Christian story has been characterized by often bitter doctrinal controversies, acrimonious theological debates, inquisitions and executions, condemnations and excommunications, violence and religious wars, divisions and schisms between and within Christian communions, and mean-spirited denunciations of those holding divergent positions.[38] As theologian Roger Olson put it in his concern over present-day

---

[35]For a comprehensive introduction to this story, see John H. Leith, ed., *Creeds of the Churches: A Reader in Christian Doctrine from the Bible to the Present*, rev. ed. (Richmond, Va.: John Knox Press, 1973).

[36]*Hybris* is the Greek word for "excessive pride" or "arrogance." In its verbal form *hybrizō*, the word designates the treatment of others "in an arrogant and spiteful manner." See 2 Corinthians 12:10, where Paul speaks of enduring "insults" *(hybresin)*.

[37]The phrase "knowing good and evil" may not be a reference to moral awareness or moral knowledge, but rather a reference to absolute, ultimate knowledge: to "be like God." The phrase would designate completeness, all-inclusiveness (like our idioms "from top to bottom" or "from east to west").

[38]A more recent example of this was the very public call (on March 1, 2007) by James Dobson of Focus on the Family to discipline or ouster Richard Cizik, who at the time was vice president for

doctrinal battles, especially within the larger evangelical community, "The incessant quarreling and cold indifference between God-fearing, Bible-believing, Jesus-loving Christians is scandalous to the secular world—as it should be scandalous to Christians."[39]

The scandalous nature of Christian pride and arrogance, which mars the Christian landscape, has also found expression in recent memory in the very troubling and arrogant judgments uttered by Christian leaders regarding events on the world stage. With prideful certainty, leaders such as Franklin Graham, Jerry Falwell and James Dobson—on the basis of the Bible's general affirmations that human sin stands under the judgment of God—pronounced that events like the terrorist attacks of 9/11 or the devastation caused by Hurricane Katrina represented the judgment of God on America for its liberal attitudes toward homosexuality and abortion or the moral decadence of New Orleans. These kinds of statements undermine the possibility for authentic Christian witness to be heard by secularists.

The passion for truth, when marred by the hubris of theological rectitude and doctrinal absolutism, often masquerades in "the outward form of godliness," while in practice "denying its power" (2 Tim 3:5). The final tragedy is that such a stance contributes to the world's brokenness, to the cumulative weight of the anger, jealousy, hatred and bitterness that fractures human communities and relationships. This kind of stance builds barriers that divide, separate and exclude.[40]

There are numerous warnings within the Bible itself against this quest for theological knowledge that transcends our finite understanding and reasoning, for doctrinal certainty that eliminates mystery, paradox and ambiguity. We are to seek the Lord, says the prophet, to trust ourselves to God's grace (Is 55:6-7) even though God's thoughts and ways cannot be confined to our thoughts and ways, even though his ways transcend ours "as the heavens are higher than the earth" (Is 55:8-9).

---

governmental affairs of the National Association of Evangelicals, for his outspoken advocacy of Christian responsibility for the care of creation, including global warming.

[39]Roger E. Olson, *The Mosaic of Christian Belief: Twenty Centuries of Unity and Diversity* (Downers Grove, Ill.: InterVarsity Press, 2002), p. 26. I recommend this work highly as a thorough and comprehensive treatment of the issue addressed in this section of the present chapter. For a classic treatment of the doctrinal controversies in the first five centuries, see J. N. D. Kelly, *Early Christian Doctrines* (San Francisco: Harper & Row, 1978).

[40]See the biblical warnings against these attitudinal vices, which are out of place in communities that claim the presence of God's reign in their midst (e.g., Eph 4:25-32; Col 3:5-11).

This call to stand in creaturely humility before the absolute truth of God is also a central feature in the book of Job. His friends argue their case for the justification of Job's suffering on the basis of their "theological certainty," which they ground in the Mosaic teaching (Deut 28): God rewards and blesses the righteous, and he punishes the unrighteous. Therefore there must have been unrighteousness in Job (e.g., Job 4:7-8; 11:4-6; 15:17-25; 18:5-21; 20:4-5; 22:4-5). The integrity of Job's right relationship with God is, however, affirmed in contradiction to the inherited theological certainty (Job 1:8; 2:3; 27:5-6). And in the midst of this "theological ambiguity" (Job 34:5-9), the book of Job calls for humility before a God whose ways are beyond comprehension (Job 33:12-14; 36:24-29; 37:5, 14-18; 38—41). This is also the point of Psalm 111:10: "The fear of the LORD is the beginning of wisdom; / all those who practice it have a good understanding."[41] This is the proper stance of humility before the God whose thoughts and ways are beyond our understanding, rather than the arrogance of knowledge.

The note of caution in the Old Testament regarding the "hubris quest" for final answers and doctrinal certainty meets us repeatedly in the New Testament. In Mark 13, the wonder of the disciples about the magnificence of the Jerusalem temple (Mk 13:1) evokes from Jesus the prediction of the temple's impending desecration (Mk 13:14) and destruction (Mk 13:2), and the teaching about the end of the age (Mk 13:24-27). The disciples' question, "Tell us, when will this be, and what will be the sign that all these things are about to be accomplished?" (Mk 13:4), is answered by Jesus in three parts. First, various historical events are yet to come before the climax of history, such as the temple's destruction and its aftermath, wars and rumors of wars, international conflicts, natural disasters and persecution for Jesus' followers (Mk 13:5-23). Second, neither the angels in heaven, nor the Son, are privy to "that day or hour," which is known only to God the Father (Mk 13:32). Third, always be ready, "for you do not know when the time will come" (Mk 13:35; see also 13:28-37). This implicit warning against end-time speculation, and the explicit affirmation of our limited knowledge in this matter, is repeated in one of Christ's post-resurrection appearances. On the basis of the common Jewish belief that the resurrection of the dead was connected with the end-time judgment and the establishment of the kingdom of God, the resurrection of Jesus was apparently

---

[41]The Hebraic concept of "the fear of the Lord" (cf. Job 37:24) has nothing to do with being "afraid of God." The Hebrew term denotes the idea "to stand in awe before God."

perceived by the disciples as inaugurating these end-time events. So they ask: "Lord, is this the time when you will restore the kingdom to Israel?" (Acts 1:6). Jesus responds: "It is not for you to know the times or periods the Father has set by his own authority" (Acts 1:7). The message seems to be, "that is none of your business!" Rather the emphasis is that "you will receive power . . . and you will be my witnesses" (Acts 1:8). Spirit-empowered presence in the world—not permission to engage in endless and often-fruitless quests for eschatological, doctrinal certainty and precision—is Jesus' mandate.

Despite these words of Jesus (that the chronology and timing of the end of time are known only to the Father, and that the disciples do not have a "need to know") an immense body of Christian literature has been produced over the centuries, particularly within the past 150 years, with competing and often diametrically opposed theories and timetables about end-time events. All of these are, of course, grounded by their advocates in biblical texts and frequently promoted as *the* biblical teaching on the subject. The result has often been division, separation of fellowship, acrimonious disputes and internecine charges of heresy.[42] On what basis have followers of Jesus—preachers, scholars, teachers—decided that they can do their Lord one better, that they know more about God's timetable than he did, and that they can then use that "superior knowledge" to bring division and often bitter controversy into the body of Christ?

We saw above that the apostle Paul certainly contended for the truth of the gospel. In his passion for that truth he could be stridently polemical when he saw the integrity of the gospel undermined by false teaching and especially by restrictive, ethnocentric beliefs that would seriously impair the mission of the gospel of God's grace to the nations. For him, that was a matter of life or death. But he was clear at the same time that the mystery of God's redemptive purposes, revealed in the Christ event (Eph 1:7-14), and which he sought to articulate in his missionary preaching, teaching and writing, is nevertheless to be received and held in creaturely humility. Why? Because "we have this treasure"—the treasure of "the light of the knowledge of the glory of God in the face of Jesus Christ"—in "clay jars, so that it may be made clear that

---

[42]For a concise, clear and fair presentation of six major eschatological views (premillennialism, postmillennialism, amillennialism, dispensationalism, pretribulationism, posttribulationism) and three mediating views (midtribulationism, partial rapture view, imminent posttribulationism), see Millard J. Erickson, *A Basic Guide to Eschatology: Making Sense of the Millennium* (Grand Rapids: Baker, 1998).

this extraordinary power belongs to God and does not come from us" (2 Cor 4:6-7). Because of our present "clay-jar" limitedness, "we see in a mirror, dimly. . . . Now I know only in part; then I will know fully" (1 Cor 13:12).[43] This affirmation of our limited understanding and knowing in the "now" is particularly potent within the context of Paul's controversy with Christians in Corinth who prized their theological knowledge, their insight into divine realities, above all else—certainly above love for their brothers and sisters in Christ (1 Cor 3:18; 8:1-2; 13:2).

The fact that we hold the treasure of God's self-disclosure in Christ—mediated to us in the biblical writings—in the "clay jars" of our humanity means that this knowing can never be a matter of *absolute certainty*. It is rather a matter of the *confidence of faith*, which is yet always open to new insights and perspectives. "We walk by faith, not by sight" (2 Cor 5:7). This caution with respect to the hubris of superior knowledge or theological absolutism is also present in what is arguably Paul's most sustained theological treatise, namely his epistle to the Romans. He spends eight chapters expounding on the meaning and significance of God's work in Christ for the human condition (Rom 1—8). Then he follows up with three chapters in which he wrestles mightily with the question of whether Israel, as a historical community of God's people, has a continuing place within God's purposes now that Christ, "the end of the law," has come (Rom 10:4; see also Rom 9—11). At the conclusion of this intense theological reflection—which has both astounded and often perplexed exegetes and commentators, due to Paul's complex, and at times convoluted, argumentation[44]—Paul stands in awe and humility:

> O the depth of the riches and wisdom and knowledge of God! How unsearchable are his judgments and how inscrutable his ways!
>
> For who has known the mind of the Lord?
> Or who has been his counselor? (Rom 11:33-34)[45]

---

[43]The Greek phrase translated "in a mirror, dimly" is *en ainigmati*. It literally means "in a riddle." The English word "enigma" is derived from this Greek term.

[44]See, e.g., the commentaries by James D. G. Dunn, *Romans 9—16*, Word Biblical Commentary, vol. 38B (Dallas: Word Books 1988); and N. T. Wright, "The Letter to the Romans," in *The New Interpreter's Bible*, vol. 10 (Nashville: Abingdon, 2002).

[45]Romans 11:34 is a citation of Isaiah 40:13 from the Greek translation (Septuagint) of the Hebrew Old Testament, the Bible of Greek-speaking Jews in the time of the early church. The Hebrew text, in English translation, reads: "Who has directed the spirit of the LORD, or as his counselor has instructed him?"

Three conclusions emerge from the above reflections:

1. Truth matters! The theological content of Scripture, its revelatory truth statements, provide the authoritative charter and foundation for the super-structure of the Christian faith. That superstructure consists of: (a) *beliefs* about God, creation, sin, Christ, salvation, church and so on; (b) more complex constructions of those beliefs into *doctrines*, such as the doctrine of the Trinity, Christology, ecclesiology and eschatology; and (c) larger *theological systems*, such as Reformed theology, Arminian theology and Anabaptist theology.

2. In our apprehension and interpretation of the truths of Scripture—and even more so in the process toward, and conclusions about, doctrines and theological systems—we are called by Scripture to practice humility, rec-ognizing (a) that the truth of God, the Word of God, comes to us by God's design in the limiting context of our "clay jars," namely human language, culture and historical circumstances;[46] (b) that the redemptive purposes and actions of God—worked out in the history of Israel, the Christ event, and the teaching and living of Jesus' earliest followers, which were trans-mitted to us in the sacred writings—are trustworthy. They give us the *confidence of faith* (2 Cor 5:6-7) that—even as we, with the biblical wit-nesses, acknowledge that God's thoughts and ways transcend our limited understanding and fragmented theologizing—God's truth is revealed in Scripture.

3. Since our knowing—that is, our understanding of the propositional truth statements in Scripture, from which we derive beliefs and formulate doc-trines and build theological systems—is always penultimate, never abso-lute, we must always guard against the intrusion of the sin of hubris, the quest to know as only God knows. The arrogance of theological rectitude and doctrinal absolutism is not only out of place in light of the biblical call to humility and awe before the unfathomable ways of God, but it is down-right dangerous.[47] Its presence in the Christian community has been divi-

---

[46]See my discussion of these in chapters five and seven of this book.

[47]For a full-scale treatment of the divisiveness and distortions in Christian believing and thinking resulting from "either-or theology"—where beliefs and doctrines become weapons of theological warfare against those who hold divergent beliefs and doctrines, all grounded in biblical texts—I strongly recommend the book by Roger E. Olson, *The Mosaic of Christian Belief: Twenty Centuries of Unity and Diversity* (Downers Grove, Ill.: InterVarsity Press, 2002). Beyond his critique of "either-or" doctrinal certainties, the significant contribution of Olson's work is in his proposals

sive, destructive and scandalous. It has been a direct affront to the desire of Jesus that the community of his followers "become completely one" (Jn 17:11, 21-23). And it has significantly undermined the purpose of Christian unity, namely "that the world may believe that you have sent me" (Jn 17:21, 23).

PASSION FOR TRUTH AND ETHICAL ENTHUSIASM

Passion for truth is a proper response to the claims of biblical revelation, as long as this task is undertaken with humility and a balancing, sober restraint. In addition to this balance, however, the preoccupation with, and passion for, theological knowledge and doctrinal certitude must also be balanced by "ethical enthusiasm." Throughout the Bible, there is everywhere an intimate connection between theology (teachings about God, Christ, Holy Spirit, salvation, etc.) and praxis (teaching about the consequences of our theological beliefs in all areas of personal and societal life). We'll briefly look at some examples.

In the Old Testament, affirmations about the holiness of God never stand alone. Their purpose is not primarily to provide raw material for the construction of a theology of the nature and essence of God. Rather, their purpose is to ground the life of God's people, their moral values and their ethical life: "You shall be holy, for I the LORD your God am holy" (Lev 19:2). Allegiance to the holy God has within it the imperative for holiness of life. Thus sexual fidelity and purity, justice in social relationships, honesty in economic transactions, concern for the welfare of the poor, compassionate treatment for the disabled—all these and more are the ethical imperatives that flow from the theological belief in the holiness of God (Lev 18:1—19:32; Ps 68:5).

Further, the Old Testament is replete with affirmations of the righteousness and justice of God (e.g., Ps 89:14; 99:4; 119:142; Is 51:4; 59:16-17).

---

for mediating "both-and" theological perspectives. For a discussion of New Testament texts and teachings that are in tension with each other, or provide alternative perspectives that lead to divergent doctrinal positions, see James D. G. Dunn, *Unity and Diversity in the New Testament* (Philadelphia: Westminster Press, 1977). Another helpful contribution in this matter of both unity and diversity in the biblical witness is George B. Caird's "Apostolic Conference Model" for doing New Testament theology. This model envisions the authors of the New Testament documents sitting around a conference table, making their unique contributions, while bearing witness to the meaning and significance of the Christ event. See George B. Caird, *New Testament Theology*, completed and edited by L. D. Hurst (Oxford: Clarendon, 1994).

Therefore, human beings created in God's image,[48] to reflect the character, nature and purposes of God within human affairs, are to live rightly and practice justice. This is particularly true of rulers, who are to imitate the great King within their earthly realms (Ps 72:1-14; 82:2-4). When God's justice is embodied in the life of his people (Is 58:6-7, 9-10), God's light and salvation will break forth to the nations (Is 51:4; 58:8, 10). Israel's worship of the Lord of hosts (Jer 7:1-4) is only authentic and acceptable if righteousness and justice characterize their national life (Jer 7:5-7; Amos 5:21-24; Mic 6:6-8). Theological affirmations about being rightly related to God, about "knowing God" who is the only God, are closely tied to the ethical and moral life of God's people. So Jeremiah says that "to know the Lord" is to do justice and righteousness and to advocate for the poor and needy (Jer 22:15-16; cf. Hos 6:3, 6).

God is "father of orphans and protector of widows . . . in his holy habitation" (Ps 68:5). Therefore, God's people "shall not abuse any widow or orphan" (Ex 22:22; Is 10:2). The fair and loving treatment of aliens in the midst of Israel, as well as indentured servants, is grounded in the theology of the exodus, God's redemptive work of liberation: "for you were aliens in the land of Egypt" (Ex 22:21; 23:9; Lev 19:33-34) and "you were a slave in the land of Egypt, and the LORD your God brought you out from there with a mighty hand and an outstretched arm" (Deut 5:15; cf. Deut 15:12-15; 24:17-18). Repeatedly, the theological grounding of the admonition to keep the Lord's commandments is Israel's theology of redemption (Deut 6:20-25; 8:11-14). This intimate connection between theological truth and ethics is also present in the New Testament.

Jesus' teaching about the in-breaking of the kingdom of God (or "kingdom of heaven")[49] during his life and ministry makes abundantly clear that

---

[48]Old Testament scholars are unanimous in the view that God as King is the predominant metaphor for God in the Old Testament. Therefore, the concept of Yahweh's royal dominion must inform our understanding of the Genesis 1:26-27 affirmation that human beings are created "in the image" of God. Throughout the cultures of the ancient Near East, human kings were often perceived as images of God, executing the will of the gods in their spheres of sovereignty. Further, it was common practice for conquering monarchs to erect a statue, an *image* of themselves in the conquered territory. That image represented the continuing reign of the monarch in that territory, even in his absence. This background is important for understanding the significance of the biblical word that humans are created in the image and likeness of God. They are to embody, in their living and relating, the character and nature of God's kingly reign.

[49]The term "kingdom of God" is the literal translation of the Greek *basileia tou theou*. New Testament scholars have recognized, however, that our term *kingdom* has a geographical connotation,

beliefs and convictions about God's kingly reign, without the embodiment and outworking of that reign in human lives and institutions, is ultimately empty. The announcement of the coming of God's reign at the beginning of Jesus' public ministry (Mt 3:2; 4:17; Mk 1:15) is at the same time a call to repentance.[50] Kingdom theology and the transformation of life and living cannot be separated.[51] John the Baptist's challenge to "bear fruit worthy of repentance" (Mt 3:8) became a prominent theme in Jesus' teaching.

In warning against false prophets, Jesus taught that they would be known by the fruit they bore (Mt 7:15-16). That is, our character, our deepest values and beliefs, are ultimately revealed in the life that we live (Mt 7:17-20; Lk 6:43-45). Therefore, participation in the sphere of God's reign is neither guaranteed nor secured by the confession of Jesus as Lord; rather, only those who embody God's will in their lives are children of the kingdom (Mt 7:21; Lk 6:46-48). In his interpretation of the parable of the sower (Mt 13:18-23; Mk 4:13-29; Lk 8:11-15), Jesus asserted that neither the hearing nor the receiving of "the word of the kingdom" is sufficient. Only those who bear the fruit of its presence in their lives are revealed as those who truly grasp its deepest significance (Mt 13:23), accept it (Mk 4:20) and "hold it fast in an honest and good heart" (Lk 8:15).

Authentic relationship with God in Christ—the consequence of being born anew by the Spirit (Jn 3:3-8) and believing in Jesus (Jn 14:12)—is manifested in our participation in the works that Jesus does. That connection is powerfully expressed in the allegory of the vine (Jn 15). Two complementary truths emerge from this allegory. One is that "abiding" in Jesus is the source of bearing fruit (Jn 15:4-5). This indissoluble connection between "abiding"

---

denoting a "realm," whereas Jesus' use of the term (in keeping with Old Testament usage), has a dynamic connotation, referring to God's kingship, or God's kingly rule in human affairs. Common in Jewish teaching in Jesus' time was the idea that God's kingly reign was realized whenever and wherever his will was obeyed. The term "kingdom of heaven" appears in the New Testament only in the Gospel of Matthew (twenty-seven times). In the parallel passages in Luke and Mark, we always find "kingdom of God." Since the Gospel of Matthew is clearly written to a Jewish-Christian audience, Matthew's use of "kingdom of heaven" is most probably a circumlocution for "kingdom of God," an indirect way of speaking about the same reality, namely the decisive in-breaking of the reign of God into human history in the Christ event, as well as in its future consummation.

[50]The Greek *metanoia* refers both to a "change of mind" and a "turning about" or "turning away from (and toward)." Acts 26:20 expresses this concisely in the phrase: "They should repent and turn to God and do deeds consistent with repentance."

[51]For a challenging study of this theme, see Glen H. Stassen and David P. Gushee, *Kingdom Ethics: Following Jesus in Contemporary Context* (Downers Grove, Ill.: InterVarsity Press, 2003).

in Jesus and a fruitful life is parallel to the contention of the Old Testament prophets that "knowing God" is authenticated in the "doing of justice." The second, complementary truth is that in the very act of keeping the Lord's commandments we abide in him (Jn 15:10). Our true theological identity as Jesus' disciples is confirmed when we do what he commands (Jn 15:14; cf. Jn 14:15, 21).

The intimate relationship between belief and praxis, theological truth and action, is at the heart of the parable of the Good Samaritan (Lk 10:25-37). Recognition of the theological truth of Deuteronomy 6:4-5 and Leviticus 19:18 about the linkage between loving God and loving the neighbor becomes realized in the imperative, "do this, and you will live" (Lk 10:27-28). The question "but who is my neighbor?" Jesus answers with the parable. Priest and Levite, representing the highest form of religiosity and theological certitude, fail to embody the central truth that love of God and love of neighbor are two sides of the same coin, while the Samaritan—the theological heretic—truly embodies the reign of God in his act of compassion (Lk 10:36-37). Jesus' final word, "go and do likewise" (Lk 10:37), is a potent reminder that the affirmation and declaration of theological verities must ultimately find expression in concrete action. Otherwise they are, in the words of Paul, "a noisy gong or clanging cymbal" (1 Cor 13:1).

Another illustrative example of the connection between theological truth claims and the ethical imperatives that emerge from them is seen in Jesus' offer of forgiveness. The forgiveness of sins is a divine act of unconditional love and grace. It is extended by Jesus repeatedly[52] and stands at the heart of the New Testament's theology of the atoning work of Christ on the cross.[53] As in the Old Testament, where God's holiness, righteousness, justice and redeeming action must be appropriated and given concrete expression in human life and society, so also the divine forgiveness mediated in and through Jesus must be appropriated, extended and lived out in transformed lives and relationships.

In the Lord's Prayer, the petition for the realization of God's reign on earth (Mt 6:10; Lk 11:2) is accompanied by the petition for the forgiveness of

---

[52]E.g., the healing of the paralytic (Mt 9:1-8; and parallels in Mk 2:1-12; Lk 5:17-26); the sinner in the house of the Pharisee (Lk 7:36-50); Zacchaeus the tax collector (Lk 19:1-9); the adulteress (Jn 8:3-11); Christ's self-giving (Mt 26:28; Lk 23:34).

[53]E.g., Acts 10:43; 13:38-39; Rom 3:21-26; 5:6-11; Eph 1:7; 4:32; Col 1:14; Heb 9:22; 1 Pet 2:24; 1 Jn 1:7-9.

sins (Mt 6:12; Lk 11:4). When God's reign encounters broken human life, the healing of that brokenness begins with the liberating act of forgiveness. That gift of grace, however, cannot be appropriated simply for one's own benefit. It is only when God's forgiveness of us is extended by us in forgiving attitudes, words and actions toward others that God's forgiveness finds realization (Mt 6:14; Mk 11:25-26; Lk 11:4). The parable of the unmerciful servant (Mt 18:23-35) is a powerful expression of this fact, namely that God's liberating forgiveness has consequences. When authentically experienced and appropriated, it leads to loving service (Lk 7:47), to a turning from sinful living (Lk 19:1-9; Jn 8:3-11), to the actualization of God's forgiveness in reconciling actions (Jn 20:23).

A final example from the Gospel record of Jesus' ministry is found in the parable that depicts the Great Judgment at the end of time (Mt 25). It is a familiar and potent passage, uncompromising in its clarity about the extremely high value that Jesus placed on concrete demonstrations of authentic faith. An invitation into the eternal kingdom of the Son of Man (Mt 25:31-34) is extended to those who have fed the hungry, given drinks to the thirsty, welcomed the stranger, clothed the naked, cared for the sick and visited the imprisoned (Mt 25:35-39). For in these acts of compassion these people have demonstrated their love for Christ ("You did it to me"; Mt 25:40) and expressed authentic, right relationships with God (Mt 25:45-46). The balance between theological truth and the outworking of that truth in relational, social and structural contexts—present in Jesus' ministry as revealed in the Gospels—is also very evidenced in the rest of the New Testament.

Luke's story of the origin and expansion of the early church (in Acts) shows that Jesus' teaching about the in-breaking and claims of the kingdom of God deeply influenced the community of his followers. Empowered by the Spirit (Acts 1:8; 2), they became Jesus' witnesses in word and deed. They shared their possessions with those in need (Acts 2:44-45; 4:32-35); spoke truth to power and challenged the authorities (Acts 4:18-20; 5:27-29; 7:2-53); organized themselves for attending to social ministries (Acts 6:1-6; 20:35); crossed restrictive ethnic/racial barriers (Acts 10); and engaged in famine relief (Acts 11:27-30).

In the Pauline epistles, theology and praxis are intimately connected. This balance is evident in the structural arrangement of several letters, where sections devoted to the theological explorations of the meaning of Christ's life, death and resurrection are followed by sections given to the practical implications and ethical imperatives of these theological affirmations for Christian life and witness in the world.[54] Thus, in Romans, Paul's theological reflections on (1) the deep-seated distortion of human life and community (Rom 1:18—3:23), (2) the redemptive work of Christ leading to justification (Rom 3:24—5:21), and (3) the dying and rising to new life in Christ, empowered by the Spirit (Rom 6—8) are the grounding for the imperative: "I appeal to you, therefore . . . by the mercies of God, to present your bodies as a living sacrifice. . . . Do not be conformed to this world, but be transformed by the renewing of your minds, so that you may discern what is the will of God—what is good and acceptable and perfect" (Rom 12:1-2). The remaining chapters explicate what it means in practice to be a living sacrifice that is not conformed to this world. Included are such specific attitudes and behaviors as: humility (Rom 12:3); cheerful works of compassion (Rom 12:8); genuine love and goodness (Rom 12:9-10; 13:8-10); assistance to those in need and hospitality to strangers (Rom 12:13); living peacefully in relationships (Rom 12:18); responding to enemies with acts of goodness and overcoming evil with good (Rom 12:17-21); responsible citizenship and support of governing authorities in their God-given responsibility to promote that which is good (Rom 13:1-7); loving the neighbor (Rom 13:8-10); refraining from judging each other (Rom 14:10); and welcoming the other (Rom 14:7).

In Galatians, Paul's passionate defense of the good news of justification by faith (Gal 1—4) is the springboard for the admonition: "For you were called to freedom . . . do not use your freedom as an opportunity for self-indulgence, but through love become slaves to one another" (Gal 5:13). What that means in the conflicted context of the churches in Galatia is that they do not "bite and devour one another" (Gal 5:15), but rather give evidence of the fruit of the Spirit in their relationships and life in the world, with fruits such as "love, joy, peace, patience, kindness, generosity, faithfulness, gentleness, and self-control" (Gal 5:22-23).

Ephesians and Colossians also clearly reflect this biblical balance between theology and praxis. In Ephesians, Paul lays theological foundations as he un-

---

[54]Paul's theology of salvation by faith, in response to God's work in Christ, worked out in such passages as Romans 1—8; Galatians 1—4; Ephesians 1—3; and Colossians 1—2, is followed by Pauline teaching about the consequences of those theological truths in Romans 12—16; Galatians 5—6; Ephesians 4—6; and Colossians 3—4, respectively.

packs the mystery of God's purposes revealed in Christ (Eph 1:3-10; 3:1-6). Paul includes such truths as God's gracious adoption of us, formerly alienated enemies (Eph 1:3-5); God's redeeming work in Christ (Eph 1:7-8); the power of God manifested in Jesus' resurrection and exaltation (Eph 2:20-22); the gift of God's gracious justification (Eph 2:8-9); the breaking down of the barrier between Jew and Gentile and the creation of a new humanity out of the two (Eph 2:11—3:6); and the power of the indwelling Christ through the Spirit (Eph 3:16-19). These are the theological foundations that ground the conviction that we have been "created in Christ Jesus for good works" (Eph 2:10) and evoke the foundations for the imperative "to lead a life worthy of the calling to which you have been called" (Eph 4:1). The good works that we were created for, and that are worthy expressions of our identity as God's adopted children, are spelled out in Ephesians 4—6. The doing of them is, first of all, made possible by a house-cleaning, a "putting away" of such vices as falsehood, destructive anger, theft, evil talk (which brings no grace to those who hear), bitterness, wrath, wrangling and slander (Eph 4:25-31), as well as fornication, impurity, greed, obscene and vulgar talk (Eph 5:3-5) and "unfruitful works of darkness" (Eph 5:11). Putting away this "former way of life" (Eph 4:22) allows good works to flourish in and through us. These include: (1) building up the community of Jesus' disciples in unity of faith and love (Eph 4:1-16); (2) becoming "imitators of God" (Eph 5:1) by being "kind to one another, . . . forgiving one another, as God in Christ has forgiven you" (Eph 4:32), living in love "as Christ loved us and gave himself up for us" (Eph 5:2), living as "children of light" by promoting "all that is good and right and true" (Eph 5:8-9), and exposing "the unfruitful works of darkness" (Eph 5:11); and (3) manifesting the fullness of the Spirit's presence and power in our various human relationships by "subordinating ourselves to one another in awe of Christ" in imitation of his sacrificial servanthood (Eph 5:21)[55] for our sake (Eph 5:1-2).[56]

---

[55]The NRSV and NIV translate Eph 5:21 with "Be subject to one another out of reverence for Christ." However, the Greek verb *hypotassō* is a compound consisting of the preposition *hypo* (meaning "under") and the verb *tassō* (meaning "to place or station a person or thing"). It is then better to convey Paul's meaning with the English "subordinate." That meaning seems also to be required by the larger context of the passage, which is controlled by the idea of Christ's giving of himself for the needs of humanity as a model for human behavior toward one another. The same juxtaposition of ideas is found in Philippians 2, where Christ's humiliation and sacrificial death is, for Paul, the paradigm for Christians' placing the needs of others above their own.

[56]In Colossians, the ethical imperatives—which are virtually identical to those in Ephesians—are grounded in theological affirmations about the person and work of Christ. Since Christians have been raised to newness of life with Christ (Col 2:9-14; 3:1), their presence and living in the world

In addition to the theology-praxis balance in the structural arrangement of the Pauline epistles noted above, *imperatives* for the nature of Christian presence and action arise from *indicative* theological affirmations throughout his epistles.[57] Let us look at a few examples:

1. Paul's understanding of oneness with Christ in his death and resurrection (Rom 6:1-11) means that believers are set free from the power of sin (Rom 6:6-7, 17, 19) in order to "walk in newness of life" (Rom 6:4). From this theological indicative flows the imperative: "Therefore, do not let sin exercise dominion. . . . No longer present your members to sin as instruments of wickedness, but . . . present your members to God as instruments of righteousness" (Rom 6:12-13).

2. The theological truth that the Christian community is "God's temple," in which "God's Spirit dwells" (1 Cor 3:16), means that divisive quarreling and jealousy (1 Cor 1:10-11; 3:3), spiritual pride (1 Cor 3:21; 4:7, 18; 5:2, 6; 8:1-3), grievances between church members fought out in public (1 Cor 6:1-8), lack of concern for the weak (1 Cor 8:7-13), humiliation of the poor (1 Cor 11:20-22) and the arrogance of spiritual giftedness (1 Cor 12—13) are all destructive to "God's temple" and stand under God's judgment (1 Cor 3:17). The imperative arising from that theological truth is this: "Pursue love . . . so that the church may be built up" (1 Cor 14:1, 5).

3. The truth that through Christ's sacrificial death (1 Cor 5:7; 6:11) our bodies have become "members of Christ" (1 Cor 6:15) means that sexual immorality (1 Cor 5:1; 6:9, 13) is simply incompatible with this new reality of being in Christ. Therefore the imperative: "Shun fornication!" (1 Cor 6:18).

4. The magnificent "hymn"[58] in Philippians 2:5-11 about Christ's condescension—from "the form of God" and "equality with God" (Phil 2:6) into "human form" by emptying himself (Phil 2:7) and humbling himself to the point of death on a cross (Phil 2:8)—has been the object of intense and

---

is to reflect that empowered newness.

[57] The grammatical terms *indicative* and *imperative* are used here to designate statements of "what is" and "what ought to be," respectively. Thus theological affirmations are "indicatives," while exhortations for a particular way of life are "imperatives."

[58] On the basis of the poetic nature of the passage, many New Testament commentators detect here a hymn about Christ, either composed by Paul himself or cited by him from a pre-Pauline, early church confession about Christ. See the discussion of this matter in Gordon D. Fee, *Paul's Letter to the Philippians*, New International Commentary on the New Testament (Grand Rapids: Eerdmans, 1995), pp. 191-94.

extensive theological debate and reflection across two millennia. The passage has pride of place in virtually every treatment of New Testament Christology. In the past century, entire volumes have been devoted to the theological exploration of these few verses,[59] as well as hundreds of journal articles.[60] And yet, much of this voluminous discussion and debate—as helpful and insightful as some of it is for our understanding of the nature and person of Christ—often misses the central point of the passage within the context of Paul's letter.

This exalted narrative about Christ's self-emptying is not given by Paul, in the first instance, as his Christology (though he most assuredly believed what he expressed there about the person of Christ); rather, Christ's self-emptying and humiliation functions as an example that the believers in Philippi are to emulate in their relations with one another: "Do nothing from selfish ambition or conceit, but in humility regard others as better than yourselves. . . . Let the same mind be in you that was in Christ Jesus, / who, though he was in the form of God, / did not regard equality with God / as something to be exploited, / but emptied himself" (Phil 2:3, 5-7). The imperative for Christian conduct arises out of the indicative Christology. Confessions about the person and work of Christ are ultimately empty and powerless if not embodied in Christian praxis.

I conclude my reflections about the biblical theology-praxis balance with two representative examples from the non-Pauline epistle literature. The letter of James provides the classic example of the view that theological truths and confessions of faith, when not translated into action, are empty. James launches his argument with the imperative, "be doers of the word, and not merely hearers who deceive themselves" (Jas 1:22). To be hearers of "the law of liberty," but not "doers who act," amounts to self-deception (Jas 1:23-25). The religiosity of those who claim to have faith, but "do not bridle their tongues . . . is worthless" (Jas 1:26). James's contention is that religion (that is, Christian faith) is only "pure and undefiled before God" when it expresses itself in "care for orphans and widows in their distress" (Jas 1:27).

---

[59]See e.g., Ralph P. Martin, *Carmen Christi: Philippians 2:5-11 in Recent Interpretation and in the Setting of Early Christian Worship* (Cambridge: Cambridge University Press, 1967). An early full-scale treatment is Ernst Lohmeyer's *Kyrios Jesus* (Heidelberg: Carl Winter, 1928).

[60]Gerald F. Hawthorne devotes four dense pages to this extensive literature in *Philippians*, Word Biblical Commentary, vol. 43 (Waco, Tex.: Word Books, 1983), pp. 71-75.

In confronting the practice of showing partiality and favoritism toward those of higher economic and social status (Jas 2:1-13), James writes: "Do you with your acts of favoritism really believe in our glorious Lord Jesus Christ?" (Jas 2:1). The truth of such a belief is validated ultimately in doing "the royal law," namely "You shall love your neighbor as yourself" (Jas 2:8), for "if you show partiality, you commit sin" (Jas 2:9). James then goes on to reflect on the relationship between faith and works and salvation (Jas 2:14-26).[61] A concise summary of the entire argument is the statement: "So faith by itself, if it has no works, is dead" (Jas 2:17; cf. Jas 2:26). To drive this point home, the author says that even the demons have a correct understanding of theology, even they believe that "God is one" (Jas 2:19). But that belief does not save them. James's concern is really this: What does saving faith look like in practice? His answer is that authentic faith, when confronted by others' needs, provides the motivation to address those needs (Jas 2:15-16).

The concern of James for the connection between belief and action is also a central feature in 1 John. The letter begins with theological affirmations about the incarnation, the nature of God as light and the forgiveness of sins on the basis of Christ's sacrifice (1 Jn 1:1-7). These theological truths are immediately related to Christian living: conducting our living and relating in God's light rather than walking in darkness (1 Jn 1:5-7). Further, the claim to "know God" (theological certainty) is shown to be authentic "if we obey his commandments" (1 Jn 2:3). The same claim, when not concretized in obedience, shows the person to be a liar (1 Jn 2:4). A life of obedience to Jesus' word reveals the truth that "the love of God has reached perfection" (1 Jn 2:5). The truth of the affirmation of the Christian's union with Christ ("I abide in him") contains within it the imperative "to walk just as he walked" (1 Jn 2:6). Light and darkness are incompatible. Therefore to claim that "I am in the light" (1 Jn 2:9), on the basis that "the true light [that is, Jesus] is already shining" (1 Jn 2:8) is incompatible with attitudes and actions that express hate rather than love (1 Jn 2:9-11; cf. 1 Jn 3:10). The theological

---

[61]This passage was understood by the Reformer Martin Luther as an outright contradiction of the Pauline insistence on "justification by faith alone," and thus he judged the letter of James as "an epistle of straw." Given the context of Luther's criticism of much in the medieval church that smacked of "salvation by works," his reading of James is understandable, though mistaken. For James was not speaking about faith *and* works as means of salvation. Rather, he is speaking about saving faith whose authenticity is revealed in the fruit it bears. The passage (Jas 2:14-26) can even be seen as an exposition of Paul's statement in Galatians 5:6 that "the only thing that counts is faith working through love."

knowledge that Jesus is the righteous one, and the conviction that through God's love we have been birthed into the family of God, is authenticated when we "do what is right" (1 Jn 2:29—3:1; cf. 1 Jn 3:7). Relentlessly, John drives home the truth of the emptiness of theological claims that are not translated into life.

The above survey of, and reflections on, the broad sweep of the biblical revelation leads to the conclusion that concern for theological knowledge, for the truth claims of Scripture, must be balanced with equal concern for its ethical imperatives. The idea that there is such a thing as "saving knowledge"— a bedrock concept in much of the evangelical tradition—is, at its core, un-biblical.[62] Knowledge, even correct theological knowledge, does not save. In and of itself it has the capacity to create theological pride and to judge the action of love as a sentimental concession to those who are weak (1 Cor 8). But if truth is not accompanied by love (Eph 4:14-16), the community of Jesus' disciples cannot be the instrument of God's redeeming love in the world. The pursuit of truth and love at the same time is the imperative of Scripture. As Max Lucado put it: "Love in Truth. Truth in Love. Never one at the expense of the other. Never the embrace of love without the torch of truth. Never the heat of truth without the warmth of love. . . . To pursue both is our singular task."[63]

Correct doctrinal confession without concrete ethical action is "dead or-thodoxy"; it is right belief without life. That is surely the point of the word of Jesus that "Not everyone who says to me 'Lord, Lord,' will enter the kingdom of heaven, but only the one who does the will of my Father in heaven" (Mt 7:21). The entire biblical witness chips away at this façade of empty "beliefism." Confessional certitude without ethical enthusiasm is, in Dietrich Bonhoeffer's words, "cheap grace" without "costly discipleship." Therefore, when the biblical balance—of truth and love, faith and action, doctrine and ethics, knowledge and praxis—is abused by the neglect of ei-ther of these balancing dimensions of the Word, then the consequence is a

---

[62]The idea of "saving knowledge" in Christianity is, in fact, a product of the Gnostic heresy that seriously threatened the integrity of the Christian faith in the second and third centuries. One of its central themes had to do with the attainment of special revelatory knowledge (Greek, *gnōsis*), by means of which those who possessed it would transcend human limitation and make their way safely into eternity. *The Gospel of Thomas*, discovered in 1946 among other sacred texts at Nag Hammadi, Egypt, reflects aspects of this Gnostic heresy.

[63]Max Lucado, *Grace for the Moment* (Nashville: Thomas Nelson, 2000), p. 244.

serious distortion of the Christian faith, as well as a powerless, anemic presence and witness in the world.

The bifurcation of Christian witness—resulting from the abuse of the whole gospel (ch. 2) with its divided emphasis on either the "personal gospel" or the "social gospel"—is also one of the tragic consequences of the "abuse of biblical balance" discussed in the present chapter. In the liberal Christian tradition, the biblical balance has been skewed largely toward ethical concerns, with particular emphasis on those aspects of biblical teaching that address larger social issues and structural evils that demean and lessen human life and community.

At the same time, there has been a significant lack of attention to the theological truth claims of the Bible in which those ethical concerns are grounded—and that provide the moral authority to empower ethical engagement of difficult social, cultural and structural issues. As commitment to revelatory, propositional truth has increasingly receded from the liberal theological horizon, ethical engagement has become increasingly guided by relativism. In the absence of absolute moral values—a major feature of postmodern thought—Christian ethical teaching and practice has become coopted by cultural and societal views and constraints.[64] The ultimate outcome of this trend, which is one of the results of the abuse of biblical balance, is the submergence of a distinctive, alternative Christian voice into the general chorus of humanistic concerns.

In the evangelical Christian tradition, the biblical balance has been skewed largely toward a preoccupation with truth, the theological content of the biblical revelation.[65] The quest for doctrinal certainty, undergirded by a passion for truth, has characterized this Christian movement. Insofar as enthusiasm for the Bible's ethical dimensions has been present, the focus has been largely on personal and relational concerns, such as sexual con-

---

[64]At a recent major denominational conclave, a leader expressed the view that, in light of the reality that today's youth culture is increasingly influenced by the Hollywood entertainment industry and MTV culture, it is simply unrealistic to expect our youth to abstain from sexual intimacy prior to and outside of marriage. Therefore, that person said that the church's educational efforts, with regard to human sexuality, ought to focus on safe sex and prevention of sexually transmitted diseases, rather than on an unrealistic concern with traditional Christian sexual mores.

[65]A survey of the catalogs of the major evangelical publishing houses (Baker Books, InterVarsity Press, W Publishing Group, Tyndale House) reveals a greater number of books devoted to biblical studies (especially commentaries and commentary series) and theological studies than publications devoted to ethical-social-cultural concerns.

duct, family values and selected "sanctity of life" issues (abortion, stem-cell research, end-of-life decisions).

Truth really matters,[66] and the evangelical passion for understanding, proclaiming and defending biblical truth has been, and will continue to be, an absolutely crucial and indispensable contribution to Christian faith and witness in the world. At the same time, the relatively minor attention to both the direct and indirect implications of biblical truth for *all* areas of human life, relationships, society and culture (including politics and economics) has significantly muted the power of our biblical-theological treasure for the marketplace.[67] Our preoccupation with the theological side of biblical truth has been, almost exclusively, a matter of "preaching to the choir," an in-house affair that has, more often than not, served to create division, distortion of community and acrimony within the body of Christ—further undermining the possibility of a positive, constructive evangelical presence in, and engagement of, the culture. The lack of significant attention to the Bible's ethical teaching, and the implications of its theologically grounded imperatives for all areas of life, has resulted in a Christian presence that is frequently ethically confused and uncertain.[68] If the evangelical tradition continues its version of the abuse of biblical balance, and therefore produces an "indistinct sound" (1 Cor 14:8), how will the larger culture "know what is being said" (1 Cor 14:9)?[69]

---

[66]Recall the earlier section in this chapter on the biblical balance between "The Quest for Correct Belief and the Restraint of Humility."

[67]Recent notable contributions by scholars who are theologically evangelical and biblically grounded are hopeful signs for redressing this imbalance. See, e.g., David P. Gushee, *The Future of Faith in American Politics: The Public Witness of the Evangelical Center* (Waco, Tex.: Baylor University Press, 2008); Stanley Hauerwas, *The Peaceable Kingdom: A Primer in Christian Ethics*, 2nd ed. (London: SCM Press, 2003); Richard B. Hays, *The Moral Vision of the New Testament: A Contemporary Introduction to New Testament Ethics* (San Francisco: HarperSanFrancisco, 1996); Alexander Hill, *Just Business: Christian Ethics for the Marketplace* (Downers Grove, Ill.: IVP Academic, 2008); David C. Jones, *Biblical Christian Ethics* (Grand Rapids: Baker Academic, 1994); Robertson McQuilkin, *An Introduction to Biblical Ethics*, 2nd ed. (Wheaton, Ill.: Tyndale, 1995); Nick S. Megoran, *The War on Terror: How Should Christians Respond?* (Downers Grove, Ill.: IVP Books, 2007); Stephen C. Mott, *Biblical Ethics and Social Change* (Oxford: Oxford University Press, 1982); Lewis B. Smedes, *Mere Morality: What God Expects from Ordinary People* (Grand Rapids: Eerdmans, 1987); Glen H. Stassen and David P. Gushee, *Kingdom Ethics;* Fred VanDyke, David C. Mahan, Joseph K. Sheldon and Raymond H. Brand, *Redeeming Creation: The Biblical Basis for Environmental Stewardship* (Downers Grove, Ill.: InterVarsity Press, 1996).

[68]That is a major burden of Ronald J. Sider's *The Scandal of the Evangelical Conscience: Why Are Christians Living Like the Rest of the World?* (Grand Rapids: Baker Books, 2005).

[69]The analogy comes from Paul's discussion in 1 Corinthians 14:6-11 of the confusing impact of ecstatic speech (*glōssolalia,* or "tongues") for outsiders.

AVOIDING THE ABUSE OF BIBLICAL BALANCE

Based on the many areas of biblical doctrine, and the many perspectives, teachings, themes and mandates for Christian living surveyed in this chapter, it is easy to see that the Bible frequently presents us with complementary (or even multiple) perspectives or emphases. When this biblical reality is not appropriately acknowledged on the theoretical level, and therefore also not expressed or embodied on the practical level, Scripture's intention is abused. What can be done to help us avoid such abuse? The following perspectives and principles—implicit or explicit—should guide our interpretive work so that it does not result in the abusive reading of, and the abusive application of, biblical truth.

1. Acknowledge the reality of having to balance complementary or multiple biblical perspectives. This is a critical, foundational assumption, and it lays the groundwork for avoiding abuse. We cannot take a head-in-the-sand approach with regard to this biblical reality without thereby refusing to take the Bible on its own terms. Sticking our heads in the sand is most certainly not an approach to the Bible that is compatible with the biblical call to be trustworthy, faithful stewards of the treasure of God's revelation.

2. Refuse to dictate in advance what Scripture reveals about any particular aspect of God and God's dealing with human life. This attitudinal stance is extremely important. It counters our tendency to prefer monofocal, singular, exclusive points of view. It stands over-against our discomfort with doctrinal ambiguity or complexity, paradox or tension. It cautions us against our proclivity toward, and demand for, cognitive consistency.

3. Approach complementary biblical materials with a "both/and" rather than an "either-or" mindset. When we begin with such a mindset, we acknowledge that God's "total truth" revealed in Scripture on any one issue is beyond our finite comprehension. Such a mindset also provides us with the opportunity—both in personal study and in communal discussion—to discover broader and deeper insights into God's revealed truth than an either-or approach would allow. We close ourselves to aspects of biblical truth when we abuse balancing biblical perspectives.

4. Heed the biblical call to practice humility. In our understanding and interpretation of scriptural teaching, and in the subsequent movement toward (and drawing conclusions about) biblically-based doctrines and theological systems, we must practice humility. Arrogance and pride with regard to what we determine to be ironclad biblical truth is, from a biblical perspective, sinful. This does not mean that we ought not contend for the truth or ought not try to get it right or ought not rigorously defend and proclaim a host of theological certainties at the core of the Christian faith; what rejecting arrogance and pride does mean is that we hold those certainties together with a gracious, grace-filled spirit that refuses to demonize and judge those who do not share those certainties with us.

5. Give heed to biblical precedents! This principle was implicit particularly in the discussion of the proclivity among both conservative and liberal Christians to rank various categories of sin or particular sins as higher or lower, weighty or marginal, important or negligible. The biblical revelation clearly shows a different way. In that way, for example, self-righteousness distorts human-divine and human-human relationships as much as adultery; biblical revelation shows injustice in economic life as being as objectionable to the Lord as bearing false witness or gossiping; and it shows greed as being as incompatible with belonging to the kingly reign of God in human life as is sexual immorality. Christian proclamation and presence must emulate these (and many other) biblical precedents.

6. Never separate components of Scripture. For example, we cannot separate theology from ethics, truth from its consequences, knowledge from its implications for action, doctrine from conduct, or believing from living. Separating components of Scripture has had, and continues to have, perhaps more serious negative consequences for the integrity of Christian witness than any other abuse of Scripture. This is the foundation for the reality, as well as charge (from the nonbelieving culture), of hypocrisy. From a balanced, biblical perspective, *enthusiastic intoxication* with biblical/theological truth without *ethical enthusiasm* results in a sterile, often-cold and judgmental Christian witness and presence, while ethical enthusiasm, without the energizing fire of intoxication with biblical truth, is anemic and, ultimately, impotent humanism.

5

THE ABUSE OF WORDS

Some years ago, my colleague Reidar Bjornard, professor of Old Testament studies at Northern Baptist Theological Seminary, wrote a primer on Old Testament interpretation for his students, and he titled the book *God Spoke Hebrew.* The point of the title was that in the process of choosing a small Semitic tribe and communicating his will and way to them, God limited himself to the confines of a very particular dialect within the larger Semitic world in the ancient Near East.

Language, though virtually indispensable as a vehicle for human communication, is also limiting, both within the community that speaks the language and across language barriers. This is so because a specific language reflects the culture of a particular people. Language gives voice to their habits and practices, their rituals and beliefs, their understanding of themselves, their history and their world. Anyone who has ever moved between or among different language groups, or been an immigrant in a country where a different language is spoken, is keenly aware of this reality.

The activity of translating from one language to another is always burdened by the fact that the words, phrases, idioms, syntax and grammar in both the original language and the translation reflect the culture and experiences of the respective language groups. It is still necessary for me, at times, to render a particular German word, phrase or idiom with a sentence or two in English in order to convey the meaning accurately and effectively. The communication of meaning—that is, the meaning the speaker or writer seeks to express in his or her own language into the new language so that the meaning does not get lost in translation—is of course the purpose of communication.

Communication of meaning via language consists of the *encoding* and *decoding* of meaning between sender and receiver. That is, meanings are given to words, phrases and idiomatic expressions by the cultural/historical/experiential context of the sender (they are *encoded*), and then *decoded* in the cultural-linguistic context of the receiver. The greater the receiver's understanding of the sender's cultural-linguistic context, the better the chances that he or she will decode the message accurately. An example will strikingly illustrate this process. When Johnny arrived home from school, he found the following note from his mom on the kitchen table: "Johnny, you know what will happen to you if you don't do what I told you about you know what." Outsiders like us understand the words in this note perfectly well; the sentence makes sense. We can even discern, in a very general way, what may be going on, but we have no idea what is going on specifically. We cannot grasp the central meaning of this communication. We cannot *decode* it accurately. It is fairly certain, however, that Johnny is able to decode this message. Why? Because Johnny and his mom share a particular relational-experiential-historical context, within which the words on the note have been encoded. Only if we enter into the same context can we participate meaningfully and accurately in the process of decoding.

Even within the same relational context, the communication of meaning is attended by the possibility of misunderstanding or miscommunicating as a result of the encoding-decoding process. We have all surely experienced the reality expressed in these words: "I know you think you understand what you thought I said, but I am not sure you are aware that what you heard is not what I meant." The words used in such a communication can be understood accurately enough, but the meaning those words carry may be missed completely.

The Word of God has come to us in the limited form of human language—primarily Hebrew and Greek—and subsequently, on a global scale, through hundreds of other languages. God's self-disclosure, the revelation of God's nature and purposes for us, participates in the dynamic and complex process of human communication, with all its possibilities for either understanding or misunderstanding, for accurate or inaccurate translation, for helpful or misleading interpretation. Examples from Paul's epistles clearly illustrate the dynamic and complex nature of communication, and the necessity of seeking to understand the situational, historical and cultural contexts within which the encoding and decoding of meanings takes place.

The Corinthian correspondence reveals that over the course of several years a very active and at times contentious relationship existed between the apostle and the church in Corinth, which he had founded on his second missionary journey (Acts 18). We know from 1 Corinthians 5:9 that Paul had written a letter to the church—most likely while in Ephesus during his third mission tour—some time before he wrote the letter we know as 1 Corinthians. From Ephesus, he also visited the church in Corinth briefly, but that turned out to be a rather painful experience (2 Cor 2:1), which he followed up with a letter written "out of much distress and anguish of heart and with many tears" (2 Cor 2:4).[1] In addition to these communications and visits from the apostle, we also know that the church sent a delegation ("Chloe's people"—1 Cor 1:11) to Paul while he was in Ephesus, with a report about serious quarrels in the church. They also sent a letter in which they enumerated several issues that they needed him to address (1 Cor 7:1—"Now concerning the things about which you wrote.")[2]

Given this situational context (even apart from a consideration of the cultural and historical context of Corinth at the time), our "listening" to Paul's correspondence is sometimes like listening in on one side of someone's telephone conversation. We hear one side of the "conversation" between him and the church in Corinth. In responding to the report from "Chloe's people" and to the issues communicated in their letter to him, Paul assumed that they knew what was in the oral report and in their letter. His response to their report about dissensions in their ranks is quite explicit. Paul even quotes

---

[1]For whatever reason, the letter referred to in 1 Corinthians 5:9 was lost, as well as the "letter of tears" referred to in 2 Corinthians 2:4. Some scholars believe that 2 Corinthians 10—13, which is a strident defense of Paul's apostleship and his work and is written in a polemical tone so different from the conciliatory tone in chapters 1-9, may be the "letter of tears."

[2]The phrase "now concerning" appears several times (1 Cor 7:1; 8:1; 12:1), indicating that Paul is apparently responding to the items of concern communicated in their letter to him.

specific slogans that seemed to be at the heart of their quarrel ("I belong to Paul" or "I belong to Apollos" or "I belong to Cephas" or "I belong to Christ"). Thus we can get some idea about what was going on from Paul's side of the conversation, though we cannot be certain what the exact meaning of their divisive slogans was, and what caused them. Further, when Paul begins his response to the issues raised in their letter to him (1 Cor 7:1), we are on similarly uncertain grounds, for Paul simply takes for granted that his readers know what they wrote, and he merely launches into his response and discussion of the issues they raised. Again, we know from his side of the communication what the major contours of the matters are, but the specifics are not always transparent.

For example, when dealing with the issue of appropriate apparel (and/or hairstyle) in the context of worship (1 Cor 11), Paul states that when women pray or prophesy in the assembly without wearing a head-covering, they bring shame on the men in the congregation (1 Cor 11:5). Why is that so? What is it about head-coverings that prevent such disgrace? Only an understanding of cultural and religious conventions in Corinth will assist us in properly answering those questions.

A few verses later, Paul states that a woman ought to have "authority on her head, because of the angels" (1 Cor 11:10). What does Paul mean by the phrase "authority on her head"? On the basis of literary and social context, translators seek to "decode" Paul's meaning.[3] Paul does not explain the phrase "because of the angels." We can assume that the Corinthians knew what Paul meant, but that meaning is not at all clear to us.[4]

Given this reality of the situationally focused and culturally embedded nature of Scripture, faithful and trustworthy interpretation of the Word of God (written primarily in Hebrew and Greek) demands that we are attentive

---

[3]The NRSV renders the text with "a woman ought to have a symbol of authority on her head." A footnote rightly indicates that the Geek text does not have the phrase "a symbol of." The translators further indicate that the wearing of the veil most likely symbolized *the woman's authority* to pray or prophesy. The paraphrase of the *Living Bible,* going way beyond the Greek text, reads: "So a woman should wear a covering on her head as a sign that she is under man's authority." (Elsewhere in this book we will take a closer look at this text.)

[4]See the commentaries on 1 Corinthians for the many attempts to get at the meaning of this phrase. Gordon Fee's discussion of both phrases ("authority on her head" and "because of the angels") is an excellent example of both thorough scholarship and humility. At the conclusion of a rigorous exegetical-historical investigation of the phrase "because of the angels," he concludes that "we must admit that we cannot be sure," in *The First Epistle to the Corinthians,* New International Commentary on the New Testament (Grand Rapids: Eerdmans, 1987), pp. 518-22.

to the meanings of words. Only when we are attentive to these basic carriers of meaning can we accurately hear what any particular biblical writer sought to convey.

A further reality that adds to the complex nature of communication, especially across language barriers, is the fact that often words don't have a literal meaning; rather they have a semantic range, a range of metaphorical meanings. Therefore, in getting at the meaning of a biblical text, particular attention has to be given to the meaning of words when they are used metaphorically. In such cases, the literal translations of words from one language to another will not accurately convey the meaning of the original word (or phrase or idiom).

A few examples from our language help to illustrate this reality: (1) Take the word *awful,* whose archaic, literary sense is "full of awe," where "awe" has the meaning of profound reverence, respect or admiration (as in "awesome"). At the same time, *awful* can also mean "extremely disagreeable" or "terrible" (as in "it was an awful accident"), or "very great" (as in "an awful lot of money" or "it was awfully kind of you"), or "beautiful" (as in "it was an awesome sunset").[5] (2) Depending on its context the word *home*—in the expression "I have come home"—can mean either that "I have come to the place where I live, my house" or "I have returned to my country" or "I am where I am supposed to be" (as in a restored relationship). (3) The word *feather* in the expression "feather in my cap" could convey, to someone learning English, the image of a literal feather stuck in my cap. But within our linguistic context, we know it is an idiomatic expression, referring to an accomplishment that I can be proud of. (4) The word *hand* has a range of metaphorical, figurative meanings beyond its literal meaning. In the expression "he dealt me a lousy hand," the word *hand* refers to a group of playing cards. In the expression "he asked for her hand in marriage," the word *hand* stands for the whole person. (5) In today's youth culture, the metaphorical meaning of the word "bad" can be the opposite of its literal meaning, to designate something which is really good, great or outstanding (as in "this is a bad car," meaning it is a "cool" car or a "hot" car. Even in this example, the adjectives *cool* and *hot,* though literally

---

[5]Biblical words for the English *fear* have a similar range of metaphorical meanings. The Hebrew *yir'â* can mean "terror" or "fear" (e.g., Ps 55:4-5), but it can also mean "reverence" and "awe" (e.g., Ps 33:8; Prov 1:7). Likewise, the Greek *phobos* can mean "fear," "dread" or "terror" (e.g., Lk 2:10; 21:26; Rom 13:3) but also "awe" or "reverence" or "astonishment" (Lk 5:26; Eph 5:21).

opposite in meaning, designate something that is considered very good!). Recently, my son referred to a great snowboarding trip from which he had just returned as both "bad" and "so sweet." Here, both *bad* and *sweet* have the meaning "great," "extraordinary" or "fabulous." An outsider or foreigner, not immersed in the youth culture and its linguistic conventions, could easily be baffled and confused!

Careful attention to the meanings of words and their metaphorical ranges of meaning is, of course, extremely important when translating meaning from one language to another. English versions of the Bible generally follow two philosophies or methodologies of translation. One is that of "formal equivalence"; the other is that of "functional equivalence" (previously termed "dynamic equivalence"). Formal-equivalent translations seek to stay as close as possible to the "form" of the original language (Bibles that follow this philosophy are, e.g., RSV, NRSV, NASB, NKJV), while functional-equivalent versions seek to capture the meaning of the original text in clear and natural language (e.g., TEV, CEV, NLT). Somewhere between these two are "mediating versions" (e.g., NIV, TNIV, NJB). In order to stay as close as possible to the original text, translators—even those guided by the linguistic philosophy of functional equivalence—often opt for the literal translation of a word, and they leave the determination of the most appropriate metaphorical meaning both to scholars who write commentaries on biblical books and to the interpretation of the reader. This is particularly true when words or phrases in the original, depending on their metaphorical meaning, have differing theological, doctrinal or practical implications.

The "abuse of words" happens when words and expressions are decoded (by teachers or readers) in ways that are not in keeping with the original encoding. When that happens, meanings are read into biblical texts that may not be there at all. The resulting understanding and application of the meaning and message of biblical texts may, at times, have a distorting, or a significant, serious and negative consequence for Christian life and presence.

THE WOMAN AS MAN'S "HELPER, SUITABLE FOR HIM"

As already discussed in chapter three, the narrative of the creation of man and woman in Genesis 2 has long provided one of the foundations for a hierarchical view of the male-female relationship (in both Judaism and Christianity). This traditional interpretation has focused its attention on the so-called principle of primogeniture, namely the chronological priority of the man's creation.[6] His being shaped *first* was held to signify his leadership and authority in relation to the woman. Though the Genesis text itself does not makes this claim, such an interpretation is seen to be supported by the affirmation that the woman was created as man's "helper suitable for him" (Gen 2:18, 20 NIV).[7] The designation of the woman as man's "helper" is understood, in traditional interpretation, as suggesting her subservient role as man's "assistant," his "domestic helper." In our context, a particular meaning of the word "helper" in the English language (such as "assistant") is used as the interpretive lens through which the Hebrew term is understood.[8]

Apart from the fact that the biblical narrative's only judgment regarding the man's chronological priority and isolation (his being "alone") is that "it is not good" (Gen 2:18), the meaning of the Hebrew word, translated "helper," simply cannot be squeezed into the mold of this particular restrictive meaning (i.e., *helper* as "assistant" or "servant").[9] The Hebrew verb ʿāzar (to help),

---

[6]The "principle of primogeniture" has been derived from the reality that in Israelite culture, as reflected in the Old Testament, importance is often attached to that which comes first, as in *firstborn*. (See appendix B for examples of this idea in the writings of the Jewish philosopher Philo of Alexandria and the church fathers Ambrosiaster, Theodoret of Cyr and Augustine.) At the same time, the climax (or last of a series) can also be of utmost importance. For example, the creation of human beings "in the image of God" is clearly the climax toward which God's creative work moves in Genesis 1. That concept is reflected in the commentary on Genesis 1:26-27 by the church father Gregory of Nyssa, who wrote: "Creation moves from lower to higher, to the perfect form, humanity," quoted in Andrew Louth, ed., *Genesis 1—11*, Ancient Christian Commentary on Scripture, Old Testament, vol. 1 (Downers Grove, Ill.: InterVarsity Press, 2001), p. 28. Further, the sequence in the creation narrative of Genesis 2 may be deliberately balancing the idea of priority: Just as ʾādām (man = masculine) emerges out of ʾădāmâ (ground = feminine), so ʾiššâ (woman = feminine) emerges out of îš (man = masculine). We have a similar balancing in 1 Corinthians 11:11-12, where Paul states that "just as woman came from man, so man comes through woman." From an overall biblical perspective, it is noteworthy that the faith of Israel is characterized by the frequent rejection of cultural norms and values. Repeatedly, the cultural preference for *first* is set aside in accomplishing God's purpose: Isaac is chosen over Ishmael, Jacob over Esau, David over Saul. Jesus' words that "the last will be first, and the first will be last" articulates this biblical rejection of cultural preference (Mt 20:16; cf. Mt 19:30).

[7]This is the translation of the Hebrew ʿēzer kĕnegdô in the NIV in Genesis 2:18. (At Genesis 2:20, it renders the same Hebrew words as "suitable helper.") The NRSV translates the phrase with "helper as his partner." Peterson, in *The Message*, translates the Hebrew as "a helper, a companion" (at Gen 2:18) and as "a suitable companion" (at Gen 2:20). The RSV translates it with "a helper fit for him."

[8]Even in English usage, the word *helper* has a range of possible meanings. Beside the meaning "assistant" or "servant" (as in "hired help"), the word can also refer to someone in a superior position (as when someone throws a lifeline to a drowning person) or in a position of authority (such as a professor, who was of great help in my dissertation research).

[9]Some early church fathers interpreted the woman's relationship to the man in that way. Ephrem

from which the noun *ʿēzer* ("helper") is derived, signifies the action of someone who saves another from extremity, who delivers from death. The noun *ʿēzer*, as a designation of someone in relationship to another person or a group of people, is used eighteen times in the entire Old Testament. Outside of its two occurrences in Genesis 2:18, 20 as a designation of the woman, the word *ʿēzer* is only and always used for God as redeemer, as the one who rescues from distress, danger, calamity and death (e.g., Ex 18:4; Deut 33:7, 26, 29; Ps 33:20; 46:1; 70:5; 115:9-11; 121:1-2).

Given this linguistic data, the word *ʿēzer*, rather than evoking the idea of someone in a subservient role, evokes the opposite. In some sense, the woman is depicted as the man's savior; her presence with the man is redemptive, whole-making. In no way does the word *ʿēzer* connote the idea of the woman as man's assistant or subordinate.

The Hebrew word that follows the word *ʿēzer*, and qualifies it, is *kĕnegdô* ("fit for him" or "suitable for him"). It underlines the note of prominence and strength expressed already in the word *ʿēzer*. The Hebrew *neged* means, literally, "in front of, in sight of, opposite to" (equivalent to the English expression "face to face"). The related noun *nāgîd* designates a leader, ruler or prince (such as a general, "in front of" his troops, leading them into battle). As a whole, the Hebrew phrase *ʿēzer kĕnegdô* ("helper suitable for him") designates the woman as the one whose creation and being leads the man out of his aloneness. Unlike the animals, who are found not to be man's *ʿēzer kĕnegdô* (Gen 2:19-20), the woman does correspond to him; she is his equal partner ("bone of my bones and flesh of my flesh," Gen 2:23), fashioned from the same essence and substance, who complements and completes him.[10] The

---

the Syrian wrote that the woman as man's helper meant that she would "help the man" with the various tasks in agriculture and animal husbandry. Augustine, likewise, understood the woman as man's helper in the sense of the relationship between ruler (the man) and ruled (the woman). Ambrose contended that the woman was called "helper" in the sense of "the generation of the human family—a really good helper," and then he gave an analogy from his own time: "We see people in high and important offices often enlist the help of people who are below them in rank and esteem" (see Andrew Louth, ed., *Genesis 1—11*, Ancient Christian Commentary on Scripture, Old Testament, vol. 1 [Downers Grove, Ill.: InterVarsity Press, 2001], pp. 68-69).

[10]The first-century Jewish philosopher Philo of Alexandria, who is generally not an advocate of women's equality, understood the *ʿēzer kĕnegdô* of Genesis 2:18, 20 to "refer to partnership . . . with those who bring mutual benefit. . . . To everyone of those who come together in the partnership of love the saying of Pythagoras can be applied, that 'a lover is indeed another self.' " See *Questions and Answers on Genesis, 1:17,* Loeb Classical Library (Cambridge, Mass.: Harvard University Press, 1937).

church father John Chrysostom (A.D. 344-407) understood the status of the woman before the Fall, as intended by God, in these words:

> In the beginning I created you equal in esteem to your husband, and my intention was that in everything you would share with him as an equal; and as I entrusted control of everything to your husband, so did I to you.[11]

Chrysostom's comment shows his understanding of the important connection between Genesis 1 and Genesis 2. (I will discuss the significance of this connection in chapter six, where I will focus my attention on the abuse of literary context.)

In light of the meaning of the Hebrew phrase *ʿēzer kĕnegdô* ("helper suitable for him") and the literary-theological connection between Genesis 1 and 2, the traditional understanding of Genesis 2:18-20—as stipulating a creationally-intended and designed subordinate role and status for women in relationship to men—is simply untenable, and it represents a serious abuse of Scripture. This critique of the traditional view of male-female hierarchy is supported by the way several other Hebrew and Greek terms are encoded in the original context of the Word of God and abusively decoded in much of the church's hermeneutical tradition.

THE USE AND MEANING OF THE TERM *ĀDĀM* IN SCRIPTURE

In the early Genesis narrative of creation and the Fall, the Hebrew word *ʾādām* (usually translated either "man" or "Adam"), is used in three different ways. Attention to this variety of uses, as well as to the way this word (transliterated into Greek) is used in the New Testament by Paul, contributes toward a more accurate decoding of its meaning in particular contexts.

In the phrase, "Let us make man in our image" (Gen 1:26 NIV), the Hebrew word translated "man" is *ʾādām*. Then follows the phrase "and let *them* have dominion" (NRSV, emphasis added). The plural pronoun *them* shows that the word *ʾādām* is used here, not as a designation of the male member of the human species, but rather as a *generic noun*, referring to humanity in general. This fact is recognized in the NRSV, which renders the Hebrew text as "Let us make humankind in our image."[12] Genesis 1:27 (my translation)

---

[11]Louth, *Genesis 1—11*, p. 92.

[12]Peterson, in *The Message*, translates the Hebrew of Genesis 1:26 with "Let us make human beings in our image," thereby recognizing the generic meaning of *ʾādām* in this text.

confirms this meaning of the Hebrew *'ādām:*

> So God created *adam* in his image,
>> in the image of God he created him,
>> male and female he created *them.*

What we have here—in the structure of the passage—is a typical example of "poetic parallelism" in the Hebrew language. The second line repeats the essential content of the first line, and the third line expands (and explicates) the fact affirmed in the first two lines. The pronoun "him" in the second line refers back to the word *'ādām* in the first line, which in the Hebrew is a masculine singular noun. But as in Genesis 1:26, the plural pronoun "them" in the third line indicates that the term *'ādām* is used again as a generic noun, designating *humanity* in its male-female polarity, complementarity and partnership.

Further warrant for this meaning of the text is found in Genesis 5:1-2. It states that *'ādām* is created "in the likeness of God" (Gen 5:1). It is clear that *'ādām,* as in Genesis 1:26-27, is used as a generic noun, in light of the fact that the text goes on to state that "male and female he created them, and he blessed them and named them humankind [*'ādām*] when they were created" (Gen 5:2). Male and female together are designated as *'ādām.* They share in a common humanity; they are both equally human, in the likeness of God. It is significant to note that the "image of God" is not bestowed on individual human beings as such, but rather on human beings in their male-female complementarity and partnership. That is to say, it is ultimately only in the context of human relationships, in human communities of love, where the "image of God," the reflection of God's character and purpose, is realized. We are created in and for relationship.[13]

This hearing of the texts in Genesis 1:26-27 and Genesis 5:1-2 has theological significance for how we hear the second creation narrative (Gen 2). There, the term *'ādām* is consistently used with the definite article (*hā'ādām,*

---

[13]Ray S. Anderson and Dennis B. Guernsey, in *On Being Family: A Social Theology of the Family* (Grand Rapids: Eerdmans, 1985), pp. 17-18, speak of this as "cohumanity": "Theological anthropology, drawing upon biblical teaching [shows that] the solitary person cannot share fully in the complete human existence. . . . According to the creation account in Genesis 2, co-humanity is the original and therefore quintessential aspect of personal and individual human existence." See also Mary Stewart Van Leeuwen, *Gender & Grace: Love, Gender and Parenting in a Changing World* (Downers Grove, Ill.: InterVarsity Press, 1990), pp. 38-41, who contends that an important dimension of the image of God is our sociability: "we are so unshakably created for community that we cannot even develop as full persons unless we grow up in nurturing contact with others," especially including "fellowship with the opposite sex."

"the man") to designate the specific male member of the human species, who is shaped by God out of the dust of "the ground" *(hā'ădāmâ)*. What is true of humanity in general (its male-female structure in the "image of God") must be true specifically. Thus, "it is not good that the man should be alone" (Gen 2:18).[14]

The intimate theological connection between Genesis 1 and 2, as reflected in both the generic and particular uses of the word *'ādām*,[15] provides a unified theological affirmation of male-female equality and complementarity. As *'ādām* (male and female) they are co-image bearers and coregents. As *'ādām* (the man) he is alone and, in that isolated existence, not up to the task of tilling the garden (Gen 2:15). The creator fills that void by shaping his *'ēzer*. "Woman is for man the savior from his void and the mate prepared to respond to his ongoingness."[16]

THE CURSEDNESS OF "PAIN" AND "TOIL"

The Genesis 3 narrative of the Fall—which depicts the human quest for ultimate, absolute knowledge and divinity, and results in the distortion of human life—became a major source of theological reflection about the origin of sin and evil during the intertestamental period (ca. 300 B.C. to A.D. 100). And Jewish reflection, which tended heavily toward blaming the woman (and her female descendants!) for sin and evil in the world,[17] strongly influenced early Christian thought.[18]

Paul's use of the Jewish interpretive tradition is clearly reflected in 1 Tim-

---

[14]See Samuel Terrien, *Til the Heart Sings: A Biblical Theology of Manhood and Womanhood* (Philadelphia: Fortress, 1985), pp. 9-10, who writes: "The ancient mentality, especially the Hebraic, considered aloneness as the negation of authentic living, for true life is not individual but corporate and social. The Hebrew word translated 'alone' (Gen 2:18) carries an overtone of separation and even of alienation. Human beings live only insofar as they are related in their environment to partners with whom they share mutuality and complementariness. Animals do not fulfill the requirements of true partnership."

[15]A third use of the word *'ādām* is as the name of the male ("Adam") in relationship to his wife, who is named Eve *(hawwâ)*, "because she would become the mother of all the living" (so the NIV in Gen 3:20; 4:1, 5:1, 3 and the NRSV at Gen 5:1, 3). In Hebrew, the word *hawwâ* resembles the word for "living" *(hay)*. The Greek translation of the Hebrew recognizes this alliteration when it translates *hawwâ* with *zōē* ("life"), and *hay* with *zōntōn* ("living").

[16]Terrien, *Til the Heart Sings,* p. 11.

[17]See appendix B for examples in the Jewish intertestamental and rabbinic literature.

[18]Examples are given in appendix B. See also Elizabeth A. Clark, *Women in the Early Church,* Message of the Fathers of the Church 13 (Wilmington, Del.: Michael Glazier, 1983), who presents some fascinating—and disturbing—points of view from the early church fathers.

othy 2:14, where he states that "Adam was not deceived, but the woman was deceived and became a transgressor." Such a view is later echoed in the writings of church fathers like Tertullian (ca. A.D. 155-225), who addressed women in these words: "You are the devil's gateway; you are the unsealer of that tree; you are the first forsaker of the divine law. . . . How easily you destroyed man, the image of God."[19] This interpretation of the Fall narrative is clearly based on a very partial, one-sided reading of the text in Genesis 3. There, both the man and the woman—who are side by side (Gen 3:6) when temptation faces them and who, together, reject the Creator-creature boundary (Gen 3:1-6)—are equally culpable (Gen 3:7) and are equally held responsible by God for their rebellion (Gen 3:8-13).[20]

However, the pervasive tendency—in the history of interpretation—to cast all or primary blame on the woman, strongly influenced the reading of the rest of the narrative of the Fall. This is evident in how the Hebrew word ʿiṣṣābôn ("pain, toil") has been translated in the narrative of the curse of the woman and the man in Genesis 3:16-18. The translational tradition, on the whole, places much more weight on the curse of the woman than on that of the man. In Genesis 3:16, the NIV renders the Hebrew ʿiṣṣābôn with "pain" and "pains" (Gen 3:16), clearly connected to the bearing of children ("in childbearing," NIV; "bring forth children," NRSV). This rendering of ʿiṣṣābôn, in the context of childbearing, immediately conjures up the woman's physical labor pains. The NRSV emphasizes this reading of the text even more strongly by translating ʿiṣṣābôn in Genesis 3:16 with "your pangs" and later with "in pain," thus evoking the image of labor pains in the process of delivery. The CEV (Contemporary English Version) is even more explicit. It combines the parallel expressions of Genesis 3:16 in the rendering, "You will suffer terribly when you give birth." The Living Bible goes even further when it renders Genesis 3:16 as: "You will bear children in intense pain and suffering."[21]

In contrast to these readings and this understanding of the curse of the woman—resulting in physical labor pains in childbirth, compounded by the man's "rule over" her[22]—the man's cursedness seems rather benign. It is im-

---

[19]Cited by A. K. Curtis, ed., "Women in the Early Church," in *Christian History* 7, no. 1 (1988): 4.

[20]See appendix B for several texts in Jewish literature, as well as in Paul's letters to Rome and Corinth, that hold Adam, the man, responsible for the entrance of sin into the world.

[21]NASB and *The Message* render both occurrences of ʿiṣṣābôn in Genesis 3:16 with "pain." This is also true of Luther's translation (*Schmerzen* = pain).

[22]Most translations render the Hebrew *māšal* as "rule over" (e.g., NRSV, NIV, NASB, CEV). The Living

portant to note here that ʿiṣṣābôn (used twice in Gen 3:16) is used again in Genesis 3:17: "Cursed is the ground because of you." Therefore, "in ʿiṣṣābôn you will eat of it." The same word, understood in Genesis 3:16 to refer to the woman's intense physical pain in childbirth, is understood in Genesis 3:17 to refer basically to "hard labor." The NRSV translates the Hebrew with "toil." This understanding of ʿiṣṣābôn as signifying "hard work" is clearly expressed in CEV's rendering: "You will have to struggle to grow enough food," and in the Living Bible's "All your life you will struggle to extract a living from it."

These emphases—on either the physical pain in childbirth or the hard toil of agricultural labor—may not be warranted, given the range of meanings of ʿiṣṣābôn. The term often refers to emotional pain (as in sorrow, grief, distress, trouble and agony), rather than physical pain.[23] Such a meaning of the Hebrew term was recognized by the KJV translators, who rendered all three uses of the Hebrew ʿiṣṣābôn (in Gen 3:16-17) with "sorrow."[24] Given this possible meaning of the Hebrew original, the experience of the man and woman's cursedness (i.e., their separation from life-giving and life-sustaining relationship with God) is very much the same, though experienced uniquely. In their complementary vocations as practiced in the context of primitive nomadic/agrarian culture—the woman in her unique function as the life-giver (Gen 3:20), and the man in his primary function as provider of food for the support and nurture of that life—both would experience sorrow, distress, agony, even despair. In the context of the ancient Near East, infant mortality was extremely high. Bearing and bringing forth children into the world was always overshadowed by the possibility (and frequent actuality) of death; thus the experience of sorrow. Likewise, the man's primary vocation in that cultural-historical context was always hindered by "thorns and thistles" (Gen 3:18)[25]

Bible renders the Hebrew as "he shall be your master" (cf. Luther's translation, *Er soll dein Herr sein* = "He shall be your lord").

[23]E.g., Ps 16:4; 127:2; Prov 10:22; 15:13. See F. Brown, G. R. Driver and C. R. Briggs, *A Hebrew and English Lexicon of the Old Testament* (Boston: Houghton, Mifflin and Company, 1906), pp. 781-82. Cf. Willem A. VanGemeren, ed., *New International Dictionary of Old Testament Theology and Exegesis*, vol. 1 (Grand Rapids: Zondervan, 1997), p. 483, who states that "the pain includes both physical and psychic dimensions." See also Jay Green, ed., *Genesis-Ruth*, vol. 1 of *The Interlinear Hebrew/Greek English Bible*, 4 vols. (Wilmington, Del.: Associated Publishers and Authors), p. 176, who renders all three occurrences of ʿiṣṣābôn in Genesis 3:16-17 with "sorrow."

[24]Cf. Luther, who translated ʿiṣṣābôn in Genesis 3:16 (the woman's curse) with *Schmerzen* ("pain"); but in Genesis 3:17 (the man's curse) with *Kummer* ("sadness" or "sorrow").

[25]Isaiah's vision of God's everlasting covenant (Is 55) includes the elimination of "thorns" and "briars," which represent adversity.

and accompanied by the possibility (and frequent actuality) of drought or pestilence, flood or hail. The labor of farmers across the world, from seed-time to harvest, is always attended by the anxiety of knowing that the crops may, and frequently do, come to naught.[26]

In light of these linguistic considerations, it is unfortunate that the traditional translations (with the notable exception of the KJV) have furthered a hearing of the text that promotes the idea of the woman's greater culpability for the origin of sin, and thus deserves the greater punishment. For if the ground is cursed because of the man's violation of God's boundaries, and he experiences hard labor in his agricultural pursuits, then the woman is thrice cursed. Not only does she experience intense physical pain in childbirth and suffer the man's mastery over her (Gen 3:16); she knows, additionally, the reality of hard labor and toil side by side with the man. For the historical reality is that women have, and continue to carry, the major load in many, if not most, agricultural societies worldwide. If we are attentive, however, to the probable encoding of the Hebrew term 'iṣṣābôn in its biblical context (as signifying emotional distress and sorrow), then our decoding reveals that both woman and man equally experience the reality of their separation from God (Gen 3:1-13) as an existence in which their unique and complementary vocations are marked by sorrow.

The equality and complementarity of man and woman, fashioned in creation (Gen 1—2), survived the Fall. Yet their partnership—designed by the Creator for mutual wholeness, for life-giving and life-sustaining relationality—was marred at its core. The historical reality of man's "rule over" woman (Gen 3:16) is a cursedness that cuts in both directions. For in the male-female relationship, the assertion of authority over the other, and the exercise of power to compel obedience and submission from the other, lessens the one and demeans the other. Across cultures, women have suffered, and in many places continue to suffer, from this cursedness, through all sorts of abuse, restriction, subjugation, mutilation and oppression. Their full humanity, de-

---

[26]An alternative reading of the assertion in Genesis 3:19—that the man would eat bread "by the sweat of your face"—would further support the idea that the woman and man are alike in their sorrow. The Hebrew scholar Thomas McDaniel argues that the Hebrew phrase in Genesis 3:19 literally means "by the dripping of your nostrils" and may refer to "weeping, the result of sorrow," which comes "when even hard work leaves one fruitless and one's progeny starving." See Thomas F. McDaniel, " 'He Shall Be Like You': Genesis 3:16," <daniel.eastern.edu/seminary/tmcdaniel/cbbp-chapter2.pdf>.

signed in creation to be exercised in equal and joyful partnership with men, has been pervasively throttled and their giftedness marginalized. Correspondingly, the full humanity of men has also been lessened and distorted by this cursedness, namely the domination-submission structure in the male-female relationship. On the one hand, the full humanity of men has been lessened by rejecting the equal partnership of women, thus restricting the enriching and whole-making giftedness of women in their lives. On the other hand, the assertion of "power over" the other (overwhelmingly by men)—which is, at its core, the rejection of authentic life-giving and life-nurturing love for the other[27]—has led to the destructive reality of the use of violence and force in human affairs between individuals, peoples and nations.

Biblical words, and how they are heard, interpreted and applied, have consequences. The above study shows how the erroneous decoding of the original, contextual meaning of the words *ʾādām* ("man, human being, Adam"), *ʿēzer* ("helper") and *ʿiṣṣābôn* ("pain, toil, sorrow") has significant and negative consequences for the man-woman relationship. In addition to the use of these words in the narratives of the creation and Fall in Genesis, and the implications of the way we "hear" them and apply them to the man-woman relationship, I will now examine Paul's use of the word *head* to designate persons in relationship to other persons or realities.

THE MEANING OF *HEAD* IN THE PAULINE EPISTLES

Paul uses the Greek word *kephalē* ("head") to designate the following persons in their relationship to other persons and realities: first, God in relationship to Christ (1 Cor 11:3); second, Christ in relationship to man (1 Cor 11:3), to the church (Eph 4:15-16; 5:25; Col 1:18; 2:19), and to the powers (Eph 1:22; Col 2:10); third, men in relationship to women, and husbands in relationship to wives (1 Cor 11:3-5; Eph 5:23). What does Paul intend to communicate by the use of this term for one member in these relationships?

We decode the meaning of words and how they are used largely on the basis of our own linguistic conventions. So let us begin to respond to this question by looking at the various meanings of the word *head* in our language. Side by side with the literal meaning (i.e., the physical head of a human being or animal), the English word *head* has a range of metaphorical

---

[27]Tony Campolo, "God as the Suffering Servant," *Tikkun* (May/June 2007): 17-19.

meanings. It can refer to: the source or origin of a river ("headwater"); an exalted position ("he is head and shoulders above the others"); an individual person ("staking their heads on" or "the teacher counted heads"); a culminating point ("the crisis came to a head"); a place of honor ("she is at the head of her class"); a natural talent or giftedness ("she has a good head for math"); and a person in a position of authority, a boss, a chief ("head of state," "head of the corporation," "head of the household").

The last metaphorical use of the word *head,* for a person in a position of authority, is very common and normal within our language. And this metaphorical meaning has been the pervasive "filter" by which Paul's use of the Greek word *kephalē* has been decoded in the traditional interpretation of the Pauline texts. For English readers of these texts, the common metaphorical meaning of *head* as ruler, leader, chief, boss or director suggests itself almost immediately. Such an understanding of *head* as connoting "authority over" leads to an understanding of the nature of the relationship in terms of a hierarchical authority structure.

Is this the meaning that Paul had in mind when he used the word *kephalē* to designate God, Christ and men in relationship to others? Would Greek-speaking Christians, as well as non-Christians, have heard and understood *kephalē* in terms of "authority over"? A survey of the linguistic evidence, both in the larger Greek world and in the Greek translation of the Old Testament (commonly called the Septuagint—the version of the Old Testament that was primarily read in Paul's churches), should help. After which, we can apply our findings to Paul's usage of this term.

Meanings of the word kephalē. The most exhaustive lexicon of the Greek language[28] covered Greek literature from circa 80 B.C. to A.D. 500. First published in 1843, it lists numerous metaphorical meanings of the word *kephalē* (in addition to its literal meaning, "head"), and it provides citations from the literature where those meanings are present. The following metaphorical meanings are given: the top or brim of a vessel; the capital of a column; the chief city or place; the crown or completion or consummation of something; the origin or source (as of a stream, or of life). The final metaphorical meaning of *kephalē* given in this lexicon is "of persons, a chief," but not a single citation from the Greek literature is given as evidence for such a metaphorical

---

[28]H. G. Liddell and R. Scott, *Greek-English Lexicon* (New York: American Book Company, 1897).

use of the word "head." The 1925 revised edition of this lexicon[29] includes several other interesting metaphorical uses of *kephalē*. In the ancient study of anatomy, the places where muscles are attached to bones, where they originate or begin, are called *kephalē*.[30] In addition to the meaning "source of a river," *kephalē* is said to refer generally to source or origin. An Orphic fragment, of the ancient Greek religious beliefs, is cited where the god Zeus is called the *kephalē* of all things. Other manuscripts of this fragment have *archē* ("beginning") instead of *kephalē*, showing that in the Greek language these terms could be used synonymously.[31] The starting point of an era can be designated by the word "head" (*kephalē chronou* = literally "head of time," i.e., "beginning of an epoch").[32] What is particularly noteworthy is that the metaphorical meaning "of persons, a chief," given in the 1897 edition without substantiation in the Greek literature, is dropped for lack of evidence in the 1925 edition. The 1996 edition of this lexicon also has no references to *kephalē* in the metaphorical sense of "person in a position of authority."[33] This lexical conclusion is also that of the *Theological Dictionary of the New Testament*.[34] On the basis of a study of the metaphorical meanings of *kephalē* outside the New Testament, H. Schlier states that "in secular Greek usage, *kephalē* is not employed for the head of a society," such as a chief or ruler.[35]

---

[29]H. G. Liddell and R. Scott, *A Greek English Dictionary*, rev. ed. S. Jones (Oxford: Clarendon, 1925).

[30]In modern anatomy, the condyloid and coronoid processes (namely the bony ridges where muscles are attached) are referred to as "muscle origins." See Carmine D. Clementi, *Anatomy: A Regional Atlas of the Human Body* (Baltimore: Urban and Schwarzenburg, 1981), pp. 72-75, 575.

[31]An informative New Testament parallel is found in John 1:1, 3, which reads: "In the beginning *(archē)* was the Word, and the Word was with God, and the Word was God. . . . All things came into being through him."

[32]The festival at the beginning of the Jewish New Year is called Rosh Hashanah. The Hebrew word *rō'š* (literally "head"), has as one of its metaphorical meanings "the beginning, the starting point."

[33]H. G. Liddell and R. Scott, *A Greek-English Lexicon*, rev. ed. H. S. Jones and R. McKenzie (London: Oxford University Press, 1996).

[34]H. Schlier, "κεφαλή, ανακεφαλαιόομαι," in *Theological Dictionary of the New Testament*, ed. Gerhard Kittel (Grand Rapids: Eerdmans, 1965), 3:673-81.

[35]F. W. Danker, *A Greek-English Lexicon of the New Testament and Other Early Christian Literature*, 3rd ed. (Chicago: University of Chicago Press, 2000), provides two examples outside the New Testament (Zosimus, a Byzantine historian in the sixth century, and Artemidorus, a professional diviner and author in the third century) where he sees *kephalē* including the figurative sense of "a being of high status." Fee, *First Epistle to the Corinthians*, p. 502, understands Zosimus to use *kephalē* in the sense of "dignity," not "authority." The citation from Artemidorus is an analogy: just as the head *(kephalē)* is the source of light and life of the whole body, so a father is the light and life of the son. The *head* in this analogy of head-body has the metaphorical sense of "source."

In contrast to the absence of clear examples of *kephalē* as denoting persons of authority, there are numerous, decisive examples of *kephalē* as denoting "source" or "origin."[36] For example, Zeus as the *kephalē* (or *archē*, which means beginning, starting point) of all things; the *kephalē* as that which gives life to the body, like parents who are the source of one's life; Esau, son of Isaac, is described by Philo as the progenitor, the *kephalē*, of the entire clan; the virtuous person, seen as the *kephalē* of the human race, just like the limbs of the body draw their life from the forces of the *kephalē* at the top.[37]

Decisive support for the above data—which shows that in ordinary Greek usage *kephalē* was not used as a metaphorical designation for persons in authority-over positions[38]—comes from the Greek translation of the Old Testament (produced ca. 250-150 B.C.). It was published for Greek-speaking Jews, who mostly lived outside Palestine as the Diaspora, and was their authoritative Bible.

How kephalē is used when translating the Hebrew into Greek. Like the English word *head* and the equivalent Greek word *kephalē*, the Hebrew word for "head" *(rō'š)* has numerous metaphorical meanings. In an exhaustive study[39] of how the Septuagint translators rendered the Hebrew word *rō'š* into Greek, the following data emerged. In the approximately two hundred times when *rō'š* refers to a physical head, the translators almost always used the

---

[36]For these examples in Greek literature, see the studies by C. C. Kroeger, "The Classical Concept of 'Head' as 'source' " in G. Gaebelein Hull, ed., *Equal to Serve: Women and Men in the Church and Home* (Old Tappan, N.J.: Fleming H. Revell, 1987), pp. 267-83; Berkeley and Alvera Mickelsen, "What Does *Kephalē* Mean in the New Testament?" in *Women, Authority and the Bible,* ed. Alvera Mickelsen (Downers Grove, Ill.: InterVarsity Press, 1986), pp. 97-110; P. Barton Payne, "Response," in *Women, Authority and the Bible,* ed. Alvera Mickelsen (Downers Grove, Ill.: InterVarsity Press, 1986), pp. 118-32.

[37]See also the references above to *kephalē* as the source or mouth of a river, to the origin of muscles and to the starting point of an epoch.

[38]S. Bedale launched the contemporary discussion, leading to a near-consensus in biblical scholarship, in his 1954 essay, "The Meaning of κεφαλή in the Pauline Epistles," *Journal of Theological Studies* 5 (1954), pp. 211-15. The most thorough attempt to counter this trend, and in support of the traditional understanding of *kephalē* (as referring to a person in authority over another or others), in both Greek literature and in the New Testament is Wayne Grudem's "Does Κεφαλή ('Head') Mean 'Source' or 'Authority Over' in Greek Literature? A Survey of 2336 Examples," *Trinity Journal* 6 (1985), pp. 38-59. Having studied this essay carefully, I am in solid agreement with Gordon Fee's critique: "For all its attempt at objectivity by means of computer research, this article is quite misleading both in its presentation and conclusions." See Fee, *First Epistle to the Corinthians,* p. 502 n. 42.

[39]Berkeley and Alvera Mickelsen, "What Does *Kephalē* Mean in the New Testament?" in *Women, Authority and the Bible,* ed. Alvera Mickelsen (Downers Grove, Ill.: InterVarsity Press, 1986), pp. 97-110.

Greek *kephalē*. About 180 times, the Hebrew *rō'š* has the metaphorical meaning "leader" or "chief" or "authority figure," or refers to something of prominence (like the place where a sovereign lives). From this it is obvious that there is a close affinity between the English *head* and the Hebrew *rō'š*. In both languages, the word *head* frequently has the metaphorical meaning "authority over." However, out of those 180 instances where *rō'š* has the metaphorical meaning "authority over" ("leader, ruler") in the Hebrew original, the translators chose overwhelmingly *not* to use the Greek word *kephalē*. About 135 times, *rō'š* (when it refers to an authority figure) is translated by the Greek *archōn* (or its derivatives), clearly meaning "ruler," "commander," "chief" or "leader." About thirty times, *rō'š* is translated by other Greek terms that convey specific "authority-over" meanings, such as *megas* ("great one") or *hēgeomai* ("to rule, to have dominion"). In the remaining occurrences (about eight), *rō'š* is rendered by the Greek *kephalē*. In several of those instances, *rō'š* simply refers to the chief city of a country.[40] There are only six Old Testament texts (out of 180) where *rō'š* designates a figure of authority and is translated by the Greek *kephalē*.[41]

In light of the fact that the Greek word *kephalē* was *not* used in the vast majority of cases when the Hebrew word *rō'š* has the metaphorical significance meaning "authority over," what may account for its use in these six texts? Isaiah 7:8-9 is a good example of Hebraic poetic parallelism, where the word *rō'š* is used in two parallel metaphorical senses: as denoting both the capital cities of two regions (indicating their prominence) and the rulers of those regions (indicating persons of authority). It is, therefore, most probable that the translator wished to preserve the Hebraic parallel structure of the

---

[40]We have the equivalent in English in the terms "the capital" and "the capitol," derived from the Latin *capitolum* and *capitellum*, closely related to the Greek *kephalē*. Note also our use of the word "cephalic," referring to the human head. We also speak of a city that is prominent in some way (as in "Paris is the fashion capital").

[41]Judg 10:18; 11:8-11; 2 Sam 22:44; Ps 18:43; Is 7:8-9; and Lam 1:5. In his discussion of the Septuagint renderings of the Hebrew *rō'š* when designating an authority figure, H. Schlier (in "κεφαλή"), adds to this list of texts Deuteronomy 28:13, 43-44. However, his reading of them is not correct. These texts are embedded in promises of God's rich blessing if Israel is obedient and warnings of calamity if disobedient. In the case of obedience (Deut 28:13), Israel will be "the head, and not the tail" (*rō'š* translated with *kephalē*), "the top, and not the bottom." In the case of disobedience (Deut 28:43-44), Israel's enemies "shall ascend above you higher and higher, while you shall descend lower and lower. . . . They shall be the head and you shall be the tail." The entire chapter has to do with prosperity (Deut 28:11-12). So the head-tail and top-bottom metaphors have nothing to do with rule or authority over others but with the contrast between prosperity (the result of divine blessing) and with want (the result of God's judgment).

passage by rendering the two parallel sets of the Hebrew *rō's* consistently with the Greek *kephalē,* even though *kephalē* did not connote "authority over" in ordinary Greek usage.[42] In the other five occurrences where *rō's* (designating a person of authority) is rendered *kephalē,* the translators may have simply opted for the literal Greek equivalent, namely *kephalē,* without attention to metaphorical nuances. This would be similar to what happens when modern translators of English versions of the Bible translate the Greek *kephalē* in Paul's epistles with the literal English equivalent "head," without regard for the possible or likely metaphorical meanings of both the Greek *kephalē* and the English *head.*

Whatever the merit of the above reflections on the possible reason why the Septuagint translators used *kephalē* for *rō's* in these instances, the overwhelming use of other standard Greek words for authority figures reveals these few texts to be the glaring exceptions that prove the rule.[43] The lexical data from common Greek usage and the data from the Septuagint translation of the Old Testament lead to the conclusion that, in ordinary Greek usage, the word *kephalē* did not have the metaphorical meaning of chief or ruler or someone having authority over. Further attestation for this conclusion is the fact that in the entire Gospel record, as well as in the rest of the New Testament outside the Pauline passages (1 Cor 11; Col; Eph), where persons in positions of authority and control are frequently mentioned, the word *kephalē* is *never* used for such individuals.[44] That would not have been the meaning Gentile and Jewish Greek-speakers would have understood in Paul's time when he used the term to designate persons in certain relationships. It is quite improbable, therefore, that Paul conveyed the idea of someone having authority over when he used *kephalē* to describe those relationships. So what *did* he mean to convey?

Kephalē as "source" or "origin." We begin with 1 Corinthians 11:3-16. In

---

[42]Isaiah 7:8-9 reads: "the *rō's* of Aram [Syria] is Damascus, and the *rō's* of Damascus is Rezin. . . . The *rō's* of Ephraim is Samaria, and the *rō's* of Samaria is the son of Remaliah."

[43]This is also the judgment of J. Murphy O'Connor, "Sex and Logic in 1 Corinthians 11:2-16," *Catholic Biblical Quarterly* 42 (1980): 482-500, who notes that "these exceptions . . . do not change the picture." See also Fee, *First Epistle to the Corinthians,* p. 503.

[44]See, for example, Mt 13:27; Lk 12:39 (*oikodespotēs* = householder, owner, master of the house); Mt 18:25-34; 20:8; Lk 12:36-37; Jn 13:16 (*kyrios* = lord, master); Lk 16:1, 3, 8 (*oikonomos* = household manager); Mk 13:35 (*kyrios tēs oikias* = master, lord of the household); Lk 23:13; Jn 7:26, 12:31; Acts 4:5; Rom 13:3; 1 Cor 2:6, 8 (*archōn* = ruler, magistrate, official, prince); 2 Tim 2:21; 2 Pet 2:1; Jude 4 (*despotēs* = lord, master, despot); Eph 3:10; 6:12; Col 1:16; 2:15; Tit 3:1 (*archē* = rulers, principalities); Rom 13:1; Eph 3:10; Col 1:16; 2:15; Tit 3:1; 1 Pet 3:22 (*exousia* = power to act, authorities); Eph 1:21 (*dynameōs* = the powers).

dealing with the issue of appropriate hairstyle and head covering, Paul employs the word "head" *(kephalē)* in both a metaphorical and literal sense. In 1 Corinthians 11:10, 13 the term clearly refers to the literal head of man and woman. In 1 Corinthians 11:3, the term is clearly used in a metaphorical sense: Christ is the *kephalē* of every man; the *kephalē* of woman is the man; and God is the *kephalē* of Christ.[45] In 1 Corinthians 11:4-5, two uses of "head" are clearly literal (the man's and woman's literal heads). Each of the other two uses can have one of two metaphorical meanings: a man who prays or prophesies with his literal head covered (1 Cor 11:4) "disgraces his head" (either "himself" or his metaphorical "head," namely Christ); a woman who prays and prophesies with her head uncovered "disgraces her head" (either "herself" or her metaphorical "head," namely man).

Our concern here is not with a comprehensive interpretation of Paul's entire, and complex, argument. (Literary and cultural context issues will be addressed in chapters six and seven of this book.) Here we will, rather, deal with the question: in what sense is Christ the *kephalē* of man, and man the *kephalē* of woman, and God the *kephalē* of Christ (1 Cor 11:3)? If Paul had a hierarchical authority structure in view in these relationships, one could reasonably expect that he would have shaped his argument in terms of descent from the top of the hierarchy to the bottom, as in the "chain of command" theory,[46] where authority moves from God to Christ to man to woman. But Paul does not structure his argument this way, because he is not at all thinking about authority structures. Rather, he is concerned about the reflection of honor and glory (and the possibility of disgrace and shame) in various relationships, especially in the relationship between men and women in the worship of the congregation, and the consequent negative impact of their behavior within the social-cultural context of Corinth.

Another clue, pointing away from a hierarchical interpretation of these relationships—together with an understanding of the metaphor *head* as not

---

[45]The NRSV translates 1 Corinthians 11:3 with "and the husband is the head of his wife," while the NIV has "and the head of the woman is man." This difference is due to the fact that the Greek word *anēr* can mean either "husband" or "man," and *gynē* can mean either "wife" or "woman" (as is acknowledged in the NRSV notes). The NIV's rendering has the better of it here, for the entire passage deals generally with acceptable hairstyle/covering of man and woman in worship, not with the husband-wife relationship.

[46]See the discussion of this theory, held by many traditionalists and popularized by Bill Gothard in the 1970s, in Diane S. R. Garland and David E. Garland, *Beyond Companionship: Christians in Marriage* (Philadelphia: Westminster Press, 1986), pp. 26-27.

denoting a "power over" relationship—is the fact that throughout the passage, appeal is made to "source" imagery: woman was made "*from* man" (1 Cor 11:8) and "came *from* man" (1 Cor 11:12); man is now "born *of* woman" (1 Cor 11:12 NIV), and all things are "*from* God" (1 Cor 11:12). Paul's clear allusion (in 1 Cor 11:8-9, 12) to the creation narrative of Genesis 2, shows that he is talking about the *origin* of woman. According to Gen 2:23-24, man is the source of the woman's life, of her being.

This metaphorical meaning of *kephalē* (as source or origin) is also the most appropriate meaning of *kephalē* for Christ in relation to man. Paul, as other New Testament writers, affirmed Christ as the one *by whom* and *through whom* all things were created (Jn 1:3; 1 Cor 8:6; Col 1:16; Heb 1:3). Therefore, Paul sees Christ as the *kephalē* (source, origin) of man (in light of Gen 2), and indeed of "every man" (1 Cor 11:3), since for Paul, the first man is in some sense representative of all (cf. Rom 5:12-19; 1 Cor 15:47).[47] By participating in worship with covered heads, men dishonor their "head," the one who is the *source* of their existence.[48]

The third metaphorical use of *kephalē* in our text is as a designation of God in relation to Christ. The traditional understanding of *kephalē* in this relationship, in the sense of hierarchical "headship," evokes the early Christian heresy of "subordinationism," where Christ is seen as under the authority of God and subordinate to him, and this represents a challenge to the classical doctrine of the Trinity. Such a reading of the text is, however, neither required nor legitimate, in light of both the linguistic data regarding the term *kephalē* and the context. In keeping with the Christ-to-man and man-to-woman relationships, defined by *kephalē* in its metaphorical meaning "source," God is the source or origin of Christ. How are these relationships to be understood?

Cyril of Alexandria—an important Christian teacher in the fifth century—in commenting on 1 Corinthians 11:3, wrote:

Thus we say that the *kephalē* of man is Christ, because he was excellently

---

[47]Alternately, Paul may have the "new creation" in mind, namely that Christ is the source of the new creation (2 Cor 5:17), the new humanity (Eph 1:10, 15). See Fee, *First Epistle to the Corinthians*, pp. 504-5. A problem for this interpretation seems to be Paul's appeal to the Genesis 2 narrative, pointing to the original creation, not the new creation in Christ. That Christ is (also) *kephalē* (source) of the new creation, namely the new humanity constituted as "the body of Christ," is clearly attested in Ephesians and Colossians. See our discussion below.

[48]See chapter seven for a discussion of the cultural background relative to this text.

made *through* him, and the *kephalē* of woman is man, because she was taken *from* his flesh, and the *kephalē* of Christ is God, because he is *from* him according to nature.[49]

Two insights emerge from this text: (1) It is clear that when Cyril read the word *kephalē* in 1 Corinthians 11:3, he understood the word in the sense of "source" (or "origin") for all three pairs of relationships. (2) Cyril's reading of the God-Christ relation reflects the early trinitarian and christological discussions, from which emerged the doctrine of the eternal generation of the Son, who is of the same essence or substance as the Father. It is doubtful that this later theological formulation was already anticipated by Paul. It is more likely that Paul was making an affirmation about the incarnation. God is the *kephalē* of Christ in the sense that the Incarnate One has his origin in God. God is the source of Christ, who comes from God, is sent by God.[50]

Concluding from the above study of 1 Corinthians 11:3, the designation of God, Christ and man as "head" in relation to Christ, man and woman, respectively, has nothing to do with authority structures, but with "head" as source or point of origin.[51] That metaphorical meaning of *kephalē* as source seems also to be the most appropriate meaning of Paul's use of *kephalē* for both Christ in relation to the church, and man in relation to woman, in Ephesians 5:23. I will deal with the larger literary-theological context of Paul's argument, within which Ephesians 5:23 functions, in chapter six of this book. Here, though, I will narrowly focus on the analogy that Paul forges between Christ as *kephalē* of the church, his body, and man as *kephalē* of woman (Eph 5:23). Since Christ's relationship to the church, and his ac-

---

[49]Emphases mine; cited in G. W. Lampe, *A Patristic Greek Lexicon* (London: Oxford University Press, 1968), p. 749. Cf. Ambrosiaster (fourth century) on 1 Corinthians 11:3: "God is the *kephalē* of Christ because he begat him; Christ is the *kephalē* of the man because he created him; and the man is the *kephalē* of the woman because she was taken from his side," quoted in Mark J. Edwards, ed., *Galatians, Ephesians, Philippians,* Ancient Christian Commentary on Scripture, New Testament, vol. 8 (Downers Grove, Ill.: InterVarsity Press, 2005), p. 104.

[50]E.g., Gal 4:4; Phil 2:6-7; cf. Jn 1:1, 14; 3:16-17, 34; 5:37; 17:21-22.

[51]Numerous commentaries and other Pauline and New Testament studies over the past few decades support this understanding of the meaning of *kephalē* in Paul's usage here; e.g., C. K. Barrett, *The First Epistle to the Corinthians* (New York: Harper and Row, 1968); Hermann N. Ridderbos, *Paul: An Outline of His Theology* (Grand Rapids: Eerdmans, 1975), pp. 379-83; S. Scott Bartchy, "Power, Submission and Sexual Identity Among the Early Christians," in *Essays on New Testament Christianity,* ed. C. R. Wetzel (Cincinnati: Standard Publishing, 1978), pp. 50-80; F. F. Bruce, *The Epistles to the Colossians, to Philemon and to the Ephesians,* New International Commentary on the New Testament (Grand Rapids: Eerdmans, 1984), p. 384.

tion toward the church, is the point of comparison in the analogy (both in Eph 5:23 and in Eph 5:25), we must ask: In what sense is Christ as "head" of the church to be understood? What is the metaphorical significance of *kephalē* here?

Christ as head (kephalē) of the church. The first thing to be noted is that Paul uses the head-body image when speaking of Christ and the church. "He is the Savior" of this body (Eph 5:23). He is the one who, through his self-giving love and sacrifice (Eph 5:2, 25), brought the church into being, brought forth the "new creation" community of all those who are "in Christ" (2 Cor 5:17), the new humanity (Eph 2:15), the body of Christ (1 Cor 12:27). What is the nature, the meaning, of this head-body image? Is it that Christ exercises sovereignty over the church? that he exacts obedience? that he controls her? That would certainly be the case if the metaphorical meaning of Christ as head of the church carried the meaning "in charge of" or "authority over" the church. But if that were the case, I suspect that the condition of Christ's church, his body in the world, would be significantly other than what it is. No, the meaning of the head-body image must be decoded in keeping with its encoding by Paul in the context of the ordinary linguistic conventions of his time. We recall that in Greek physiology, the head was understood to be that part of the human body from which the rest of the body receives its life.[52] This is explicitly stated by Artemidorus: "the *kephalē* is the source of life and light for the whole body."[53] In the same way, Christ as *kephalē* is the Savior of the church, his body. He is the *kephalē*, the source and origin of the church's life and being.

This understanding is explicitly confirmed in the remaining three texts where Christ is designated as *kephalē* in relation to the church. In Ephesians 4, Paul speaks of the various gifts of Christ "for building up the body of Christ" (Eph 4:12) toward maturity in Christ (Eph 4:13-14). He brings this challenge to a climax by calling this body to "grow up in every way into him who is the *kephalē*, into Christ, *from* whom the whole body . . . promotes the body's growth in building itself up in love" (Eph 4:15-16). The prepositional phrase "from whom" clearly indicates that the body's "growth in love" is en-

---

[52]This concept was most surely derived from the observable fact that in capital punishment, when the head was severed, the body died; hence, the head is the source of the life of the body.

[53]See note 35 in this chapter. Cf. the Gospel of John, where Jesus is repeatedly presented as both the source of life and light (Jn 1:4; 8:12; 9:5; 10:10-11, 15; 14:6; 20:31).

ergized and enabled by the *kephalē*. Christ is not only the source or origin of the church's life in the beginning of its existence (Eph 5:23); he is also the source *(kephalē)* of its ongoing life.

In Colossians 1:18, Christ is called "the head of the body, the church." As in Ephesians 4:15-16 and Ephesians 5:23, the image of the organic unity of head and body is in the foreground. As Novatian of Rome (third century) argues, "the head matches its own limbs and the limbs their own head, a natural bond uniting both in complete harmony."[54] Within this organic relationship, the head is at the same time the source of the church's life.[55] That is affirmed in the expressions following the head-body image, in Colossians 1:18, where Christ, the *kephalē*, is also called the "beginning" *(archē)* and "the firstborn from the dead" *(prōtotokos)*. Two observations are in order here: (1) In the analysis of the linguistic evidence regarding the various metaphorical meanings of *kephalē*, we noted that *kephalē* (as source) was interchangeable with *archē* (beginning, origin). Christ stands at the beginning of the church's life. He is her originator, her *archē*. (2) The designation of Christ as "firstborn from the dead" is, of course, a reference to his resurrection (Rom 8:29; cf. 1 Cor 15:20). Paul is convinced that Christ's resurrection released the power that both birthed the church and sustains it (Rom 6:4; 8:11; Eph 2:4-6; cf. Jn 11:25-26). The life that energizes the church is his risen life, the life of the *head* that flows into the *body* and nourishes it (cf. Eph 5:29).

The final text where Christ is named as *kephalē* in relation to the church

---

[54]Cited in Gerald Bray, ed., *1-2 Corinthians*, Ancient Christian Commentary on Scripture, New Testament, vol. 7 (Downers Grove, Ill.: InterVarsity Press, 1999), p. 104. Cf. Theodore of Mopsuestia (ca. 350-428), who also wrote that Christ is called "head of the church" because the church received her "spiritual rebirth" from him. Theodoret of Cyr (ca. 393-466) understood Christ as "head of the church" and as "firstborn from the dead," in terms of Christ's humanity, through which he accomplished the church's salvation. Ambrosiaster (fourth century) spoke of the head-body (Christ-church) metaphor in terms of the life-giving union of the church with its Creator. See the commentaries by these early Christian leaders on Colossians 1:18 in Peter Gorday, ed., *Colossians, 1-2 Thessalonians, 1-2 Timothy, Titus, Philemon*, Ancient Christian Commentary on Scripture, New Testament, vol. 9 (Downers Grove, Ill.: InterVarsity Press, 2000), p. 17.

[55]Bruce, *Epistles to Colossians, Philemon and Ephesians*, p. 68, thinks that in addition to this meaning of *kephalē*, there is "in accordance with another figurative sense of 'head' the thought that he is the church's Lord." Cf. also Peter T. O'Brien, *Colossians, Philemon*, Word Biblical Commentary, vol. 44 (Waco, Tex.: Word Book Publishers, 1982), pp.48-51; O'Brien comments on Ephesians 4:18 that "headship over the body refers to Christ's control over his people as well as the dependence of all the members on him for life and power." I think both Bruce and O'Brien introduce here more than the text allows. While it is certainly true that Christ was believed to be the Lord *(kyrios)* of the church, the nature of that lordship is other than the exercise of "power over" or "control of"; it is rather the lordship of redeeming, transforming love.

is Colossians 2:19. It is the head, says Paul, *from whom* the whole body is nourished and held together and grows. In the final analysis, this growth "is *from* God." How? Because in Christ, "the fullness of God was pleased to dwell" (Col 1:19; cf. Col 2:9), and "you have come to fullness in him" (Col 2:10). The entire thrust of this text, intensified by the repeated use of the preposition *from*, leads unambiguously to the conclusion that when Paul speaks of Christ as the *kephalē* of the church he is evoking the image of Christ as the *source* of the church's life.

This understanding of Christ as head of the church must now inform our understanding of man as *head* in relation to woman (in Eph 5:23). For, Paul says, "man is the head of woman, just as Christ is the head of the church" (my translation). Christ as *kephalē* of the church is therefore the model for man as *kephalē* of the woman. As Christ (designated "head") is the source of the church's life, so man (designated "head") is the source of woman's life. In what sense is this to be understood?

Most English translations of Ephesians 5:23 render the Greek *anēr* (which refers to either "man" or "husband") and *gynē* (which refers to either "woman" or "wife") with "husband" and "wife." There is no question that the text, as a whole, deals with the husband-wife relationship.[56] But the fact that *anēr* is used without the definite article (as in 1 Cor 11:3), points to *anēr* as referring not to specific husbands, but to man in general. The reference to the Genesis 2 creation narrative in Ephesians 5:31 shows that Paul—as he reflects on the nature of the marriage relationship—has in mind the picture of the woman's being shaped out of the man as a basis for marriage (Gen 2:24, cited in Eph 5:31). As we saw above, this is exactly what Paul has in mind in 1 Corinthians 11, the only other Pauline text where man is designated as "head" in relationship to woman. There too he refers explicitly to the creation of woman *from* man (1 Cor 11:8). Thus it seems most probable that when Paul says that "man is the *kephalē* of woman," in analogy to Christ as "the *kephalē* of the church," he means that man is the source out of whom woman was formed (as per Gen 2:21-23). The church father Ambrosiaster (fourth century) recognized this meaning of the text when he commented: "Here is Paul's analogy: As the church takes its beginning from Christ . . . so too does the woman take hers from man."[57] There is no question that he read *kephalē* in the sense of "source"

---

[56]See also our discussion of this text in its larger context in chapter 6.
[57]Cited in Edwards, *Galatians, Ephesians, Philippians*, p. 195. While Ambrosiaster understood

or "origin," rather than "chief" or "authority-over."

So far, I have described four relationships that are defined by the word *head* in the Pauline writings: God-Christ, Christ-man, Christ-church and man-woman. From this study, it is apparent that the most appropriate metaphorical meaning of *head* in these relationships is that of "source" or "origin." There is a fifth relationship that is defined by the use of the term *kephalē*, namely the relationship between Christ and the powers (in Eph 1:22; Col 2:10). In what sense is Christ as "head" to be understood in these relationships?

Christ as head (kephalē) of the powers. In Colossians, the stage is set by the affirmation that in (or by) Christ—who is "the image of the invisible God" and "the firstborn of all creation" (Col 1:15)—"all things in heaven and on earth were created . . . whether thrones or dominions or rulers or powers—all things have been created through him and for him" (Col 1:16). Christ is the source of their existence. These affirmations about Christ's cosmic preeminence (he is "before all things" and "in him all the fullness of God was pleased to dwell"—Col 1:17, 19) are determinative for our reading of Colossians 2:9-10. There we read that Christ—in whom "the whole fullness of deity dwells bodily" (Col 2:9)—is "the head of every ruler and authority" (Col 2:10). In light of, and in keeping with, Colossians 1:16 (where the powers are said to be the result of Christ's creative work), the metaphorical meaning of Christ as *kephalē* (in relation to the powers—Col 2:10) is surely, again, that Christ is the source of their being.[58] That understanding—which stands in opposition to the prevailing notion that Christ is "head" over the powers in the sense of exercising authority over them[59]—is confirmed, I believe, by Paul's affirmations a few verses later about what happened at the cross. In the cross, Paul argues (Col 2:14-15), Christ "disarmed the rulers and authorities . . . triumphing over them in it." Through his act of self-giving, suffering love, the powers have been emptied[60] of their power. His relationship to the pow-

---

Ephesians 5:23 to refer to the Genesis account of the creation of woman from man, he went on to contend that "the woman is subject to man because she takes her beginning from him." This interpretive tradition became, of course, pervasive in the church throughout the centuries. Its most explicit formulation, in the translational tradition, is found in Today's English Version (TEV 1966), which renders 1 Corinthians 11:3 with "the husband is supreme over his wife," and Ephesians 5:23 with "a husband has authority over his wife."

[58]See Bruce, *Epistles to Colossians, Philemon and Ephesians*, p. 102.

[59]Bruce, in ibid., goes on to say that, because Christ is their source, he is "therefore also their ruler" (see n. 57).

[60]Cf. Jn 12:31; 14:30; 16:11, where Christ on the cross (Jesus' being "lifted up," Jn 3:14; 12:32) defeats "the ruler of this world."

ers is not defined by the exercise of hierarchical power over them. He is the source of their being. But his triumph over their rebellion and opposition to God's redemptive purpose is "not by might, nor by power" (Zech 4:6) but by means of self-giving love.

It is possible that, in addition to the metaphorical meaning of *head* as "source," Christ as head of "every ruler and authority" carries another metaphorical meaning. In studying the range of metaphorical uses of *kephalē* in Greek literature, it has been shown that at times the idea of "exalted position" is conveyed. That is certainly a possible meaning in our text. A major theme of Colossians is that Christ stands above all real and perceived powers in the universe. Therefore, and because his followers have been "raised with Christ" (Col 3:1) and "have come to fullness in him" (Col 2:10), there is no need to either live in fear of them or to engage in religious practices that appease them (Col 2:16-23). Christ is the head, the exalted One, in whom "we live and move and have our being" (Acts 17:28).

That meaning of *kephalē*—as carrying the metaphorical significance of "exalted position"—seems also to be present in our final text (Eph 1:20-22). Through God's power at work in Christ's resurrection from the dead, he has been exalted to the highest place (Eph 1:20; cf. Phil 2:9), "far above all rule and authority and power and dominion, and above every name that is named (Eph 1:21; cf. Phil 2:9).[61] In this exalted position, which Paul describes with the metaphor of supremacy ("all things under his feet," cf. Ps 8:6), he is "the *kephalē* over all things for the church, which is his body" (Eph 1:22-23). Exalted rank or position—with regard to the powers—is clearly one of the possible meanings of the metaphor here. At the same time, the affirmation that Christ is *kephalē* "for the church" can be understood in the sense of origin. "Christ is divinely appointed as source of the church's life."[62]

Therefore, on the basis of both external evidence (usage in Greek literature and the Greek translation of the Old Testament) and internal evidence (exegetical study of the relevant texts), we conclude that Paul did not use the word *head* in the sense of "authority over" (chief, ruler, boss, master).

---

[61]The various terms Paul uses here, all of which convey the idea of hierarchical authority, are precisely the common terms used by the Septuagint translators in their rendering of the Hebrew *rō'š* ("head") when it is used as a designation of persons in positions of authority.

[62]Bruce, *Epistles to Colossians, Philemon and Ephesians*, p. 274.

PAUL'S UNDERSTANDING OF "SUBMISSION"

The words studied thus far are all related, directly or indirectly, to the question of how we are to understand the man-woman (and husband-wife) relationship. There is one final word related to this matter, which is perhaps the strongest word in support of a hierarchical understanding. That word is the Greek word *hypotassō*. It is a compound verb, consisting of the preposition *hypo* and the verb *tassō*. The preposition *hypo* means "under" or "below." The verb *tassō* means "to place or station a person or thing," "to appoint to or establish an office."[63] As a compound verb, it is usually translated "to submit to," or "to be subject to," or "to accept the authority of" someone or some institution or power. The word appears about thirty times in the New Testament, and it is used five times in specific texts where the relationship between men-women and husbands-wives is being addressed in some way (Eph 5:22-24; Col 3:18; 1 Tim 2:11; Tit 2:5; 1 Pet 3:1-5).[64]

As with other words, *hypotassō* has a range of nuances and meanings, depending on its use in particular contexts. This is reflected in the variety of ways it is rendered in English translations, illustrated in the following examples. In Luke 2:51 we are told that the boy Jesus returned from Jerusalem to Nazareth with his parents, "and was *obedient* to them." Struggling with the question of Israel's future in relation to God's purposes, Paul says that "they have not *submitted* to God's righteousness" (Rom 10:3). Addressing Christians in Rome, Paul calls on them to "*be subject* to the governing authorities" (Rom 13:1, 5). In 1 Corinthians 16:15-16, Paul appeals to the Christians in Corinth to honor and give special recognition to Stephanas and his household for their faithful service among them, and exhorts them "to *put yourselves at the service* of such people." In 1 Peter 2:18, slaves are instructed "*to accept the authority* of your masters."[65]

Regardless of the variety of English words used by translators, most of the

---

[63]W. Bauer, W. F. Arndt and F. W. Gingrich, *A Greek-English Lexicon of the New Testament and Other Early Christian Literature* (Chicago: University of Chicago Press, 1957).

[64]First Corinthians 14:34 has not been included in this list of texts because of the serious questions about the authenticity (i.e., the Pauline authorship) of 1 Corinthians 14:34-35, on the basis of both external (textual transmission) and internal (exegetical and contextual) evidence. Textual scholar Gordon Fee, in an exhaustive study (in *First Epistle to the Corinthians*, pp. 699-708) concludes that "the case against these verses is so strong, and finding a viable solution to their meaning so difficult, that it seems best to view them as an interpolation [by an early copyist]" (p. 705; cf. p. 708).

[65]The emphasized words or expressions in this paragraph are all NRSV renderings of the Greek word *hypotassō*.

above examples—representing other occurrences of the word in the New
Testament—convey the idea, at least on the surface, of submission to another
or others in some form of obedience. The one exception (out of the examples
given) is the meaning indicated by the NRSV rendering of *hypotassō* as "put
yourselves at the service of," in 1 Corinthians 16:16.[66] The immediate context
seems to require such a meaning. Paul stated in 1 Corinthians 16:15 that
Stephanas and members of his household placed themselves as servants at the
disposal of the fellowship from the very beginning. Therefore, Paul urged the
believers to honor Stephanas's household by putting themselves at their service.[67] The more literal sense of the compound verb *hypotassō*—"to place
[oneself] under"—seems most fitting in this context.[68]

On first appearance, the use of *hypotassō* in Romans 10:3 seems to convey
the sense of obedience: "They have not submitted to God's righteousness."
On further reflection, however, that supposed meaning becomes problematic. For in Paul, "God's righteousness" is a special term for God's saving,
justifying work in Christ (Rom 1:16—3:26). It designates the activity of God
that restores the severed divine-human relationship. God's righteousness is
God's relation-restoring, steadfast love and faithfulness, reaching toward a
world in revolt by means of the event of Christ.[69] How is "submission" to this
redemptive event to be understood? Paul is insistent everywhere that the human response to the work of God's grace in Christ is by means of faith (Rom

---

[66]Peterson's paraphrase in *The Message* renders 1 Corinthians 16:16 with, "I want you to honor and
look up to people like that." The NIV translates it with "submit to such as these," and CEV with
"obey." Both NIV and CEV assume that Stephanas and members of his household were established
elders or people in various positions of official authority. That assumption, however, is open to
serious doubt on two counts: (1) Paul urging the believers in Corinth to submit (in the sense of
"obey") would involve such submission to a rather large number of "authority figures" in Corinth,
not just "Stephanas and his family" (1 Cor 16:15 CEV) but to "leaders like them and . . . for all others who work hard with you" (1 Cor 16:16 CEV). It is virtually impossible to postulate such a large
group of authority figures in the fledgling fellowship in Corinth. (2) The Pauline congregations,
at this early stage of their existence (early A.D. 50s), were not yet very structured in terms of ecclesiastical authority, but largely charismatic and rather fluid, as is clear from 1 Corinthians 12—14
(and especially 1 Corinthians 14:26-33).

[67]There is a play on words between 1 Corinthians 16:15 and 16. Paul uses the past tense *(etaxan)* of
the verb *tassō* (to place, to set, to appoint) in 1 Corinthians 16:15 and *hypotassō* in 1 Corinthians
16:16.

[68]Fee, *First Epistle to the Corinthians*, p. 830, contends that the meaning of *hypotassō* here is "submission in the sense of voluntary yielding in love," quoting W. Bauer, W. F. Arndt and F. W. Gingrich, *A Greek-English Lexicon of the New Testament and Other Early Christian Literature* (Chicago:
University of Chicago Press, 1957), p. 855.

[69]See the discussion of Isaiah 61:10 in chapter six of this book, and the literature cited there for
Paul's concept of "the righteousness of God."

1:16-17; 3:21-26; 4:1—5:1; 10:4; Gal 3:2, 23-26; Eph 2:8). So to "submit to God's righteousness" is not a matter of obedience or of yielding to authority, but rather a "giving oneself over to" God's grace in faith.[70]

A third text (1 Pet 2:13-24) conveys another nuanced meaning of submission. The author calls on his readers to "accept the authority" of emperors and governors (1 Pet 1:13) and instructs servants to "accept the authority of your masters with all deference," even when suffering unjustly (1 Pet 2:18-20). The basis for that challenge is the unjust suffering of Christ, who left them an example to follow (1 Pet 2:21). The references to submission "for the Lord's sake," and in imitation of Christ's self-giving, show that the submission in view here is not to be understood as simple obedience to externally imposed or expected authority but a giving of oneself freely for a greater purpose. "As servants of Christ," says Peter, "live as free people" (1 Pet 2:16).[71]

It is clear from the above survey that, while the Greek word *hypotassō* (to be subject to, to submit) usually carries the sense of obedience to authority, it also has an expanded range of meanings, and the specific meaning of the term must ultimately be discerned from the larger context in which it is used. Noted above are several texts in which this word is used in the context of the woman-man and wife-husband relationship. I will deal with 1 Timothy 2:11, Titus 2:5 and 1 Peter 3:1—and their instructions about submission—in chapter seven, since the proper understanding of these texts is dependent to a significant degree on discerning the historical-cultural situations to which they are addressed. For the present, we focus our attention on Ephesians 5:21-24.[72]

The word *hypotassō* appears two times in the Greek text, while in most English translations the equivalent ("be subject" in the NRSV, or "submit" in the NIV) appears three or four times. A somewhat literal rendering of the Greek text will show the reasons for these differences:

---

[70]Cf. James D. G. Dunn, *Roman 9—16*, Word Biblical Commentary, vol. 38B (Dallas: Word Books, 1988), p. 588, who defines *submission* here as "complete dependence . . . on grace for which God looks."

[71]J. Ramsey Michaels, *1 Peter,* Word Biblical Commentary, vol. 49 (Dallas: Word Books, 1988), pp. 137-38, translates 1 Peter 2:18 with "you servants must, with deep reverence [toward God] defer to your masters." Cf. Fee, *First Epistle to the Corinthians*, p. 890 n. 29, who suggests that 1 Peter 2:18 means "to submit to undeserved brutality in the sense of not fighting back, as over against submission = obedience."

[72]Col 3:18-19 is, in essence, an abridged form of Paul's extended discussion in Ephesians 5:21-33. Our understanding of the nature of the wife's submission to her husband (in Eph 5) will significantly inform, if not determine, the interpretation of Colossians 3:18-19.

[21]*Submit* to one another in awe of Christ. [22]Wives *** to your husbands as to the Lord. . . . [24]For as the church *submits* to Christ, so also wives *** to their husbands in everything. (My translation)

This literal translation shows that the construction of Ephesians 5:22 has no verb (indicated by three asterisks). That means that the reader has to supply the verb from the participial phrase in Ephesians 5:21 ("submit to one another"). A further consequence of this connection between Ephesians 5:21 and 22 is that the nature of the mutual submission called for in verse 21 is determinative for a proper understanding of the nature of wives' submission to their husbands in verse 22. The situation is similar in the two lines of text in Ephesians 5:24. Paul drew a parallel between the relationship of the church to Christ and that of wives to husbands. The verb *submit* in the first line has to be "imported" into the second line (where the asterisks are). Thus the nature of the church's relationship to Christ is determinative for the nature of the wife-husband relationship. Given these connections, how are we to understand the meaning (or nature) of the submission of wives to husbands, and of the church to Christ? Several observations can be made in response to this question:

1. The "mutual submission" enjoined on the believers (in Eph 5:21) is unique in the known literature of the New Testament world. It is a radical, if not revolutionary, challenge spoken into a culture that prized hierarchical power relationships. One-sided submission—characterized by the exercise of power and authority by one party and obedience by the other—was understood to preserve social cohesion and order. This is similar to the expression that was often heard among those who wanted to preserve the status quo during the civil rights struggle: if people "knew their place" and "stayed in their place," we would not have such social turmoil and dislocation. But when people are *locked* in place by hierarchically defined power relationships, freedom for growth toward human wholeness and fulfillment is severely restricted, if not impossible. Mutual submission challenges the exercise of hierarchical power and the structures that promote it.

2. Mutual submission is to be undertaken not on the basis of some lofty ethical principle but "in awe of Christ" (my translation; or "out of reverence for," NRSV). The significance of that expression emerges from attention to its context. Paul introduces this section of his letter with these words: "Be

imitators of God, as beloved children, and live in love, as Christ loved us and gave himself up for us, a fragrant offering and sacrifice to God" (Eph 5:1-2). What "imitation of God" and living in Christ-like, self-giving love specifically looks like in human relationships is Paul's concern in Ephesians 5—6, including instructions to husbands and wives. Thus mutual submission is to be in awe of Christ's self-giving love.

3. In Ephesians 5:22, the relation of wives to their husbands is further qualified by the phrase "as you are to the Lord." Its function here is surely related to the qualifier "in awe of Christ" (in the previous verse), and conveys the idea that the wife's relation with (submission to) her husband is in response to, and imitation of, Christ's example.

4. As noted earlier in this chapter in the discussion of the meaning of Christ as "head" of the church, that metaphor has nothing to do with hierarchical power structure but rather conveys the image of Christ as the source of the church's origin and continuing existence. This concept in Ephesians 5:23 provides the clue for the nature of the church's "submission" to Christ in Ephesians 5:24. Christ and the church are not related in a structure of authority and obedience, of ruler and subject. Rather, the church "submits itself to Christ" (NIV) in the sense of giving itself over to Christ in awe of and response to his self-giving, redemptive, life-giving and life-sustaining love. And that is, again, the model for the relation between wife and husband. The nature of her submission to her husband is not defined by the cultural norm of servant-master, but by the new way of Christ. She is challenged to give herself over to her husband totally ("in everything") in imitation of Christ. What prevents this self-giving of the one to the other from becoming another form of an over-under power relationship is mutual submission. Paul addresses the husband's side of mutual submission in Ephesians 5:25-33.[73]

All of the words discussed so far in this chapter—which have been shown not to warrant the understandings and meanings assigned to them in much of the interpretive tradition—have been used in the tradition as important building blocks in the construction of the so-called biblical view of the man-woman

---

[73]We will seek to understand the entire text of Ephesians 5:21-33—which I have dissected somewhat in terms of my attention to the specific terms *head* and *submission*—on the basis of the larger literary and theological context, in chapter six.

relationship, namely a patriarchal, hierarchical understanding of that relationship. Of particular significance in this construction of the hierarchical view has been the Pauline use of the word *head* (in the sense of authority over) for the man-woman (husband-wife) relationship. And the hierarchical understanding of that relationship has been undergirded by the assumed theological paradigm for that man-woman relationship, which is provided by the metaphors of God as "head" of Christ, and Christ as "head" of the powers, "head" of the church, and "head" of man—also understood as authority-over relationships. Each of these links in the chain—including the links provided for this chain by the traditional understandings of the words in the Genesis creation accounts ("helper," "fit for," "pain/toil," "adam") and the Pauline concept of *submission*—is terribly weak, and thus the entire chain (i.e., the hierarchical understanding of the man-woman relationship) is a fragile, if not seriously flawed, creation. Or to change the metaphor, the entire "house" of the traditionalist interpretation of the biblical material on the man-woman relationship[74] turns out to be a rather rickety "house of cards" where the removal of just one card can lead to the collapse of the whole house.

The traditional Christian view regarding women has thus been nurtured for centuries by understandings and interpretations of words that are, at best, problematic, and may therefore be decidedly unbiblical, the consequence of the abuse of words. This means that this Christian interpretive tradition has significantly contributed to the long and tragic history of women's inferior status, of their restricted roles in home, church and society, and of their frequent subjugation and abuse in hierarchical marriage relationships.

Paul's Use of the Term *Flesh*

One of the topics in the discussion of the abuse of biblical balance in chapter four was the construction of a hierarchy of sins. Certain sins are singled out for special attention and placed at the top of the hierarchy, while others are characterized as less important. I noted that so-called sins of the flesh (such as sexual promiscuity, homosexual practice and adultery) are generally viewed as more serious transgressions within the conservative traditions of Christian faith, while sins of attitude (such as prejudice and self-righteousness) and broader social sins (such as injustice and structural, economic inequities) are

---

[74]Other aspects of this biblical material have been considered in chapter three, "The Abuse of Selectivity." Others will be discussed in chapters six and seven.

generally considered more serious in liberal Christian traditions. The study showed that this hierarchical categorization of sin is essentially a violation of biblical balance. I also noted that, in conservative expressions of this imbalance, one of the reasons for the focus on sins of the flesh has been the pervasive influence of the Greek philosophy of dualism on Christian thought and belief. In this view, human nature consists of a lower nature (the physical dimension: body, flesh) and a higher nature (the spiritual dimension: soul, spirit, mind). In early Greek thought, the lower nature was understood as a burden or hindrance to the higher aspirations of the soul. In later Hellenistic thought (in the New Testament period) it was viewed even more negatively, as evil in itself. On the basis of this view of human nature, it is easy to see why "the flesh," the physical dimension of human life, became identified specifically with human sinfulness.

This understanding of human nature stands in tension with a central biblical view, grounded in creation and affirmed in the biblical doctrine of the resurrection of the body. That view is that the whole person, including the physical dimension, is defined as "good" (Gen 1:31), and that the whole person, in its alienation from God and in its bondage to sin, is the object of God's redemptive work in Christ. It is not the soul (or spirit)—which has been conceived as a separable part or faculty of the individual, the locus of personhood—that is destined for salvation. That is the Greek view: the release of the soul from the prison, the tomb *(sēma)* of the body *(sōma)*.[75] In the biblical view, personhood or individuality is located in the inseparable interface between the material and spiritual dimensions. It is within this overarching biblical perspective that Paul's use of the term *flesh* must be understood.

We are concerned here with a particular use of the term *flesh*. Therefore, a comprehensive study of this subject is beyond the scope of this work.[76] However, a brief survey of the broad range of Paul's use of the word *flesh* is neces-

---

[75]W. D. Stacey, *The Pauline View of Man in Relation to Its Judaic and Hellenistic Background* (London: Macmillan, 1956), provides a concise review of Greek views of human nature.

[76]For comprehensive analyses of the New Testament's view of human nature, and especially Paul's—including not only the term *flesh*, but also *body, spirit, soul, mind*—see ibid.; Robert Jewett's *Paul's Anthropological Terms* (Leiden: E. J. Brill, 1971); W. G. Kümmel, *Man in the New Testament* (London: Epworth, 1963); Robert Gundry, *Sōma in Biblical Theology with Emphasis on Pauline Anthropology* (Cambridge: Cambridge University Press, 1976); C. F. D. Moule, "Paul and Dualism: The Pauline Conception of Resurrection," in *Essays in New Testament Interpretation,* ed. C. F. D. Moule (Cambridge: Cambridge University Press, 1982). On "flesh and spirit," see F. F. Bruce, *Apostle of the Heart Set Free* (Grand Rapids: Eerdmans, 1977), pp. 203-11.

sary in order to appreciate the distinctive use of the term in expressions such as "according to the flesh" or "in the flesh."

1. *The physical body.* The most normal use of "flesh" (Greek *sarx*) is in reference to the tissues of the body. Jesus had a body of flesh (Col 1:22; cf. Jn 1:14—"the Word became flesh"). It is in the flesh that pain is experienced (2 Cor 12:7).

2. *The entire body.* By extension, *flesh* is sometimes used as a synonym for the entire body. Paul's absence from his churches can be "in [the] body" (*sōma*, 1 Cor 5:3) or "in the flesh" (my translation from the Greek, *sarx*, literally means "flesh" in Col 2:5). The life of Jesus may be expressed "in our bodies" (2 Cor 4:10) or "in our mortal flesh" (2 Cor 4:11).

3. *Physical origins.* Another use of the word *flesh* is in reference to human life in general and especially to our physical origins. Paul speaks of the Jewish people as "my kindred according to the flesh" (Rom 9:3). Natural birth results in "children of the flesh" (Rom 9:8; cf. Jn 3:6). Christ is connected to David by means of fleshly descent (Rom 1:3).

4. *Human perspectives.* A fourth usage is in reference to human ways of thinking or to limited human understanding. So Paul speaks of having had "confidence in the flesh" (Phil 3:4-6), that is, confidence in his Jewish heritage and ability to keep the law. Paul says that Jesus should not be regarded "according to the flesh" (that is, "from a human point of view," 2 Cor 5:16 NRSV). In 2 Corinthians 10:2-4 (NASB), *flesh* refers to merely human standards and perspectives (cf. also Jn 8:15; 1 Cor 1:26; 2 Cor 1:12 NASB).

5. *Human limitations.* Sometimes Paul uses *flesh* to designate our creatureliness, finitude, mortality. He addresses the Romans in a certain way because of "the weakness of your flesh" (Rom 6:19 NASB). It is "in my flesh" (i.e., in concrete, earthly life) where Paul lives out his servant ministry (Col 1:24; cf. Phil 1:22).

6. *The whole person.* Finally, *flesh* at times stands for the entire self, the whole person. By observing the law, "no flesh [no human being] will be justified" (Gal 2:16 NASB). Those who belong to Christ, says Paul, "have crucified the flesh with its passions and desires" (Gal 5:24). *Flesh* designates here the whole person, as shown in Galatians 2:19, where he says "I have been crucified with Christ" (cf. Rom 6:6).

7. *The "ethical" use of the word* flesh. Beside these various uses and meanings of the term *flesh* stands a very unique use of the term by Paul. This involves its use in connection with life under the law, influenced and characterized by legalistic perspectives and observances. In Galatians 3:3 Paul speaks of return to Torah obedience (and especially the practice of circumcision) as "ending with the flesh." Relationship with God on the basis of certain religious practices (Col 2:16-17) comes from "a fleshly mind" (Col 2:18 NASB). Life lived on the basis of the law is "living in the flesh" (Rom 7:5). In these texts, *flesh* designates a particular way of living, a particular way of being in relationship to God and to others. Some have referred to this use of the term *flesh* as the "ethical" use. Here, *flesh* has nothing to do with anything like our physical nature but rather with an orientation of life.[77]

This ethical use of the term is especially prominent in Romans and is particularly used in contrast to an orientation of life empowered by the Spirit. A stark contrast is drawn between walking (i.e., living) "according to the flesh" and "according to the Spirit" (Rom 8:4-5). This contrast is followed by a parallel contrast, which clearly speaks of two opposing orientations: setting the mind "on the flesh" or setting the mind "on the Spirit" (Rom 8:5-6). These contrasts are followed by a third set, that between being either "in the flesh" or "in the Spirit" (Rom 8:8-9). That Paul is not using *flesh* in these contrasts to designate our physical nature is clear from the fourth set of contrasting affirmations in Romans 8:8-9. The statement, "those who are in the flesh cannot please God" is paired with "but you are not in the flesh." Obviously, they had their existence "in the flesh"; they were "fleshly creatures." But because "the Spirit of God" dwelt in them (Rom 8:9), the totality of their life, including the physical, was now determined by a new reality, namely the life of the resurrected Lord, mediated by the Spirit (Rom 8:11).[78] That is what Paul means in Galatians 2:20 when he confesses that "The life I now live in the flesh I live by faith in the Son of God." Here, "in the flesh" refers to the body, while in Romans 8:8-9, "in the flesh" refers to life outside Christ, life turned away from God, a life that is

---

[77]J. Murphy-O'Connor, *1 Corinthians,* The New Testament Message (Wilmington, Del.: Michael Glazier, 1979), p. 42: " 'Flesh' means the whole person as oriented away from God."

[78]In Romans 8:9-11, Paul uses several phrases interchangeably: life "in the Spirit"; life indwelt by "the Spirit of God"; belonging to "the Spirit of Christ"; "Christ is in you"; the life-giving "Spirit of him who raised Jesus from the dead."

out of synch with God's purposes and turned away from others. This latter dimension of life lived "in the flesh" (in the ethical sense) is expressed powerfully in Galatians 5:13-15. Paul says, "Do not use your freedom as an opportunity *for the flesh*" (NASB, rendered literally from the Greek), and then defines that way of the flesh as living and devouring one another, rather than the way of the Spirit (Gal 5:16), which is expressed when, "through love," they become "slaves to one another" (Gal 5:13).

Beside a whole variety of uses of the term *flesh*, Paul's most distinctive contribution is the use of the term in an ethical sense. In that use, it refers neither to a person's physical nature, nor to a lower element in human nature,[79] but it refers to persons in their psychosomatic-spiritual totality, in their condition of opposition to God, and in the embodiment of that opposition in ways of living and thinking that are distortive and destructive.

This analysis of Paul's use of the word *flesh* confirms the finding in chapter four that a dualistic understanding of human nature—where a lower nature is the source of the weightiest "sins of the flesh"—is an erroneous reading of these texts. The fact that sins of the flesh or works of the flesh include sins that originate in the heart and mind[80]—such as enmity, envy, anger, jealousy, bitterness and idolatry (e.g., Gal 5:19-21)—ought to caution us against two dangerous habits: one, the tendency to single out the more obvious or physical sins, and at the same time to minimize the sins that are more subtle, which can hide behind the façade of rectitude; and two, the concomitant tendency toward judgmentalism and self-righteousness. Much of our Christian presence and proclamation is seriously undermined in the public square by these dangerous habits, which are encouraged and abetted by the abusive decoding of biblical terms.

AVOIDING THE ABUSE OF WORDS

By means of studying several important terms related to the biblical understanding of the man-woman relationship and by studying Paul's use of the term *flesh*, we can see that how we understand the literal and figurative mean-

---

[79]See G. E. Ladd's discussion in *A Theology of the New Testament*, rev. ed. (Grand Rapids: Eerdmans, 1993), pp. 511-13.

[80]In biblical anthropology, the heart was considered the core of the person, out of which arise all thoughts and desires and decisions (see e.g., Ps 119:2; Is 38:3; Mt 5:8, 28; 15:19). In Greek thought, it is the mind that is seen to direct the life of the person. Therefore, it is significant that, in Romans 12:2, Paul focuses on the mind as that part of the person that is in need of transformation.

ings of these terms can have a huge impact on our perception of the biblical view of the man-woman relationship and on the nature of Christian life. When particular words are "heard" in ways that are not in keeping with the original encoding by the author in the historical/cultural context of his time, our hearing and acting in our Christian life and relationships can be seriously, negatively affected.

While our study of this matter is limited to a few significant terms, the possibility of either correct understanding or misunderstanding, of trustworthy reading or abusive reading, is present in the interpretation of all biblical texts, especially where significant biblical words have a range of metaphorical meanings. How do we avoid this form of Scripture abuse? Several guiding principles and resources are suggested here.

1. Remember that the biblical revelation was given within the confines of human language. Approach the study of any biblical text, and of the significant words in that text, with the acknowledgment that the biblical revelation was given to us within the confines of human language. Such an acknowledgment provides for an appropriate attitude and approach toward the study of Scripture that is in keeping with its actual, historical character, namely the work of numerous authors across the span of more than a millennium. The Word of God comes to us in Scripture within the earthen vessel of human languages—not like the words of the Qur'an, believed to be the recitations of divine instructions recorded by Muhammad, nor like the content of the Book of Mormon, believed to have been inscribed by an archangel on divinely given gold tablets. This overarching perspective must provide the parameters within which the hearing of biblical words takes place.

2. Recognize that "hearing" the biblical revelation includes the possibility of understanding and misunderstanding. The biblical revelation, as God's Word to us, participates in the dynamic reality of human communication and always involves the possibility of both understanding and misunderstanding. When we take this reality seriously, we are confronted by the fact that communication—both within a particular language and (especially) across languages via translation—is centrally characterized by the encoding and the decoding of meanings. This truth about language and communication should challenge us to exercise due caution against too easily equating the meaning of biblical words (in the original Hebrew, Aramaic and Greek) with "equivalent" words in our own languages.

3. Be attentive to the range of meanings particular words have in the original and translated languages. In our study of several words, especially the use of the word *head* to designate various persons in relationship to one another, I explained the fact that various figurative meanings of the same word were present in the biblical languages, within a variety of historical and cultural contexts. An understanding of these contexts, and the literary conventions of the people within them, must inform our discerning of the meaning of biblical words. Particularly important in this regard is the recognition that translators—especially those who function with the "formal equivalency" translation theory—often translate words from one language to another in a literal way. While perfectly acceptable and accurate on the level of "formal equivalency," such renderings frequently do not convey the specific metaphorical meaning present in the original language, nor the equivalent metaphorical meaning of the word in the language of the translator.

4. We must take seriously the contexts in which words are created and used. Since words—as basic carriers of meaning—are embedded in the historical and cultural reality of a people, and give expression to the experiences and understandings of that people, the literary/theological and historical/cultural contexts out of which, and within which, words are used must be carefully considered. I will give particular attention to those contexts for the interpretation of biblical texts, and the discernment of the meanings of words, in chapters six and seven. As illustrated through the study of words like *flesh, pain, submission* and *head,* their "plain meaning" cannot simply be read off the page. This is especially so for us as readers of these texts, since we bring our own understanding of the various nuances and meanings of these words *in our language* to the reading and hearing of biblical words *in the original language.* (Helpful for this undertaking are cultural and historical background studies, such as the *IVP Bible Background Commentary: Old Testament* and *IVP Bible Background Commentary: New Testament,* as well as the *Dictionary of New Testament Background* and the *Dictionary of Biblical Imagery* [all InterVarsity Press].)

5. Linguistic tools and resources are critically important to avoid the abuse of words. For all interpreters of Scripture, whether they are able to work in the biblical languages or not, a wealth of resources is available for the student of Scripture to assist in this important area of biblical interpretation. Important linguistic resources are such reference tools as concordances for the major

English versions (NIV, NASB, NRSV), Bible dictionaries, and Hebrew-English and Greek-English lexicons and concordances.

A survey of the online catalogs of the major Christian publishing houses (such as InterVarsity Press, Eerdmans, Zondervan, Thomas Nelson, Baker, Abingdon and Westminster John Knox) in their biblical studies and biblical references sections reveals dozens of excellent, up-to-date resources for determining the appropriate meanings of words within various biblical texts and by the various biblical authors. (A good place to begin is with the extensive InterVarsity Press "black" [so named for their black covers] dictionary series.) At the same time, the wealth of computer software resources in this area of biblical studies is almost inexhaustible (e.g., the Logos Bible Software or *The Essential IVP Reference Collection* in Macintosh and Windows 3.0).

In addition to these language tools and resources, commentaries on the various books of the Bible (whether working directly from the Hebrew and Greek texts or from modern English translations, such as the NIV or NRSV) are invaluable. Though commentators seek generally to be as objective in their exegetical and hermeneutical work as possible, it is almost inevitable that their commentaries reflect their own ecclesial and/or theological orientation and perspectives. For that reason, it is helpful to consult a variety of commentaries from varying perspectives. Also important, especially for students of the Bible who cannot work in the original biblical languages, is the use of several English translations. How these translations render particular words can sometimes alert the reader to the possibility that the original word in the Hebrew or Greek or Aramaic texts has a range of meanings. Such a discovery can then lead to a study of that word, using the linguistic resources mentioned above.

6

THE ABUSE OF CONTEXT

LITERARY AND THEOLOGICAL

It has been said that in real estate transactions the three top criteria for determining the value of a particular property are (1) location, (2) location and (3) location. Similarly, it may be said that in biblical interpretation the three most important criteria for hearing the biblical text accurately and applying it appropriately are (1) context, (2) context and (3) context. The point here is that faithful and trustworthy interpretation of biblical texts must take seriously the nature of the written Word of God—as it has been given to us within its various contexts.

Because the nature of Scripture is incarnational, which includes such factors as its historical and situational particularity and its cultural sensitivity, as well as the very specific instrument of language and literary structures in and through which the Word of God addresses us. Biblical verses, extended passages, instructions, theological affirmations and so on come to us within particular documents, such as law books, historical records, collections of prophetic utterances, Gospels and epistles. These literary productions have particular life settings: they were written in specific historical situations, to people in a variety of cultural settings, by authors who spoke from their particular understandings and with faith convictions that were shaped by their personal and communal encounter with God's self-disclosure in prophetic word and redemptive deed. All this is what we mean by *context*.

The task of "rightly explaining the word of truth" (2 Tim 2:15) calls for careful attention to the various contexts in which that word of truth was first spoken (or written). In this chapter, we will address the issue of the abuse of *literary* context and *theological* context. By literary context, I refer to the way particular verses or passages are related to the immediate textual materials that surround them, the flow of the larger argument or presentation in which they are located (the chapter or book as a whole), and the larger literary context of a collection of documents (such as the Pauline epistles, the Gospels, Old and New Testaments). Included under the rubric of literary context are also such things as the literary structure or form of a passage, its syntax and its grammatical connection to surrounding material.

By theological context, I refer to the connections or affinities between the theological affirmations of a particular verse or passage, the theological themes in the literary material immediately surrounding it, and the overarching theological concepts in broader literary contexts. For example: How is a particular idea in a Pauline verse or passage to be understood in light of the larger context of Paul's major theological convictions? Or how do we deal with the tension between, on the one hand, a significant amount of Old Testament material in which God is understood as the warrior God who leads Israel into battle to crush her adversaries, and on the other hand, the God revealed in Christ as "the Prince of Peace" (Is 9:6; cf. Lk 2:14), who calls us to love our enemies (Mt 5:44) and who loves and died for his enemies (Rom 5:10)?[1]

From these brief definitions of how I'll use the categories of literary and theological context within this chapter, it is clear that they are often closely interconnected. At times, therefore, I will have to address both contexts when dealing with a particular text. At other times, one or the other will be the primary, or exclusive, focus. I will begin with two striking contempo-

---

[1] I am reminded of the profound statement by the German pastor Martin Niemoeller, a member of the Confessing Church movement, which opposed Hitler: "I have learned that God is not the enemy of my enemies. God is not even the enemy of God's own enemies." That insight reflects the Pauline statement in Romans 5:10: "For while we were enemies, we were reconciled to God."

rary examples of "context abuse." Those will be followed by a selection of numerous examples (out of dozens that could be given) that illustrate how texts are often abusively taken out of their contexts to support all kinds of beliefs or practices, but that do not have serious negative consequences. Then, in the second part of the chapter, I will explore context abuses that have substantial consequences for the viability and integrity of Christian witness and presence.

TWO CONTEMPORARY EXAMPLES OF CONTEXT ABUSE

In a recent talk show program on national television, the prominent evangelical Christian leader James Dobson, after being introduced as one of the country's great moral spokespeople, was asked whether the recent killing of the terrorist Al-Zarqawi by the U.S. military was a moral act and, therefore, justifiable. He replied that it was a moral act and justified because "even the Bible says you live by the sword, you die by the sword."[2] This citation from Matthew 26:52 was *interpreted* to mean that those who use the sword, who use violent means to destroy the lives of others—like the terrorist Al-Zarqawi who had clearly been involved in multiple acts of terror and the destruction of hundreds of lives—deserve to die "by the sword." In other words, Al-Zarqawi got what was coming to him. He deserved to die. The action of the U.S. military was a moral act on the basis of a divine principle of retributive justice, clearly articulated by Jesus, and therefore "biblical."

But is such action "biblical"? Is that what Jesus taught? A look at this saying of Jesus—spoken in the context of his arrest in Gethsemane—shows that Jesus said these words to a disciple who tried to defend him with his sword against the arresting soldiers.[3] "Put your sword back into its place," said Jesus, "for all who take the sword will perish by the sword." The context reveals that the intent of Jesus' words was not at all to justify the use of the sword. Indeed, it was quite the opposite. With these words, Jesus was telling his followers to put their swords away. The point Jesus was making was basically that violence

---

[2]James Dobson, in an interview with Sean Hannity and Alan Colmes, *Hannity & Colmes*, Fox News, June 9, 2006.

[3]Compare Matthew 26:47-53 and John 18:1-3, 10-11. Matthew's account is more general, referring to "a large crowd with swords and clubs, from the chief priests and the elders of the people," and the defender of Jesus as "one of those with Jesus." John's account is more specific, referring to "a detachment of soldiers together with police from the chief priests and the Pharisees," and identifying Jesus' defender as Simon Peter.

begets violence. Retribution in kind calls forth retribution in kind; there is no end to it.[4] That, says Jesus, is not God's way. If it were, Jesus could call down "twelve legions of angels" to defend himself (Mt 26:53).

It is certainly possible that a case can be made for the use of force for the greater good in the context of a sinful, broken world, where choices sometimes have to be made between greater and lesser forms of evil.[5] But such a case cannot be made on the basis of the verse cited. Dobson took the verse out of its literary context to make a point *exactly opposite* of its intended purpose! Such an abuse of Scripture—by not taking seriously the context of a particular saying or teaching—has serious consequences. In the case of this example, the idea is conveyed to the larger world that this is *the* Christian position on the matter. For millions of devout listeners, it can become a justification for supporting the policies of a particular administration or government regarding the use of force in international relations. It can also serve to call into question the integrity of some Christian traditions—such as the Mennonite and other Anabaptist groups—who are committed to nonviolence, as somehow sub-Christian or "not in keeping with biblical teaching."

More recently, during a visit to relatives in Germany, I encountered the teaching of a popular evangelical lecturer, who has quite a following among conservative Christians throughout that country.[6] He is passionately supportive of the political state of Israel and its right to the entire land of Palestine, and therefore, he is strongly opposed to a U.S. policy in favor of the creation of a Palestinian state in the West Bank and Gaza. After the terrible tragedy of Hurricane Katrina, this Christian leader taught that Katrina was God's punishment on the United States for the administration's pressure on Israel to

---

[4]That is precisely the problem with the ideology of vengeance. It is an endless spiral. Around the time of this writing, a leading Hezbollah terrorist, who had committed untold atrocities, was assassinated in a car-bomb explosion in Syria. His followers, convinced that the assassination was the work of Israelis and Americans, have vowed to avenge his death by terrorist reprisals. More lives will be lost; and the cycle of violence continues. As the nineteenth-century philosopher Nietzsche put it: "Whoever fights monsters should see to it that in the process he does not become a monster" (*Basic Writings of Nietzsche,* trans. Walter Kaufmann [New York: Modern Library, 2000], p. 279).

[5]The just-war tradition, beginning with Augustine of Hippo in the early fifth century, is evidence of intense and thoughtful Christian wrestling with the question of the legitimacy of the use of force in human affairs. (See appendix C for a summary of just-war assumptions and criteria.)

[6]Ludwig Schneider, of the German news agency "Israel Heute" ("Israel Today"). His interpretation (see below) of Zechariah 2:8 is also voiced by numerous orthodox Jewish rabbis and conservative Christians in this country who see the modern state of Israel as continuous (and identical) with ancient Israel. See the website <www.4cministry.org/documents/articles/SpecialTopic-KatrinaSpecial.pdf>.

dismantle Jewish settlements in Gaza and the West Bank—settlements considered by many to be impediments to the formation of an independent Palestinian state. The basis for such a view is grounded in the prophetic word of Zechariah 2:8, where we read that those who oppose the people of Israel—"one who touches you touches the apple of my eye"—will be punished by God.[7] Is this a valid understanding and application of this (and similar) biblical texts? When Zechariah 2:8 is read in its context, it is clear that this passage addresses specifically the situation of Israel, Judah and Jerusalem whose inhabitants had been scattered among the Gentiles by the Assyrians and Babylonians (Zech 1:19-20). Therefore, those who scattered the people of God would stand under God's judgment. There is no indication that this word is to be understood in a futuristic, prophetic sense, pointing to distant future events, nor is there an indication that the modern state of Israel is somehow identical with the Old Testament people of God, and therefore under God's special protection against its adversaries.[8] Further, the context reveals that God's judgment was pronounced based on specific opposition to Israel by its ancient pagan neighbors. It is quite a hermeneutical leap to apply this text to the tens of thousands of people on whom the disaster of Katrina was inflicted in the U.S. Gulf coast—especially when the majority of these people were, most likely, members of "the people of God" whom Paul calls "the Israel of God" (Gal 6:16).

The message that emerges from the abusive reading of this and similar texts is that faithful, Bible-believing Christians ought to support the state of Israel. Its policies regarding the settlements in Palestinian territories—clearly designed to gain land and bargaining power in any future negotiations—should be unequivocally supported by Christians. For did not God give this land to the people of Israel? Therefore it belongs to them. And to think or act otherwise is to oppose the purposes of God and thus to incur God's judgment.[9] What such an abusive interpretation of a biblical text does is also to

---

[7]Cf. Gen 12:3; Ps 105:8-11; Is 60:12. In contrast is the view expressed, in an open letter to President George W. Bush, by a significant group of evangelical leaders, who urged the administration to pursue policies designed to promote justice for both Palestinians and Israelis. (See appendix D, where a copy of this letter is reprinted.)

[8]The transference of the promises of God for ancient Israel to the contemporary state of Israel is problematic at best. Paul, for one, seems to be convinced that, in Christ, the promises of God have found fulfillment, and therefore all those who are the descendants of Abraham by faith are the true children of Abraham, whether Jew or Gentile (Rom 4; Gal 3:6-9, 14, 29).

[9]This view is based on the belief that the establishment of the state of Israel in 1948 is a fulfillment

ignore other texts in both the Old and New Testaments: texts that transcend the ethnocentric exclusiveness of Israel (e.g., Is 19:24-25) and postexilic Judaism (e.g., Jonah); texts that oppose its continuing rejection of the Gentile world as "unclean" (Acts 10); and texts that envision a new Israel, the "Israel of God" (Gal 6:16), consisting of communities of both Jew and Gentile who are not tied to national boundaries or a piece of real estate (Eph 2:15-22).

Further, the view espoused by this kind of abusive reading communicates the idea that God uses natural phenomena, such as hurricanes, to punish people for opposing his will. While there are such events in the biblical narrative—like the plagues on Pharaoh's Egypt because of his refusal to set the Hebrew slaves free—there is no biblical warrant for extrapolating generally applicable theories from these events to how God acts generally. Such extrapolation can lead to great emotional and spiritual harm for faithful believers who are struck by natural calamities and are then plagued by the question: Why is God punishing us like this?

Such an act of indiscriminate "divine punishment," which ostensibly targets the acts of a government but results in the loss of thousands of innocent lives, is theologically very problematic, if not heretical. A similar theological heresy was promoted by prominent evangelical leaders like Jerry Falwell, who interpreted the terrorist acts on 9/11 as God's punishment of the United States for its moral deterioration (especially in such areas as homosexual rights, sexual promiscuity, abortion and gay marriage), or by Jeremiah Wright on the other side of the theological divide, who identified it as God's judgment on America's racism. Identifying these acts of terror as judging acts of God communicates a vision of God in the image of the terrorists, who target political entities or ideologies without any concern for "collateral damage." Does the God revealed in the cross act like this? What does this kind of theological perspective, based on an abusive reading of the Bible, communicate to the unbelieving world? I believe these sorts of theological aberrations seriously undermine the central biblical message of God's redeeming love in Christ. This is not just a matter of questionable or bad theology that is of exclusive interest in intra-Christian discussion and debate; it is a matter of

---

of prophetic predictions, that after exile and dispersion among the Gentiles, God would restore Israel to the land (e.g., Jer 9:13-15; 23:5-8; Ezek 11:16-20). However, biblical scholars are generally agreed that these and other prophecies refer to the destruction of Jerusalem in ca. 586 B.C. (not A.D. 70) and to the return from Babylonian exile in ca. 538 B.C. (not the 1948 creation of the modern state of Israel).

Christian integrity that has serious negative consequences for the persuasive power of the Christian faith in the world!

ILLUSTRATIONS OF A VARIETY OF CONTEXT ABUSES

In the following examples, we move from *immediate contexts* (within particular phrases and verses) to *larger contexts* (paragraphs, chapters, whole books) to *comprehensive contexts* (such as the Gospels, Pauline epistles, Old Testament, New Testament). While our exploration of texts within smaller contextual units will be largely confined to hearing those texts within those units, it will at times be necessary to appeal to larger units of context for the most accurate understanding of the message and meaning of those smaller units.

Immediate contexts. Beginning with several examples that illustrate the importance of context on the micro level, within individual verses, these examples also illustrate the importance of a literary convention in Hebrew poetry, namely "parallelism." Whereas, in the English language, poetry is largely characterized by meter and rhyme, Hebraic poetry is characterized by various forms of parallelism. A common form is "synonymous parallelism," where a basic idea is expressed in one or two lines, and then the same idea is expressed one or more times in subsequent lines but in a variety of different words or images. Another frequently used form is "antithetic parallelism," where the affirmation of one line is set in contrast to a second line. A third common form is "progressive parallelism," in which an idea expressed in the opening line is amplified in subsequent lines. In order to fully and accurately grasp the meaning of such poetic texts (especially in the Prophets, Psalms and Proverbs) this unique form of Hebrew poetry must be kept in mind.

Psalm 121:1-2.

> I will lift up mine eyes unto the hills, from whence cometh my help.
> My help cometh from the LORD, which made heaven and earth. (KJV)

These well-known opening sentences of the Psalm are an excellent illustration of Hebraic poetic parallelism. The citation is deliberately taken from the KJV, to show how Hebraic parallelism can be misunderstood. In this translation (as also in Luther's translation), lifting up one's eyes "to the hills" was understood in the sense of looking upward, beyond one's immediate situation, to the Lord. A favorite hymn that we sang in my youth in a German Baptist congregation was titled "Unto the Hills." It began with the words,

"Lift up your eyes to the hills, from them comes your help" (translated from the German), and then continued with the affirmation of Psalm 121:2, that the help comes from the Lord.

Newer translations (including the NKJV) consistently render Psalm 121:1 not as an indicative, but as a question: "I lift up my eyes to the hills—from where will my help come?" Verse 2 ("My help comes from the LORD") is then seen as the answer to the question. In this way of hearing the text, the two verses are understood as a case of "antithetic parallelism." Verse 2 is in contrast to verse 1, in this sense: "I lift up my eyes to the hills; shall my help come from there? Certainly not! My help comes from the Lord." We know from the historical books (Kings and Chronicles) and many of the prophets that Israel was constantly tempted to run after the gods of the Canaanites, and they often succumbed to that temptation. These gods were worshiped particularly at shrines on the hilltops (e.g., 1 Kings 14:24; 2 Kings 12:3; 16:4; 2 Chron 28:4; Jer 2:20; Ezek 6:13; 20:28; Hos 4:12-13). Within such a context, our text takes on special significance. Over against the practices of her pagan neighbors, as well as in opposition to the idolatrous practices of many in Israel, the psalmist says, in effect: "I will not look to the hills, to the shrines of the other gods for help. No! My help comes from the Lord who made heaven and earth!" Heard this way, the text becomes much more than an affirmation of trust and confidence, more than a pointer to God as the source of courage and comfort in times of adversity. It is all of that. But given the historical context within which the text functions, it is at its core a rejection of the claims of all "false gods" to be our help—from material possessions, to status, to military power, to pietistic formality. A significant dimension of the meaning of this text is lost when the literary structure of the text and its larger cultural context are not adequately considered.

Proverbs 29:18. The first half of Proverbs 29:18 states:

> Where there is no vision, the people perish. (KJV)

This biblical affirmation has become the motto for many Christian (and indeed secular) organizations when thinking about their future or their mission, or when doing strategic planning to envision where the organization wants to be in five or ten years and what it wants to accomplish. It is a good motto and expresses an empirical truth, namely, that when individuals, institutions and churches do not have a target to shoot at, they will likely miss it.

Without a vision for the future, they stagnate. However, it is quite certain that this is not what Proverbs 29:18 means. The verse is a good example of antithetic parallelism. The first half of the verse, "Where there is no vision, the people perish," is contrasted with the second half of the verse: "but happy are those who keep the law." In the Old Testament, both visions and the law are instruments of divine revelation, intended to guide God's people in the way of the Lord. They are the foundation of the people's lives, energizing them for the journey—not some goal or ideal they are trying to reach or accomplish. Both lines in this poetic verse affirm the same truth, but in opposite ways. One does it negatively and one positively: those who live life without attention to God's will—revealed in visions of that will to the prophets[10]—are in a stormy port without an anchor or at sea without a compass.[11] But those who live life in keeping with the will of God, revealed in the law, flourish (cf. Ps 1). These passages show that significantly different messages are heard from the passages when the internal context of the verse is allowed to shed light on the words.

Isaiah 61:10. This passage is an excellent example of "synonymous parallelism":

> He has clothed me with the garments of salvation,
> > he has covered me with the robe of righteousness.[12]

In this pair of lines the second line reaffirms the confession of the first line, but with different words. What is striking is that the terms denoting God's *salvation* and *righteousness* are used synonymously. That means that the *righteousness* of God is not a reference to God's essential character as such, or to God's moral nature, but it is a term that denotes God's saving action toward Israel. It does not designate a quality of God, but rather, defines the action of God's steadfast love and faithfulness toward Israel and the world. Such an understanding of God's righteousness is confirmed by numerous texts where the words "steadfast love" and "faithfulness" are used singly or as a pair in synonymous parallelism with God's "righteousness" or God's "salva-

---

[10]This is recognized in more recent translations. The NKJV has "revelation" or "prophetic vision"; NIV has "revelation"; and NRSV has "prophecy."

[11]The Hebrew rendered "perish" (in Prov 29:18) is more accurately translated "cast off restraint," in the sense of having rejected the guidance of divine revelation (so NKJV, NRSV and NIV).

[12]Sometimes the poetic structure is "A=B"; at other times it is "A, what's more, B" or "A, that is to say, B."

tion" (e.g., Ps 85:4, 10-11; 89:13-14; 98:3; Is 11:5).

This insight about a particular meaning of "God's righteousness" in the Old Testament is important for understanding the special way that Paul used the term "God's righteousness" when he wrote about the historical coming of "God's righteousness" in Christ (Rom 1:16-17; 3:21-22). When the term "God's righteousness" is taken as a definition of God's essential, moral character, then the act of justification (literally "being put right [with God]"—Rom 3:23, 26, 28, my translation) can be understood in one of two ways: either (1) as the *impartation* of that divine righteousness into us, so that we stand before God not as sinners, but as those who are now marked by his righteousness; or (2) as the *imputation* of that divine righteousness, by which we are declared to be righteous (a judicial act), even though we are in fact sinners. But if Paul understood "God's righteousness" as the activity of God's redeeming, reconciling, relation-restoring love, embodied in Christ, then our justification is a restored, reconciled relationship with God. And within the dynamic of this reconciled relationship, we are being transformed into the image of Christ. Thus, how we understand the term "righteousness of God" in Isaiah 61:10 (and similar passages, such as Ps 85:4, 10-11; 89:13-14; 98:3; Is 11:5) and also in Paul has significant implications for how we understand what happens when we respond in faith to "God's righteousness."[13]

Hosea 4:6.

My people are destroyed for lack of knowledge. (Hos 4:6)

A person could derive from this passage the idea that not having correct theological knowledge about such important concepts as God and sin and salvation, or not holding to right doctrines, leads to ultimate destruction and separation from God. This was, in fact, the position taken by the early Christian heresy of Gnosticism, a central tenet of which was that the possession of a particular kind of knowledge would enable one to gain salvation.[14] A modern

---

[13]See my discussion of Paul's concept of the "righteousness of God" in *Set Free to Be: A Study in Romans* (Valley Forge, Penn.: Judson Press, 1975), pp. 11-26; and "Righteousness, Righteousness of God," in *Dictionary of Paul and His Letters: A Compendium of Contemporary Biblical Scholarship,* ed. Gerald F. Hawthorne, Ralph P. Martin and Daniel G. Reid (Downers Grove, Ill.: InterVarsity Press, 1993), pp. 827-37. Cf. also Paul Achtemeier, *Romans,* Interpretation: A Bible Commentary for Teaching and Preaching (Atlanta: John Knox Press, 1985), pp. 61-66.

[14]The *Gospel of Thomas,* in the New Testament Apocrypha, is a good example of such a view. It consists primarily of short sayings attributed to Jesus (occasionally with parallels in the canonical Gospels) that communicate special, esoteric knowledge necessary to gain eternal life. See E. Hen-

version of this idea, though clearly attached to the canonical Christian Scriptures, is the idea of "saving knowledge." This kind of knowledge ostensibly consists of assent to biblical truths and doctrinal affirmations considered necessary for salvation. Without this "saving knowledge," people are considered "lost," or certainly "defective." A physician at the Christian college I attended as an undergraduate gave a series of lectures on a long list of dietary laws and rules about ritual washings in relationship to the "clean" and "unclean" categories in Leviticus. He maintained that if Christians observed all of these laws and rules, this compendium of divinely revealed knowledge, we would all be much healthier and would not succumb to many common diseases.[15]

But are these interpretations what the author of Hosea had in mind? In the second half of the verse, we read:

You have forgotten the law of your God.

This part of the verse clearly indicates what sort of knowledge was lacking among God's people: it was the knowledge of his will for his people, revealed in the law. They had rejected God's revelation. And to reject the revelation of God's will is to reject God, to be without knowledge of God. This is the deeper sense in which "lack of knowledge" needs to be understood.

The absence of the knowledge of God in Israel is addressed several times in Hosea. Just a few verses prior to our text, we read that there is "no knowledge of God in the land" (Hos 4:1). What God desires is not burnt offerings, but "the knowledge of God" (Hos 6:6). However, "Israel has forgotten his Maker" (Hos 8:14). Their cry, "My God, we—Israel—know you!" was a sham (Hos 8:2). This lack of knowledge is addressed by the call of the prophet: "Come, let us return to the LORD. . . . Let us know, let us press on to know the LORD" (Hos 6:1, 3), and by the promise of God: "I will take you for my wife in faithfulness; and you shall know the LORD" (Hos 2:20). The Hebrew word for "know" denotes intimate knowing of the other, not knowledge about the other.[16] This then, according to Hosea 4:6, is the kind of knowledge that the people of God lacked.

---

necke, *New Testament Apocrypha* (London: Lutterworth Press, 1963).

[15]His lectures were later published in a book. See Samuel I. McMillan, *None of These Diseases* (Old Tappan, N.J.: Fleming H. Revell, 1979).

[16]The Hebrew word "to know" is *yādaʿ*, which is also the word used in the Old Testament for sexual intercourse. The repeated use of this word in Hosea is particularly striking, since Israel is depicted as God's bride who has committed adultery with her other lovers (namely the Canaanite gods).

Larger contexts.

1 Corinthians 3:16-17. Paul's affirmations in this text, that "you are God's temple" and that "God's Spirit dwells in you," have been used within different Christian traditions as a basis for the construction of various legalistic structures, collections of rules and regulations for the conduct of believers. These were further grounded in the warning of the text that "if anyone destroys God's temple, God will destroy that person." The personal pronoun *you* was understood to refer to individuals and, specifically, to our individual bodies. Since God's Spirit dwells in our bodies, and thus makes them temples of God, we better make sure that we keep ourselves from any sort of defilement.

While there are many good reasons, including biblical ones, for abstaining from such things as tobacco and drugs, or for using alcohol (if at all) in moderation,[17] or for sex within the boundaries of the marriage covenant[18] —in order not to destroy our bodies—our text in 1 Corinthians 3:16-17 does not speak to this at all.

Both the immediate and larger contexts show that Paul is speaking about the Christian community, the church, as "God's building" (1 Cor 3:9), which had been "built" by numerous servants of God (Apollos and Paul—1 Cor 3:5, 10) on the foundation of Christ (1 Cor 3:11). It is this "building" that is "God's temple." This understanding of what Paul means is confirmed by the plain grammar of 1 Corinthians 3:16-17 (though that gets lost in literal translation into English). In the phrases, *"you* are God's temple" and "God's Spirit dwells in *you"* and *"you* are that temple," the pronoun *you* in the Greek is *plural.* What Paul is saying, therefore—in contrast to both the temple in Jerusalem and the heathen temples in Corinth—is that "you all together," or you as the community of Jesus' disciples, "are God's temple."[19] In our larger passage (and throughout the epistle) Paul is deeply concerned for the unity of the church, so that it might be, as the dwelling place of God's Spirit, an alterna-

---

[17]In Ephesians 5:18, Paul says "do not get drunk with wine," and in 1 Timothy 5:23, Timothy is advised to "take a little wine for the sake of your stomach." There is also scientific evidence that the moderate use of alcohol has health benefits, but it is universally recognized that exorbitant use is destructive.

[18]In 1 Corinthians 6:13-18, Paul says that since our bodies are members of Christ, one should not become one with a prostitute; we should "shun fornication." The Greek word for "fornication" is *porneia,* which refers to all sorts of sexual immorality.

[19]In its two uses, *temple* is a singular noun. If Paul had meant to say that *each member* of the church in Corinth was a temple of God, the noun would have had to be plural ("You are the temples of God"), or the pronoun "you" would have been singular ("Each one of you is a temple of God").

tive community, God's option in the midst of the brokenness of human society. That important truth is missed when these verses are interpreted as referring to individuals.[20]

Acts 2:4-11. In his description of the Pentecost experience, Luke tells us that all members of the community of Jesus' followers "were filled with the Holy Spirit and began to speak in other tongues" (Acts 2:4 NIV). How are we to understand this phenomenon of "speaking in other tongues" in this text?

The historic Pentecostal faith tradition, and more recently, some other charismatic expressions of Christianity, have understood this phenomenon in the sense of ecstatic speech ("glossolalia") akin to one of the gifts of the Spirit described by Paul in 1 Corinthians 12—14, and as a paradigmatic experience for all Christians, a primary (even necessary) evidence of the fullness of the Spirit in a Christian's life. This reading of the text is seen to be reenforced by Acts 10:45-46 and Acts 19:6, where the outpouring of the Spirit is also accompanied by a "speaking in tongues."

Such an interpretation is, however, not in keeping with a careful reading of Acts 2:4 within the context of the entire passage. The disciples are empowered by the Spirit to "speak in other tongues" (NIV; "languages" in NRSV; Greek *glōssais*). The crowd who heard them was bewildered, because it "heard them speaking in the *native language [dialektō]* of each" (Acts 2:6, emphasis added). Their amazement was highlighted because these disciples were Galileans,[21] and yet they heard them "in our own native language *[dialektō]*" (Acts 2:8). They were further astonished by this phenomenon because "in our own tongues" (Acts 2:11 NIV; "languages," NRSV; *glōssais*, Greek) they heard them tell of God's mighty deeds.

In the context of this passage, it is clear that the Greek words *glōssais* ("tongues, languages") and *dialektō* ("dialect, language") are used interchangeably.[22] The phenomenon that is reported is that the disciples, filled and empowered by the Spirit, are proclaiming the good news of Jesus Christ in a variety of *intelligible* languages, understood by the pilgrims who have come to Jerusalem from multiple provinces and countries throughout the Ro-

---

[20]Cf. Ephesians 2:21-22, where Paul says that individually we are built *together* to form "a holy temple in the Lord," and "a dwelling place for God."

[21]Galileans "were disdained for their indistinct pronunciation with its confused or lost laryngeals and aspirates." W. J. Larkin Jr., *Acts*, The IVP New Testament Commentary (Downers Grove, Ill.: InterVarsity Press, 1995), p. 51.

[22]Therefore, the NRSV renders all four references—both *glōssais* and *dialektō*—with "languages."

man Empire (and beyond) for the Jewish feast of Pentecost (Acts 2:9-10).[23] This understanding of the passage is reinforced by the larger context, where Peter explains this miraculous communication by citing Joel 2:28, where an outpouring of God's Spirit is promised, resulting in the empowerment of both men and women to prophesy (Acts 2:16-18). Prophetic speech, both in the Old and New Testaments, is the Spirit-empowered proclamation of the Word of God. It can be predictive speech (*fore*telling), but it is primarily and dominantly proclamation (*forth*-telling). The "speaking in other tongues" (both *glōssais* and *dialektō*) is, therefore, decidedly different from the spiritual gift of "glossolalia" in 1 Corinthians 12—14. There, Paul is dealing with an ecstatic speech manifestation, which he defines as "unintelligible utterance" (1 Cor 14:2, 6-11), and calls for limiting its expression primarily to the sphere of personal prayer (1 Cor 14:2, 13-19). Therefore, on the basis of both immediate and larger contexts, the "speaking in tongues" in Acts 2:4-11 is not the spiritual gift of "glossolalia" as ecstatic, unintelligible utterance.[24]

Acts 2:38. At the conclusion of his Pentecost sermon, Peter calls for repentance, invites converts to be baptized, assures them of the forgiveness of their sins and announces that "you will receive the gift of the Holy Spirit." What is this "gift of the Holy Spirit"? Those who understand "tongues" in Acts 2:4-11 in terms of the spiritual gift of glossolalia (as in 1 Cor 12—14) have often identified "the gift" of the Holy Spirit (in Acts 2:38) as the gift of tongues. Since one of the manifestations of the Spirit's presence was tongues *(glōssais* or *dialektō)* in Acts 2:4-11, and also in Acts 10:45-46 and Acts 19:6, it has been understood to be a significant, if not the most significant, gift and evidence of the fullness of the Spirit.

The context, however, will not permit this interpretation. The main theme of Acts 2 is that the Spirit of God has been given to ("poured out on") Jesus' followers (Acts 2:4, 17-18) in fulfillment of Jesus' promise (Acts 1:8; cf. Jn

---

[23]In this, the beginning of the church, commentators across the centuries have seen the counterpoint to the story of the confusion of tongues in Genesis 11:1-9. There, the confusion of tongues is depicted as the ultimate sign of humanity's distortion, the result of its quest to "be like God" (Gen 3:5) and to build a tower "with its top in the heavens" (Gen 11:4). In Acts, the proclamation of the good news crosses the boundaries of fragmented humanity, calling all into a new humanity. Language barriers—a sign of human division—can no longer stand in the way.

[24]See F. F. Bruce, *The Book of Acts*, The New London Commentary on the New Testament (London: Marshall, Morgan & Scott, 1954), pp. 56-58, who refers to both the Acts and Corinth manifestations of "glossolalia" as "ecstatic utterances," but distinguishes them in terms of content: recognizable words about the mighty works of God versus "speech which no hearer could understand."

14:16-17, 26; 15:26; 16:7). Just prior to our text about the "gift of the Holy Spirit" (Acts 2:38), Peter spoke of the risen Lord who received from the Father the promise of the Holy Spirit, who had been "poured out" on the disciples. In his defense before the high priest's council, Peter said that the Holy Spirit was given by God (Acts 5:32). Later texts in Acts speak of "receiving" the Holy Spirit (Acts 8:15-17; 19:2), or of the Spirit falling or coming on them (Acts 10:44; 11:15; 19:6).

Taken together, these texts clarify that the promise, "you will receive the gift of the Holy Spirit," does *not* mean "you will receive the gift of tongues from the Holy Spirit" but rather, "you will receive God's gift, *the Holy Spirit.*" This interpretation is further confirmed by a parallel text in Acts 10, where "the Holy Spirit fell" on the household of the Gentile Cornelius (Acts 10:44). This coming of the Spirit fills Peter's fellow Jewish believers with amazement and the recognition "that the gift of the Holy Spirit had been poured out even on the Gentiles" (Acts 10:45). Here also, the *Holy Spirit* is God's gift.[25]

1 Corinthians 13:9-10.

> For we know only in part, and we prophesy only in part; but when the complete comes, the partial will come to an end.

What is "the complete" that Paul anticipates, which in turn will bring "to an end" that which is partial?[26] One of the most popular answers to this question is given in those theological traditions that believe the charismatic gifts that Paul speaks about in 1 Corinthians 12—14 have ceased to be so. These charismatic gifts, including tongues, healing and special revelatory knowledge—which they agree were legitimate and important in the *early* decades of the church's life—are understood to be those "partial" manifestations that "will come to an end" (1 Cor 13:8-10), that "will cease" (1 Cor 13:8). This rejection of charismatic gifts is based on particular views of what "the complete" (or "perfection," NIV) refers to. Several answers have been given. Some are based on Paul's analogy of the contrast between the child and the adult (1 Cor 13:11). The Corinthians' valuing of charismatic gifts (especially the gift of

---

[25]Cf. 1 Cor 1:22. See Robert W. Wall, "The Acts of the Apostles," in *The New Interpreter's Bible*, vol. 10 (Nashville: Abingdon, 2002), p. 68, who states (regarding Acts 2:38) that "Peter does not have in mind the role the Spirit plays in a charismatic congregation [1 Cor 12—14] where . . . the Spirit supplies different spiritual gifts."

[26]At issue here is what the word *complete* refers to. The word itself (*teleion*, in Greek, is the adjective of the verb *teleioō*) means "to bring to an end, to complete" something; it can also have the sense of "the perfection" of something (as rendered in the NIV).

tongues), and their quest to attain those gifts, is identified as immature, as that which will come to an end when the perfection or completion of love has been attained.[27] A second major answer identifies "the complete" as a reference "to the full revelation given in the New Testament itself, which when it would come to completion would do away with the 'partial' forms of charismatic revelation."[28] Can these readings of 1 Corinthians 13:9-10 be maintained?[29] Careful attention to both the immediate and larger contexts reveals these understandings of the text to be the result of the abuse of context.

We will look first at the larger literary context within which our text functions and then focus on the more immediate context in 1 Corinthians 13. Commentators agree that 1 Corinthians 12—14 constitutes both a literary and a theological unit, introduced by the phrase, "Now concerning spiritual gifts" (1 Cor 12:1). It is concerned as a whole with the issue of the place and use of spiritual gifts in the life of the congregation,[30] which Paul addresses comprehensively in these three chapters. In 1 Corinthians 12, he contends that all the manifestations of the Spirit (gifts, services, activities, 1 Cor 12:4-6, 8-9) are given "for the common good" (1 Cor 12:7) and are empowered and allotted "as the Spirit chooses" (1 Cor 12:11). The analogy between the human body and the church as the body of Christ (1 Cor 12:12-27) shows what "the common good" looks like: a church where members, endowed with varieties of gifts, recognize that all gifts are indispensable (1 Cor 12:22) and respect and honor that variety. Paul's argument implies that this was not the way the Corinthians saw the matter. As 1 Corinthians 14 reveals, there must have been factions in the church that elevated certain gifts, and especially "glossolalia," as a badge of spiritual superiority (as in some charismatic traditions today). Paul acknowledges that some gifts are greater than others (1 Cor 12:31; 14:5), but he doesn't mean that those with the greater gifts have spiritual superiority, since it is the

---

[27]E.g., Bruce, *1 and 2 Corinthians*, New Century Bible (London: Oliphants, 1971), p. 128.

[28]Gordon D. Fee, *The First Epistle to the Corinthians*, New International Commentary on the New Testament (Grand Rapids: Eerdmans, 1978), pp. 644-45 n. 23. He identifies Reformed and Dispensational theologians, based on the exposition of 1 Corinthians 13:8-13 by B. B. Warfield, as the contexts for various expressions of this view.

[29]Gordon D. Fee and Douglas Stuart, *How to Read the Bible for All Its Worth: A Guide to Understanding the Bible*, 2nd ed. (Grand Rapids: Zondervan, 1981), pp. 64-65, call the view that prophecy and tongues have ceased to function in the church once the New Testament was completed *"one thing the text cannot mean* because good exegesis totally disallows it."

[30]It is highly probable that this issue was one of the concerns brought to Paul's attention in the letter that had been sent to him (1 Cor 7:1: "Now concerning the matters about which you wrote"). This is indicated by the repetition of the phrase, "now concerning" (1 Cor 7:1; 8:1; 12:1).

Spirit who bestows the gifts (1 Cor 12:11). Rather, *greater* is related to the extent to which the particular gift functions in "build[ing] up the church" (1 Cor 14:3-4, 6, 26).[31] The relative importance of prophetic proclamation and tongues (the focus of Paul's discussion in 1 Cor 14) is determined by their primary function and result: prophetic proclamation builds up the church (1 Cor 14:3), while those who speak in tongues "build up themselves" (1 Cor 14:4).

This is the larger context within which 1 Corinthians 13 (and specifically 1 Cor 13:9-10) must be understood. First Corinthians 13 is bracketed by the exhortations to (1) "strive for the greater gifts" (1 Cor 12:31) and (2) "strive for the spiritual gifts, and especially that you may prophesy" (1 Cor 14:1). But even this quest for the gifts that build up the church must be undergirded and accompanied by "a still more excellent way" (1 Cor 12:31), the way of the pursuit of love (1 Cor 14:1).[32] These bracketing statements provide the more immediate context for our text (1 Cor 13:9-10). All gifts of the Spirit— tongues, prophetic powers, revelatory knowledge and insight, or even a faith that can overcome all obstacles—if not ultimately grounded in and seasoned by love, are as nothing (1 Cor 13:2-3). As important as they are in and for the life of the church, they are not absolute. They are temporal, intended for equipping and building up the church for its life and mission in the world. They "will come to an end . . . they will cease" (1 Cor 13:8) "when the complete comes" (1 Cor 13:10). What is that completeness, that perfection?

Given the immediate context, the point of the adult-child analogy (1 Cor 13:11) is not the contrast between immaturity and maturity, but rather the fact that when a person becomes an adult, childhood ceases.[33] In the same way, when the complete comes, the temporal functions of the gifts of the Spirit (intended for the life and mission of the church "to the end of the earth"—Acts 1:8) will cease. The verse immediately following (1 Cor 13:12) is the specific key to what Paul has in mind when he speaks of the perfection that brings the functioning of the gifts to a conclusion. He contrasts between "now" and "then," between seeing indirectly[34] and seeing "face to face," be-

---

[31]Paul's guiding principle for actions or attitudes in the life of the church is the principle of "edification": Does it lift others up? Does it lead to their growth in faith? Is it for their good? Does it build up the body? (See 1 Cor 8:1, 9, 13; 9:12, 19-22; 10:23-24, 31-33; 11:21-23, 33; 12:7.)

[32]Cf. 1 Cor 8:1, where Paul states that "love builds up."

[33]Similarly, Fee, *First Corinthians,* p. 647, argues that the child-adult analogy "has basically to do with two modes of existence, not with 'growing up' and putting away childish behavior."

[34]The Greek phrase literally reads: "For now we see through a mirror *en ainigmati*" ("dimly" [NRSV]; "a poor reflection" [NIV]). The sense may be that in a mirror "one sees not the thing itself, but its

tween "know[ing] in part" and "know[ing] fully, even as I have been fully known by [God]." These contrasts point decisively to the contrast between this present time ("now") and the eschaton ("then"). Given Paul's rabbinic background, this language has its origin in the contrast between "this present age" and "the age to come." As vital as the gifts of the Spirit are for Christian life and witness "in the here and now," they fade in comparison with what is yet to come. Paul knew that the gift of God's Spirit to the church—and, with that Gift, the spiritual gifts for the church—is but a down payment, a first installment (2 Cor 1:22). But *then*, in the eschaton, we will see face to face that which we *now* perceive only in part. As Barth put it so eloquently: "Because the sun rises, all lights are extinguished."[35]

When both the immediate and larger contexts of a passage are taken with utmost seriousness, then certain readings of a text—influenced and sometimes determined in advance by theological views brought to the text from the outside—are often shown to be erroneous. In the case of our text, two opposing views regarding the gifts of the Spirit stand under the critical judgment of "contextual faithfulness." On the one hand is the view that gifts of the Spirit, and particularly that of glossolalia, are to be valued above all others and are the highest manifestation (and evidence) of the presence of the Spirit in personal and congregational life. On the other hand is the view that the gifts of the Spirit, and especially the more "extraordinary" gifts (like tongues, prophetic insight, healing) were given to the church in its infancy, but are no longer valid and should not be sought. In this view, the formation of the New Testament canon and the formation of ecclesiastical order and structure are believed to have put an end to the need for these gifts. As we have seen, neither view is valid. In their "over-against-ness" they weaken and divide the life of the church, and they undermine both the integrity and power of its witness in and to the world.

Luke 17:20-21.

. . . the kingdom of God is *within* you. (NIV)
     . . . the kingdom of God is *among* you. (NRSV)

The NIV has a footnote that an alternative reading for the word *within* is

---

mirror image" and therefore "indirectly" (W. Bauer, W. F. Arndt and F. W. Gingrich, *A Greek-English Lexicon of the New Testament and Other Early Christian Literature* [Chicago: University of Chicago Press, 1957]).

[35]Karl Barth, *The Resurrection of the Dead* (London: Hodder & Stoughton, 1933), p. 86.

among. Likewise, the NRSV has a footnote that an alternate reading for *among* is *within.* These footnotes in our standard translations indicate some uncertainty about the meaning of the Greek text, and therefore about the meaning Jesus intended. The Greek *entos hymōn* can mean either "within you" or "among you."

This statement by Jesus is the final part of his response to the question of the Pharisees about "when the kingdom of God was coming" (Lk 17:20). He first tells them that the kingdom of God "is not coming with things that can be observed." He most likely meant that it would not be accompanied by apocalyptic lightning strikes and thunderclaps. Those kinds of observable signs, he tells his disciples in the next paragraph, are reserved for the future coming of the Son of Man (Lk 17:22-37). Nor can one turn to external events—such as a conquering Messiah marching into Jerusalem to defeat the despised Roman occupiers[36]—and say "here it is" or "there it is." No, says Jesus, the kingdom of God (or perhaps better, "the reign of God") "is *within* [or *among*] you."

What is Jesus' meaning? In some Christian circles, Jesus' teaching here is understood in the sense of "within you"—referring to an inner spiritual reality, an awareness that the reign of God manifests itself in and through the moral core present in each human being, the law of God engraved on the human heart (cf. Rom 2:15). When that immanent spiritual law is followed, God's kingdom is *within,* and the "reign of God" is thus manifesting itself. Other Christians, who also read the text in terms of "within you," understand Jesus' teaching to point to the reality of the divine presence within individuals. They see the "reign of God within" in terms of the guiding presence of God's Spirit within believers (cf. Jn 14:15-17), or in later Pauline terms, the indwelling Christ (Eph 3:17) who, as the risen Lord, reigns in believers' hearts (cf. Col 3:15).

As good and valid as some of the above ideas are (on the basis of *other* biblical material), they are not what Jesus is talking about *here.* The immediate context is simply against it. Jesus is speaking to the Pharisees, who are, for the most part, seen throughout the Gospel record as strident opponents of Jesus' actions and teaching (e.g., Lk 6:1-11), and for whom he had quite severe

---

[36]This was the popular expectation of Judaism in the time of Jesus. The dejected disciples on the road to Emmaus, after Jesus' crucifixion, express this popular view precisely: "we had hoped that he [Jesus] was the one to redeem Israel" (Lk 24:21; NRSV footnote reads, "to set Israel free").

words at times (see the "woes" pronounced on them, including the judgment that they are "full of greed and wickedness" and "neglect justice and the love of God"—Lk 11:37-53). It is therefore impossible to conclude that Jesus would tell them that the "reign of God" was present and functioning "within" them. Thus the alternative reading of the Greek text, namely "the kingdom of God is *among* you" (or, even more precisely, *"in your midst"*) is the only possible option. But what did Jesus mean by that expression? The Gospels, on the whole, are clear that the reign of God broke into history in the person and teaching of Jesus (see Mt 3:2; 4:23; Mk 1:14-15). In Luke, Jesus begins his ministry in messianic self-consciousness by citing Isaiah 61:1-2: "The Spirit of the Lord is upon me, for he has anointed me" (Lk 4:18). Jesus chose a passage in Isaiah that was understood to describe the task of the Lord's Anointed One, the Messiah.[37] So for Luke it is Jesus, the messianic king, who embodies the breaking in of God's reign. Jesus' statement, "Today this scripture has been fulfilled in your hearing" (Lk 4:21), announces unambiguously the entrance of the kingdom of God in the life and ministry of Jesus. This was confirmed in Jesus' demon exorcism activity: "But if it is by the finger of God that I cast out the demons, then the kingdom of God has come to you" (Lk 11:20).[38]

We conclude—on the basis of the immediate context—that Luke 17:21 should read, "For the kingdom of God is among [or in the midst of] you"; and—on the basis of the larger context in Luke and the Gospel record—that this reign of God is present "in their midst" in the person and work of Jesus. This means that the common understandings, which have to do with the "spiritual interiority" of God's reign, miss the essential teaching of the text: the nature of God's kingdom, or more specifically, the characteristics of the nature of God's reign, can only be discerned as they are present in the concrete, bodily life of Jesus. He is the paradigm for what the reign of God looks like in human life and relationships and institutions. Christian spirituality— which focuses on our relationship with God—is related to but not identical with kingdom reality. God's kingship in the world in and through Christ's followers is a matter of moving outward, not inward, of imitating Christ in

---

[37]Craig A. Evans, *Luke*, New Testament Biblical Commentary (Peabody, Mass.: Hendrickson, 1990), p. 70.

[38]The parallel saying in Matthew 12:28 reads: "If it is by the *Spirit of God* that I cast out demons" (emphasis mine). Matthew's text recognizes that the metaphor "finger of God" refers to the power of God's Spirit at work in Jesus.

transforming personal and corporate presence and prophetic witness.

By affirming that the reign of God is identical with the person of Christ, because the reign of God is embodied in him, our text implies these things explained above. The spiritualizing and interiorizing of the reign of God, which results from abusing the context of our text, has a way of "disembodying" the Christian faith, robbing it of its power for concrete action in the world of human relationships and in the larger world of social interaction and institutions.[39]

Comprehensive literary-theological contexts.

Genesis 1:26-27; 2:18-23; 3:16. These texts—about the creation of humanity (*'ādām)* as male and female in God's image (Gen 1:26-27), the creation of the woman as man's "helper" (Gen 2:18-23) and the curse of the man's rule over the woman (Gen 3:16)—have been discussed and analyzed from a number of perspectives in previous chapters, where we dealt with selectivity (chapter three), biblical balance (chapter four), and the encoding and decoding of words (chapter five). Their presence together here is to illustrate the importance of their literary and theological interconnectedness, in order to avoid abusive distortion of their meaning.

Critical scholars generally assign greater antiquity to the creation narrative of Genesis 2, and a later date to the composition of the prose poem of cosmic creation in Genesis 1. But whatever the merits (or demerits) of such dating, the juxtaposition of these two Israelite faith traditions about creational beginnings, at the opening of the book of Genesis, has theological significance.[40] The two narratives, though decidedly different in content, sequence and focus, complement each other in significant ways. The affirmations made about humanity in Genesis 1:26-27 provide the overarching theological and anthropological perspective, in light of which the creation of man and woman in Genesis 2:18-23 must be understood. In Genesis 1:26-27, human beings, in male-female polarity, are created in the image of God. In that male-female polar complementarity they are, together, given the mandate to exercise sov-

---

[39]See the challenging reflections on this matter of the historical concreteness of the kingdom of God in Mortimer Arias, *Announcing the Reign of God: Evangelism and the Subversive Memory of Jesus* (Lima, Ohio: Academic Renewal Press, 1984).

[40]Helmut Thielicke, *How the World Began: Man in the First Chapters of the Bible*, trans. John W. Doberstein (Philadelphia: Muhlenberg Press, 1961), argues persuasively that we miss the great theological insights of these narratives if we read them as literalistic-historical accounts rather than as theological faith affirmations in the form of poetry and narrative.

ereignty within and over the rest of the created order. These affirmations are powerful theological convictions that stand radically over and against the cultural-religious environment within which Israel's faith traditions were being shaped.[41]

The *general* male-female nature and structure of humanity presented in Genesis 1 is articulated in Genesis 2 in terms of its particularity in the man-woman relationship (Gen 2:18-23) as the grounding for the covenant relationship of marriage (Gen 2:24-25; cf. Mk 10:5-9). Viewed from the perspective of Genesis 1:26-27, the reason why the animals cannot be man's "suitable helper" is because they are not created "in the image of God." They are not the man's equal, cannot correspond to him "face to face," cannot be his partners in exercising responsible sovereignty over the creation.[42] Further, the woman's creation from the man (Gen 2:21-22), as "bone of my bones and flesh of my flesh" (Gen 2:23), signifies that she is made from the same essence and substance, a further confirmation of the Genesis 1:26-27 affirmation of their equality—both before God (as image of God) and in relationship with each other.[43] These literary and theological connections—together with our analysis of the important terms used in Genesis 2 (see chapter five)—make it impossible to interpret the Genesis 2 narrative of man and woman in terms of either essential or functional inequality. The concept of a creationally intended male-female hierarchy (of either superior-inferior, leader-follower or authority figure-assistant) is the result of the abusive reading of Scripture, and as such, it is contrary to the order of creation.

This literary and theological unity of Genesis 1 and 2 provides the overarching theological anthropology for our hearing of the male-female condition that is a result of the Fall in Genesis 3. The rule of the man over the woman (Gen 3:16) must be seen as a dramatic departure from the order of creation. The Creator's good design and intent for the man-woman relationship has become twisted and distorted. The hierarchical over-under condi-

---

[41]G. E. Wright, *The Old Testament Against Its Environment*, Studies in Biblical Theology, vol. 2 (London: SCM Press, 1957), shows that the Old Testament's central theological affirmations must be understood as polemical formulations against the mythologies and religious beliefs of its environment.

[42]Refer to the discussion in chapter five of these special terms used in Genesis 2 for the woman in relationship to the man.

[43]These affirmations must be heard in light of the common ancient Near Eastern notion that women were shaped from inferior material, while men were of a higher order of existence. Thus we have here a polemical assertion.

tion of the male-female relationship is in bondage to sin. It is, therefore, *not prescriptive* (as God's intention for the man-woman relationship) *but descriptive* (the nature of that relationship when marred by sin). This means that the narrative of the curse regarding man and woman cannot be allowed to function as a normative paradigm for that relationship throughout history.

Within the larger literary and theological context of the whole of Scripture, the human condition—in its distortion of divinely intended creational wholeness and the resulting enslavement to sin, including the distorted man-woman relationship—is the object of God's redeeming and transforming work. This work culminated in Christ. There is Jesus' challenge to over-under power and authority structures in human relationships, and Paul's conviction that "in Christ" we have been set free from enslavement to sin. What all this means is that male-female hierarchy is out of place in the new creation (2 Cor 5:17).[44]

Galatians 3:27-28.

> As many of you as were baptized into Christ have clothed yourselves with Christ. There is no longer Jew or Greek, there is no longer slave or free, there is no longer male and female; for all of you are one in Christ Jesus.

This text, which has been called the "Christian Charter of Freedom," has at the same time been subject to misunderstanding and to abusive interpretation. Throughout most of the history of Christian interpretation and application, this text has been interpreted largely in *spiritual* terms. To be "baptized into Christ" has been understood as "the entry of the believer into the spiritual relationship of the Christian with Christ which takes place in conversion-initiation," and being clothed with Christ "is simply a figurative usage to describe more expressively the spiritual transformation which makes one a Christian."[45] In keeping with this spiritual transformation of individuals, the "no longer" of the three sets of relationships (Jew-Greek, slave-free, male-female) has also been largely understood as a transformation on the spiritual level. Because we are all "one in Christ," and are spiritual brothers and sisters, the superior-inferior categories in race, social status and gender have become irrelevant. In relationship with Christ, we are all on the same spiritual level.

[44]See our discussion below on the meaning of Galatians 3:27-28, as well as on the comprehensive literary-theological context of Ephesians 5:21-33.

[45]So James D. G. Dunn, *Baptism in the Holy Spirit* (London: SCM Press, 1970), pp. 109-10.

This spiritualizing tradition of the interpretation of Galatians 3:27-28 goes back to the church fathers. Jerome (A.D. 347-420) interpreted the oneness in Christ in purely spiritual terms, holding that within that spiritual unity the "diversity of race, condition and body is taken away." Augustine (A.D. 354-430) commented on our text as follows: "Differences of race or condition or sex are indeed taken away by the unity of faith . . . yet within the orders of this life they persist."[46]

It is certainly true that being children of God "in Christ Jesus" (Gal 3:26), being "baptized into Christ" (Gal 3:27) and being "one in Christ Jesus" (Gal 3:28) are profoundly spiritual realities. They are the result of faith (Gal 3:24-25) and involve both inner spiritual renewal and a spiritual relationship with Christ. Yet to limit the meaning of the text to this spiritual dimension does not do it justice. The totality of human life, including the concrete social-historical particularity of human life in community, is being addressed by this text. As a whole, the letter to the Galatians deals with the issue of the relationship between Jewish and Gentile believers in the Christian community. Specifically, it is concerned with whether Gentile believers must become Jews before they can be full Christians (Gal 2:3-14). In a sustained argument, Paul insists that only by faith in Christ are people restored to right relationship with God (Gal 2:15—6:16). It is further clear from Paul's strong criticism of Jewish believers who had withdrawn from fellowship with Gentile believers (Gal 2:11-14) that he was deeply concerned about the viability of the very concrete, social communities of Christ's followers. For Paul, "being baptized into Christ" on the basis of faith is, at the same time, being baptized "into one body" (1 Cor 12:13); and that body is "the body of Christ" of which individual believers are members (1 Cor 12:27; cf. Rom 12:4).

This concern for the very practical expression of the spiritual reality of life *in Christ* within the social reality of *the body of Christ* is also clearly articulated in Ephesians. Jew and Gentile (the "circumcision" and the "uncircumcision" in Eph 2:11) have been brought together in "one new humanity in place of the two" (Eph 2:15). The hostility between them has been brought to an end, for they are reconciled "in one body" (Eph 2:16). That body is constituted "in Christ Jesus" (Eph 2:13) as "the body of Christ" (Eph 4:12).

In light of this larger theological context, overcoming the Jew-Gentile,

---

[46]Mark J. Edwards, ed., *Galatians, Ephesians, Philippians,* Ancient Christian Commentary on Scripture, New Testament, vol. 7 (Downers Grove, Ill.: InterVarsity Press, 1999), p. 51.

slave-free and male-female divisions, alienations and over-under power relationships is, for Paul, not just a matter of spiritual transcendence but of social-
relational transformation. These three dual categories are social realities with
real-life interactions. Jews and Gentiles, free persons and slaves, men and
women—marked, shaped and conditioned by the old-order norms in these
relationships—were baptized into the new "in Christ" communities. They
had become members of a new form of humanity, a new creation in which the
old order of things "has passed away" (2 Cor 5:17). The "old wineskins" by
which these pairs of relationships were defined could not contain the new
wine of the Spirit. New wineskins were needed (cf. Mk 2:22). The dividing
walls of racial and religious superiority of Jew over Gentile, which Paul addressed specifically in Galatians and Ephesians, had to be abolished (Eph
2:15) so that the "one Spirit" of the resurrected Lord could shape "one body,"
namely a new community marked not by racial and religious superior-inferior
power categories but by the power of transforming love (Gal 5:22-26; Eph
4:1-16).

Scholars are largely agreed that the formulation of the three relational
categories mentioned in Galatians 3:28 has a prior history, perhaps as a formula in baptismal ceremonies,[47] where individuals from these three pairs of
groups were baptized into "the body of Christ" (as is the case in Gal 3:27-28).
What is virtually certain is that the Pauline formulation is a direct challenge
to the affirmations of superiority that were uttered by male Jews in daily
prayer, when they thanked God that he had not made them a Gentile, a slave
or a woman.[48] In Galatians, Paul applied the significance of the formulation,
"there is no longer," to the crucial matter of the relation between Jewish and
Gentile believers. If that matter could not be solved, the whole project of
Christ's work for "both Jew and Greek" would come to naught, and the vision
of the creation of a "new humanity" would remain but a vision. But since he
used the entire formula, even though the slave-free and male-female relations
are not at issue in Galatians, there is every reason to believe that Paul here
articulated a vision for the transformation of these relational "power-over"

---

[47]Some have pointed to similar formulations in 1 Corinthians 12:12-13 (where baptism is also mentioned) and Colossians 3:9-11 (where baptismal imagery is present in the context). See Daniel P.
Fuller, "Paul and Galatians 3:28," *TSF Bulletin* (November-December 1985): 9.

[48]F. F. Bruce, *The Epistle to the Galatians: A Commentary on the Greek Text* (Grand Rapids: Eerdmans, 1982), p. 187: "It is not unlikely that Paul himself had been brought up to thank God that
he was born a Jew and not a Gentile, a freeman and not a slave, a man and not a woman."

structures into relationships of equality as brothers and sisters in Christ. As F. F. Bruce[49] puts it so strikingly, "superiority and inferiority of status or esteem could have no place in the society whose Founder laid it down that among his followers 'whoever would be first . . . must be slave of all' " (see Mk 10:44).

The Pauline epistles and the record of Acts shows that the battle for the full equality of Gentile and Jew in the churches—though difficult and beset by relapses—was fought and won. In Christ's body, there could be "no longer Jew or Greek." It is equally clear that the seeds of the "no longer" principle for the transformation of the freeman-slave and the male-female relationships were sown into more stony ground. It was ground saturated with centuries-old, deeply ingrained attitudes, mores and practices that promoted the social and essential inferiority of slaves and women. And yet the seeds were sown for the eventual abolition of these dehumanizing, demeaning and marginalizing power-over relationships. In numerous places in the New Testament churches, these seeds germinated and grew.[50] But this initial growth virtually ground to a halt for centuries, as the old orders of hierarchical power patterns reasserted themselves, and in many ways, persist in our own time within the life, practices and attitudes of the body of Christ.[51] The tragedy is that abusive readings of Scripture have significantly contributed to and perpetuated this state of affairs. In the case of Galatians 3:27-28, the "spiritualizing" of the text has robbed the text of its power to challenge the legitimacy of the socially and historically grounded power structures and superior-inferior status relationships. The radically transformative vision of the "no longer" principle in our text has been blurred by the abuse of literary and theological context. We have done violence to its essential meaning and message. It cries out to be heard again for what it truly is: the "Charter of Christian Freedom."

---

[49]Ibid., p. 190.

[50]On the issue of the "free-slave" reality in the New Testament period and within apostolic teaching, see the significant studies by Willard M. Swartley, *Slaves, Sabbath, War and Women: Case Studies in Biblical Interpretation* (Scottdale, Penn.: Herald Press, 1983); William J. Webb, *Slaves, Women and Homosexuals* (Downers Grove, Ill.: InterVarsity Press, 2001). With regard to the male-female relationship, we have shown throughout this study (chapters three, five and six) the numerous ways the "no longer" principle was embodied in the early Christian communities.

[51]Examples are to be seen in many white churches where black people are still not welcome, and in Christian denominations and churches across the globe where women continue to be restricted in the use of their gifts and are under the "leadership" of male authority figures.

Romans 7:15, 18-19.

I do not do what I want, but I do the very thing I hate. . . . I can will what is right, but I cannot do it. For I do not do the good I want, but the evil I do not want is what I do.

These verses are part of a chapter in Romans that has been "one of the most hotly debated passages in New Testament scholarship."[52] No wonder the average reader, who depends on scholarly insight and clarity, is confused! This study is not the place to enter into a detailed exegetical discussion of this text. For that, excellent studies are available.[53] Our concern here is to hear these verses within the larger literary and theological context of Paul's argument in Romans 5—8, in order to address a very problematic understanding of the nature of Christian existence, a consequence of the abuse of context.

On plain reading, these verses seem like the candid confession of a divided self, a basic split within the human personality. It is an acknowledgment of utter weakness, an affirmation of absolute powerlessness. Paul's final analysis of the situation expressed in these statements is the helpless cry, "Wretched man that I am" (Rom 7:24). If the experience described in these verses is a description of the Christian life, then that description stands in stark contrast to the kind of joy, freedom and newness with which Paul describes the nature of Christian life throughout his letters, and specifically in the chapters of Romans that precede and follow this troubling passage. If chapter 7 is a description of the believer's experience, then it is decidedly unattractive. If the coming of God's relation-restoring love in Christ, and its result in the justification of sinners (Rom 1:16—3:26), does not lead to a new kind of life, then the gospel of God's saving grace is not "good news" at all, but rather "bad news." Who needs this?

---

[52]Frank Thielmann, *Paul and the Law: A Contextual Approach* (Downers Grove, Ill.: InterVarsity Press, 1994), p. 198. In note 13 (p. 295) he lists the central questions the text has evoked: "Who is the 'I' of the passage? Do the past tenses in verses 7-13 refer to Paul's own past, to Israel, to Adam or to something else entirely? Do the present tenses in verses 14-25 mean that the struggle described there is experienced by the believer? Does Paul slip into a dualistic view of good and evil in verses 14-25, portraying sin as a power out of even God's control? Is his view of human nature unconvincingly pessimistic?"

[53]For studies of all the issues raised by this text, see commentaries and special studies. I recommend especially James D. G. Dunn, *Romans 1—8*, Word Biblical Commentary, vol. 38A (Waco, Tex.: Word Books, 1988); N. T. Wright, *Romans*, The New Interpreter's Bible, vol. 10 (Nashville: Abingdon, 2000); Hermann Ridderbos, *Paul: An Outline of His Theology* (Grand Rapids: Eerdmans, 1975), pp. 126-29; Paul Achtemeier, *Romans*, pp. 108-41; Peter Stuhlmacher, *Paul's Letter to the Romans: A Commentary* (Louisville, Ky.: Westminster John Knox, 1994), pp. 101-31 (and excursus no. 11, pp. 114-21).

And yet a common and pervasive understanding of Romans 7 among rank-and-file Christians is that Paul was writing here about an internal battle in the believer's heart, or more specifically an ongoing conflict between a "higher nature" and a "lower nature," a "fleshly self" and a "spiritual self."[54] Even *that* hearing of the text lessens the severity of the actual situation described. In this scenario, there is at least the possibility of occasionally tipping the scales, of winning some of these battles, of at times acting and thinking in ways that are pleasing to the Lord. But in the text as it stands, there is only defeat. In a course I recently taught called "A Biblical Theology for Marriage and Family," a student described the terribly abusive relationship of a Christian couple who, though at times successful in getting beyond their dysfunctional and destructive behavior, found themselves more often than not reverting to the old ways, and they took refuge in the common hearing of Romans 7 as justification for their experience: this is the way it is; we are in bondage; the devil made me do it![55] For many Christians, this way of reading Romans 7 has become an escape hatch from responsible Christian life and action. They understand this chapter as "depicting Paul's present enslavement to sin, and some even use it to justify living sinfully, saying: 'If Paul could not keep from living in sin, how can we?' "[56] For many others, it has been a slightly comforting mirror image of their own struggles to be faithful disciples, but for others it has been a source of discouragement. Still others have been turned off by what they perceive to be a picture of Paul's conflicted personality, and they opt instead for a "power of positive thinking" version of the faith: if I think rightly and do my best and go for it, I can do it. All of these responses are, in some way, the unfortunate but inevitable consequences of the abuse of literary and theological contexts.

Instead, let's turn to a clarifying examination of those contexts. In order to highlight the statements of impotence in Romans 7, we'll need to look at the diametrically opposite affirmations in the surrounding passages. In Romans 7:14, Paul states, "I am of the flesh, sold into slavery under sin," but just a few verses earlier (Romans 6:18) he declares that believers have been "set free

---

[54]Recall the discussion in chapter five of Paul's understanding of living "according to the flesh" and "according to the Spirit."

[55]Achtemeier, *Romans,* p. 109: "Paul is clear: 'The devil made me do it' will no longer work as an excuse."

[56]Cited with permission from my colleague Craig S. Keener from an unpublished manual on "Biblical Interpretation," prepared for theological students in Nigeria, 2005, p. 27.

from sin" and are now "slaves of righteousness." In Romans 7:18, he confesses "that nothing good dwells within me," but in Romans 8:11 he declares that "the Spirit of him who raised Jesus from the dead" dwells in all believers. In Romans 7:25 he acknowledges that he is a slave to the law of sin, but in Romans 8:2 he states that Christ by the power of his Spirit has set us "free from the law of sin and of death." These contrasts make clear that if Romans 7 is a description of the Christian's normal experience, then Paul is hopelessly contradicting himself.

Let us place these contrasting affirmations into the larger context of Paul's thought and argument in the surrounding chapters, beginning with a summary of Paul's discussion in Romans 1—8. In light of the universal human rebellion against God, as well as Jewish faithlessness within its covenant relationship with God (described in Rom 1:18—3:20), Paul concludes by declaring that "all have sinned and fall short of the glory of God" (Rom 3:23). But in the face of this desperate human reality, God has acted. In Christ, God's righteousness—that is, his relation-restoring and alienation-overcoming love[57]—has been revealed and embodied (Rom 1:16-17; 3:21-22). All who respond by faith to that redemptive work of God in Christ's life and atoning death are "justified," are "set right," and brought back into life-giving and life-sustaining relationship with God (Rom 3:23—4:25). That foundational analysis is brought to a conclusion in Romans 5:1-11, concisely expressed in the headline sentence of this passage: "Therefore, since we are justified by faith, we have peace with God through our Lord Jesus Christ" (Rom 5:1). In the next major section of his argument (Rom 5:12—8:17), Paul goes on to unpack what that act of relation-restoring love accomplished and what that peace with God—expressed also in terms of reconciliation with God (Rom 5:10-11)—looks like.

The human condition, summarized in Romans 3:23 ("all have sinned"), is characterized by three realities: enslavement to death, to sin and (specifically for Paul's Jewish believers in Rome) to the law. The primary focus of Romans 5:12-21 is the human reality of the bondage to death, the result of our corporate belonging to, and participation in, the "adamic humanity." But, through

---

[57]Recall our brief discussion of this understanding of the meaning of "the righteousness of God" earlier in this chapter (in the examination of Is 61:10). For a thorough analysis of this term in Paul against the Old Testament background, see my book *Set Free to Be* (Valley Forge, Penn.: Judson Press, 1975), pp. 11-32.

Jesus Christ who is the antitype of "the one man"[58] (Rom 5:15), the grace of God has brought the dominion of death to an end (Rom 5:14, 17) by bestowing the gift of life (Rom 5:17-18), indeed, eternal life (Rom 5:21).

In Romans 6:1-23 Paul addresses human bondage to sin, which is at the core of our belonging to the "adamic humanity." That bondage has also been shattered. How? We have "died to sin" (Rom 6:2), says Paul, because "we have been buried with him by baptism into death" and have been raised with him to "walk in newness of life" (Rom 6:4). We are united with Christ in his death and in his resurrection, which is symbolically acted out in baptism (Rom 6:4-5). In the background of this "participation" in the event of Christ stands the Jewish (and Pauline) concept of "corporate solidarity." Just as we are in solidarity with the first Adam, in whom is launched the story of human lostness and brokenness, so by faith we are in solidarity with the second Adam, who launched the story of human redemption and wholeness. The old self, enslaved by sin, "was crucified" with Christ (Rom 6:6) so that "we might no longer be enslaved to sin. For whoever has died is freed from sin" (Rom 6:6-7). As participants by faith in his resurrection (Rom 6:9; Col 2:11-12) we have been made "alive to God in Christ Jesus" (Rom 6:11). In connection with these declarations of liberation from the dominion of sin, Paul introduces an exhortation: "Therefore, do not let sin exercise dominion in your mortal bodies" (Rom 6:12), and "no longer present your members to sin as instruments of wickedness" (Rom 6:13). Why this exhortation? Because freedom from sin's enslavement does not mean its absence from the "adamic humanity" within which we still live.[59] Justification does not immunize us against the reality of sin. We do not become automatons who live by the dictates or controlling force of a new ethical-moral core of righteousness within us. Rather, we have been "set right" (justified), brought back into reconciled relationship with God and placed on the path toward wholeness (sanctification; see Rom 6:19, 22). On that path we are being transformed into the image of Christ (2 Cor 3:18; 4:4). What we have in this dual affirmation— freedom from the bondage to sin (which Paul states repeatedly in Rom 6:6-7,

---

[58]In 1 Corinthians 15, Paul makes the type-antitype imagery of Romans 5 explicit: "the first man, Adam"—"the last Adam [Christ]"; "the first man"—"the second man"; "the man of dust"—"the man of heaven" (1 Cor 15:45-49).

[59]We are reminded of Jesus' prayer for his disciples in John 17:15: "I am not asking you to take them out of the world, but I ask you to keep them from the evil one." Cf. also 1 Cor 5:10, where Paul articulates the principle "in the world but not of the world."

14, 17-18, 20, 22), and the exhortation not to give ourselves to it again (Rom 6:12-13, 16)—is the Pauline "already-not yet" dialectic: You have been set free from sin's bondage; now embody that freedom in your life. Justification is ultimately *not* the transformation of our personality or the transformation of our ontology, the core of our being, *but rather* the transformation of relationships, the overcoming of alienation and the establishment of reconciliation. In that reconciled relationship, there is authentic freedom in two directions: freedom to live in openness to the empowering reality of the Spirit of Christ, and also freedom to yield ourselves to the enticement of sin. In Galatians, Paul affirms the same truth: "For freedom Christ has set us free. Stand firm, therefore, and do not submit again to the yoke of slavery" (Gal 5:1; cf. Gal 5:13).

In Romans 7:1—8:17 Paul addresses, first of all, Jewish believers at the point of their relationship to the law ("for I am speaking to those who know the law," Rom 7:1). He has already spoken of a close connection between the law, sin and death (Rom 5:13, 20), and he has indicated that they are no longer under law but under grace (Rom 6:14-15; cf. Rom 10:4). Those brief hints he now takes up in Romans 7. He begins with the rhetorical question: "Do you not know . . . that the law is binding on a person only during that person's lifetime?" Then he illustrates the truth of that assertion with an analogy from the law governing marriage, which binds partners only as long as both live (Rom 7:2-3), and applies that insight to their present situation: "You have died to the law" in dying and rising with Christ (recalling what he said in Rom 6:3-4).[60]

Having only hinted at the intimate connection between sin, death and the law, Paul now takes up two questions that lurk just barely in the background: (1) How is God's law implicated with sin and death, and what is the reality of life under law? (2) What does a life that is free from the bondage of law, sin and death look like? A careful analysis of the structure of Paul's argument, in response to these two questions, reveals the following. Romans 7:5 answers, in headline form, the first question; and the content of that headline sentence is then unpacked in Romans 7:7-24. Romans 7:6 answers, in headline form, the second question; and the content of that heading is then unpacked in

---

[60]It is unfortunate that the standard translations make a paragraph division between Romans 7:1-3 and Romans 7:4. The marriage analogy (in Rom 7:1-3) and its application (in Rom 7:4) belong together. The new thought-unit begins in Romans 7:5-6.

Romans 8:1-17. For purposes of clarity, a visual presentation of the structure of Paul's argument can be helpful:

Implied Question 1	Implied Question 2
What is the connection between the law, sin and death, and what is the reality of life under the law?	What does a life that is free from the bondage of the law, sin and death look like?
Headline Response **7:5**	**Headline Response** **7:6**
While we were living in the flesh, our sinful passions, aroused by the law, were at work in our members to bear fruit for death.	*But now we are discharged from the law, dead to that which held us captive, so that we are slaves not under the old written code but in the new life of the Spirit.*
Unpacking the Headline **7:7-24**	**Unpacking the Headline** **8:1-17**
(summary of argument)	(summary of argument)
Because of sin's power and its enslaving hold on me, the attempt to live life in response to God's law—which is holy and just and good—ends in utter failure. I delight in God's law, but I find myself incapable of measuring up to it. What wretchedness!	Christ has liberated us from the stranglehold of sin, death and the law; and by the Spirit of the living Christ dwelling within us, we are empowered to live a life that is free from the enslaving power of sin, death and the law, as the free children of God.

When we observe this structure of Paul's argument, the idea that Romans 7:7-24 is a description of Christian existence becomes impossible. He clearly juxtaposes two radically different experiences and time frames: *what was -> what is; then -> now; while we were -> but now we are; we were living in the flesh -> now we are not in the flesh.* This decisive alternative indisputably confirms what we already discovered from the larger context: Life outside Christ, in the adamic humanity, is marked by the bondage to sin and death. That bondage has also overpowered the good gift of God's law within Judaism, and it has turned it into the experience of legalistic chains. But life in Christ, life indwelt by Christ, life empowered by the same Spirit of God who raised Jesus from the dead (Rom 8:9-11), is the life of Christian freedom, energized for the "obedience of faith" (Rom 1:5; 16:26). Once again, we see that when a text is read within its larger literary and theological context, we can avoid misreading it or developing a distorted understanding, with all its attendant negative consequences.

A brief final reflection is in order regarding Romans 7. Since Romans 7:7-24 is decidedly not a description of Christian existence, what does it describe, and why was Paul speaking in the first person singular ("I") and in the present tense?[61] My brief response to these questions is as follows: (1) Paul was describing life lived on the basis of legalistic obedience under the Mosaic law; (2) Paul wrote in the first person singular and present tense for dramatic, rhetorical effect. Whether he was describing his actual, conscious experience and his view of the law in an autobiographical way is open to debate. As a pharisaic Jew, Paul would, most likely, not have said what he says here about the connection between sin and the law. That would have been preposterous. Rabbinic Judaism understood the law as a gift of God, a sign of his grace and favor.[62] But in retrospect, from the point of view of his encounter with Christ and his life "in Christ," Paul gained the conviction that the life that he had lived in strictest conformity to the law (and done so quite successfully!—Phil 3:4-8) had within it the seeds of death. It inexorably led to self-righteousness before God and to the judgmental exclusion of others.

What then is the relevance, for Christian existence, of this Pauline analysis of life under the law? Its relevance lies in the recognition that where the real thing is present, the distortion of it is never far behind. The story of Christianity, from Paul's time to the present, is replete with Christian forms of legalistic piety and religious formalism, which have in them the seeds of death. That is why the apostle exhorts both Jewish and Gentile believers not to trade in their freedom in Christ for a new form of bondage (Rom 6:12-13; 8:12-13; Gal 5:1, 13).

---

[61]For a thorough exploration of these questions and various answers that have been proposed, see the suggested literature cited in note 53 above.

[62]Solomon Schechter gives a helpful description of the Jewish understanding of the law in *Aspects of Rabbinic Theology* (New York: Schocken Books, 1961), pp. 148-69. The groundbreaking work of E. P. Sanders, *Paul and Palestinian Judaism* (Philadelphia: Fortress, 1977), argues that the rabbinic understanding of the law can be described as "covenantal nomism." God's covenant with Israel was seen as a gift of God's grace, the gift of salvation, while keeping the law was a way to remain faithful to the covenant (not a means to gain salvation).

Ephesians 5:21-33. In chapter five, I explored the meaning of two significant concepts in this passage about the husband-wife relationship. In decoding the Pauline concept of *submission* (or "subjection"), we saw that the submission of the wife to the husband and the church to Christ have nothing to do with authority and power exercised by one party, and reciprocated with obedience and subjection by the other party. Rather, submission involves a radical self-giving in response to the other's sacrificial love and self-giving. Further, our decoding of Paul's use of the term *head* led to the conclusion that Christ as "head" in relationship to the church, and man as "head" in relationship to woman, has nothing to do with the so-called doctrine of headship, designating a hierarchical power structure. Rather, Paul employed the term *head* in its metaphorical sense of "source of life" to define these relationships. Our purpose in dealing with the passage here is to show how reading and hearing it—within the larger theological context of the New Testament and the larger literary context of Ephesians as a whole—confirms these meanings of *submission* and *head*, and informs the way the entire passage needs to be understood.

The husband-wife relationship, both within human cultures and within the Christian tradition, has been pervasively understood in terms of the presence and exercise of power. Who is in charge? Who has the final say? Who has the right to decide? These implicit or explicit questions have largely been answered in favor of a one-sided exercise of power: "leadership of" or "control over" or "responsibility for." In the Christian tradition, this way of understanding the nature and use of power in the husband-wife relationship has been grounded in a particular theological presupposition. Namely, that God is primarily a God of order, where divine power, exercised in "control of" and "authority over" are primary dimensions, and are therefore paradigmatic for the husband-wife and man-woman relationships.[63] Especially in the Old Testament, God is often pictured as exercising power and control over creation and the affairs of nations. Yet even in the Old Testament, God's relationship with Israel and his redemptive action in and through Israel toward the world is not primarily characterized by this "order-control" model.[64] Indeed, if the final, complete revelation of the nature and purpose of God is the incarnation,

---

[63]In the following reflections on issues of power and authority I am indebted to stimulating insights by S. Scott Bartchy, in a lecture titled "Issues of Power and a Theology of the Family," given at the Consultation on a Theology of the Family conference at Fuller Theological Seminary, Pasadena, Calif., 1984.

[64]E.g., the servant passages in Isaiah 42—53.

as the New Testament affirms,[65] then the theological-redemptive paradigm
for human relationships in the new humanity must be grounded in that revelation. In order to appreciate fully the radical nature of that paradigm, we will
look at the way power is normally present in human relationships.

In a study of interpersonal relationships, behavioral scientist Rollo May[66]
identifies five kinds of power commonly present and expressed in a variety of
ways in those relationships.

1. *Exploitive power.* This is the overt use of force, compliance or domination
   exercised *over* others, usually for one's own benefit, or "for the good of the
   other" (in a paternalistic sense, where the one determines what is "good"
   for the other). This kind of power is often marked by physical abuse.

2. *Manipulative power.* This kind of power is also exercised *over* others; but it
   is more covert. It limits the choices of the other by psychological and verbal manipulation and abuse. The imposition of guilt trips on another and
   demeaning the worth or intelligence of the other is typical here.

3. *Competitive power.* This is power exercised *against* the other. May acknowledges that, in some areas of life (e.g., in sports, business, education),
   this kind of power can be positive, stimulating one toward higher achieve-
   ment and performance. But in interpersonal relationships, it typically assumes a "win-lose" posture.

4. *Nutrient power.* This is power exercised *for* the other. It is best illustrated
   in its positive form by parents' love for and normal care of their children.
   The welfare of others is the driving force. But in mature relationships
   among adults, particularly in unequal power relationships, nutrient power
   is often experienced as smothering, resulting in lack of self-worth, one-
   sided dependency and insecurity.

5. *Integrity power.* This is power exercised *with* the other. In relationships characterized by this kind of power, the partners assist each other in recognizing
   their potential; they act to facilitate, encourage, and support each other's giftedness and give each other space to grow toward wholeness. May believes
   that integrity power has a transcendent dimension because it goes beyond
   ordinary expressions of power in human relationships and institutions.

---

[65]Jn 1:1-14; Col 1:18-20; 2:9; Heb 1:1-3.
[66]Rollo May, *Power and Innocence: A Search for the Sources of Violence* (Scranton, Penn.: W. W. Norton, 1972).

In contrast to these pervasive expressions of power in human relationships (with the exception of integrity power), the radical nature of the use of power in the incarnation stands out in bold relief. In Jesus' life, ministry and teaching, the nature and uses of power and authority are transformed. A radically new vision is given birth: Authentic power is not used to control but to serve. We'll consider several christological texts that underline this affirmation.

Mark 8:27-38. In this text, Peter's confession of Jesus' messianic identity is acknowledged by Jesus,[67] and it is immediately followed by the prediction of Jesus' impending suffering and death. This word about suffering and servanthood is rejected by Peter, for his understanding of the person and work of the Messiah is very much that of his Jewish context. According to common belief, the Messiah was to be the conquering, triumphant king who would deliver Israel from its bondage to Rome.[68] Jesus' rebuke of Peter's ideology—which he called demonic—reveals that Jesus rejected the trimphalistic tradition as not in keeping with God's purpose. Then follows Jesus' teaching that those who would be his disciples are called into the same servant life as their master. To cling to life and power is to lose life; to give oneself away in service to others is to discover it.

Mark 9:30-37. This is the second prediction of Jesus' impending suffering. This prediction is followed, remarkably, by the discussion among the disciples about who among them was the greatest. The contrast between Jesus' sacrificial servanthood and their concern about status and power is stark. This is immediately followed by Jesus' statement that "Whoever wants to be first must be last of all and servant of all" (Mk 9:35). Prominence, status and leadership are redefined by Jesus in terms of servanthood. Luke connects the disciples' dispute about who was to be regarded as the greatest (Lk 22:24) with the Lord's Supper, the symbolic enactment of his sacrificial suffering and death (Lk 22:14-23). Jesus responds that the models of the world's power structures (Lk 22:25) are not to guide them: "But not so with you" (Lk 22:26). The model for Jesus' new community is Jesus himself: "I am among you as one who serves" (Lk 22:27).

Mark 10:32-45. The third prediction of Jesus' suffering is followed by James and John's question about the privilege of sitting at his right and left hand—positions of power and authority—when he reigns in glory (surely, in

---

[67]Cf. Mt 16:17: "Flesh and blood has not revealed this to you, but my Father in heaven."
[68]Cf. Lk 24:21: "We had hoped that he was the one to redeem Israel."

their minds, when he would establish the messianic reign in Israel in the near future). Again, Jesus reminded them that they were called to participate in his servant life. In the world, says Jesus, rulers lord it over others (Mk 10:42), "but it is not so among you; but whoever wishes to become great among you must be your servant, and whoever wishes to be first among you must be slave of all" (Mk 10:43-44). Then, in Mark 10:45, in direct reference to the prophecy about the Son of Man in Daniel 7:13-14, Jesus' words turned upside down the expectation associated with that Son of Man. In Daniel, the Son of Man "was given dominion and glory and kingship, that all . . . should serve him." Jesus explicitly identified himself as that Son of Man, but rather than expecting to be served, he was ready to serve others, even at the cost of his own life: "For the Son of Man *came not to be served* but to serve, and to give his life a ransom for many" (Mk 10:45, emphasis mine). Both the prophetic expectation of a conquering Messiah and the apocalyptic expectations for the heavenly Son of Man were reinterpreted by Jesus in terms of the Servant of Yahweh[69] in Isaiah 53.

Philippians 2:3-8. This is Paul's significant contribution to the christological frame of reference for individuals and their relationships in the new humanity. Jesus' condescension and suffering (Phil 2:6-8) is presented as the paradigm: "Let the same mind be in you that was in Christ Jesus" (Phil 2:5). This is the theological-christological model for Christian conduct and relationships within the new humanity: "Do nothing from selfish ambition or conceit, but in humility regard others as better than yourselves. Let each of you look not to your own interests, but to the interests of others" (Phil 2:3-4).

These christological texts reveal Jesus' very intentional rejection of the exercise of power in order to control or dominate. In Jesus' new community, the power plays of this world, characterized by domination, exploitation, manipulation and win-lose competition are out of place. Jesus' power is not expressed as control from above, but strength from beneath; it does not coerce or demand, but it serves and invites. But, some have argued, is not all of this set aside by the early Christian confession that "Jesus is Lord" (Rom 10:9)? Quite the contrary is, in fact, true. He is the authoritative paradigm for human relationships as *servant*, not as sovereign. He is a different kind of Lord

---

[69]The radical nature of that identification particularly stands out in light of the fact that the figure of the suffering servant in Isaiah is never identified with the Messiah or the Son of Man in pre-Christian Judaism.

than Caesar. In his incarnate servanthood, he is the image of God for us and our journey of transformation into that same image (2 Cor 3:18; 4:4). The confession of this Jesus as Lord challenges the legitimacy of all earthly "lords" in their exercise of distortive power. The same confession was also a powerful statement about the serving nature of divine power. It is the exercise of this kind of power that challenges ordinary understandings of power, station and privilege, and it is, therefore, also paradigmatic for all relationships in the new community of Jesus' disciples. From this larger theological context, we are ready to move to the more immediate theological and literary context of our text (Eph 5:21-33) within Ephesians as a whole.

On the basis of the redemptive work of God's grace in Christ (Eph 1:7-8; 2:8-9), Christians are "God's workmanship, created in Christ Jesus to do good works" (Eph 2:10 NIV). In Christ, men and women are being brought together as a dwelling place of God's Spirit (Eph 2:21-22). Paul certainly understood God's Spirit as the energizer and enabler of the new way of Jesus in the lives of his disciples (Eph 3:16-17; cf. Rom 8:11-14). They are to be "filled with all the fullness of God" (Eph 3:19) and grow together toward maturity in Christ as the body of Christ (Eph 4:13-16). These affirmations and exhortations reach their climax in Ephesians 5:1-2: "Therefore, be imitators of God . . . and live in love, as Christ loved us and gave himself up for us." What that imitation of God, as embodied in the way of Christ, looks like in specific behaviors (Eph 5:3-16) comes to a focus in Ephesians 5:17-18: "Understand what the will of God is. . . . Be filled with the Spirit." That fullness of the Spirit manifests itself in four ways in the common life of Jesus' new community and in the concrete, ordinary relationships of its members. These four ways are stated in four participial clauses that "exegete"[70] (or "interpret") how the fullness of the Spirit expresses itself (Eph 5:19-21).[71]

It is unfortunate, and misleading, that the standard translations (e.g., NIV, RSV) separate Ephesians 5:21 (the fourth participial clause) from both what precedes it and what follows it, as if it were an isolated exhortation. Paul's grammatical construction argues against this "interpretive" rearrangement of the text. Equally important is the fact that without the fourth participle in

---

[70]The participial clauses are what Greek grammarians call "epexegetical participles." They "exegete" (interpret, unpack) the significance of the verb.

[71]For a very helpful and complete interpretation of these four participial clauses, see Markus Barth, *Ephesians 4—6*, Anchor Bible (New York: Doubleday, 1974), pp. 583-85.

Ephesians 5:21 (literally, from the Greek, "submitting yourselves to one another in awe of Christ"), the following sentence in Ephesians 5:22 ("Wives, to your husbands as to the Lord") lacks a verb, which must be supplied from the participle of Ephesians 5:21 ("submitting yourselves").[72] What these literary and grammatical connections signify is that "mutual submission" is one of the evidences of the fullness of the Spirit, and the exhortation to this mutual submission (or subordination) *sets the agenda* for the nature of the husband-wife relationship, which follows in the household code (Eph 5:22-33).[73] I have already noted (in chapter five) that the guiding principle of "mutual submission" is grounded christologically. It is to be "in awe of Christ," a clear reference to the exhortation in Ephesians 5:1-2 to live in our relationships in imitation of Christ's self-giving. So husbands and wives are challenged to practice this mutual submission, which at its core is a radical alternative to the culturally prescribed (and one-sided) order of the wife's submission to her husband's authority over her.

Given the cultural context, the Pauline description of the way husbands are to embody the "mutual submission" principle "in awe of Christ" is nothing short of revolutionary. Husbands are to love their wives "as Christ loved the church and gave himself up for her" (Eph 5:25). This astounding comparison between Christian husbands and Christ has, as its point of comparison, *not* "lordship language" (in the sense of power and control) *but* sacrificial servant language. The only point at which the husband is called on to identify himself with Christ's behavior or role is the extreme extent of Christ's love for the church (Eph 5:29-33).[74]

In this interpretation of Ephesians 5:21-33, I have brought to bear four hermeneutical methods in order to avoid abusive readings of this text: First,

---

[72]The Greek word translated "submit" (NIV) or "subject" (NRSV) is *hypotassō*, which literally means "to place, or set under [something or someone]." While the English words "to submit" or "to subject" express the idea of obedience to a person who has authority or power over one, the word "to subordinate" expresses more the idea—which I believe is present in our text—of giving oneself to another or others in loving service, in imitation of Christ. Recall this discussion in chapter five.

[73]Given the grammatical flow of the passage, I think that F. F. Bruce, *The Epistles to the Colossians, to Philemon and to the Ephesians*, New International Commentary on the New Testament (Grand Rapids: Eerdmans, 1984), p. 383, is wrong when he states that "while the household code is introduced by a plea for mutual submissiveness, the submissiveness enjoined in the code itself is not mutual."

[74]See appendix D for my expanded translation of Ephesians 5:21-33, on the basis of both the linguistic work in chapter five and the theological-literary context perspectives worked out in the present chapter.

we investigated the "encoding" and "decoding" of significant and critical terms *(head* and *submit)* used by Paul in Ephesians 5 and related texts. Second, we sought to hear the broader New Testament theological context regarding the nature and exercise of power, and we paid specific attention to christological texts that reveal a new paradigmatic pattern for human relationships. Third, we observed the narrower literary and theological context of Ephesians as a whole, in terms of the broad sweep and direction of Paul's argument. Fourth, we looked at the immediate literary and grammatical context, namely how Ephesians 5:21-33 is connected with the flow of Paul's overall argument—both as a bridge from that which precedes it and as agenda-setting for what follows it. When all of these elements are brought together for the interpretation of the husband-wife passage, it is extremely difficult to construe Ephesians 5:21-33 as apostolic instruction—in keeping with prevailing cultural norms—for wives to submit themselves to their husbands' leadership and authority, and for husbands to exercise authority (even "benevolent authority") over their wives.

AVOIDING THE ABUSE OF LITERARY AND THEOLOGICAL CONTEXTS

The significance of "hearing" the contexts within which any particular biblical text is located, in order to interpret the meaning of that text correctly, cannot be overstated. Indeed, contexts may be the most important lenses through which to determine the meaning and significance of the Word of God, which addresses us in and through the words of the biblical text. The analysis of numerous biblical verses and passages has revealed how the meanings and messages of biblical texts can easily be distorted when those contexts are not taken with utmost seriousness. How can such abusive readings of biblical texts be avoided? The following guidelines and principles—implicit in our discussion of how literary and theological contexts are often abused— need to be observed.

1. Ask "What is its context?" This is the first question that should follow the reading of a particular verse or passage. Then the initial reading of the text should aim to answer the question: "What does the text say?" This identification of what the text says should be followed immediately by the question: "What does the text mean?" In order to begin to answer that question, one of the most important tasks is to understand the various contexts within which it is located.

2. Analyze, first, the immediate literary context and then the larger context **(from verse, to paragraph, to chapter, to book).** The analysis of the contexts of any biblical text should begin with the most immediate literary context of the word or verse or passage, and proceed to the larger context (from verse to paragraph to chapter to whole book), in the order of concentric circles. Such systematic attention to the connections of the considered text to the larger literary units to which it belongs represents faithfulness to the *way* the author communicates in order to grasp *what* he communicates.

3. Resist the temptation to bring preconceived notions of what a text should **mean.** One of the most common abuses in the interpretation of Scripture results from the tendency to read a text *in light of* or *determined by* understandings brought to the text from outside its own theological and/or literary contexts. In other words, we should never interpret a text out of its own context and then use it as a *pretext* in support of particular beliefs and doctrines that we held prior to the study of that text. On the microlevel that is called *eisegesis* (importing a meaning into the text) rather than proper *exegesis* (unpacking the meaning that is in the text). When we eisegete a text, "contextual faithfulness" is seriously undermined.

4. Ask "What would the implied audience of this text, when it heard or read **the text within the author's context, have heard?"** This is a fundamental question that must be asked. A text cannot mean what the immediate and larger contexts—whether literary or theological—do not allow, nor can a text mean what the original audience could *not* possibly have heard or understood it to mean. (An example of this discussed above is the text from 1 Corinthians 13:9-10, which the original recipients in Corinth could not possibly have understood as a reference to the completion of the New Testament canon one hundred years later!)

5. Interpret any text from the perspective of the larger literary and/or theo- **logical argument of which it is a part.** This hermeneutical principle is particularly important when interpreting texts that are an integral part of a sustained theological reflection about and/or argument in support of Christian praxis, or the life and mission of the church, or the relationship of Christians with the outside world, such as in the Pauline epistles. (Recall our discussion of Romans 7 and Ephesians 5 as illustrations.) Questions involved in the application of this principle are: What is the grammatical structure and syntax of the passage? What role does it play in the development of the argument?

How and what does it contribute? What is the overarching theological idea within the argument? How does that theological perspective affect the passage or verse under consideration? When such questions are carefully pursued, the quest for the meaning of the text within its context has a good chance of yielding positive results.

Throughout the reflections in this chapter, we noted that an understanding of the cultural context and the particular historical situation addressed by a text are equally important for faithful hearing and interpretation of God's Word. In the next chapter of this study, we will turn to an examination of the abuse of the meaning of biblical texts that occurs when those contexts are not taken seriously.

7

THE ABUSE OF CONTEXT

HISTORICAL SITUATION AND CULTURAL REALITY

A fundamental assumption about the nature of the Bible, discussed in chapter one, is its "incarnational" nature, in analogy to the incarnate reality of the Word made flesh (Jn 1:14). This means that the Word of God, his "lamp to [our] feet and a light to [our] path" (Ps 119:105), comes to us within the confines of human language and within the context of human history, and it participates in various cultural realities and addresses individuals and peoples in diverse situations. In that sense, the entirety of Scripture is historically and culturally embedded and conditioned. This reality of Scripture does not lessen its overarching authoritative character, just as the "enfleshed" nature of the living Word of God in Jesus does not lessen his authoritative presence. What it does mean is that our hearing, interpreting and application of Scripture must not take place without careful attention to this contextualization, this "human location" of Scripture.

When we are attentive to this reality, we find that God's word—spoken in and through the biblical witness over the course of over a thousand years—is not static, but "living and active."[1] God's reclamation project, attested to and narrated in Scripture, encounters the broken, distorted human objects of that divine work in their particular real-life situations and becomes "incarnate" in those situations. That is, God speaks through his servants and prophets into the ongoing story of a people within ever-changing historical and cultural situations. Therefore, that speaking addresses God's people at the point of their need, their reality within these changing historical and cultural realities. Theologians have spoken of this in terms of "progressive revelation" or the "progressive unfolding" of God's revelation. These terms communicate the truth that God did not reveal the totality of his redemptive project to Israel in its infancy. New and deeper truths about God, about the human reality of alienation from God, and about God's purposes for dealing with that alienation were disclosed to and through God's servants in subsequent stages of redemptive history.

Sometimes, as we saw in chapter three and chapter four of this book, new truths and understandings of God's ways in later periods stand in significant tension with, or even in critical opposition to, earlier truths and understandings. What this data revealed was another dimension of the incarnational nature of Scripture. When God surrenders his speaking to historically/culturally conditioned and limited (even sinful) hearers and witnesses, "God makes his words vulnerable"[2] to misunderstanding or partial understanding. Such misunderstood and partially understood truths are then—in light of the redemptive movement of God's revelation toward its climax in Jesus Christ—seen to be what they are, namely problematic or distorted perceptions of God's truth.

In addition to the above two dimensions of the incarnational nature of revelation, attested to in the Bible, there is a third one. Authoritative words of Scripture are, at times, so specifically addressed to particular cultural contexts or historical situations that their authority does not transcend those situations or contexts. At other times, situations and contexts are addressed by authoritative words that shed the light of God's truth on those particularities, and at the same time transcend them and have abiding authority for

---

[1]This phrase is from Telford Work, *Living and Active: Scripture in the Economy of Salvation* (Grand Rapids: Eerdmans, 2002). For the foundational understanding of the nature of Scripture in analogy to the incarnation, see his presentation of the thinking of the church fathers Athanasius and Augustine in pp. 33-63.

[2]Ibid., p. 46.

Christians in all times and places and cultures.

These dimensions of the incarnational nature of the biblical revelation confront us with what may be the most sensitive, difficult and controversial issue in the interpretation of the Bible: How do we discern between those things in Scripture that are culturally or historically relative and, therefore, limited in their inspired authority to the people and situations addressed at that time, and the things that are transcultural and transhistorical, where the authoritative Word of God is binding for all Christians at all times and in all cultures?[3] Some would immediately object that this question raises an issue not appropriate for Bible-believing Christians. For isn't the entire Bible the authoritative Word of God? Since the ultimate source of this Word is God, who by his Spirit inspired the writers of the various biblical documents, must we not then accept the authority of all parts of Scripture equally? As one popular Christian slogan puts it, "The Bible says it, I believe it, and that settles it!" For these people, even to raise the above question seems like an act of heretical thinking. They see such a hermeneutical process of discernment— between what is historically/culturally relative and what has abiding authority—as leading inevitably to a liberal watering down of the Bible's authority, to an open-ended slippery slope of selectivity based on the subjectivity of the interpreter, to a picking and choosing from a biblical smorgasbord in relation to one's personal tastes.

Are these objections valid? The answer is both yes and no. They have validity insofar as decisions about what is and what is not culturally/historically relative are made on the basis of our own likes and dislikes, our own cultural conditioning, our particular theological traditions, denominational doctrinal positions, and personal experiences. The objections are not valid, however, insofar as they represent a rejection of both the necessity and legitimacy to engage in that discernment process.

ALL CHRISTIANS DO IT!

The fact of the matter is that all Christians, across the theological spectrum from ultrafundamentalist to radical liberal, are involved in this decision-making process, whether or not they acknowledge it in theory. Many who are

---

[3]Cf. James Orr, *Revelation and Inspiration* (Grand Rapids: Eerdmans, 1952), pp. 177-78, who argues that while in some places the level of inspiration is at a "maximum," in other places it is operating on a "lower plane" with "feebler energy."

staunch proponents of the above objections, and thus reject the *legitimacy* of such decisions on theoretical grounds, nevertheless tacitly acknowledge the *necessity* of such discernment in practice. This is true even among the most conservative defenders of the verbal inspiration of the Bible, who affirm all parts of Scripture—all laws, rules, teachings, instructions, exhortations, narratives—as equally authoritative. They often affirm that the Bible is literally true at every point and, therefore, at every point it exercises a literal authority. But in practice, this affirmation becomes quite nuanced. An important distinction is quickly made between interpreting the Bible *literally* or *literalistically*. To read and interpret the Bible *literally* is to do so with full recognition of the literary character of its various parts. But, to my knowledge, no sane Christian has ever taken Jesus' words in Matthew 5:29-30—about tearing out an eye or cutting off a hand that causes one to sin—with wooden literalism, or *literalistically*. To take these words literally, however, is to recognize the literary convention of hyperbole in order to drive home a point or a message. Likewise, Paul's wish in Galatians 5:12—that those who pressure Gentile believers to be circumcised would castrate themselves—is a polemical hyperbole. It is doubtful that Paul intended that wish literalistically. Much of the language in the book of Revelation (and other prophetic/apocalyptic passages in books like Daniel and Ezekiel) is symbolic and figurative, often referring to events or persons or institutions in the time of the writer.[4] These recognitions are the result of taking the text literally, in keeping with its own nature. To read these texts literalistically would be to miss their intended meaning, both for the earliest readers and for us.

Beyond this matter of interpreting the Bible literally or literalistically, most Christians reveal in their practice that they do make decisions about what they consider culturally/historically relative and what they affirm as having abiding authority. Let's consider some representative samples.

---

[4]The importance of due attention to *literary genre* for nonabusive interpretation is touched on in this chapter and noted elsewhere throughout our study. A thorough treatment of this important topic is, however, beyond the purview of this study, deserving an entire book. For an excellent study, see Gordon D. Fee and Douglas Stuart, *How to Read the Bible for All Its Worth*, 2nd ed. (Grand Rapids: Zondervan, 1993). For helpful insights into the symbolic, figurative language of apocalyptic literature, see several commentaries on Revelation. An accessible introduction into the topic is Craig S. Keener, *Revelation*, The NIV Application Commentary (Grand Rapids: Zondervan, 2000), pp. 21-43. Commendable also are Robert H. Mounce, *The Book of Revelation*, New International Commentary on the New Testament, rev. ed. (Grand Rapids: Eerdmans, 1998); and Kenneth H. Maahs, *Of Angels, Beasts and Plagues: The Message of Revelation for a New Millennium* (Valley Forge, Penn.: Judson Press, 1999).

1. Mosaic law mandates, by the Lord's decree, that whoever "strikes father or mother" or "curses father or mother" shall be put to death (Ex 21:15, 17). Yet Christian parents would hardly want capital punishment to be inflicted on their sons or daughters in retribution for such acts.

2. The principle of "retributive justice," articulated in Exodus 21:24-25—"eye for eye, tooth for tooth, hand for hand, foot for foot, burn for burn, wound for wound, stripe for stripe"—practiced by some Islamic communities on the basis of this Old Testament teaching, has not been practiced in the vast majority of Christian communities.

3. What Christian farmer has followed the injunctions of Exodus 23:10-11, to let their fields, vineyards and orchards rest and lie fallow every seventh year, so that the poor may use the land and orchards for their livelihood? Or what Christian landowner, in areas of the country where there are poor aliens (undocumented immigrants?), hears the command of Leviticus 19:9-10—to leave some crops for the poor and aliens—as applying to them?

4. Many of the ordinances in the book of Leviticus regarding "clean" and "unclean" foods are routinely ignored by most Christians, including those who affirm the full authority of the Bible. According to Leviticus 11:6-7, rabbits and pigs are off the table; so are lobsters, shrimp, crabs, scallops, oysters and mussels (Lev 11:9-12).

5. Rules about moral or religious uncleanness are particularly problematic for Christians. In Leviticus 15, normal bodily discharges of semen or blood, both during regular menstrual cycles or sexual intercourse, render people unclean. Both men and women were commanded to bring a sin offering, implying that their "uncleanness" was a moral infraction (Lev 15:15, 30). It is doubtful that most Christians accept this negative evaluation of natural processes created by God, or that they come before the Lord in repentance to receive "atonement."

6. While most Christians would agree with biblical teaching that adultery is against God's will, and likely the majority would affirm that homosexual practice is contrary to God's created design, few would advocate, or want to practice, the biblical mandate that such persons "shall be put to death" (Lev 20:10-13).

7. Many Christians' view of both poor people and rich people is influenced

by the statement in Proverbs 10:4 that "a slack hand causes poverty, / but the hand of the diligent makes rich." Yet many others recognize that this wisdom saying is not universally true. There are many causes of poverty (like drought, disease, oppression and economic injustice); laziness is perhaps the least of the causes. And there are countless hard and diligent workers who never become wealthy. Thus the insight of this proverb can hardly be understood as having transcultural, authoritative meaning.

8. Proverbs 31:6-8 advocates giving "strong drink" and "wine" to those in distress and poverty, so they can "forget their poverty" and "remember their misery no more." What Christian counselors, including those in certain Christian groups who advocate "biblical counseling," would actually apply this biblical instruction in their practice?[5]

9. Jesus' action of washing his disciples' feet (Jn 13:1-11) is followed by these words: "you also ought to wash one another's feet. For I have set you an example, that you also should do as I have done to you" (Jn 13:14-15). This instruction is every bit as clear as Jesus' words instituting the Lord's Supper (Communion, Eucharist, Mass): "Do this in remembrance of me" (Lk 22:19; cf. 1 Cor 11:24-26). Yet, while the vast majority of Christians celebrate the Lord's Supper regularly, only a few small Christian communions practice the ritual of footwashing.

10. In his narrative of the early church in Judea, Luke tells us that the believers, empowered by the Spirit, created a community where everything individuals owned was held in common (Acts 4:34-35). There is no command or instruction attached to this narrative. Yet throughout the centuries, Christians have gone back repeatedly to "New Testament Christianity," seeking authoritative models or patterns for the organization of Christian communities and Christian practices. Such authoritative models and patterns have been detected in New Testament narratives and statements about matters like church leadership and baptismal prac-

---

[5]For studies about the unique nature of the authority of the biblical Wisdom literature, see Roland Murphy, "The Interpretation of Old Testament Wisdom Literature," *Interpretation* 23 (1969): 289-301; R. B. Y. Scott, *The Way of Wisdom in the Old Testament* (New York: Macmillan, 1971); Walter Brueggemann, *In Man We Trust: The Neglected Side of Biblical Faith* (Louisville, Ky.: John Knox, 1983); David Bartlett, "The Authority of Wisdom," in *The Shape of Scriptural Authority* (Philadelphia: Fortress, 1983); Wayne S. Tower, "The Renewed Authority of Old Testament Wisdom for Contemporary Faith," in *Canon and Authority*, ed. G. W. Coats and B. O. Long (Philadelphia: Fortress, 1977), pp. 132-47.

tices. But there is scant evidence that the community of goods, empowered by the Spirit (and thus "inspired") has been affirmed as an authoritative biblical model.

11. The letter to Gentile Christians in Antioch, by the apostolic leaders of the church in Jerusalem, included the instruction that they should abstain from meat that has blood in it (Acts 15:29). This instruction, however, was not just a kind request. Rather, it was given by the authority of the apostles and by the inspiration of the Holy Spirit (Acts 15:28—"For it has seemed good to the Holy Spirit and to us"). In spite of this clearly inspired and authoritative instruction, the vast majority of Christians (who are "Gentile" Christians), do not eat kosher meat, and many rather enjoy a juicy steak!

12. Paul's instruction to both women and men in the church in Corinth is quite straightforward. When in worship and participating in praying and the proclamation of God's Word (prophesying), women should wear a head covering, and men should not be so covered (1 Cor 11:5-7, 13-15). In most of the church's history (and in some communions to this very day), these apostolic instructions were understood as inspired words that have abiding authority.[6] During the last half century, however, the traditional requirement of women's head being covered has largely been abandoned in many sectors of the church, including the vast and diverse evangelical church bodies.

13. Another instruction of Paul, addressed to the church in Corinth, concerns the issue of orderly worship. To avoid the possibility of confusion for both insiders and outsiders (1 Cor 14:1-25), Paul lays down very clear parameters for ordered worship (1 Cor 14:26-32), since "God is a God not of disorder but of peace" (1 Cor 14:33). The order Paul laid down was actually quite open and flexible, providing for the participation of numerous Spirit-led persons to share "a hymn, a lesson, a revelation, a tongue, or an interpretation" (1 Cor 14:26). This participation, though charismatic, was ordered by certain criteria: it was to be one at a time, and it had to contribute to the building up of the church. Paul concludes these and

---

[6]In the commencement worship ceremonies of the seminaries where I taught, the male faculty members instinctively removed their caps during prayer, while the women faculty members retained theirs. This practice reveals the hold that the traditionally understood text of 1 Corinthians 11 has on Christian practice.

other instructions by stating that "what I am writing to you is a command of the Lord" (1 Cor 14:37). Despite the strong language of divine authority behind these apostolic teachings, most Christian communions throughout the church's history have not structured their worship experiences in such a manner.

14. Apostolic instructions for women's hairstyle and clothing in 1 Timothy 2:9-10 and 1 Peter 3:3 are, for the most part, quite clear: modest and inexpensive clothing, no braided hair, and no gold or pearl jewelry. While in some Christian traditions, such as in the Wesleyan Holiness Movement, these instructions were understood to have abiding authority until very recently, the vast majority of Christians have not followed these apostolic injunctions.

These representative examples—from among dozens more that could be selected—reveal clearly that, for whatever reasons, many Christians and Christian communions—many of whom otherwise affirm the full authority of the Bible and seek to live their lives and "do church" in faithful response to biblical teaching—in fact consider certain instructions or biblical models or commands not to be authoritative for them. One could protest here and say: Just because Christians "do it" does not necessarily justify it. However, that objection becomes problematic when we look back to the earliest days of the church as revealed in the earliest New Testament documents. There we find that Jesus' earliest followers already considered certain aspects of Old Testament teaching not to be authoritative for them. Is it possible that they were unfaithful or mistaken, thus starting Christians on the slippery slope toward liberalism? But even that objection is invalidated by the recognition that Jesus himself got that ball rolling, not his followers, and that the Spirit-inspired prophets and teachers before him challenged some Israelite faith traditions that in earlier stages of Israel's history were understood as divinely inspired and commanded. So the question is not whether it is legitimate and necessary to make discernments between what is culturally/historically relative and what has abiding authority. Rather, the question is (1) are the discernments made for good, legitimate reasons that are based on biblical precedents, and (2) are they made on the basis of carefully articulated and consistently applied principles—in order to avoid the ever-present tendency and temptation to arbitrariness, selectivity and subjectivity in this area of biblical interpretation.

It is a lack of the use of biblically grounded and sound principles, which are carefully and consistently applied in this process of discernment, that leads to the abusive reading and application of the Bible.

BIBLICAL PRECEDENTS

The best foundation for the legitimacy and necessity of engaging in the process of distinguishing between what is culturally/historically relative (and therefore authoritative primarily or only for the situation to which it was originally written) and what has abiding authority (for all Christians, at all times, in all places and cultures) is the fact that this process was already present within the Bible itself, beginning with the Old Testament and continuing into the New Testament.

In the discussion in chapter three on the abuse of selectivity and in chapter four on the abuse of biblical balance, I noted several areas in biblical faith where earlier convictions or certainties were later set aside, critiqued as inadequate or balanced by an alternative perspective. For example, an early conviction in Israel's faith tradition was the direct connection between righteous, faithful living, on the one hand, and God's reward for that life through such blessings as health, wealth, offspring, fame and long life, on the other hand. But the validity of that direct relationship was seriously questioned by later authorities, especially in Ecclesiastes and the book of Job, as well as by Jesus and his followers. This means that the direct and overly simplistic equation of righteous living and God's reciprocal blessing—though very much a part of the biblical witness—cannot provide an authoritative basis for a "health and wealth" theology and a lifestyle based on that theology.

Major sections of the Pentateuch (the first five books of the Bible) are devoted to descriptions of Israel's sacrificial cult (especially in Leviticus and Numbers). There are instructions for the construction of the tabernacle, the altar for sacrificial offerings, the choice of animals and their proper preparation, appropriate agricultural and animal offerings for various offenses, priestly vestments, sacrificial procedures and practices, and so on. All of this was narrated with the conviction that God gave specific instructions regarding these matters, that they were therefore authoritative and that infringement would have negative consequences for the people. Yet the legitimacy and appropriate place of the sacrificial system in the life of Israel and her relationship with God was deeply questioned and critiqued in the later prophetic tradition. On the one hand, the voice of the Lord through prophetic voices critiqued the sacrificial practices because they were nothing but a formal pretense of piety, while unrighteousness and injustice abounded in the land. Typical in this regard is Hosea:

> For I desire steadfast love and not sacrifice,
> the knowledge of God rather than burnt offerings. (Hos 6:6)

Even stronger were the Lord's words through the prophet Amos:

> I hate, I despise your festivals,
> and I take no delight in your solemn assemblies.
> Even though you offer me your burnt offerings and grain offerings,
> I will not accept them. (Amos 5:21-22)

Why? Because what God really desired was justice and righteousness (Amos 5:24).

On the other hand, the value, or even the very legitimacy, of the institution of the sacrificial system was called into question by God:

> What to me is the multitude of your sacrifices?
> says the LORD;
> I have had enough of burnt offerings of rams
> and the fat of fed beasts;
> I do not delight in the blood of bulls
> or of lambs, or of goats.
> When you come to appear before me,
> who asked this from your hand? (Is 1:11-12)

The "sacrifice" that counts before God is justice (Is 1:17). Jeremiah echoed this same questioning of the legitimacy of the sacrificial cult as an appropriate or acceptable system of religious ritual for Israel's continuing relationship with God:

> Thus says the LORD of hosts, the God of Israel: Add your burnt offerings to your sacrifices, and eat the flesh. For in the day that I brought your ancestors out of the land of Egypt, I did not speak to them or command them concerning burnt offerings and sacrifices. But this command I gave them, "Obey my voice, and I will be your God, and you shall be my people. (Jer 7:21-23)

What we have here is the questioning of one biblical authority (the Mosaic tradition) by another authority (the prophetic tradition). There is, of course, no question but that the sacrificial system had profound theological significance for Israel's understanding of its covenant relationship with a holy God, in both the wilderness period immediately after the exodus and after settlement in the land of Canaan.[7] In contrast to the surrounding cultures—where sacrificial practices, which were outwardly very much like those in Israel, were intended to appease and procure the favor of the gods—the sacrificial cult in Israel signified the covenant realities of God's grace, mercy and forgiveness when it encountered repentance and faith. However, as the historical record (Samuel, Kings and Chronicles) reveals, the sacrificial cult gradually lost its unique theological focus—under the impact of Canaanite religions and the deterioration of Israel's moral life—and became empty religious performance. Against this background, the prophetic critique must be seen. While cultic practices, shared by all peoples in the ancient world, became a vehicle for a radically different understanding of God within Israel,[8] its abuse was seen by the divinely inspired prophets to indicate its inadequacy in Israel's continuing history with God. Their authoritative, prophetic words about Israel's moral obligations ("justice" and "righteousness" in Amos 5:24) took center stage. The temporal and historically relative character of the sacrificial cult, announced in this prophetic critique, is confirmed in the New Testament. Paul names Christ "the mercy seat,"[9] in whom God meets sinners in reconciling love (Rom 3:25). In Hebrews, Christ is presented as the sacrifice to end all sacrifice (Heb 9:11-12, 26).[10]

---

[7]For thorough discussions of the place and significance of the sacrificial cult in Israel, see the standard works on Old Testament theology by Gerhard von Rad, Walther Zimmerli and Walther Eichrodt. For a basic, yet concise and thorough, study, see William Dyrness, *Themes in Old Testament Theology* (Downers Grove, Ill.: InterVarsity Press, 1980), pp. 143-60; Hans-Joachim Kraus, *Worship in Israel: A Cultic History of the Old Testament* (Richmond, Va.: John Knox Press, 1966); and Walter Kaiser, *Toward an Old Testament Theology* (Grand Rapids: Zondervan, 1978).

[8]Cf. Psalm 50:8-14, which shows that the purpose of the sacrificial system in Israel was decidedly different than in the surrounding cultures, where sacrifices *were* intended to feed the gods and to thereby procure their favor. Contrarily, as Dyrness, *Themes*, p. 156, states, "The sacrificial system was a part of God's means for creating a people who would hear his voice and follow him."

[9]In Romans 3:25, Paul uses the word *hilasterion* ("place of atonement") to designate Christ. It is the term used in the Septuagint for the cover on the Ark of the Covenant, usually translated "mercy seat" (Ex 25:21-22; Lev 16:12-15 NRSV). At the mercy seat, the God of Israel met his repentant people—represented in the sacrificed life of the sin offering on the Day of Atonement—in forgiving mercy.

[10]According to some forms of dispensationalism, a restored nation of Israel will rebuild the Jerusalem temple and reinstitute the priestly order, including the sacrificial system, in the millennium. This view is clearly based on a reading of Scripture that does not recognize Scripture's own evalu-

A third biblical precedent—in which authoritative instructions are set aside and judged to be historically/culturally relative and therefore no longer authoritative for us—is in the instructions about what is "clean" and "unclean" (concentrated especially in Lev 10—15). Laws and rituals of purification to remove "uncleanness" were intended to set the people apart for relationship with God and for the worship of God: "You shall be holy, for I the LORD your God am holy" (Lev 19:2; see also Lev 11:44-45; 20:7, 26; 21:8). To be "set apart" (become holy) meant not being contaminated by that which was considered unclean, such as certain animals, foods, bodily fluids, contaminated objects, dead or diseased animals or humans, and non-Israelites (contaminated by pagan religious practices, such as witchcraft). In many cases we cannot recover specific reasons why certain things were defined as either clean or unclean. We do know that the larger context for these categories was that of keeping God's people undefiled and separated from the worship practices and customs of their neighbors.[11] It is clear from the subsequent history of Israel that the ritual religious purity practices and legislation were finally inadequate to bring about the deeper purity of life, which the clean-unclean categories symbolized. God's words in Isaiah make it clear that cleanness before God is attained not by means of purification rituals: "Wash yourselves; make yourselves clean . . . says the Lord" (Is 1:16, 18). How? By removing "the evil of your doings from before my eyes," and by doing justice, rescuing the oppressed and defending the cause of the most vulnerable (Is 1:16-17).

This initial prophetic insight, which challenged the adequacy and continuing legitimacy of divinely given legislation in the earlier faith tradition, came to full flowering in the teaching of Jesus: "Listen to me . . . there is nothing outside a person that by going in can defile, but the things that come out are what defile" (Mk 7:14-15). With that word (and the further explanation in Mk 7:17-23) "he declared all foods clean" (Mk 7:19). Jesus' invalidation of clean-unclean categories was embodied in his actions in numerous ways: he associated and spoke in public with a Samaritan woman, who was by

ation of the historically relative nature of the sacrificial cult. Cf. Millard J. Erickson, *A Basic Guide to Eschatology: Making Sense of the Millennium* (Grand Rapids: Baker, 1998), p. 103.

[11]Some animals, defined as unclean, such as pigs, mice, serpents and hares, were associated with pagan religious ideas and practices. See Walther Eichrodt, *Theology of the Old Testament* (Philadelphia: Westminster Press, 1961), 1:134; and W. S. Lasor, D. A. Hubbard and F. W. Bush, *Old Testament Survey: The Message, Form and Background of the Old Testament*, 2nd ed. (Grand Rapids: Eerdmans, 1996), pp. 86-88.

definition of unclean racial mixture (Jn 4); the hero of a parable was a Samaritan who touched a wounded man, making himself doubly unclean (Lk 10:29-37); Jesus was touched by a woman with a hemorrhage, thus unclean (Lk 8:43-48); he was not hesitant to accept the ministrations of an unclean "woman of the street" (Lk 7:36-50), to touch the unclean leper (Mt 8:1-3), and to have table fellowship with the unclean tax collector Zacchaeus (Lk 19:2-10) and other "sinners" (Lk 15:2).

Jesus' rejection of the ritual law[12] as having abiding authority was taken up by his followers—though reluctantly at first. Steeped in the ritual-purity tradition, Peter rejected the divine invitation (given in a vision, recorded in Acts 10:9-13) to eat the "unclean" food set before him with the protest, "By no means, Lord; for I have never eaten anything that is profane or unclean" (Acts 10:14). The divine response was: "What God has made clean, you must not call profane" (Acts 10:15). The subsequent narrative makes it clear that the unclean animals in the vision symbolize another category of unclean, namely uncircumcised Gentiles—those with whom contact and association would make Jews unclean (Acts 10:28; 11:1-2). "God has shown me," confesses Peter finally, "that I should not call anyone profane or unclean" (Acts 10:28).

Through the witness of Jesus' earliest disciples, Paul learned Jesus' lesson well: "I know and am persuaded in the Lord Jesus that nothing is unclean in itself" (Rom 14:14). That even includes "food offered to an idol," and later sold in the marketplace (1 Cor 8:7-8; 10:25-31; cf. Tit 1:15). In his epistle to the Colossians, Paul asks the provocative question: "Why do you submit to regulations, 'Do not handle, Do not taste, Do not touch'?" (Col 2:20-21). The context makes it clear that he is referring to Jewish food laws and other clean-unclean regulations. He mentions the "legal demands" under which they once lived (Col 2:14), as well as "matters of food and drink" (Col 2:16). What is particularly significant is that Paul speaks of these rules and regulations as

---

[12]Seventh-day Adventists have interpreted the clean-unclean food regulations of the Old Testament not in terms of ritual purity but in terms of dietary laws: "because our bodies are the temple of the Holy Spirit . . . we are to adopt the most healthful diet possible and abstain from the unclean foods identified in Scripture." Cited from the Seventh-day Adventist Church's website, "Adventists Beliefs: Fundamental Beliefs," no. 22 <www.adventist.org/beliefs/fundamental/index.html>. This reading of the biblical material is very problematic at several points: (1) it does not recognize the cultural/religious context of the clean-unclean food laws; (2) it misconstrues 1 Corinthians 3:16-17 as a reference to individual human bodies rather than to the body of Christ, the church; (3) it fails to take seriously the New Testament's invalidation of the clean-unclean categories and therefore their nonbinding and nonauthoritative character.

"human tradition" (Col 2:8) and "things that perish with use; they are simply human commands and teachings" (Col 2:22). It is astounding that Paul the rabbi, schooled in the Torah—which he affirmed as authoritative Scripture (cf. 2 Tim 3:16)—could make such a statement. This evaluation of the "limited humanness" of these Old Testament regulations was only possible on the basis of the conviction that—through the death and resurrection of Christ, in which all Christ's followers participate (Col 2:12)—these aspects of earlier authoritative teaching have been surpassed by "the substance" that "belongs to Christ" (Col 2:17). What Paul points to here is a "christological hermeneutical principle," which will be further explained later.

A fourth biblical precedent for distinguishing between that which is culturally/historically limited in terms of its authority, and that which has abiding authority, is in the area of sabbath observance. The institution of the sabbath is narrated in Exodus 20 as the fourth of the Ten Commandments: "Six days you shall labor and do all your work. But the seventh day is a sabbath to the LORD your God; you shall not do any work. . . . For in six days the LORD made heaven and earth . . . but rested on the seventh day" (Ex 20:9-11). Here the sabbath is based on God's resting after the work of creation. In the second major narrative of the giving of the Ten Commandments (Deut 5:6-21), the sabbath commandment is said to be given "so that your male and female slave may rest as well as you" (Deut 5:14).[13] This purpose of the sabbath law is grounded in the theology of the Exodus: "Remember that you were a slave in the land of Egypt, and the LORD your God brought you out from there with a mighty hand . . . *therefore* the LORD your God commanded you to keep the sabbath day" (Deut 5:15, emphasis mine).

As with other laws, the deepest significance and purpose of the sabbath law—as an opportunity to celebrate the Creator's magnificent handiwork, as a gift of God's grace to avoid (as we would say today) "burnout," and as a special provision of relief for all who labor for masters over them—was soon eclipsed by formal, external, legalistic observance. They lost sight of the justice dimension:

New moon and sabbath and calling of convocation—
I cannot endure solemn assemblies with iniquity.

---

[13]Cf. Ex 23:12, where the purpose of the sabbath law is "so that your ox and your donkey may have relief, and your homeborn slave and the resident alien may be refreshed." The sabbath law is clearly understood here as a gift, not a legal restriction.

Your new moons and your appointed festivals
> my soul hates;
they have become a burden to me,
> I am weary of bearing them. (Is 1:13-14)

In the postexilic period, until the time of Jesus, when Israelite faith became increasingly focused on the Torah rather than the sacrificial cult, the meaning of the sabbath regulation ("You shall not do any work on the sabbath") became the object of much rabbinic discussion. Those discussions eventually resulted in several dozen specific rules and regulations that clearly defined what constituted "work" and what activities were consequently off limits on the sabbath.[14] The establishment of this body of regulations became known as "fencing the Torah." This "fence" was intended to protect the law. Strict observance of these regulations was intended to assure that the law ("Remember the sabbath day, and keep it holy") would not be violated.[15] The Pharisees and scribes in the time of Jesus were the custodians of these "Torah fences," which in the case of the sabbath law regulated all kinds of activities, such as: how far you could walk,[16] what you were permitted to carry, whether you could start a fire that had gone out (and how), and what kind and how much cooking you could do.[17]

It is within this cultural and religious-historical context that Jesus' conflict with the religious leaders regarding sabbath observance must be seen. In his teaching and practice, he challenged their understanding, interpretation and application of the fourth commandment at a fundamental level, in two ways: (1) he rejected their understanding of the sabbath law in terms of "restriction" and emphasized instead its "gift" character; (2) he laid down the principle that human need has precedence over laws and rules, even though those laws and rules were given under divine authority in the Torah. In response Jesus'

---

[14]The Mishnah tractate, *m. Šabb.* 7:2, lists thirty-nine classes of work that are proscribed. The tractate as a whole and the supplemental tractate *'Erubin* (together about thirty-five pages in the Mishnah), expound on these thirty-nine classes of work and their practical implications in minute detail. See H. Danby, *The Mishnah: Translated from the Hebrew with Introduction and Explanatory Notes* (London: Oxford University Press, 1933), pp. 100-136.

[15]When we consider that, according to Exodus 31:12-17, violation of the law of the sabbath was punishable by death, it is understandable why the teachers of the law in Judaism created such a vast collection of defenses to enable strict Torah observance.

[16]Acts 1:12 describes the distance from Mount Olivet to Jerusalem as "a sabbath day's journey" (2,000 cubits, about a half of a mile). That was the distance a person was allowed to walk on the sabbath; more than that was defined as "work." See *m. 'Erub.* 4:3; 5:7.

[17]E.g., *m. Šabb.* 1:10; 17:1, 4; 19:1.

opponents' criticism of him and the disciples for plucking grains of wheat on the sabbath and eating them (Mt 12:1-8; Mk 2:23-28; Lk 6:1-5)—a violation of the rule against harvesting and threshing on the sabbath!—Jesus laid down this fundamental principle: "The sabbath was made for humankind, and not humankind for the sabbath" (Mk 2:27). The point is clearly that the law was not given to restrict and restrain and box in, but as a gift to enable life, to make it more livable. Here Jesus made explicit what was already implicit in Exodus 23:12 and Deuteronomy 5:14, namely that the sabbath law is a gift to enable greater human wholeness. The second principle, that human need takes precedence over the law, is underscored by an example from the Old Testament (1 Sam 21:1-6), where divine law was set aside in response to human need.

These basic principles were also operating when Jesus performed healings on the sabbath. Criticized for healing a man's crippled hand (Mt 12:9-14; Mk 3:1-6; Lk 6:6-11), Jesus pointed out that if it is permissible on the sabbath to save the life of a sheep, it is certainly "lawful to do good on the sabbath" (Mt 12:12).[18] In the narrative of the healing of the crippled woman (Lk 13:10-17), the criticism was this: "There are six days on which work ought to be done; come on those days and be cured, and not on the sabbath day" (Lk 13:14). But for Jesus, the need of the woman overrode the legality of particular days: "Does not each of you on the sabbath untie his ox . . . and lead it away to give it water?" If that is permissible, argued Jesus, "ought not this woman . . . bound for eighteen long years, be set free from this bondage on the sabbath day?" (Lk 13:15-16).[19]

In the Gospel of John, Jesus' healing of the paralytic (Jn 5:8-18) and the blind man (Jn 9)—both acts of compassion that were whole-making and life-enriching—were overshadowed by the concerns of the custodians of the law about "no work" on the sabbath. The cripple was told by Jesus to "stand up, take your mat and walk" (Jn 5:8). Their response was: "it is not lawful for you to carry your mat" (Jn 5:10). In the case of the blind man,

---

[18]In Mark 3:4 and Luke 6:9, this statement is given as a rhetorical question: "Is it lawful to do good . . . on the sabbath?" Their silence (Mk 3:4) reveals that the only possible answer is "yes." Cf. Lk 14:1-6.

[19]*M. Šabb.* 19:1 states that "any act of work that can be done on the eve of the Sabbath does not override the Sabbath." That is, any work that can be done before the sabbath should not be done on the sabbath. This principle is underlined by *m. Šabb.* 18:3, which says that when a child is ready to be delivered on the sabbath, midwives "may profane the Sabbath for the mother's sake."

Jesus violated the "no work" rule by making mud, putting it on the blind man's eyes and telling him to go wash his eyes in the pool (Jn 9:6-14). Both the "gift" character and the "for us" character of the law took absolute priority for Jesus over the legalists' "you shall not do any work" character of the sabbath commandment.

In addition to the two guiding principles articulated by Jesus (discussed above), there is a third one, pronounced by Jesus in response to his critics' condemnation of him and his disciples for "work" on the sabbath. In their legalistic interpretation of the fourth commandment, they failed to take into consideration the prophetic word of God: "I desire mercy and not sacrifice" (Mt 12:7, citing Hos 6:6). For Jesus, ritual observance is subordinate to the exercise of compassion. Here Jesus confirmed the truth already articulated in the prophetic word of Isaiah 1:12-17, that God is much more concerned about our doing good to others and having compassion and seeking justice than ritual acts and external observance of holy days and festivals, including the sabbath. The priority of human need and God's desire for compassion in human society are the principles front and center in John 7:19-24. Jesus responded to the anger of his opponents over his healing a man on the sabbath by pointing out that they were perfectly willing to circumcise a man on the sabbath day "in order that the law of Moses may not be broken" (Jn 7:23).[20] You are willing, said Jesus in effect, to break one ritual law in order to obey another one, but you are not willing to acknowledge that the healing of a man's entire body on the sabbath (Jn 7:23) takes precedence over the law of the sabbath. Is not the healing of a crippled man more important than the rite of circumcision?[21]

Above all these challenging principles, however, stands even a higher challenge, namely Jesus' authority to both reinterpret the law in terms of its deepest intentions and to go beyond it. That is the significance of his pronouncement that "the Son of Man is lord even of the sabbath" (Mk 2:28; see also Mt 12:8; Lk 6:5). He stands in sovereignty above the law in its historically contingent context.[22] The deepest meaning of this truth is articulated in

---

[20]Circumcision was to be administered on the eighth day after birth (Lev 12:3). Since the eighth day often fell on the sabbath, there was a conflict between that law and the law of the sabbath. The rabbinic discussion of this matter is present in *m. Šabb.* 18:3; 19:1-6. It is very likely that Jesus was quite familiar with this discussion and indirectly appealed to it in John 7:22-23.

[21]Cf. Matthew 23:23, where Jesus distinguished between lesser and "weightier matters of the law."

[22]This is particularly true of the ritual law. Throughout Jesus' teaching, the moral law of the Old

John's narrative of the healing of the paralytic (Jn 5). Jesus was opposed "because he was doing such things on the sabbath" (Jn 5:16). His response was the cryptic line: "My Father is still working, and I also am working" (Jn 5:17). This somewhat-enigmatic expression becomes perfectly clear in the context of the rabbinic discussion about God's relation to his own law, particularly the sabbath law. The question was: does God keep the sabbath law?[23] The common answer was that God rested on the seventh day from his work of creation. But since God is both the giver and sustainer of life, he obviously continues to be at work, even on the sabbath. That is why babies are born even on the sabbath. That is why life goes on even on the sabbath. In his response to his opponents' criticism, Jesus identified himself with that ongoing working of God, which in the rabbinic mind was the sole prerogative of God.[24] He thus assumed this divine prerogative—to give and sustain life—for himself: "For just as the Father has life in himself, so he has granted the Son also to have life in himself" (Jn 5:26).

It is this same authority[25] by which Jesus relativized several other divinely given laws. This is the case, for example, with the "law of retributive justice" given in Exodus 21:23-24: "Life for life, eye for eye, tooth for tooth, hand for hand, foot for foot, burn for burn, wound for wound, stripe for stripe" (cf. Lev 24:17-21; Deut 19:21). Jesus set this law aside: "it was said, 'An eye for an eye and a tooth for a tooth.' But I say to you . . . if anyone strikes you on the right cheek, turn the other also" (Mt 5:38-39). The law of retaliation would have called for striking back. But Jesus challenged his hearers not to live by this law, so that the endless cycle of vengeance—encouraged and sustained by that law—might be brought to an end.

Related to this strain in Jesus' teaching is his rejection of the use of force and violence in human affairs, even against one's enemies. Jesus' teaching echoes and brings to a climax the voices that had already been raised, protesting the powerful strain of divinely sanctioned force against idolaters, pagan neighbors and enemies in the Israelite faith tradition. Even in the Old Testa-

---

Testament was not overturned, though Jesus often pointed his listeners beyond formal, external obedience toward its deepest meaning (as for example in the "antitheses" of Mt 5:21-48).

[23]F. F. Bruce, *The Gospel of John: Introduction, Exposition and Notes* (Grand Rapids: Eerdmans, 1983), pp. 126-27.

[24]Jesus' identifying himself with God in his prerogative to be "working" on the sabbath in life-giving and life-sustaining ways is the basis for the Pharisees' charge of blasphemy (Jn 5:17-18).

[25]See Matthew 7:29, where Jesus' authority is recognized as higher than that of the custodians of the law.

ment, there are evidences within the faith tradition that the use of violence in human affairs is not the will of God.

For example, in David's charge to his son Solomon to build a temple for the worship of the Lord, David relates to him this word of God's judgment on him: "But the word of the LORD came to me, saying, 'You have shed much blood and have waged great wars; you shall not build a house to my name, because you have shed so much blood in my sight on the earth'" (1 Chron 22:8). That word of judgment is followed by the promise that his son Solomon "shall be a man of peace" (1 Chron 22:9). Within a description of the reign of Solomon in 1 Kings 3, God responded to Solomon's prayer for wisdom with these words: "Because you have asked this, and have not asked for yourself long life or riches, *or for the life of your enemies* . . . I give you a wise and discerning mind" (1 Kings 3:11-12, emphasis mine).

Jehu's extermination of the entire house of Ahab (2 Kings 9—10) was understood by the chronicler to have received divine approval (2 Kings 10:30). Yet the prophet Hosea pronounced God's word of judgment and punishment on the house of Jehu for that bloodbath (Hos 1:4-5). Side by side with this rejection of violence as God's way was the prophetic voice of Isaiah, proclaiming the future coming of God's anointed, under whose reign "they shall beat their swords into plowshares, and their spears into pruning hooks" (Is 2:4; Mic 4:3). He would be "the Prince of Peace" (Is 9:6). The prophet Zechariah envisioned that Coming One to ride into Jerusalem, not on a warhorse in full battle armor, but in humility on a lowly donkey (Zech 9:9). Chariot, warhorse and battle bow shall be removed, and he "shall command peace to the nations" (Zech 9:10).

Finally, the book of Jonah is a decisive rebuke of an ethnocentric, hate-and-destroy-your-enemy ideology within Israel's faith tradition. The main character in the story, Jonah, is a representative of that tradition. He did not want to speak God's word of judgment in Nineveh—the capital city of the Assyrians, Israel's archenemy that destroyed Samaria in 721 B.C.—because he knew that "you [the Lord] are a gracious God and merciful, slow to anger, and abounding in steadfast love" (Jon 4:2). In contradiction to Jonah, who was apparently perfectly happy to announce the impending destruction of Nineveh (Jon 3:3-4) and was very displeased and angry at God when the result of his preaching was Nineveh's repentance and turning to the Lord (Jon 3:5—4:1), God had compassion for the thousands of lost and confused citizens in Nineveh.

Jesus brought the seeds of this contrary faith tradition to fruition in his life and teaching. His birth was accompanied with the heavenly announcement of peace (Lk 2:14). He rejected the triumphalistic messianic ideology, wedded to the use of the sword, and assumed the role of the suffering servant of Isaiah 53 (Mk 8—10). He rebuked the disciples for asking him to "command fire to come down from heaven and consume" the Samaritan town that had refused them lodging (Lk 9:51-55). In fulfillment of Zechariah's vision (Zech 9:9) he entered Jerusalem on a lowly donkey and took to task the religious establishment, rather than rallying the revolutionary Zealots and the people for a battle against the hated Roman occupiers (Mt 21). To the disciples who would defend him from arrest with the use of the sword (Mt 26:51), Jesus announced the principle that "all who take the sword will perish by the sword" (Mt 26:52). In concert with Isaiah's vision of the messianic peace-bringer, he called his disciples to be peacemakers (Mt 5:9). He echoed the message of Jonah—that God loves Israel's enemies—by telling his followers to imitate the perfection of God by loving their enemies and praying for those who persecute them (Mt 5:43-48).

Jesus' rejection of both the law of retributive justice and the use of force in human affairs took root in the lives of Jesus' new community. Paul who, in allegiance to the faith tradition, had persecuted those he considered to be God's enemies (Acts 9:1-2; Gal 1:13), was compelled by the example and constraining love of Christ (2 Cor 5:14) to proclaim a message of peace and reconciliation: "Bless those who persecute you. . . . Live in harmony with one another. . . . Do not repay anyone evil for evil. . . . Live peaceably with all. . . . Never avenge yourselves. . . . 'If your enemies are hungry, feed them.' . . . Overcome evil with good" (Rom 12:14-21). Both Jesus' teaching and the embodiment of that teaching in his life compelled Paul toward a reevaluation of what he had believed to be God's will, as expressed within the Scriptures of his people and the faith traditions built on it. And so he became an imitator of Christ (1 Cor 11:1), calling all of Christ's followers to do the same (Eph 5:1).

Another rejection by Jesus of Old Testament authoritative teaching is found in the narrative of the woman accused of adultery in John 8:1-11.[26] Je-

---

[26]In the earliest and best Greek texts of the Gospel of John, this passage is absent. In some later texts, it appears after John 7:6 or John 21:25 or after Luke 21:38. Textual scholars are virtually unanimous in their view that the passage was most likely not in the original text of the Gospel of John. However, numerous Johannine scholars believe that it is a historically authentic piece of tradition from the life of Jesus, continuing side by side with the written Gospels in oral trans-

sus affirmed the truth of the moral law about adultery: it is sin, a violation of God's purpose (Jn 8:11). What Jesus did reject is the imposition of the punishment of stoning, required in the law (Jn 8:5, referring to Lev 20:10 and Deut 22:23-24). His word to the scribes and Pharisees is: "Let anyone among you who is without sin be the first to throw a stone at her" (Jn 8:7). With that penetrating challenge, Jesus invalidated the legitimacy of anyone ever again to imposing this Mosaic judgment, for what executioner can ever claim to be without sin? Instead of joining the teachers of the law in the act of condemnation, Jesus touched the sinner's life with grace and forgiveness. The Mosaic law, received as authoritative divine instruction—which names sin for what it is and judges it—is swallowed up in the divine mercy. It is a "severe mercy" that recognizes the gravity of the sin, annuls it in the divine forgiveness (cf. Rom 3:25) and creates the foundation for the transformation of life (Jn 8:11: "Neither do I condemn you. Go your way, and from now on do not sin again"). As in other examples discussed above, Jesus judged an earlier scriptural teaching as historically relative, as a limited, or even distorted human perception about the will of God. It must not, therefore, be seen as authoritative for the new humanity brought into being through Christ.

Just as Paul, in imitation of Jesus, understood the clean-unclean distinction in terms of historical/cultural relativity, and with his Lord rejected the use of force and retributive justice, judging it as contrary to God's will in human affairs, so he also followed him in evaluating the rigorous observance of the sabbath law as historically/culturally relative. His definition of clean-unclean distinctions as "human tradition" and "human commands and teachings" (Col 2:8, 22), also applies to the observance of "festivals, new moons, or sabbaths" (Col 2:16). They only foreshadowed what was yet to come, namely Christ (Col 2:17; cf. Rom 10:4; Gal 3:23-26). This understanding of the relative nature of sabbath observance was also Paul's concern in Galatians. In light of his debate with the Judaizers (Jewish Christians who demanded that Gentile converts obey Jewish religious customs and practices), Paul speaks of their observance of "special days and months and seasons and years" (Gal 4:9-10) as being "enslaved to them." And this enslavement, said Paul, is equiva-

---

mission. See, e.g., Bruce M. Metzger, *A Textual Commentary on the Greek New Testament* (New York: United Bible Societies, 1971), pp. 220-21, who says that "the account has all the earmarks of historical veracity. It is obviously a piece of oral tradition which circulated in certain parts of the Western church and which was subsequently incorporated in various manuscripts at various places."

lent to their former enslavement (in their Gentile religious context), "to beings that by nature are not gods" and "to the weak and beggarly elemental
spirits" (Gal 4:8-9).[27]

Both Jesus' and Paul's evaluations of sabbath observance as historically
relative—and, therefore, certainly not as a measure of Christian faithfulness—
took a back seat in much of the practice of the church in subsequent centuries.
Rules regarding sabbath observance were gradually transferred from the Jewish sabbath on the seventh day of the week (Saturday) to the first day of the
week (Sunday). Thus the day on which Christians worshiped Christ as
the resurrected and living Lord became increasingly a Christian version of the
Jewish sabbath. The Christian college I attended in the 1960s provided a
lengthy list of activities we were not allowed to engage in on the "Christian
sabbath," very reminiscent of the various activities that were defined as "work"
by the Jewish rabbis. Some Christian groups today are still very much committed to relatively strict sabbath observance, either within the confines of
Sunday, the Christian day of worship, or within the literal Jewish sabbath on
Saturdays.[28] What has clearly been defined by Jesus and Paul as culturally/
historically relative has in these cases been maintained by some Christians as
a requirement, or even as normative for Christian faithfulness to the authority
of Scripture. Such adherence to the dictates of certain scriptural teachings
(especially, but not exclusively, in the Old Testament), and thereby the implicit
rejection of the teaching of Jesus and Paul that have evaluated these same
teachings as not having abiding authority, raises the question of what our ultimate foundational authority is—a question we'll return to later.

A final example that reveals Paul's indebtedness to the example of Jesus in
his rejection of certain Mosaic legislations is Paul's response to a serious case
of sexual immorality *(porneia)* in the church at Corinth: "a man has his father's wife" (1 Cor 5:1 NIV).[29] From Paul's perspective, this case was a clear

---

[27]Cf. Leon Morris, *Galatians: Paul's Charter of Christian Freedom* (Downers Grove, Ill.: InterVarsity
Press, 1996), p. 133: "For Paul, the multiplicity of ecclesiastical activities in which the Galatians
engaged before they responded to the gospel stamped them as slaves, not of the one true God, but
of spirit beings that were behind the demand for such acts."

[28]E.g., the Seventh-day Adventists: "The fourth commandment of God's unchangeable law requires the observance of this seventh day Sabbath ['from sunset to sunset,' Friday evening to
Saturday evening] as the day of rest, worship, and ministry in harmony with the teaching and
practice of Jesus, the Lord of the Sabbath." Cited from the Seventh-day Adventist Church's website, "Adventists Beliefs: Fundamental Beliefs," no. 20 <www.adventist.org/beliefs/fundamental/
index.html>.

[29]The Greek *porneia* generally referred to prostitution, but in Hellenistic Judaism it was used to

violation of Leviticus 18:8, as well as a form of sexual immorality not condoned "even among pagans."[30] The enormity of this form of sexual immorality is evident in the consequences pronounced on it in various biblical texts. In Amos 2:6-7, it appears among several transgressions—such as, "they sell the righteous for silver"; "trample the head of the poor into the dust"; and "push the afflicted out of the way"—for which God's judgment falls on Israel. In Deuteronomy 27:20, this immorality is part of a list of transgressions for which its practitioners are cursed (Deut 27:11-26). In Leviticus 18, the sexual relations between a son and his father's wife (Lev 18:8) is one of several other "abominations" that result in being "cut off from their people" (Lev 18:29), that is, permanently excluded from the covenant community of Israel.[31] In some deep sense, such an exclusion is the equivalent to a death sentence, which according to Leviticus 20:11 is imposed on both parties for this form of sexual transgression.

Given this background, it is not at all surprising that Paul calls for the separation of the offender from the Christian community at Corinth.[32] What *is* surprising is that he does not pronounce a curse[33] or call for much more severe punishment for the offender. Even his call for exclusion echoes the redemptive way of Jesus with the adulterous woman (Jn 8). The purpose of the exclusion is neither rejection nor banishment nor condemnation, but the man's restoration[34] and salvation.[35] Once again we see Paul the rabbi—look-

---

collectively designate all extramarital sexual relations, as well as particular expressions, such as in 1 Corinthians 5, where it stands for a man being in sexual relationship with his father's wife, i.e., his stepmother.

[30]Gordon D. Fee, *The First Epistle to the Corinthians*, New International Commentary on the New Testament (Grand Rapids: Eerdmans, 1987), p. 200, states that "what is forbidden by all ancients, both Jewish and pagan, is the cohabiting of father and son with the same woman."

[31]In the Roman world, some forms of incestuous sexual relationships were punishable by banishment to a remote island. See Craig Keener, *The IVP Bible Background Commentary: New Testament* (Downers Grove, Ill.: InterVarsity Press, 1993), pp. 461-62.

[32]Commentators are agreed that the woman in this relationship could not have been a member of the church, for Paul would surely have addressed her also.

[33]As in Deut 27:20. Paul was certainly capable of such harsh judgment when the truth of the gospel was at stake (see Gal 1:8-9).

[34]Many commentators think that the person referred to in 2 Corinthians 2:5-11 is the same as the one who has been excluded from the community (according to 1 Cor 5): "This punishment by the majority is enough for such a person; so now instead you should forgive and console him, so that he may not be overwhelmed by excessive sorrow. So I urge you to reaffirm your love for him" (2 Cor 2:6-8).

[35]Excellent discussions of Paul's words—"hand this man over to Satan for the destruction of the flesh, so that his spirit may be saved in the day of the Lord" (1 Cor 5:5)—are found in the major commentaries, especially Fee, *First Corinthians*, pp. 198-214. Richard B. Hays, *First Corinthians*,

ing at a grave distortion of God's good purpose for sexual fidelity through the eyes of his Lord—go beyond the largely punitive dimension of some biblical legislation. Some aspects of Mosaic law are rejected; others are tempered by grace and transformed into instruments of restoration.

BIBLICAL FOUNDATIONS FOR DISCERNMENT

The central issue addressed in this chapter is that of discerning within Scripture that which is historically and culturally relative and that which has abiding authority for Christian life and faith in all times, places and cultures. Several conclusions have emerged up to this point.

1. Given the incarnational nature of the Bible, Christian engagement in such a process is virtually *inevitable*. It seems impossible not to be engaged in this process if we take two contexts seriously: one, the historical-cultural contexts of biblical teaching and narrative, and two, the ever-changing historical-cultural contexts of the Christian communities reading and interpreting the Bible. This inevitability is evidenced in the *actuality* of Christian practice. Whether or not acknowledged in theory, believers make these discernments in interpreting biblical teaching and applying it to their lives all the time.

2. A second conclusion to be drawn from our study of this issue is that the inevitability and actuality of Christian practice is not finally the result of Christians arbitrarily deciding that certain instructions, rules or teachings in the Bible are not authoritative for them. Rather, the actuality of this Christian practice is in fact grounded in biblical precedent. The fact that, within Scripture itself, biblical authors, and Jesus in his teaching and practice, are engaged in this process of discernment gives biblical *legitimacy* to the inevitability and actuality of Christian practice. The biblical precedents that we have surveyed above provide authoritative parameters to guide Christian practice and constrain it from degenerating into arbitrary subjectivity. When faithfully engaged, within these guiding biblical con-

---

Interpretation: A Bible Commentary for Teaching and Preaching (Louisville, Ky.: John Knox, 1989), p. 86, voices a concise summary of the near consensus among the exegetes: "Paul hopes that the community's censure and expulsion of the incestuous man will lead to this result: his fleshly passions and desires will be put to death. Thus the eschatological fate of this man, after undergoing discipline and repentance, will be salvation." See also my *Hard Sayings of Paul* (Downers Grove, Ill.: InterVarsity Press, 1989), pp. 96-102, for a concise analysis of this text.

straints, the process of distinguishing between the culturally-historically relative and that which has abiding authority becomes a legitimate activity in the trustworthy interpretation and application of the Bible.

3. A third conclusion that emerges from our study—in light of the redemptive movement in Scripture from Moses through the prophets to Jesus to the early church—is that the process of discernment that we are concerned with is not only inevitable and legitimate, but *crucial* and *necessary*. A refusal to engage in the process is to deny the redemptive forward movement of God's revelation in Scripture with its endpoint in Jesus Christ. It is to petrify dimensions of this revelation—intended for specific cultural and historical contexts and situations—into icons of abiding authority. To assign normative status to that which inspired prophets, wisdom teachers and apostles deemed relative is to lessen the ability of the Scriptural revelation to speak God's new words to ever-new cultural and historical contexts. To make *normative* what Jesus' life and teaching make *relative* is to resist God's ultimate way (Jn 14:6), and to throttle the living and active authority and message of Scripture in our time.

It has been said that a true conservative is one who reaches back into the hearth of history, takes out the glowing embers, and leaves the ashes behind. This image provides an apt analogy for the task of distinguishing between the culturally and historically relative, and that which has abiding authority. In the "hearth" of Scripture, there are ashes, no longer useful, but which nonetheless give powerful testimony to living and active embers that once burned brightly in the fire of divine inspiration and instruction for the people of God. We acknowledge them; we recognize the service performed by the burning embers that produced them. But our present concern has to be with the glowing embers that continue to give warmth to the life of God's people, provide light for their path, and empower them for effective witness and transforming mission in the world today. When we carry the glowing embers *and* the ashes of God's revelation in Scripture into the present, we not only carry unnecessary burdens, but we impose those burdens on those who are invited to new and vibrant life in Jesus Christ.

From these general conclusions—that it is *inevitable, legitimate* and *necessary* to distinguish between the authoritative word that is limited to its original cultural-historical context and that which has abiding authority—we can derive several core, guiding criteria that in turn provide the larger framework for the process of discernment that we are exploring.

Core criterion one: Christ the center. Jesus' affirmation that "the Son of Man is lord of the sabbath" (Mt 12:8) not only announces his sovereignty to interpret and reinterpret the sabbath law, and thus to stand authoritatively above it, but his affirmation implies, at the same time, his authority over the entirety of the Scriptures of Judaism: he stands authoritatively above the temple and its sacrificial cult (Mt 12:7), the prophets (Mt 12:41) and the sages (of whom Solomon was the epitome; Mt 12:42). This understanding of Jesus as "greater than" the entire faith tradition of Judaism is pervasive throughout the New Testament and is articulated in a variety of ways. For John, he is the Word through whom all things came to be (Jn 1:3), who is the source of all life and understanding (Jn 1:4), who comes to "tabernacle" among God's people as the reflection of God's glory (Jn 1:11, 14) and who, in his incarnation, is the ultimate revelation of God that has superseded Moses through whom the law was given (Jn 1:17-18). He is thus the Word that stands before and above the words of Scripture; the one to whom both law and prophets[36] bear witness (Jn 1:45; 5:46-47).[37] In him, the truth of God is embodied (Jn 14:6); therefore, the words that he spoke are the very words of God (Jn 17:8, 14).

In the Synoptic Gospels, the narrative of the transfiguration of Jesus points in the same direction. Moses and Elijah appear with Jesus, representing the law and the prophets (Mk 9:2-8).[38] A heavenly voice designates Jesus as "my Son, the beloved" and instructs the disciples to "listen to him" (Mk 9:7). While "the law and the prophets" are clearly carriers of divinely inspired, authoritative teaching, Jesus now takes center stage. Scholars are generally agreed that Matthew understood Jesus as the new Moses, who ascends the mountaintop (Mt 5:1) to deliver the new law of the Lord (Mt 5:2—7:28) to

---

[36]The authoritative Scripture in Judaism at the time of Jesus was generally grouped into three categories: the Law, the Prophets, and the Writings. "From the initials of these three divisions in Hebrew, the Bible is often referred to among Jews as the *TeNaKh,*" which was formed from the initial letters of *Tôrâ* (law, direction), *Něbî'îm* (prophets) and *Kětûbîm* (writings) writes F. F. Bruce, *The Canon of Scripture* (Downers Grove, Ill.: InterVarsity Press, 1988), p. 19. In the New Testament, the entire scriptural faith tradition is usually referred to as "the law and the prophets" (Mt 5:17; 7:12; Lk 16:16; Acts 24:14; 28:23; Rom 3:21). See Roger Beckwith, *The Old Testament Canon of the New Testament Church* (Grand Rapids: Eerdmans, 1985), pp. 105-7, for the great variety of designations of the entire Hebrew Old Testament or discreet parts.

[37]Cf. Jn 6:14—"This is indeed the prophet who is to come into the world." John's affirmations that Moses and the law bear witness to and speak of Jesus seem to be references to Deuteronomy 18:15, 18.

[38]Cf. the parallels in Matthew 17:1-8 and Luke 9:28-36.

the new covenant community of his disciples (Mt 26:26-28).[39] "Jesus is not only greater than Solomon and the temple (Mt 12:6, 42), but greater than Moses as well."[40]

The author of the epistle to the Hebrews contends that "God spoke to our ancestors in many and various ways by the prophets" (Heb 1:1).[41] This speaking of God, which was "long ago," is contrasted with the assertion that "in these last days he has spoken to us by a Son" (Heb 1:2), who "is the reflection of God's glory and the exact imprint of God's very being" (Heb 1:3). There is no question but that this contrast anticipates the repeated use of the comparative adjective *better*, which "is used thirteen times in Hebrews to contrast Christ and His new order with what went before Him."[42] The statement about his superiority to "the angels" (Heb 1:4) is significant, for Jewish tradition affirmed that God's law was mediated to Moses by angels (Acts 7:53; Gal 3:19; Heb 2:2). That law, states Hebrews, could not make perfect (Heb 7:19), "because it was weak and ineffectual" (Heb 7:18). Likewise, Jesus is "the mediator of a better covenant" (Heb 8:6) to replace the old covenant, which was not "faultless" (Heb 8:7).[43] Finally, both sanctuary (representative of the sacrificial cult) and the law are but "shadows" of the true reality, now revealed in Christ (Heb 8:5; 10:1).

Paul is in accord with these New Testament voices about the partial and preliminary nature of divine revelation prior to Christ. Like in Hebrews, the entire legal tradition is but "a shadow of what is to come" (Col 2:17).[44] As in the gospel tradition, that which has come in and through Christ is superior to the law[45] and to Moses (2 Cor 3:15-17). Beyond these comparisons, Paul's affirmation of Christ as the final, complete revelation of God comes into bold relief. In Jesus Christ, the righteousness of God has become historically present (Rom 1:16; 3:21). Christ is "the end of the law" (Rom 10:4)[46] in whom

---

[39]E.g., Robert H. Gundry, *Matthew: A Commentary on His Literary and Theological Art* (Grand Rapids: Eerdmans, 1982), pp. 65-73 and 342-46.

[40]Craig Keener, *A Commentary on the Gospel of Matthew* (Grand Rapids: Eerdmans, 1999), p. 437.

[41]Here, "by the prophets" is a reference to the totality of God's revelation, which preceded Christ.

[42]F. F. Bruce, *The Epistle to the Hebrews,* New International Commentary on the New Testament (Grand Rapids: Eerdmans, 1964), p. 9. The texts are Heb 6:9; 7:7, 19, 22; 8:6; 9:23; 10:34; 11:16, 35, 40; 12:24.

[43]Cf. Hebrews 8:13, where the old covenant is said to have become "obsolete."

[44]That tradition includes "matters of food and drink . . . observing festival, new moons, or sabbaths" (Col 2:16) and "regulations, 'Do not handle, Do not taste, Do not touch' " (Col 2:20-21).

[45]Recall our discussion of Romans 7 in chapter six. Cf. Gal 3:19-26.

[46]The English "end" renders the Greek *telos,* meaning either "abrogation or annulment of the law"

the wisdom of God is embodied (1 Cor 1:24, 30). More than that, he is "the image of the invisible God" (Col 1:15; cf. 2 Cor 4:4) in whom "all the fullness of God" (Col 1:19) "dwells bodily" (Col 2:9).

This pervasive and multifaceted witness to Christ as the one in and through whom God's self-disclosure comes to its fullest and final expression, superseding all that has come before him in the progressive unfolding of God's redemptive work, has absolutely crucial and primary significance for the hermeneutical task before us. In distinguishing between that in Scripture which is culturally and historically relative and that which has abiding authority, God's ultimate self-disclosure in Christ is the irreducible hermeneutical key. As the "light of the world" (Jn 8:12; 9:5), it must be allowed to shine both backward (across the pages of the Old Testament revelation) and forward (across the pages of the New Testament revelation). Christ, in his person and work, his life and acts, is the *hermeneutical lens* through which the entire preliminary faith tradition of Israel and the subsequent witness of Jesus' earliest followers must be evaluated. The common practice in Christian biblical interpretation of bypassing God's final, complete revelation in the person of Christ and going directly to the Old Testament is significantly flawed. Similarly flawed is the interpretation of New Testament passages without the light of God's revelation in Christ enlightening our reading and hearing of the meaning and message of those passages. We must learn to read the words of the Bible through the eyes of the "Word." Both Paul and John are one in the conviction that the glory of God, that is his redemptive presence, is most fully disclosed in the crucified one.[47] Therefore, in the written Word of God, whatever *blossoms* in the light of the cross has abiding authority for Christian faith and life and mission; and whatever *withers* in the light of the cross is culturally and historically relative.[48]

---

[47](as final authority for the life of the new humanity in Christ), or "the climax, completion, endpoint of the law" (in the sense that in Christ, the purpose of the law has been accomplished). Cf. J. D. G. Dunn, *Romans 9—16*, Word Biblical Commentary, vol. 38B (Dallas: Word Books, 1988), pp. 596-97, who holds that the term "is probably intended in the primary sense of 'termination, cessation' but that Paul may have "intended 'end' here to have also the fuller or further sense of 'fulfillment, goal.' "

[47]Jn 3:14; 12:13, 32; 17:1; 1 Cor 1:18-24; 2 Cor 4:4-6. In the Gospel of John, Jesus' "hour" is, first of all, always a reference to his crucifixion, and at times also to his exaltation and return to his Father (cf. Jn 7:30; 8:12; 13:1). See G. R. Beasley-Murray, *John*, Word Biblical Commentary, vol. 36 (Waco, Tex.: Word Books, 1987), pp. 34-35, 211.

[48]For the images "what blossoms in the light of the cross" and "what withers in the light of the cross," I am indebted to my colleague Thomas F. McDaniel, who proposes this hermeneutical

The truth that God's will and way with and for humanity is supremely disclosed in Christ, "who loved us and gave himself for us" at the cross (Eph 5:2), has profound implications for our process of hermeneutical discernment. For example, what happens when we shine the light of Christ of the cross on texts that deal with the man-woman/husband-wife relationship, or with the relationship between master and servant, or with the use of force in human affairs?

The implication for the man-woman relationship is that the exercise of power over and control of the other withers, but the subordination of each to the other in self-giving love blossoms. For this is precisely what we see Paul doing in his christological grounding of this relationship in Ephesians 5. The implication for the master-servant relationship is that the ideology of social hierarchy—of the idea that some human beings are inferior to other human beings on the basis of race, ethnicity, economic class or nationality—withers. While seeing and treating this "other" as created in the image of God and loved by God, and therefore deserving of love and compassion and respect, blossoms. Again, this is what we see Paul doing when he applies the christological perspective by telling masters not to treat their slaves harshly, that both master and slave "have the same Master in heaven" with whom "there is no partiality" (Eph 6:9), and when Paul declares boldly—over against all cultural and historical norms and practices—that in Christ "there is no longer slave or free" (Gal 3:28).

Finally, what is the implication for the use of force in human affairs when the light of the cross is shed on it? The implication is that the human proclivity to strike out, to hit back, to seek revenge, to demolish, to inflict hurt, to isolate and weaken the other, withers in light of the cross. Contrarily, the costly and vulnerable act of loving and feeding the enemy, turning the other cheek, repaying evil with good, seeking harmony, working for peace (Mt 5; Rom 12)—all these blossom in the light of the cross.

One of the great tragedies of our time—in terms of Christian witness and presence and impact on our culture—is the propensity of the majority of evangelical, conservative Christians to jump all too quickly and easily on political and nationalistic bandwagons that advocate and support the use of

---

approach for the interpretation of Scripture, with a primary focus on the Old Testament. For a detailed explication of his thoroughgoing christological hermeneutical procedure, see "Key for Interpreting the Bible," Palmer Theological Seminary <tmcdaniel.palmerseminary.edu>.

force in order to solve conflicts among peoples and nations. What drives many Bible-believing followers of Jesus, who are deeply committed to the sanctity of God-given life—and thus rightly in the vanguard of the battle against abortion-on-demand and demonstrably cruel abortion practices—at the same time into the front ranks of advocacy of and support for the defeat and destruction of real or perceived enemies? I believe that the bottom-line answer to this question lies in the abusive interpretation and application of Scripture. This abuse of Scripture results from not recognizing that there are dimensions of the biblical revelation that are historically and culturally relative, and that these must be discerned in light of the primary and transcultural/ transhistorical authority of Jesus Christ, the living Word. When Scripture is viewed in a flat, one-dimensional way—and the mountaintop of God's self-disclosure in Christ is not the vantage point from which the entire territory of the biblical revelation is viewed and interpreted—then it is possible to find support in the Bible for the use of force in settling disputes; then it is possible to vote with the character in the book of Jonah for the destruction of enemies; then it is possible to claim biblical precedent, and even divine sanction, for "shock and awe" attacks on enemies and infidels; then it is possible to be committed to the ideology of retaliation or "retributive justice." For do not Exodus 21:24 and Deuteronomy 19:21 advocate an eye for an eye and a tooth for a tooth? But from the mountaintop of God's self-disclosure (and literally in Mt 5:1), we hear the voice of Jesus: "You have heard it was said 'An eye for an eye, and a tooth for a tooth.' But I say to you . . ." (Mt 5:38-39).

Core criterion two: Jesus' words and acts. I have argued above that Jesus *is God's Word to us,* and that the fullest and final revelation of that Word is seen in God's way with humanity at the cross. As such, the divine self-disclosure of that Word and Way stands behind and above the words of Scripture, whose words need to be understood in light of that Word and that Way. But in addition to the crucial centrality of that biblical truth for the interpretation and application of biblical texts, there is a related truth, namely that Jesus also *speaks* God's words and *lives* God's words (Jn 14:24; 17:8). Both the speaking and living of God's words in the life and ministry of Jesus are intended to serve as an authoritative pattern for all interpersonal and social relationships and for all institutions within the new humanity, as well as in the larger world *(kosmos)* for which he gave his life (Jn 3:16). This speaking and living of God's words by Jesus is another crucial hermeneutical key—in addition to the disclosure of God's Word and Way in the cross—for distinguishing between the culturally and historically relative and that which has abiding authority in Scripture.

In our discussion of biblical precedents for this process of discernment, we noted numerous teachings of Jesus that both challenged the abiding validity of certain convictions and practices in the scriptural faith tradition and set them aside as no longer operative, or as inadequate or distorted expressions of God's will and way. His rejection of the principle of retaliation and of retributive justice, his specific teaching about loving the enemy and his admonition against the use of force, his assertion that human need and compassion take priority over ritual performance—all these are hermeneutical filters through which we must hear and interpret the whole of Scripture.

Jesus' spoken words also provide clues for dealing with issues that are not specifically or directly addressed by him and for which Christians seek "biblical" answers. Take the volatile and emotionally charged wrestling with the matter of homosexuality in our time. There are clear statements in the Bible that declare homosexual intercourse to be contrary to God's creational design and intention (Lev 18:22; 20:13; Rom 1:26-27; 1 Cor 6:9; 1 Tim 1:10). For the majority of Christians, that is the bottom line. Many others have argued that the judgment of homosexual acts in Leviticus is paralleled by the judgment of other acts that defile and make impure, but which most Christians have decided are culturally and historically relative. It has further been argued that the Pauline assessment of homosexual acts as sin (Rom 1:26-27), as not in line with the kingdom (1 Cor 6:9) and as "contrary to the sound teaching that conforms to the glorious gospel" (1 Tim 1:10-11) must be understood within the context of Greco-Roman culture where "pederasty" (the use of boys or young men for the sexual gratification of older men) was widely practiced, and that Paul has that practice specifically in mind.[49] In addition, an argument

---

[49]For both clear and compassionate explorations of this difficult issue, I recommend Stanley Grenz, *Welcoming but Not Affirming: An Evangelical Response to Homosexuality* (Louisville, Ky.: Westminster John Knox, 1998); Thomas E. Schmidt, *Straight and Narrow? Compassion and Clarity in the Homosexuality Debate* (Downers Grove, Ill.: InterVarsity Press, 1995); Robert J. Gagnon, *The Bible and Homosexual Practice: Texts and Hermeneutics* (Nashville: Abingdon, 2002); Willard Swartley, *Homosexuality: Biblical Interpretation and Moral Discernment* (Scottdale, Penn.: Herald Press, 2003); L. R. Holben, *What Christians Think About Homosexuality: Six Representative Views* (North Richland Hills, Tex.: Bibal Press, 1999); Judith K. Balswick and Jack O. Balswick, *Authentic Sexuality: An Integrated Approach* (Downers Grove, Ill.: InterVarsity Press, 1999); and Richard B. Hays, *The Moral Vision of the New Testament: A Contemporary Approach to New Testament Ethics* (San Francisco: HarperSanFrancisco, 1996).

voiced frequently is that Jesus never said anything about homosexuality. Therefore, he must not have considered it an important matter worthy of his attention. Apart from the criticism that an "argument from silence" is always a weak argument,[50] the reason for Jesus' silence on this matter is most likely the fact that homosexuality was virtually unknown in Jewish Palestine (it was considered *the* Gentile vice) and, therefore, unlikely to have come to Jesus' attention. Yet there are words of Jesus that provide guiding perspectives on the matter. First, in his response to the issue of divorce (Mk 10:2-9), Jesus cites from the two creation narratives that "from the beginning of creation, 'God made them male and female'" (Mk 10:6) and, on that basis, the husband and wife "shall become one flesh" (Mk 10:7-8). While the matter addressed is that of divorce, Jesus clearly affirmed divine intentionality for the male-female polarity of humanity and for the specific expression of that polarity in male-female sexual union. It is thus an affirmation that has authoritative import for the creational form of sexual union. But second, in light of Jesus' dealing with both the adulteress and her judges and would-be executioners (Jn 8:1-11), Christian self-righteousness, condemnation and judgmentalism toward homosexual individuals is halted by Jesus' word, "Let anyone among you who is without sin be the first to throw a stone at her" (Jn 8:7). Jesus' word affirms the creation order of male-female sexual union, and thereby confirms the view of the Old Testament and Paul as having abiding authority. At the same time Jesus' word rejects the punitive, condemnatory word of Leviticus 20:10, 13—which imposed the death penalty for both adultery and homosexual acts—as historically relative. Jesus' words, whether directly or indirectly, provide guiding perspectives and control beliefs. They help us discern between relative and abiding authority in the biblical revelation.

Side by side with the hermeneutical filter of the words of God spoken by Jesus is the equally important filter of the words of God that Jesus lived. While his words are specific *articulations* of the Word, his actions are particular *embodiments* of the Word. In the discussion about gender issues, and specifically in the matter of husband-wife relationships, some have argued that since Jesus did not say anything specifically about male-female roles or about authority in marriage, he must not have wanted to challenge the dominance of males in family life and society. Therefore, the texts in the New

---

[50]There are many human issues addressed in various parts of Scripture on which we have no word from Jesus, but that does not make them unimportant.

Testament where women/wives are restricted in relationship to men/ husbands and said to be in subjection to them must have abiding authority (1 Cor 14:34-35; Eph 5:22-24; Col 3:18; 1 Tim 2:11-15; Tit 2:5). Contrary to this claim, it must be asserted that the entire New Testament affirms that both in his teaching and in his life, Jesus radically challenged the prevailing cultural and religious understandings about power, status and privilege and their use in all human relationships. Jesus' teaching challenged hierarchical power structures and relationships as not acceptable in the new humanity that he was bringing into being. That broad, frontal challenge, on the theoretical level of his teaching, is very specifically embodied in his actions, the words of God lived.

In chapter three, I documented how, in contrast to the dominant cultural reality and religious perceptions regarding the status and value of women in first-century Judaism, the attitudes and actions of Jesus were nothing short of revolutionary. In his life and ministry, he modeled a radically different way for the relationship between men and women. He addressed women with respect; engaged them in substantive theological discussion; welcomed them into his circle; invited them to become learners; reached out with compassion toward those who were broken, rejected and "unclean"; and defended them against the criticism and judgmentalism of the custodians of the religious cultural traditions. Consequently, from Galilee to the cross, women proved to be his most faithful disciples. Several are named (Mary Magdalene, Joanna, Susanna, Mary, Martha) among "many others" (Lk 8:1-3) "who had followed him from Galilee" (Lk 23:49, 55). And it was one of these, Mary Magdalene, whom he entrusted with the good news of his resurrection to tell to his other (male) disciples (Jn 20:17-18).[51]

I do not think that the significance of this reality from the Word of God embodied in the acts and attitudes of Jesus can be overstated for those who are called to be "imitators" of Christ. Jesus is the way and shows the way. To ignore the normative pattern of this way and to bypass the authoritative nature of this lived way is to become mired in culturally encapsulated attitudes, understandings and structures that are an offense to the God who created

---

[51]According to Luke, Mary Magdalene and several other women disciples ("Joanna, Mary the mother of James, and the other women with them," Lk 24:10) are together entrusted with the good news for Jesus' other disciples. The other (male) disciples, in turn, in lockstep with the popular and religiously sanctioned view that women's testimony could not be trusted, "did not believe" the women, for their witness "seemed to them an idle tale" (Lk 24:11).

man and woman in his image, called them into equal and complementary partnership, and in Christ came to set them free from the cursed, demeaning and lessening reality of hierarchical bondage. The continuing denial of this absolute, essential and functional equality in large sectors of the Christian community here and abroad is based on a variety of abusive readings of Scripture, with two serious consequences: (1) it continues to contribute to, abet and reinforce the widespread abuse of women; (2) it is, therefore, a major roadblock to the advance of the gospel.

Closely related to the "hermeneutical filter" of the lived word of Jesus for the man-woman relationship is the hermeneutical filter of his lived word for the relationship between people of faith and all those whom we tend to define as "the other." There is plentiful evidence that deep-seated fear, resentment and hate of "the other"[52] are deeply ingrained realities both within the faith community of ancient Israel and within Christian communities, from the beginning to this present day. The tragedy is that these emotional forces, which come to expression in prejudice, bigotry, exclusion and discrimination, have all too often been reinforced by elements in the scriptural faith tradition, or by justifying interpretations of particular texts. A good example is the centuries-old interpretation of the Genesis narrative of the curse of Ham (Gen 9:20-27). Ham and his descendants are cursed to be slaves by Noah, and the blessing of God is pronounced on Noah's other descendants, whom the race of Ham's descendants would serve as slaves. Since the Hamites were believed to have migrated into Egyptian territory (Gen 10:6-20), dubious historical reconstruction led to the conclusion that the dark-skinned peoples of the African continent were the descendants of Ham. As such, they were "biblically" identified as a slave race, and so-called Christian nations (England, Spain, Portugal and the American colonies) were justified in engaging in the slave trade and enslaving Africans. As preposterous as this sounds to (hopefully) most Christians today, Christian groups in the American South separated from their northern branches during the fierce debates over slavery on the basis of this traditional reading of the Genesis 9 text. Such a reading was further supported by appeal to the New Testament "household codes" (Eph 6:5-8; Col 3:22-24; 1 Pet 2:18-21), where slaves are admonished to obey their masters "in everything" and to suffer quietly when mistreated.

---

[52]For a powerful, penetrating analysis of this reality, see Miroslav Volf, *Exclusion and Embrace: A Theological Exploration of Identity, Otherness and Reconciliation* (Nashville: Abingdon, 1996).

This example of the centuries-long "biblical" justification of the institution of slavery is part of a larger ideology within the biblical story of God's people that views the other—particular ethnic or racial groups or personal and national enemies, as well as certain classes or types of people, such as "sinners" or adherents of pagan cults—as inferior, unclean, deserving of exclusion or even of extermination. Much of the story of Israel is a story of violence and bloodshed. There is the slaughter of all the men of Shechem and the enslavement of their wives and children by the sons of Jacob in retaliation for the rape of their sister Dinah (Gen 34). There is the extermination of the army of the Amalekites, with the divine promise that "the remembrance of Amalek" will be blotted out "from under heaven" (Ex 17:8-14). There is also the total destruction of all the inhabitants (men, women and children) of Jericho and Ai under Joshua (Josh 6—8), followed by genocidal campaigns throughout the land of Canaan.[53] Then there is Gideon's slaughter of the Midianites (Judg 7—8), followed by Jephthah's vengeance against the Amorites (Judg 11) and the destructive internecine warfare between Israelite tribes (Judg 12—20). The records of the united monarchy (under Saul, David and Solomon) and the kingdoms of Israel and Judah, recorded in the books of Samuel and Kings, echo these themes of violence and bloodshed during the earlier periods of conquest and settlement. This ideology of vengeance and retribution, which frequently led to genocidal warfare against both declared and hapless enemies, was understood to be sanctioned by God. It was apparently so deeply ingrained in the collective consciousness of the people that its legacy is even present in Israel's worship liturgy. The so-called imprecatory passages in the Psalms[54] contain prayers for God to inflict wrath on the personal enemies of the psalmist or the national enemies of Israel. There is the violent and repellent language of Psalm 109:6-19, which asks that no kindness and pity be granted to the widows and orphaned children. Psalm 58:10 affirms that "the righteous will rejoice when they see vengeance done; / they will bathe their feet in the blood of the wicked." Psalm 137:7-9 is a cry for vengeance against the Babylonians for their sacking of Jerusalem in 586 B.C., and contains this cruel wish:

---

[53]A repeated affirmation, preceding each campaign, is that the Lord had given the inhabitants into the hands of Joshua's forces (Josh 6:2; 10:8). Following each slaughter, a repeated summation is that Joshua "utterly destroyed every person in it; he left no one remaining" (Josh 10:28; cf. Josh 6:21; 8:22-24; 10:40; 11:21-22).

[54]See, e.g., Psalms 2:9; 21:8-12; 35:4-8; 58:6-10; 68:22-23; 69:22-28; 83:9-18; 109:6-14; 137:8-9.

Happy shall they be who take your little ones
and dash them against the rock! (Psalm 137:9)

As we saw earlier in this chapter, there were voices in the Israelite faith tradition that did not share this theme of vengeance, retribution and despising "the other." David was forbidden from building the temple because he "shed much blood" in the wars he conducted (1 Chron 22:8). God's judgment was pronounced on Jehu for the bloody extermination of the house of Ahab (Hos 1:4-5). The book of Jonah, against the desire of the prophet to see Nineveh destroyed, pronounces God's mercy and steadfast love on Israel's enemy.

To these voices has to be added an astounding vision by the prophet Isaiah, which he proclaimed to Judah and Jerusalem in the waning years of the eighth century B.C. It was a time of political crisis in which the very survival of the kingdom of Judah was at stake, threatened by the Assyrian empire to the north and Egypt to the south.[55] In that context, Isaiah spoke a message from God that was nothing short of revolutionary, and deeply troubling for the custodians within Israel of an ethnocentric exclusivism and the ideology of retribution. The text reads:

> On that day, Israel will be the third with Egypt and Assyria, a blessing in the midst of the earth, whom the LORD of hosts has blessed, saying: "Blessed be Egypt my people, and Assyria the work of my hands, and Israel my heritage. (Is 19:24-25)

In this startling vision we see Israel's nemesis (Assyria in the north) and its former oppressor and continuing threat (Egypt to the south) united with Israel by their common calling to be a blessing to the nations (Is 19:24) and by their common identity as the people of God: "Blessed be Egypt my people, and Assyria the work of my hands, and Israel my heritage" (Is 19:25). In these remarkable closing words of Isaiah's vision, these terms, which were previously restricted to Israel and solely designations of Israel by God, are now applied to both Egypt and Assyria.[56] Egypt is called "my people" (a designation for Israel in Is 10:24; 43:6; Hos 1:10; 2:23; Jer 11:4). Assyria is given the honor of being called "the work of my hands" (a special designation of Israel

[55]John D. Watts, *Isaiah 1—33*, Word Biblical Commentary, vol. 24 (Waco, Tex.: Word Books, 1985), pp. 261-62.
[56]John Oswaldt, *The Book of Isaiah, Chapters 1—39* (Grand Rapids: Eerdmans, 1986), p. 381.

in Is 60:21; 64:8; Ps 119:73; 138:8). Walter Brueggemann gets at the heart of Isaiah's vision:

> Israel's long-standing enemies are now renamed and redefined according to pet names now to be used for Assyria and Egypt as well as for Israel. . . . By this astonishing renaming, the enemies are renamed as fellow members of the covenant and are invited to accept new identity in the world. But we also notice that to make this possible, Israel must relinquish its exclusive claims and its unrivaled relation to Yahweh and be willing to share the privileges of such identity.[57]

Not surprisingly, the idea that God is not the enemy of Israel's enemies was extremely difficult to grasp and accept. The possibility that God is in the business of creating a new community of belonging out of former enemies could not be seriously entertained. And so, in the age-old contest between exclusion and embrace, God's inclusive embrace lost out to the ideology of exclusion and rejection. Such a response is clear from the subsequent translations and interpretations of this prophetic text. When the Hebrew Bible was translated into Greek around 250-100 B.C. for the Jewish Diaspora—immersed as it was in alien, Hellenistic territory—the Hebrew text of Isaiah 19:25 was translated as follows:

> Blessed is my people who are in Egypt, and who are in Assyria, and Israel which is my inheritance. (Is 19:25 LXX)[58]

Thus a blessing that originally included Assyria and Egypt was transmuted into a blessing for Diaspora Jews living *in* Assyria and *in* Egypt. To the audience of that era, the Assyrians and Egyptians—strangers, enemies, aliens, foreigners, culturally different, ritually unclean, religious infidels (i.e., "the other")—could not possibly be the objects of God's reconciling forgiveness and loving embrace. So they were placed outside the circle of acceptability.

This restriction of Isaiah's vision in the Greek Old Testament is further seen in the Targum. These Aramaic paraphrases of the books of the Hebrew Bible, intended for reading in the synagogue, reflect traditional Jewish thinking in the time of the New Testament. It is at once clear that the Targum of

---

[57]Walter Brueggemann, *Isaiah 1—30*, Westminster Bible Commentary (Louisville, Ky.: Westminster John Knox, 1998), pp. 165-66.

[58]Arie Van der Kooij, "The Old Greek of Isaiah 19:16-25: Translation and Interpretation," in *LXX: VI Congress of the International Organization for Septuagint and Cognate Studies, Jerusalem 1986*, ed. Claude E. Cox (Atlanta: Scholars Press, 1987), pp. 127-28.

Isaiah 19:25 represents a significant shift of meaning from the original:

> Blessed be my people whom I have brought out of Egypt. Because they sinned before me, I carried them into exile in Assyria. But now that they have repented, they shall be called my people my inheritance, even Israel.[59]

God's designations (in the original Hebrew) of Egypt as "my people" and of Assyria as "the work of my hands" were stripped from these "others" and returned to their "rightful owners." The ongoing tragedy of this tendency to make ethnocentric, exclusive claims on God is that it represents a denial of the divine yearning to embrace "the other." This is the troubling story that has also manifested itself in numerous ways in the history of Jesus' followers—who in this matter have often not been very faithful followers of their Lord. The conflict between exclusion and embrace was at the very heart of the conflict between Jesus and the religious establishment of his day. He constantly crossed the boundaries by which God's people excluded people and groups, seeking to embrace and reclaim "the other": the Samaritan woman—a despised member of another ethnic, religious group (Jn 4:1-30); the Roman centurion—a feared representative of Rome's oppressive power (Lk 7:2-10; Jn 4:46-54); the publicans—Caesar's despicable collaborators and tax collectors (Mt 9:9-13; Lk 19:2-8); the Syrophoenician woman—a "Gentile dog" (Mk 7:24-30); the ritually unclean (Mk 1:40-42; Lk 10:29-37); and the morally defiled (Lk 7:36-50; Jn 8:1-11).

This "lived word" in Jesus' ministry provides—in addition to his "spoken word" ("love your enemies and pray for those who persecute you," Mt 5:44)—a hermeneutical filter for discerning which elements in the biblical story must be left behind, which are not authoritative perspectives, instructions or patterns that Christians are called to perpetuate and implement. Among conservative Christians, there is a strong tendency to support the use of military power. This stance is often grounded in the divinely sanctioned military conquests against and extermination of Israel's adversaries.[60] The related tendency among Christians toward ethnocentric exclusivity and cultural-religious purity—which manifests itself in fear, prejudice, bigotry and exclusion of the other—is also seen to be justified by aspects of

---

[59]Bruce D. Chilton, "The Isaiah Targum," in *The Targums,* vol. 2 of *The Aramaic Bible* (Wilmington Del.: Michael Glazier, 1987), p. 13.

[60]See the thoughtful work on Israel's divinely sanctioned use of force, in Peter C. Craigie, *The Problem of War in the Old Testament* (Grand Rapids: Eerdmans, 1978).

the faith tradition preserved for us in the Old Testament. But such grounding of Christian perceptions, attitudes and actions in "biblical authority" is only possible if contrary voices in the Old Testament are ignored, and if the ultimate authoritative criterion of Jesus' spoken word and lived word is bypassed. When the light of God's living Word, manifested supremely in the act of suffering love on the cross—where Jesus died for God's enemies (Rom 5:10)—is shed on the biblical texts that are used as justification for such Christian perceptions, attitudes and actions, they wither. They are revealed as historically and culturally relative.

Core criterion three: Prophetic anticipation and apostolic implementation. In our discussion of biblical precedents, we saw that there were, at times, prophetic voices[61] that stood critically over against certain elements and beliefs in their faith tradition. The concerns and affirmations of those voices often came to full flowering in Christ, and they were further given specific shape in both the spoken words and the lived words in Jesus' ministry. In seeking to discern those elements in Scripture prior to Jesus that are historically-culturally relative, the *continuity* between the prophetic voices that challenged the faith tradition and the lived and spoken words of the Word is very significant. For while contrary prophetic voices give us a tentative hermeneutical filter and place question marks over the legitimacy of certain elements in the tradition, the confirmation of those contrary prophetic voices by the person, words and acts of Jesus remove the question marks and replace them with exclamation marks. Questioning earlier and pervasive beliefs, values and practices gives way to a radical challenging of them and a denial of their legitimacy or continuing validity. The continuity between prophetic questioning and Jesus' affirmation of the validity of that questioning discloses the presence of the redemptive movement within Scripture. Prophetic questioning points forward in an exploratory sort of way. In the Word, lived and spoken, the exploratory questioning is both validated and confirmed: "In Christ . . . everything old has passed away; see, everything has become new" (2 Cor 5:17). Or to put it another way, the vision of God to transform the broken, old order toward its intended wholeness—anticipated and announced in these prophetic voices—becomes fully embodied in the living Word. But that is not the end of the story. For God's vision, lived and spoken by Jesus,

---

[61]I am using the term "prophetic voices" not in the narrow sense of the classical prophets, but in the broader sense of Jewish usage, which included Joshua through the Kings as "the former prophets."

was deposited into the community of his disciples. God's vision is entrusted to the church's mission (Jn 17:8).

That is indeed the story of the earliest decades of the Christian movement, documented in the pages of the New Testament: how and where God's vision took on flesh and bone in the concrete lives and communities of Jesus' disciples; how the *vision* was implemented in the *mission*. When we survey that story, we find that the challenging and, at times, radical dimensions of that vision fell like seeds into the soil of apostolic preaching and practice, which was not uniformly fertile. Some seeds of the vision took immediate root and grew to maturity rather quickly. Other seeds fell into the more resistant soil of sanctified tradition and grew more slowly toward maturity. Still others fell into the soil of historical, cultural and situational contexts where they lay dormant, awaiting future germination, growth and fruitfulness. Tracing a few examples from the biblical precedents discussed above will illustrate the redemptive movement from God's vision (articulated by contrary prophetic voices) to the embodiment of that vision in the Word, to the implementation of that vision in the life and mission of the community of Jesus' disciples.

God's vision for the restoration of humanity's relationship with God was foreshadowed in the external ritual of Israel's sacrificial system. But there were later prophetic voices that recognized the serious limitation of such ritual transactions, claiming instead that authentic relationship with God was evidenced in steadfast love, not sacrifice, in knowing God, not burnt offerings, in joyful obedience, not the blood of bulls, in justice, not solemn assemblies, and in goodness, not incense. In order to realize that vision—the New Testament shows—God reached toward humanity in the ultimate sacrifice of steadfast love, embodied in the servant life of Jesus (Eph 5:2), thus ending forever the human illusion that God's love can be earned, that God's favor can be manipulated by ritual transactions. The seeds of this revolutionary vision grew rapidly. The community of Jesus' followers, both Jewish and Gentile, became the only religious movement in antiquity without temple and sacrificial cults. Instead, Jesus' followers were called to live sacrificial lives: to give themselves as "living sacrifices" to the will and way of God (Rom 12:1), to become servants to one another (Jn 13:14) by loving one another (Gal 5:13), to reach toward others in mercy (Mic 6:8; Mt 5:7) as, in the "mercy seat" of Christ, God reached in mercy toward us (Rom 3:25). So in the movement of the disclosure of God's way, sacrificial ritual was judged as inadequate, temporal and preliminary, replaced by the transforming power of lived sacrifice.

A second illustration of the redemptive movement of God's vision—from its tentative articulation in prophetic voices to its embodiment in Christ, to its implementation in his new community—is the matter of retaliation and the use of force in human affairs. We have seen that in the midst of, and over against, a pervasive holy-war ideology in much of Israel's story—from the patriarchs in Genesis through the conquests in Canaan and the kingdoms of Judah and Israel[62]—prophetic voices articulated a divine vision for righteousness, justice, mercy and peace in human affairs. This countercultural vision, which rejected the holy-war tradition, including the eye-for-an-eye ideology of retributive justice, became powerfully embodied in the nonviolent life of the Servant Messiah,[63] the Prince of Peace. He lived and spoke that vision into being. That vision found fertile soil in the lives and communities of his followers. Unlike earlier and subsequent messianic movements, which were fanned by holy-war ideology and ultimately crushed by superior force, the Christian movement spread across the Roman Empire purely in the power of serving and self-giving love, in imitation of the way of God in Christ (Eph 5:1-2). The vision of God, embodied in Jesus and spoken by him, echoed in the speaking of his followers: repay evil with good, do not avenge yourselves, pray for your persecutors, feed your enemies, live in peace. That teaching became the bedrock of the lives of the earliest Christian communities and the way of their presence in the world.

A third element in God's vision fell on more resistant, less fertile soil. One of the biblical precedents in which authoritative instructions are set aside and judged to be historically and culturally relative, and therefore no longer authoritative for us, is in the Old Testament legislation regarding what is clean and unclean. The purpose for this Mosaic legislation was to keep God's people undefiled and separated from the worship practices and customs of their pagan neighbors. But the subsequent history of Israel reveals that religious

---

[62]The "holy war" tradition persisted beyond the exile. It emerged again in the Maccabean revolt in the second century B.C., in numerous messianic movements in the following two centuries, in the Jewish war against Rome in A.D. 66-70, and in the vision of the Qumran covenant community's battle between "the children of light" against the "children of darkness."

[63]Contra the pervasive expectation in Judaism for the triumphant Messiah who would cast off the yoke of Rome (cf. Lk 24:21). In pre-Christian Judaism, the suffering servant of Isaiah 53 was never identified with the Messiah.

purity legislation and practices were finally inadequate to bring about the deeper purity of life that the clean-unclean categories symbolized. In the midst of this reality, the lonely voice of Isaiah articulated a contrary vision: purity before God is not attained by means of purification rituals and keeping separate from those defined as unclean, but rather by removing "the evil of your doings from before my eyes" and by doing justice, rescuing the oppressed, and defending the cause of the most vulnerable and needy (Is 1:16-17). The radical nature of that prophetic perception of God's vision came to full flowering in the life and ministry of Jesus. For him, things, or "specific others" or "categories of others," were never unclean or untouchable: foods, diseased people, Samaritans, Gentiles, sinners. For Jesus, those defined as unclean were the objects of God's redeeming, transforming love. But when the seeds of this vision fell into the soil of Jesus' followers, it met with strong, initial resistance. Centuries of religious teaching and cultural tradition had conditioned the soil of their lives and attitudes to resist this radical challenge: "By no means, Lord; for I have never eaten anything that is profane or unclean" (Acts 10:14). This resistance, which symbolized resistance to follow God's vision with regard to fellowship with and inclusion of unclean others, was gradually overcome by the Spirit's transforming work in Jesus' disciples and the relentless, Spirit-empowered teaching and practice of Paul, Jesus' apostle to the Gentiles. He knew that Christ had "broken down the dividing wall" (Eph 2:14) between Jew and Gentile, built by defining the two groups "clean" and "unclean," respectively. Therefore, in Christ, "there is no longer Jew or Greek" (Gal 3:28).[64]

Paul's conviction that the superior-inferior distinction between ("clean") Jews and ("unclean") Gentiles is "no longer" valid does not stand alone. It is paralleled by the conviction that the over-under status of the master-slave and man-woman relationship is also "no longer" valid (Gal 3:28). The truth expressed in this inspired declaration about the new creation in Christ (2 Cor 5:17) is already articulated at the very beginning of the biblical story: *all human beings are created in the image of God.* That creational design, that vision of a humanity of equality and harmony in the presence of God, became distorted at the very dawn of the human story (Gen 3—11). In the Bible's depic-

---

[64]*Gentile* and *Greek* are used interchangeably in the New Testament, and especially in Galatians, where the Jew-Gentile divide is the central focus. See F. F. Bruce, *The Epistle to the Galatians: A Commentary on the Greek Text* (Grand Rapids: Eerdmans, 1982), pp. 111, 187.

tion of a small slice of that human story (as lived by the descendants of Abraham), it is eminently clear that the divine vision, announced in the creation story, became obscured by and buried under the distorted reality of human culture. Gender and social over-under power structures carried the day. Indeed, they were increasingly understood to have their origin in divine decree,[65] and thus normative structures reflecting divine order, where the lesser serve the greater. At some points in the Old Testament, the creational divine vision breaks through, as in legislation to protect the most vulnerable,[66] and in prophetic voices that call for mercy and justice and kindness, especially for the powerless at the bottom of these social structures—which had been accepted as normative over the course of centuries. As we saw in chapter three, negative views of women's inferior nature and their servant status in relation to men seems to have become increasingly entrenched during the intertestamental period (see appendix B). And the status of slaves and indentured servants in the Jewish world had not improved since Old Testament times, though it was less severe than in the surrounding Greco-Roman world.

Within and over-against these cultural realities, the creational vision of God reasserts itself in the life and teaching of Jesus. The Lord makes himself a servant, and thereby challenges all other human "lords" to imitate him: "I have set you an example, that you also should do as I have done to you" (Jn 13:12-15).[67] Jesus' teaching about the subversion of over-under power categories is a fundamental, frontal challenge to both male-female patriarchy and master-servant hierarchy ("It is not so among you," Mk 10:42-44; cf. Mk 9:34-35; Lk 22:24-27).[68]

When the seeds of this recovered vision, as embodied in the life of Jesus and articulated in his teaching, fell into the soil of apostolic teaching and the practice of the earliest Christian communities, the results were mixed. In both cases, the recovered divine vision was affirmed: "There is no longer slave or free, male or female" (Gal 3:28; see also 1 Cor 12:13; Col 3:11). In the case of the master-slave structure, the recovered vision led to more humane treatment

---

[65]As we saw elsewhere in this study, Genesis 2—3 became fertile soil for Jewish grounding of male-female hierarchy as divinely purposed. And the curse of Ham in Genesis 9 provided authoritative justification for master-slave social arrangements.

[66]See William Webb, *Slaves, Women and Homosexuals: Exploring the Hermeneutics of Cultural Analysis* (Downers Grove, Ill.: InterVarsity Press, 2001), pp. 74-79.

[67]Jesus' countercultural treatment of, and relationship with, women represents a particular embodiment of this challenge.

[68]Recall our extended discussion of this matter in chapter 6.

of slaves (Eph 6:9; Col 4:1): Paul recognized that slaves were, at the same time, also brothers and sisters in the Lord, for with God " there is no partiality" (Eph 6:9; Philem 15-16). However, the redemptive movement of the vision from Jesus into the practice of the early church stopped significantly short of its full realization in the breaking of this dehumanizing power structure. The seeds that were planted for this radical transformation lay largely dormant for many centuries, imprisoned in that dormancy by "biblical justifications" of the institution.[69] It was the horrible realities of the transatlantic slave trade and the dehumanizing institution of race-based slavery in the Americas during the seventeenth through nineteenth centuries that reawakened the Christian conscience to the evil of such power-over social structures.

As argued throughout this study, the vision for male-female equality in both the essence of the female being and in function—announced in the creation narratives and powerfully embodied in the incarnate life and speaking of the Word—initially found more fertile soil for significant growth. The Pauline affirmation of that vision in the "no longer" principle is reflected concretely in the life and practices of the early Christian communities. Numerous New Testament texts reveal that men and women alike were empowered by the Spirit to proclaim the good news of the gospel; that women were free in Christ to pray and proclaim the word in public worship with authority; that women were leaders and teachers, deacons and co-laborers together with men in the gospel; that women and men were challenged to imitate Christ's servant model by giving themselves to one another in mutual submission and self-giving love.

This enthusiastic flowering of the vision in release from entrenched patriarchal structures was not, however, uniform. There were social realities and significant problem-situations, as well as cultural pressures and missional necessities that, in some circumstances, limited implementing the vision for full equality and partnership in all areas of home, church and society. Such factors have been clearly identified in the case of the two texts in the Pauline literature that restrict the vocal participation and leadership of (some)[70]

---

[69]See Willard M. Swartley, *Slaves, Sabbath, War and Women: Case Studies in Biblical Interpretation* (Scottdale, Penn.: Herald Press, 1983), pp. 31-66, for an account of Christian defense of slavery on scriptural grounds.

[70]That these restrictions did not apply to all women in these Pauline churches seems clear. According to 1 Corinthians 11, women did have authority to participate in both prayer and proclamation in the worship of the church. And according to Acts 18:24-26, the ministry team of Priscilla and

women in the churches in Corinth (1 Cor 14:34-35) and in Ephesus (1 Tim 2:11-15).[71] This is not the place to review the exhaustive exegetical work and social-cultural analysis that has shown why Paul, in these two situations, was constrained to call for these restrictions.[72] By way of concise summary, the overarching consensus in these studies is that the apostolic restrictions dealt with very specific problems, such as disruptive behavior in worship (1 Cor 14), heretical teaching and inappropriate grasping for power (1 Tim 2), and missional necessity for respectful social behavior (1 Pet 3). Of importance for our purposes here is the recognition that these texts represent marginal exceptions to the otherwise courageous implementation of the vision for male-female equality.

From these reflections on the matter of master-slave and male-female relationships, two critical insights emerge that further guide us in discerning what is historically-culturally relative and what has abiding authority. First, the fact that there is redemptive movement from creational vision to incarnational embodiment means that all texts that stand between the declaration and embodiment of the vision, and that reflect a reality that falls short of the vision, cannot have abiding authority. Such texts would represent a broken, or

---

Aquila participated together in the instruction of the highly educated Apollos in the church at Ephesus.

[71]In addition to the text in Ephesians 5:21-33, aspects of which we have carefully studied in chapters five and six, there is the similar text in 1 Pet 3:1-6, where wives are exhorted to accept the authority of their husbands. That exhortation is part of a series, where all are called on to accept the authority of all governing institutions, and slaves are admonished to accept the authority of their masters. We saw in chapter three that governing authority is limited elsewhere in the New Testament, and we also saw in the present chapter that the christological hermeneutical filter invalidates the authority of the slavery structure. In light of these limitations, the wife's submission to the husband's authority must be understood not as an authoritative absolute, but as relative within that particular historical situation. For an excellent discussion of the "household code" in 1 Peter 2:13—3:7, within the situation in which the church found itself, see J. Ramsey Michaels, *1 Peter*, Word Biblical Commentary, vol. 49 (Waco, Tex.: Word Books, 1988).

[72]See the major commentaries on these texts published in the past few decades (e.g., by Gordon D. Fee, C. K. Barrett, Charles H. Talbert, Richard B. Hays and Ben Witherington III on 1 Corinthians; Gordon D. Fee and J. N. D. Kelly on 1 Timothy). See also the excellent, specially focused studies, such as Craig S. Keener, *Paul, Women and Wives: Marriage and Women's Ministry in the Letters of Paul* (Peabody, Mass.: Hendrickson Publishers, 1992); David Scholer, "1 Timothy 2:9-15 and the Place of Women in the Church's Ministry," in *Women, Authority and the Bible*, ed. Alvera Mickelsen (Downers Grove, Ill.: InterVarsity Press, 1986); Gilbert Bilezikian, *Beyond Sex Roles: What the Bible Says About a Woman's Place in Church and Family* (Grand Rapids: Baker Book House, 1986); Patricia Gundry, *Women Be Free: The Clear Message of Scripture* (Grand Rapids: Zondervan, 1977); Aída Besançon Spencer, *Beyond the Curse: Women Called to Ministry* (Peabody, Mass.: Hendrickson, 1989); R. T. France, *Women in the Church's Ministry: A Test Case for Biblical Interpretation* (Grand Rapids: Eerdmans, 1995).

limited, or distorted understanding of God's vision for these relational, social realities.

Second, the partial or limited implementation of the vision in apostolic teaching and churchly practice should not carry normative authority, as judged in light of its embodiment in Christ. From these insights, an important hermeneutical principle emerges: *One must distinguish between vision and limited implementation of that vision.* The vision is normative. Limited implementation—or attitudes and practices in tension with or in opposition to the vision—is relative. Vision announces divine intentionality; it declares what *ought* to be. When *what is* stands in tension with the *ought*, "what is" can then be judged to be relative.

The tragedy in much of the history of the church is that the relativity of the limited implementation of the vision for the male-female and master-slave relationships became normative. The redemptive movement of the vision into the life and teaching of the church was throttled. The vision moved from the church's horizon. That tragic reality continues into this very day. While the external system of slavery in the Americas was abolished a century and a half ago, its legacy in terms of prejudice and bigotry and discrimination is still all too real—even in Christian attitudes and actions. And the demeaning and lessening reality of male-female hierarchy is still with us in large sectors of the worldwide Christian community. It still prevents the gifts of countless women from being used, experienced and brought to bear on the mission of the church in the world. It still abets the abuse of women by reinforcing the lingering cultural attitudes about the secondary status of women with religious, "biblical" justifications.

AVOIDING THE ABUSE OF HISTORICAL SITUATION AND CULTURAL REALITY

We have covered a significant amount of territory in this chapter. It may be helpful to briefly review that territory by way of a summary of major affirmations and findings. Within this summary, principles and criteria for avoiding this abuse of Scripture will be articulated.

1. Scripture is communicated in particular, changing historical and cultural contexts. The fundamental assumption of the entire chapter is that the incarnational nature of Scripture must be taken seriously. Scripture participates in, and is addressed to, Israel and the Christian community in their particular, and changing, historical and cultural contexts.

2. Scripture can transcend a historical, cultural context, be limited to that context and/or be misunderstood in many contexts. This "human embeddedness" of Scripture means (a) that it can speak authoritatively to particular cultural and historical situations with an authority that transcends those situations; (b) that an authoritative word addressed to a particular situation may be limited to that context; and (c) that perceptions of God's words or ways, within the context of the limited and sinful recipients, may reflect misunderstandings and distortions of those words and ways.

3. We must distinguish between what is relative and what transcends all contexts. These aspects of the incarnational nature of Scripture (in points 1 and 2 above) raise a *fundamental hermeneutical issue:* How do we distinguish between that in Scripture which is culturally and historically relative and, therefore, limited in its authority to the people and situations addressed? And how do we distinguish between that which is transhistorical and transcultural and is authoritative for all Christians in all times and all places?

4. All Christians, from the first century to the present, have been and are engaged in this discernment process. This is true whether or not they acknowledge the assumptions about the nature of Scripture affirmed above (points 1-2). That fact points to the *inevitability* of making such decisions. It also raises the specter of subjectivity and arbitrariness.

5. These pitfalls can be avoided if we ground our discernment in biblical precedent. We discovered numerous places throughout the scriptural canon where the writers are engaged in the process of discernment. Careful observation of how they do it provides guidelines for engaging in it responsibly. In light of biblical precedents, we affirmed both the *legitimacy* and *necessity* of discerning between that which is relative and that which transcends the original situation.

6. Precedents found in Scripture. From our study of the precedents in Scripture, we derived three core hermeneutical criteria:

a. Christ is the center. He is the Word of God, in light of whom the entirety of the words of Scripture must be viewed. God's redemptive self-disclosure— ultimately focused in the cross—is the ultimate hermeneutical filter for understanding all of Scripture.

b. Jesus' words and acts are normative and paradigmatic. The incarnate being of the Word becomes historically particular in the lived and spoken word. Thus

Jesus' actions and teaching are a critical hermeneutical filter.

c. There should be concurrence between prophetic anticipation and apostolic implementation. Congruence between prophetic voices that oppose elements in the biblical faith tradition and between the words and ways of God as disclosed in the incarnation provides a complementary hermeneutical criterion. Continuity between God's words and ways in the incarnation and between apostolic teaching and practice provides a second complementary hermeneutical criterion.

7. We must judge the vision in Scripture as having normative authority rather than its limited implementation. The redemptive movement of God's vision and purpose for human life, which reaches its fullest expression in the incarnation, is finally surrendered into the earthen vessel of the life and ministry of the community of Jesus' disciples. Whenever there is incongruity between the vision and its practical implementation, the latter must be judged to reflect cultural/historical/situational limitation, rather than normative authority.

8. The cross of Christ is the ultimate hermeneutical key. The ultimate, irreducible hermeneutical key for discerning between that which is relative and that which has transcending, abiding authority is the revelation of God's glory (Jn 1:14; 17:1, 22)—his character and way for humanity—in the cross of Christ. Whatever withers in light of the cross reflects historically and culturally limited authority or the recipients' lack of appropriate perception of God's will and way. Whatever blossoms in light of the cross has transcendent, abiding authority.[73]

---

[73]Insightful hermeneutical principles for distinguishing between biblical texts that are culturally relative and those that transcend their original setting and have normative authority for Christians in all times are proposed by Gordon D. Fee and Douglas Stuart in *How to Read the Bible for All Its Worth*, pp. 70-76. A very helpful essay is that by S. Scott Bartchy, "Power, Submission and Sexual Identity Among the Early Christians," in which he deals with the issue of determining what is either relative or of abiding authority in New Testament teaching and practice regarding the man-woman relationship, in *Essays on New Testament Christianity*, ed. C. R. Wetzel (Cincinnati: Standard Publishing, 1978), pp. 50-80.

8

CONCLUDING REFLECTIONS
AND CHALLENGES

As indicated in the introduction, this was not to be a book about biblical interpretation as such, though in its entirety it *does* biblical interpretation and *is* biblical interpretation. Nor is it a book about methodology in biblical interpretation, though issues of method are raised, explicitly or implicitly, throughout this study. Nor is it a book about principles of biblical interpretation, though principles for the trustworthy interpretation of Scripture are both named and practiced. All of these undertakings are, of course, both worthy and absolutely essential for the continuing vivacity of Scripture, its responsible interpretation in and for the church, and its active presence in the church and for the world. But there is already much good literature available on these important matters, both for the average reader and the expert.

The reader has surely perceived that this is not an exhaustive or comprehensive study on the matter of the abuse of Scripture. It does not systematically explore all possible ways in which Scripture is misinterpreted and misapplied. Nor are all parts of Scripture equally represented, though an effort has been made to be as representative as possible in the choice of biblical texts and the selection of issues addressed in Scripture. Apart from a few references, the book of Revelation has not received special attention. The issues in this particular literary genre are so numerous that only extensive explorations would do them justice, and such an exploration was beyond our more limited and immediate purpose.[1]

Rather, my goal has been twofold: (1) to demonstrate not so much how Scripture *should* be interpreted properly and correctly, but how Scripture *is in fact* all too frequently and pervasively misinterpreted, mishandled, misunderstood and misapplied in and by the Christian community, both individually and collectively; (2) to demonstrate repeatedly, via multiple examples, that the abuse of Scripture has consequences.

Biblical interpretation is often seen—certainly by those outside the fold—as an esoteric exercise, like a Shakespeare society quibbling over the interpretation of Shakespeare's metaphors, of relevance to no one outside the guild. Likewise, biblical scholars are often seen to be quibbling over the meaning of passages, parsing words and phrases to determine whether particular passages support an Arminian or Calvinistic reading of the text; whether a passage speaks about the impending fall of Jerusalem in A.D. 70 or the apocalypse at the end of time; whether the book of Revelation speaks to its own time at the close of the first century or is purely futuristic; whether all the letters attributed to Paul are directly from his hand. These sorts of matters are sometimes extremely interesting and often very important for a full understanding of the faith. But at times they have little or no significant consequences for the participants in the exercise, or are of little, if any, use for the living of the Christian life, or are totally irrelevant to those outside the circle.

On the contrary, the abuses of Scripture addressed in this book, for the most part, have serious consequences. For these not only do violence to the meaning and message of Scripture, but do collateral damage, in two ways:

---

[1]While matters of literary genre are noted a number of times, I have chosen not to unduly burden this book with a topic that easily deserves a book-length treatment of its own. The issues raised by literary genre are vast, since within the confines of the canon there are about a dozen different types—legal codes, historical narratives, prehistoric theology in narrative or poetic forms, wisdom, prophecy (both pronouncement and prediction), apocalyptic, love songs, Gospels (as biography and/or theology), personal letters, epistles, etc. While there are general principles of biblical interpretation applicable to all (in such matters as syntax and grammar), each has a distinct character and requires understanding and principles unique to each genre. An excellent primer in these matters is Gordon D. Fee and Douglas Stuart, *How to Read the Bible for All Its Worth*, 2nd ed. (Grand Rapids: Zondervan, 1993).

First, the abuse of Scripture undermines and blunts the veracity of the gospel we seek to proclaim, and it impairs the effectiveness of Christian witness and presence. Second, when we abuse Scripture, we contribute to abuse and brokenness in the world. We unwittingly, and at times wittingly, contribute to its level of violence, to bitterness between people groups, to bigotry and prejudice, to judgmentalism and the exclusion of "the other."

Thus the title of the book, *Abusing Scripture: The Consequences of Misreading the Bible,* is apt. The main purpose has been to lead the reader into and through a variety of ways in which Scripture is misinterpreted, to show how its meaning and message is thereby misunderstood, and to point to significantly negative and often tragic consequences this abusive reading of Scripture can have. The intent has been to shake things up a bit, to rattle the safe cage in which we talk to each other about interpreting the Bible, so we can get it just right for our nuanced, in-house theological discussions and debates, while the "sharks" out there swim quietly by our cage and barely notice.

While the focus throughout the book has been to alert my sisters and brothers in the community of Jesus' disciples to the serious, negative consequences of the abuse of Scripture, I want in the following concluding reflections to lift up some challenging possibilities for Christian witness, presence and mission that open up before us when we refuse to abuse Scripture. At a few places, I have already pointed in that direction; echoes of those, I hope, can be profitably heard again.

What would happen if both the "left" hand and "right" hand of the theological divide within the Christian family finally capitulated in their respective abuses of the whole gospel, and instead joined hands and promoted the *whole* gospel together? When personal gospel and social gospel walk side by side, when the Bread of Life and bread for the world are offered by the same hand, when those who work for political peace can do so unflinchingly in the name and power of the Prince of Peace, when those who are passionate about getting people saved can promote with equal passion the saving of the environment, and when those who call and work for justice will also talk about and work for the justification of sinners—what might happen? Is it possible that such a united Christian voice, witness and presence would be more thoughtfully listened to, more respectfully considered, and more warmly embraced in the marketplaces of our time? One thing is certain: such a whole gospel could not be as easily ignored, nor could sectors within the broad spectrum of the Christian community be as easily coopted or hijacked by political parties or sectarian ideologies.

What would happen if we ceased abusing the Bible's balanced and inclusive agenda by only giving attention to certain parts and ignoring or minimizing others? For one thing, we would rob the secular media of its ability to present to the world a caricature of who we are and what we are for, showing primarily only what we are against. On the basis of that caricature, evangelicals are summarily dismissed as misguided, single-agenda, obscurantist zealots. But when we reject the abuse of biblical balance, we can speak as loudly and persuasively about compassion for illegal aliens as about abortion; about responsible stewardship of the earth as about premarital sexual abstinence; about poverty and its dehumanizing power as about family values; about the continuing and all-too-pervasive racism in our midst as about ethical concerns in stem-cell research; about sinful social and economic structures as about the integrity of marriage; about gossip and slander in our churches as about homosexuality; about self-righteousness and judgmentalism as about adultery. Could it be that with such a balanced agenda, our proclamation, witness and presence in our culture might be taken more seriously than it presently is?

We have seen how the abuse of words related to a biblical understanding of man and woman—and their relationship to one another in the church, home and marriage—has contributed important building blocks for the construction of the so-called biblical view of that relationship, in terms of hierarchical authority and power. We further saw how the abuse of literary and theological contexts about the man-woman relationship (such as 1 Cor 11 and Eph 5) have contributed their share to the centuries-old and still-pervasive traditional understanding of this relationship in terms of "power over": authoritative husband and submissive wife, leader and follower, authority figure and servant, head of the house and keeper of the house. It is clear that this Christian interpretive tradition has significantly contributed to the long and tragic history of women's inferior status; of their restricted roles in home, church and society; and of their demeaning subjugation and abuse in many hierarchical marriage relationships. What would happen if we would cease and desist from these abusive readings of Scripture? If we could learn with Paul that, in the new humanity in Christ, power-over relationships in which one is exalted and the other is debased are an affront to the God who created both man and woman in his image? That they are an affront to the God whose vision for man and woman is a partnership of mutual self-giving, a partnership where each one uses all of his or her gifts in the journey of becoming whole and the mission of helping others become whole? What would be the impact on our culture—and throughout the world through Christian witness and presence, especially in places where women are terribly used and abused, oppressed and demeaned—if the voice of evangelical faith were in the forefront of passionate advocacy for the absolute equality and dignity of women and men in all areas of home, church and society? What if educational programs were launched in the churches within the worldwide evangelical movement, helping Christian men learn to become partners with their wives and setting them on the journey of relinquishing the need to exert power and authority over women? We can only speculate what would be if the Christian church had been in the vanguard of promoting equal rights for women—rather than resisting it and giving the field to the secular, often antireligious and angry, feminist movement.

In our discussion of the abuse of historical and cultural context in the interpretation of biblical passages, we noted significant negative consequences in the matters pertaining to the rejection and exclusion of others, to the use of force and military might, and to the human propensity for retaliation and demands for retributive justice. Abuse of Scripture in these areas has, perhaps, done more to undermine the gospel and the trustworthiness of our Christian presence and witness in the world than any other single abuse of Scripture. But . . . what if? What would happen if Christians across the broad spectrum of theological traditions (and especially within the community of those who affirm the Bible as their absolute authority) would learn to view in light of the cross those biblical passages that sanction force and retaliation, and thus judge those passages as "not biblical" in the sense of having legitimizing authority for followers of the Prince of Peace? What would happen if, on the basis of such an orientation, Bible-believing Christians were the last, rather than among the first, to jump on the bandwagon to use force against our enemies, or to preserve our "national self-interest"? I am not arguing here for a thoroughgoing, absolute kind of pacifism—although there are Christian traditions, such as the historic "peace churches" (e.g., Mennonites, Brethren, Quakers) who have borne courageous witness to such an understanding of the calling of the gospel. I have deep respect for that position. Yet, given our sinful world and sinful political/structural realities, there are occasions when the use of force seems the choice of last resort for self-defense, or for the defeat of ruthless conquerors, or for the intervention in and termination of genocidal bloodbaths (see appendix C on the just-war theory). What I am contending for is a christologically focused preference for peacemaking rather than warmongering, for restraint rather than aggression, for responding to our enemies with goodness rather than with evil.

What if, for example, Focus on the Family—on the basis of the christologically centered hermeneutic discussed in chapter seven—would match its passion for halting the destruction of the innocent unborn with an equal passion for halting the destruction of the innocent children in Iraq? What would happen if the Moral Majority would be as strident in opposition to corporate greed—which often results in the lessening and demeaning and impoverishing of human life—as it is in opposition to the moral deterioration of our society? What would happen if the National Association of Evangelicals were as committed to the reversal of the spread of weaponry in our land as it is to doctrinal purity within its membership? Or more outrageously: what if these and other like-minded organizations, and the vast number of churches and individual Christians who are referred to in the media as the "religious right," would join with such movements as Evangelicals for Social Action and Call to Renewal in their advocacy for "plowshares" rather than "swords," for bread rather than bullets, for justice rather than judgment?

Such a broad movement of historically diverse Christian faith traditions could speak to our leaders at all levels of government—with a united voice of advocacy at the voting booth—demonstrating that we are truly disciples of the Prince of Peace, the author and protector of life, the friend of sinners, the lover of enemies, the reclaimer of rejects, and the protector of the poor. Such a broad coalition of Christian voices could speak the truth of Christ about human life and human institutions to "the powers" who make and execute national and international policies and programs. What if, instead of advocating for military might and its use in international affairs, a united Christian voice—informed by the centrality of the cross of Christ in biblical interpretation—would advocate for policies that focused on "overcoming evil with good"? Such advocacy might promote policies of reconstruction rather than isolation, of assistance rather than military threat, of reconciliation rather than rejection. What if a united Christian voice advocated for policies that assist "enemy nations" to overcome poverty in their lands through agricultural innovation and technological assistance; that create health-care partnerships with disease-wracked nations who are not our friends; and that promote programs through which undocumented immigrants in our midst are treated with compassion, even though they broke the rules to get here?

Answers to these questions are wanting, since such united Christian advocacy has not been attempted. But one thing, I believe, is certain. The abuse of Scripture—practiced by all who bypass the hermeneutical key of Christ's centrality and refuse to let the light of the cross shine on the reading of all biblical texts—continues to be a debilitating force that undermines the credibility of Christian witness. It lessens the effectiveness of Christian presence. It denies the possibility of a transforming Christian advocacy for policies and programs that reflect God's way revealed in the cross, God's alternative to the distortion and brokenness of human life and society.

Perhaps the "what if" questions raised above, and the possibilities voiced in these concluding reflections, represent fragments of an unrealistic, utopian dream. But . . . NO! We are called to hope. And my hope is that this book will contribute, in some small way, to the continuing Christian journey toward realizing the hope expressed by our Lord: that we may be one, and that the world will come to know, through our united witness and presence, the transforming love of God.

APPENDIX A

THE GOSPEL OF PERSONAL SALVATION
AND THE SOCIAL GOSPEL

The bifurcation of the whole gospel has been a significant reality, particularly within American Protestantism, for over a century. Its origin lies in bitter theological struggle in the last decades of the nineteenth century and the early decades of the twentieth, known as the "Modernist-Fundamentalist Controversy." Fueled by the Enlightenment and the scientific revolution, there emerged a liberal Protestantism that questioned or rejected the transcendent and supernatural elements of the orthodox Christian faith, and focused its attention on the ethical and social teachings of the Old and New Testaments. A primary concern became those teachings that address people and nations on the level of social ills, economic injustice, oppressive cultural and political structures, racial hatred, and the needs of the poor. A significant pointer in that direction was Walter Rauschenbusch's *A Theology for the Social Gospel*.[1] In reaction, the evangelical, pietistic stream within Protestantism—

---

[1]Walter Rauschenbusch, *A Theology for the Social Gospel* (New York: Macmillan, 1922). Though Rauschenbusch's work promoted this trend in liberal Protestantism, his continuing commitment

fearing that the precious gospel of Jesus the Savior, of his atoning death on the cross, of his resurrection from the dead, and of the benefits of this divine work of redemption for individuals, was being cast on the trash heap of history—largely rejected the social gospel and closed its eyes to the social teachings in Scripture, as well as those teachings' implications for sinful social and political structures and policies, and it retreated into private, personal piety, emphasizing the evangelistic task of saving souls.[2]

This divorce within Protestantism, this bifurcation of the whole gospel, is both a tragedy and a heresy, because the two elements belong together.[3] Both personal salvation and social justice were the passionate concerns of great evangelical leaders in the eighteenth and nineteenth centuries, like William Wilberforce in Great Britain and Charles Finney in America.[4] Both the modernists and the fundamentalists lost sight of this great heritage in their fierce controversy, and they bequeathed their imbalanced, one-sided versions of the gospel to their somewhat "kinder and gentler" offspring, namely mainline Protestantism and modern evangelicalism.

Significant voices contested this bifurcation of the gospel, particularly in the last half of the twentieth century, and contended for keeping these two dimensions of the gospel together. Carl F. H. Henry, theologian and long-time editor of *Christianity Today*, challenged the neglect of the social dimensions of the gospel in his *The Uneasy Conscience of Modern Fundamentalism*.[5]

---

to the comprehensive implications of the gospel, including the reality of personal sin and salvation through the atoning work of Christ, was largely ignored in the polarizing controversy between liberalism and fundamentalism. (In the early decades of the twentieth century, the terms *fundamentalism* and *evangelicalism* were interchangeable. *Fundamentalism* expressed a concern for the "fundamentals" of the orthodox Christian faith; only later did it come to denote a very rigid, narrowly legalistic and absolutist expression of the Christian faith, which today is largely identical with the "religious right.")

[2]George M. Marsden chronicles this struggle in his *Fundamentalism and American Culture: The Shaping of Twentieth-Century Evangelicalism, 1870-1925* (New York: Oxford University Press, 1980).

[3]See the passionate plea for, and biblical-theological grounding of, such a whole gospel in Ronald J. Sider, *One-Sided Christianity? Uniting the Church to Heal a Lost and Broken World* (Grand Rapids: Zondervan, 1993).

[4]Donald W. Dayton documents this in his *Discovering an Evangelical Heritage* (New York: Harper & Row, 1976). See also the thorough study by Timothy L. Smith, *Revivalism and Social Reform in Mid-Nineteenth Century America* (New York: Abingdon, 1957). A major film (2007), titled *Amazing Grace*, is the powerful story of William Wilberforce's tenacious struggle, as a member of the British Parliament, to have the slave trade outlawed throughout the British Empire. In mid-nineteenth century America, the noted evangelist Charles Finney was also significantly engaged in the battle to abolish slavery.

[5]Carl F. H. Henry, *The Uneasy Conscience of Modern Fundamentalism* (Grand Rapids: Eerdmans, 1947). The enduring potency—and necessity—of Henry's plea is evidenced in the decision by the

In his introduction to this volume, Harold J. Ockenga wrote:

> If the Bible-believing Christian is on the wrong side of social problems such as war, race, class, labor, liquor, imperialism, etc., it is time to get over the fence to the right side. . . . A Christian world- and life-view, embracing world questions [and] societal needs . . . ought to arise out of Matthew 28:18-21 as much as evangelism does. Culture depends on such a view, and fundamentalism is prodigally dissipating the Christian culture accretion of centuries, a serious sin.[6]

Baptist theologian Culbert Rutenber issued a ringing call for social involvement, grounded in the evangelical faith, in his *The Reconciling Gospel*.[7] In 1971, Carl Henry followed his earlier challenge with the publication of *A Plea for Evangelical Demonstration*, which began with these words: "A sensitive Christian conscience must openly confront enduring and intractable social injustices."[8]

Arguably the strongest, most articulate and passionate evangelical voice, calling both evangelicals and other Christian traditions to surrender their half-gospels and become advocates for, and embodiments of, the whole gospel, is that of Ronald J. Sider. In 1973, he organized a major meeting of evangelical leaders, devoted exclusively to social concerns. One of the outcomes of this gathering was "The Chicago Declaration of Evangelical Social Concern," which both acknowledged the deplorable neglect of social concern in the evangelical movement and called for a confrontation with the social, economic and other structural injustices in our nation.[9] Another outcome was Sider's founding of Evangelicals for Social Action (ESA),[10] which has recruited, trained and influenced a great number of new evangelical leaders in the past three decades to be champions of a holistic gospel.

Perhaps Sider's most significant contribution in this movement toward a recovery of evangelical social concern was the publication of his *Rich Chris-*

---

publisher to issue a reprint of this volume in 2003.

[6]Ockenga's reference to "the right side" has nothing to do with a political or religious position but with the "correct" position, in keeping with biblical truth.

[7]Culbert Rutenber, *The Reconciling Gospel* (Valley Forge, Penn.: Judson Press, 1960).

[8]Carl F. H. Henry, *A Plea for Evangelical Demonstration* (Grand Rapids: Eerdmans, 1971).

[9]Sider, *One-Sided Christianity?* p. 19.

[10]ESA is a national membership organization devoted to reducing poverty, promoting social justice and caring for the creation. It "emphasizes both the transformation of human lives through personal faith and also the importance of a commitment to social and economic justice as an outgrowth of Christian faith." See ESA's website <www.esa-online.org>.

tians in an Age of Hunger.[11] It not only made an irrefutable biblical case for God's special concern for the poor, the oppressed, the marginalized and the sufferers of injustice, but it also challenged, especially, evangelicals to make God's concern a priority, side by side with their passion for evangelism. Sider's publications,[12] which address various facets of the whole gospel and their implications for Christian presence and witness, together with likeminded colleagues across the evangelical and ecumenical landscape,[13] have made a significant contribution to reversing the century-long near-abandonment of social justice concerns by evangelicals.[14] Yet we have a long way to go in both acknowledging and embodying the whole gospel.[15] Avoiding the either-or approach in hearing and applying biblical teaching should contribute decisively to the recovery of the whole gospel in Christian witness and action.

[11]Ronald J. Sider, *Rich Christians in an Age of Hunger* (Downers Grove, Ill.: InterVarsity Press, 1977). The volume has gone through several editions, culminating in the twentieth-anniversary revision, *Rich Christians in an Age of Hunger: Moving from Affluence to Generosity* (Dallas: Word Publishing, 1997). This work has recently been named by *Christianity Today* as the seventh most-influential book in the past fifty years.

[12]His extensive writings, in addition to those already noted, include *Christ and Violence* (Scottdale, Penn.: Herald Press, 1979); *Completely Pro-Life: Building a Consistent Stance* (Downers Grove, Ill.: InterVarsity Press, 1987); *Cup of Water, Bread of Life* (Grand Rapids: Zondervan, 1994); *Good News and Good Works: A Theology for the Whole Gospel* (Grand Rapids: Baker Books, 1999); *Just Generosity: A New Vision for Overcoming Poverty in America* (Grand Rapids: Baker Books, 1999).

[13]Jim Wallis, *Faith Works: How to Live Your Beliefs and Ignite Positive Social Change* (New York: Random House, 2005); *Agenda for Biblical People* (New York: Harper, 1976); *God's Politics: Why the Right Gets It Wrong and the Left Doesn't Get It* (San Francisco: HarperSanFrancisco, 2005); Daniel Buttry, *Christian Peacemaking: From Heritage to Hope* (Valley Forge, Penn.: Judson Press, 1994); David P. Gushee, ed., *Toward a Just and Caring Society: Christian Responses to Poverty in America* (Grand Rapids: Baker Books, 1999); Donald B. Kraybill, *The Upside-Down Kingdom* (Scottdale, Penn.: Herald Press, 1978); David O. Moberg, *Wholistic Christianity* (Elgin, Ill.: Brethren Press, 1985); Gabriel Fackre, *Word and Deed: Theological Themes in Evangelism* (Grand Rapids: Eerdmans, 1975); Vinay Samuel and Chris Sugden, eds., *The Church in Response to Human Need* (Grand Rapids: Eerdmans; Oxford: Regnum Books, 1987); Nicholas Wolterstorff, *Until Justice and Peace Embrace* (Grand Rapids: Eerdmans, 1983).

[14]In "Evangelical Voters, Practice What You Preach," Beliefnet.com <www.beliefnet.com/story/162/story_16252_1.html>, Sider reports that "In mid January [2006], over one hundred evangelical leaders wrote President Bush, urging him to do more to empower poor people in his second term. Last October [2005], the National Association of Evangelicals (the largest evangelical network in the USA, representing 30 million evangelicals) adopted a new document as the official framework for its political engagement." This document, "For the Health of the Nation: An Evangelical Call for Civic Responsibility," calls for a biblically based agenda that includes "justice for the poor, protecting human rights, seeking peace and caring for creation."

[15]This is the concern addressed by Ronald J. Sider in his *The Scandal of the Evangelical Conscience: Why Are Christians Living Just Like the Rest of the World?* (Grand Rapids: Baker Books, 2005).

APPENDIX B

VIEWS OF WOMEN IN INTERTESTAMENTAL
JUDAISM AND EARLY CHRISTIANITY

A decisively negative view of women was pervasive in Judaism. In a passage on the worst form of evil (in Sirach 25:13-23), we read: "Any wound, only not a heart-wound! Any wickedness, only not the wickedness of a woman!" This assessment is grounded in the observation that "from a woman, sin did originate, and because of her we all must die" (Sirach 25:24). Therefore, "if she go not as thou wouldst have her, cut her off from thy flesh (Sirach 25:26—meaning, "If she does not obey you, divorce her"). These sentiments are further expressed in Sirach 42:14, where "the wickedness of a man" is judged as "better . . . than the goodness of a woman."[1]

In a legendary conversation between Eve and Adam after the Fall (in The Books of Adam and Eve), she addresses Adam as "my lord" throughout, and confesses that "I have brought trouble and anguish upon thee" (v. 3). In another passage, she asks Adam whether he would slay her, for per-

---

[1]Translations from R. H. Charles, ed., *The Apocrypha and Pseudepigrapha of the Old Testament: The Apocrypha*, vol. 1 (1913; reprint, Oxford: Clarendon, 1969).

haps then "the Lord will bring thee into paradise, for on my account thou hast been driven thence" (3.2; cf. Slavonic Version 28.2 and 35.1). The interpretation of Genesis 3:16 as a divine command is clearly expressed in 32.1, where the archangel Joel, speaking on behalf of God, castigates Adam for listening to a suggestion by Eve: "I did not create thy wife to command thee, but to obey."[2]

A rabbinic interpretation of Genesis 18:15 (where Sarah is caught in a lie) concluded that women were by nature deceptive, and therefore their testimony could not be trusted. To teach a woman the Torah was tantamount to teaching her promiscuity. Indeed, it was considered better to burn up the Torah rather than deliver it into the hands of women. Talking much with women was considered a source of evil that would ultimately lead to Gehenna.[3]

In his reflections on Genesis 2:21, the first-century Jewish philosopher-theologian Philo of Alexandria asked why the woman, unlike the man (and the animals!) was not formed from the earth. His answer is that, "First, because woman is not equal in honor with man. Second, because she is not equal in age, but younger. Third [God] wishes that man should take care of woman as a very necessary part of him, but woman, in turn, should serve him as a whole."[4] It is interesting that Philo justified this interpretation of the Genesis text by appealing to the cultural conventions of his own day, where the woman changed her habitat from her family to her husband. In reference to Genesis 3:1-2 he asks: "Why does the serpent speak to the woman and not to the man?" His answer is: "A woman is more accustomed to be deceived than men. . . . Because of softness, she easily gives way and is taken in by plausible falsehoods which resemble the truth."[5]

His younger contemporary, the Jewish historian Josephus, wrote: "From women let no evidence be acceptable because of the levity and temerity of their sex, neither let slaves bear witness because of the baseness of their soul . . . for they will not attest the truth."[6] These attitudes are comprehensively

---

[2]R. H. Charles, ed., *The Apocrypha and Pseudepigrapha of the Old Testament: The Pseudepigraph*, vol. 2 (1913; reprint, Oxford: Clarendon, 1969), p. 134.

[3]Craig S. Keener, *Paul, Women and Wives: Marriage and Women's Ministry in the Letters of Paul* (Peabody, Mass.: Hendrickson Publishers, 1992), documents this rabbinic tradition throughout his study (e.g., pp. 83-84 and notes).

[4]Philo of Alexandria *Questions and Answers on Genesis*, 1.17 (trans. Ralph Marcus, Loeb Classical Library, supplement 1 [Cambridge, Mass.: Harvard University Press, 1953]).

[5]Philo of Alexandria *Questions and Answers on Genesis* 1.33.

[6]Josephus *Jewish Antiquities* 4.8.15, par. 219.

expressed in one of the "Eighteen Benedictions" prayed regularly by Jewish men, in which God is praised for not having created them either as slaves, Gentiles or women.[7]

Jewish practice in the first century reflected the impact of these perspectives. In keeping with the negative view of their reliability and trustworthiness, women's testimony was not acceptable in a court of law. They were restricted from studying Torah. In synagogue worship, they were segregated behind a curtain and not permitted to participate actively and vocally in the worship liturgy. The main sanctuary of the temple was reserved for Jewish men, while women were relegated to a lower level outside the main sanctuary, called "the court of women."[8]

There were also voices within the Jewish tradition that did not join this negative chorus regarding the value and status of women. In some Jewish texts, the first man—not the woman—is held responsible for the entrance of sin and death into the world. In reflecting on the origin of sin and evil, the author of 4 Ezra states that God gave Adam but one command to observe, "but he transgressed it" (4 Ezra 3:7). He went on to say, "For the first Adam, clothing himself with the evil heart, transgressed and was overcome" (4 Ezra 3:21; cf. 4 Ezra 7:11-12). Then there is the lament in 4 Ezra 7:18, "O thou Adam, what hast thou done! For though it was thou who sinned, the fall was not thine alone, but ours also who are thy descendants!"[9] Paul's use of "Adam" (Rom 5:14; 1 Cor 15:22) and "one man" or "a human being" (Rom 5:12; 1 Cor 15:21) as the antithesis to "the one who was to come" or "Christ" (Rom 5:14; 1 Cor 15:22; cf. 1 Cor 15:45-49) is in line with these exceptions to the overwhelming insistence in Jewish thought on Eve's culpability. Unfortunately, these alternative voices were largely muted in the louder chorus and did not influence the development of Christian views in the first centuries in any significant way. To the contrary, in the writings of the early fathers during the first few centuries, there is ample evidence that the prevailing negative

---

[7]Paul reflects this formula in Galatians 3:28. See Leon Morris, *Galatians: Paul's Charter of Christian Freedom* (Downers Grove, Ill.: InterVarsity Press, 1996), p. 121; and F. F. Bruce, *The Epistle to the Galatians: A Commentary on the Greek Text* (Grand Rapids: Eerdmans, 1982), p. 187, who cites both the rabbinic sources for this threefold formula of superior social, racial and gender structure, as well as similar formulations in Greek literature.

[8]See Frank and Evelyn Stagg, *Women in the World of Jesus* (Philadelphia: Westminster Press, 1978); and Joachim Jeremias, *Jerusalem in the Time of Jesus: An Investigation into Economic and Social Conditions During the New Testament Period* (Philadelphia: Augsburg Fortress, 1979).

[9]Charles, *Pseudepigrapha*, vol. 2.

view about women in Judaism, which relegated them to subservient status in relation to men (husbands), reigned.

The commentaries by early church fathers on Genesis 1—3 clearly reflect traditional Jewish interpretations of these texts. Ephrem the Syrian (A.D. 306-373) seems to echo the view expressed in The Books of Adam and Eve when he states: "She [Eve] hastened to eat before her husband . . . that she might become the one to give command to that one by whom she was to be commanded." Irenaeus (A.D. 202-235) wrote: "As the human race was subjected to death through the act of a virgin, so was it saved by a virgin; thus the disobedience of the one virgin was precisely balanced by the obedience of another." (It is to be noted that several other church fathers contended that Adam and Eve had no sexual relations before the Fall. Thus Eve was considered a virgin before she was tempted.[10]) Commenting on Genesis 2:20, Augustine states that "he [Adam] rules and she [Eve] obeys. He is ruled by wisdom; she, by the man."[11]

In their reflections on New Testament passages regarding the relationship between men (husbands) and women (wives), the early church fathers often brought their understanding of Genesis 1—3 to bear, and in so doing, also revealed their indebtedness to the thinking of their Jewish forbears. For example, Ambrose of Milan (A.D. 333-397) states that "she who was made as a helper needs the protection of the stronger. . . . Yet, while he believed he would have the assistance of his wife, he fell because of her."[12] In reference to Genesis 2:23, Ambrosiaster (fourth century) says that "although man and woman are of the same substance, the man has relational priority. . . . He is greater than she is by cause and order, but not by substance."[13] Likewise, Theodoret of Cyr (A.D. 393-466) holds that "Man has first place because of the order of creation." In speaking of the significance of this primacy of man, he states that "the woman was created to serve [man], not the other way around."[14]

As reflected in their commentaries on the critical New Testament texts

---

[10]Andrew Louth, ed., *Genesis 1—11*, Ancient Christian Commentary on Scripture, Old Testament, vol. 1 (Downers Grove, Ill.: InterVarsity Press, 2001), p. 78.

[11]Ibid., p. 68.

[12]Gerald Bray, ed., *1-2 Corinthians*, Ancient Christian Commentary on Scripture, New Testament, vol. 7 (Downers Grove, Ill.: InterVarsity Press, 1999), p. 105.

[13]Ibid., p. 107.

[14]Ibid., p. 109.

(e.g., 1 Cor 7; Eph 5; 1 Tim 2), which are the basis for traditional Christian teaching about the subordinate roles of women and wives in male-female hierarchy, early Christian leaders largely read these texts in light of their understanding of the creation and Fall narratives in Genesis—and in keeping with both the Jewish interpretive tradition and the prevailing cultural norms. Like in Judaism, there were also contrary voices among the Greek fathers of the church, who heard those texts speak to them differently. Both traditional and contrary voices among them have been noted throughout this study where these New Testament texts are discussed.

APPENDIX C

When Augustine (early fifth century in North Africa) formulated the earliest "just-war" criteria, he was motivated by a strong desire to provide an alternative to the crusading spirit of his day, in which a high value was placed on using all means available to utterly destroy an enemy. Augustine was not looking for a way to "justify" the use of violence for political ends. Rather, he sought to reduce the amount of violence in the world.

Paul Ramsey, the noted American ethicist at the University of Chicago after World War II, described the just-war tradition as an explication of the *public implications* of the great commandment of "love for the neighbor," even as he argued that this commandment sets limits on the use of armed force.

Assumptions

1. It has its origin in a desire to place moral limits on what would otherwise be unbridled use of force and militarism.

2. There are circumstances in which the first, and most urgent, obligation in the face of evil is to stop it.

3. There are times when waging war is morally necessary to defend the innocent and to promote the minimum conditions of international order.

4. It maintains a clear distinction between "warring" and "dueling":

   a. warring is the use of force for public ends by public authorities who have an obligation to defend the security of their citizenry.

   b. dueling is the use of force for private ends by private individuals.

5. It views armed force as something that can be used for good or for evil, depending on who is using it, why, to what ends and how.

6. It seeks to provide "statecraft" (i.e., political policy and action) with a "moral compass," thereby helping governing authorities achieve the classical goals of politics: justice, freedom, order, general welfare and peace.

Principles

1. Is war the response of last resort when all other nonmilitary means of dealing with the adversary have been exhausted?

2. Is the war waged for a just cause?

3. Is it grounded in right intentions?

4. Is it waged by competent, constituted authority?

5. Is there a reasonable chance of success?

6. Is the use of force *proportional* and *discriminate,* and related to *morally worthy ends?*

APPENDIX D

LETTER TO PRESIDENT BUSH
FROM EVANGELICAL LEADERS

Published July 29, 2007
President George W. Bush
The White House
1600 Pennsylvania Ave. NW
Washington D.C., 20500

Dear Mr. President:
We write as evangelical Christian leaders in the United States to thank you
for your efforts (including the major address on July 16) to reinvigorate the
Israeli-Palestinian negotiations to achieve a lasting peace in the region. We
affirm your clear call for a two-state solution. We urge that your administration not grow weary in the time it has left in office to utilize the vast influence of America to demonstrate creative, consistent and determined U.S.
leadership to create a new future for Israelis and Palestinians. We pray to that
end, Mr. President.

We also write to correct a serious misperception among some people including some U.S. policymakers that all American evangelicals are opposed
to a two-state solution and creation of a new Palestinian state that includes
the vast majority of the West Bank. Nothing could be further from the truth.
We, who sign this letter, represent large numbers of evangelicals throughout
the U.S. who support justice for both Israelis and Palestinians. We hope this
support will embolden you and your administration to proceed confidently
and forthrightly in negotiations with both sides in the region.

As evangelical Christians, we embrace the biblical promise to Abraham: "I will bless those who bless you" (Genesis 12:3). And precisely as evangelical Christians committed to the full teaching of the Scriptures, we know that blessing and loving people (including Jews and the present State of Israel) does not mean withholding criticism when it is warranted. Genuine love and genuine blessing means acting in ways that promote the genuine and long-term well being of our neighbors. Perhaps the best way we can bless Israel is to encourage her to remember, as she deals with her neighbor Palestinians, the profound teaching on justice that the Hebrew prophets proclaimed so forcefully as an inestimably precious gift to the whole world.

Historical honesty compels us to recognize that both Israelis and Palestinians have legitimate rights stretching back for millennia to the lands of Israel/Palestine. Both Israelis and Palestinians have committed violence and injustice against each other. The only way to bring the tragic cycle of violence to an end is for Israelis and Palestinians to negotiate a just, lasting agreement that guarantees both sides viable, independent, secure states. To achieve that goal, both sides must give up some of their competing, incompatible claims. Israelis and Palestinians must both accept each other's right to exist. And to achieve that goal, the U.S. must provide robust leadership within the Quartet to reconstitute the Middle East roadmap, whose full implementation would guarantee the security of the State of Israel and the viability of a Palestinian State. We affirm the new role of former Prime Minister Tony Blair and pray that the conference you plan for this fall will be a success.

Mr. President, we renew our prayers and support for your leadership to help bring peace to Jerusalem, and justice and peace for all the people in the Holy Land.

Finally, we would request to meet with you to personally convey our support and discuss other ways in which we may help your administration on this crucial issue.

Sincerely,

Ronald J. Sider, President
Evangelicals for Social Action

Don Argue, President
Northwest University

Raymond J. Bakke, Chancellor

Bakke Graduate University

Gary M. Benedict, President
The Christian and Missionary Alliance

George K. Brushaber, President
Bethel University

Gary M. Burge, Professor
Wheaton College and Graduate School

Tony Campolo, President/Founder
Evangelical Association for the Promotion of Education

Christopher J. Doyle, CEO
American Leprosy Mission

Leighton Ford, President
Leighton Ford Ministries

Daniel Grothe, Pastoral Staff
New Life Church, Colorado Springs

Vernon Grounds, Chancellor
Denver Seminary

Stephen Hayner, former President
InterVarsity Christian Fellowship

Joel Hunter, Senior Pastor
Northland Church
Member, Executive Committee of the NAE

Jo Anne Lyon, Founder/CEO
World Hope International

Gordon MacDonald, Chair of the Board
World Relief

Albert G. Miller, Professor
Oberlin College

Richard Mouw, President
Fuller Theological Seminary

David Neff, Editor
Christianity Today

Glenn R. Palmberg, President
Evangelical Covenant Church

Earl Palmer, Senior Pastor
University Presbyterian Church, Seattle

Victor D. Pentz, Pastor
Peachtree Presbyterian Church, Atlanta

John Perkins, President
John M. Perkins Foundation for Reconciliation and Development

Bob Roberts Jr., Senior Pastor
Northwood Church, Dallas

Leonard Rogers, Executive Director
Evangelicals for Middle East Understanding

Andrew Ryskamp, Executive Director
Christian Reformed World Relief Committee

Chris Seiple, President
Institute for Global Engagement

Robert A. Seiple, Former Ambassador-at-Large,
International Religious Freedom
U.S. State Department

Luci N. Shaw, Author, Lecturer
Regent College, Vancouver

Jim Skillen, Executive Director
Center for Public Justice

Glen Harold Stassen, Professor
Fuller Theological Seminary

Richard Stearns, President
World Vision

Clyde D. Taylor, Former Chair of the Board
World Relief

Harold Vogelaar, Director
Center of Christian-Muslim Engagement for Peace and Justice

Berten Waggoner, National Director
Vineyard USA

APPENDIX E

This rendering of the text is based on the exegetical/theological work on this text that was done in chapters five and six.

²¹Give yourselves to one another in awe of Christ's self-giving.

²²Wives, give yourselves to your husbands in imitation of Christ's example. ²³Remember that in creation, man is the source of woman's life, just as the church, as Christ's body, receives its life from Christ, the source of her life. ²⁴Just as the church gives itself over to Christ's self-giving love, so also ought wives to give themselves totally to their husbands.

²⁵Husbands, love your wives just as Christ loved the church and gave himself up for her in self-giving, sacrificial love. ²⁶*[He did this to make the church holy by cleansing her with the washing of water by the word, ²⁷so as to present her to himself in splendor, without spot or wrinkle or anything of the kind—yes, so that the church may be holy and without blemish].*¹ ²⁸In the same way, husbands

---

¹I have placed verse 26 in brackets and italics to indicate that it represents a brief christological-soteriological expansion of the affirmation of Christ's self-giving in verse 25. It is inconceivable

should love their wives as they do themselves. He who loves his wife loves himself. [29]For no one ever hates his own body, but nourishes and tenderly cares for it, just as Christ nourishes and tenderly cares for the church, [30]because we belong to his body.

[31]This is why the Scripture says that "a man will leave his father and mother and be joined to his wife, and the two will become one flesh." [32]This is a great mystery, which is also true for the intimate relationship between Christ and the church.

[33]So husbands, just as you love yourselves, so give yourselves to your wives in serving love. And wives, when your husbands love you in that selfless way, they deserve your deepest respect.

---

for Paul to have thought that the husband's self-subordinating love for his wife does for the wife what Christ did for the church (including husbands and wives!), namely making his wife holy by purifying her. The only point of comparison is this: husbands are to love their wives in sacrificial, self-giving love, just as Christ loved and gave himself for the church.

BIBLIOGRAPHY

Achtemeier, Paul. *Romans*. Interpretation: A Bible Commentary for Teaching and Preaching. Atlanta: John Knox Press, 1985.

Alsdurf, James, and Phyllis Alsdurf. *Battered into Submission: The Tragedy of Wife Abuse in the Christian Home*. Downers Grove, Ill: InterVarsity Press, 1998.

Anderson, Ray S., and Dennis B. Guernsey. *On Being Family: A Social Theology of the Family*. Grand Rapids: Eerdmans, 1985.

Arias, Mortimer. *Announcing the Reign of God: Evangelism and the Subversive Memory of Jesus*. Lima, Ohio: Academic Renewal Press, 1984.

Arnold, Clinton. *Powers of Darkness: Principalities and Powers in the Letters of Paul*. Downers Grove, Ill.: InterVarsity Press, 1992.

Balswick, Judith K., and Jack O. Balswick. *Authentic Human Sexuality: An Integrated Approach*. Downers Grove, Ill.: InterVarsity Press, 1999.

Barrett, C. K. *The First Epistle to the Corinthians*. New York: Harper & Row 1968.

Bartchy, S. Scott. "Power, Submission and Sexual Identity Among the Early Christians." In *Essays on New Testament Christianity*, edited by C. R. Wetzel. Cincinnati: Standard Publishing, 1978.

Barth, Karl. *The Resurrection of the Dead*. London: Hodder & Stoughton, 1933.

Barth, Markus. *Ephesians 4—6*. Anchor Bible. New York: Doubleday, 1974.

Bartlett, David. "The Authority of Wisdom." In *The Shape of Scriptural Authority*. Philadelphia: Fortress, 1983.

Bauer, W., W. F. Arndt and F. W. Gingrich. *A Greek-English Lexicon of the New Testament and Other Early Christian Literature*. Chicago: University of Chicago Press, 1957.

Beasley-Murray, George R. *John*. Word Biblical Commentary 36. Waco, Tex.: Word Books, 1987.

Beckwith, Roger. *The Old Testament Canon of the New Testament Church.* Grand Rapids: Eerdmans, 1985.

Bedale, S. "The Meaning of κεφαλή in the Pauline Epistles." *Journal of Theological Studies* 5 (1954): 211-15.

Berkhof, Hendrik. *Christ and the Powers.* Scottdale, Penn.: Herald Press, 1977.

Bilezikian, Gilbert. *Beyond Sex Roles: What the Bible Says About a Woman's Place in Church and Family.* Grand Rapids: Baker, 1986.

Brauch, Manfred T. *Hard Sayings of Paul.* Downers Grove, Ill.: InterVarsity Press, 1989.

———. *Set Free to Be: A Study in Romans.* Valley Forge, Penn.: Judson Press, 1975.

Brauch, Manfred T., and Karen Onesti. "Righteousness, Righteousness of God." In *Dictionary of Paul and His Letters: A Compendium of Contemporary Biblical Scholarship,* edited by Gerald F. Hawthorne, Ralph P. Martin and Daniel G. Reid. Downers Grove, Ill.: InterVarsity Press, 1993.

Bray, Gerald, ed. *1-2 Corinthians.* Ancient Christian Commentary on Scripture, New Testament, vol. 7. Downers Grove, Ill.: InterVarsity Press, 1999.

Brown, F., G. R. Driver and C. R. Briggs. *A Hebrew and English Lexicon of the Old Testament.* Boston: Houghton Mifflin, 1906.

Brown, Raymond E. *101 Questions and Answers on the Bible.* New York: Paulist Press, 1990.

———. *Jesus, God and Man.* New York: Macmillan, 1967.

Bruce, F. F. *1 and 2 Corinthians.* New Century Bible. London: Oliphants, 1971.

———. *Apostle of the Heart Set Free.* Grand Rapids: Eerdmans, 1977.

———. *The Book of Acts.* The New London Commentary on the New Testament. London: Marshall, Morgan & Scott, 1954.

———. *The Canon of Scripture.* Downers Grove, Ill: InterVarsity Press, 1988.

———. *The Epistle to the Galatians.* A Commentary on the Greek Text. Grand Rapids: Eerdmans, 1982.

———. *The Epistle to the Hebrews.* New International Commentary on the New Testament. Grand Rapids: Eerdmans, 1964.

———. *The Epistles to the Colossians, to Philemon and to the Ephesians.* New International Commentary on the New Testament. Grand Rapids: Eerdmans, 1984.

Brueggemann, Walter. *Isaiah 1-30.* Westminster Bible Commentary. Louisville, Ky.: Westminster John Knox Press, 1998.

———. *In Man We Trust: The Neglected Side of Biblical Faith.* Louisville, Ky.: John Knox Press, 1983.

Buttry, Daniel. *Christian Peacemaking: From Heritage to Hope.* Valley Forge, Penn.: Judson Press, 1994.

Caird, G. B. *New Testament Theology,* completed and edited by L. D. Hurst. Oxford: Clarendon, 1994.

Charles, R. H., ed. *The Apocrypha and Pseudepigrapha of the Old Testament: The Apocrypha.* 1913; reprinted, Oxford: Clarendon, 1969.

Charlesworth, James H., ed. *Jews and Christians: Exploring the Past, Present and Future.* New York: Crossroad, 1990.

Chilton, Bruce D., trans. "The Isaiah Targum." In *The Aramaic Bible, Vol. II: The Targums.* Wilmington, Del.: Michael Glazier, 1987.

Clark, Elizabeth A. *Women in the Early Church.* Message of the Fathers of the Church. Wilmington, Del.: Michael Glazier, 1983.

Clementi, Carmine D. *Anatomy: A Regional Atlas of the Human Body.* Baltimore: Urban and Schwarzenburg, 1981.

Clouse, Robert G., and Bonidell Clouse, eds. *Women in Ministry: Four Views.* Downers Grove, Ill.: InterVarsity Press, 1989.

Copeland, Kenneth. *The Laws of Prosperity.* Newark, Tex.: Kenneth Copeland Publications, 1974.

Craigie, Peter C. *The Problem of War in the Old Testament.* Grand Rapids: Eerdmans, 1978.

Cullmann, Oscar. *Immortality of the Soul or Resurrection of the Dead? The Witness of the New Testament.* London: Epworth, 1958.

Curtis, K. "Women in the Early Church." *Christian History* 7, no. 1 (1988): 17.

Danby, H. *The Mishnah: Translated from the Hebrew with Introduction and Explanatory Notes.* London: Oxford University Press, 1933.

Danker, F. W. *A Greek-English Lexicon of the New Testament and Other Early Christian Literature.* 3rd ed. Chicago: University of Chicago Press, 2000.

Dayton, Donald W. *Discovering an Evangelical Heritage.* New York: Harper & Row, 1976.

Dunn, James D. G. *Baptism in the Holy Spirit.* London: SCM Press, 1970.

———. *Romans 1-8.* Word Biblical Commentary 38A. Waco, Tex.: Word Books, 1988.

———. *Romans 9-16.* Word Biblical Commentary 38B. Waco, Tex: Word Books, 1988.

———. *Unity and Diversity in the New Testament.* Philadelphia: Westminster Press, 1977.

Dyrness, William. *Themes in Old Testament Theology.* Downers Grove, Ill.: InterVarsity Press, 1979.

Edwards, Mark J. *Galatians, Ephesians, Philippians.* Ancient Christian Commentary on Scripture, New Testament, vol. 8. Downers Grove, Ill.: InterVarsity Press, 1999.

Eichrodt, Walther. *Old Testament Theology.* Vol. 1. Philadelphia: Westminster Press, 1961.

Enns, Peter. *Inspiration and Incarnation: Evangelicals and the Problem of the Old Testament*. Grand Rapids: Baker Academic, 2005.

Erickson, Millard J. *A Basic Guide to Eschatology: Making Sense of the Millennium*. Grand Rapids: Baker, 1998.

Evans, Craig A. *Luke*. New International Biblical Commentary. Peabody, Mass.: Hendrickson, 1990.

Fackre, Gabriel. *Word and Deed: Theological Themes in Evangelism*. Grand Rapids: Eerdmans, 1975.

Farmer, William R. *Jesus and the Gospel: Tradition, Scripture, and Canon*. Philadelphia: Fortress, 1982.

Fee, Gordon D. *The Disease of the Health and Wealth Gospels*. Vancouver, B.C.: Regent College Publishing, 1985.

—————. *The First Epistle to the Corinthians*. New International Commentary on the New Testament. Grand Rapids: Eerdmans, 1978.

—————. *Paul's Letter to the Philippians*. New International Commentary on the New Testament. Grand Rapids: Eerdmans, 1995.

Fee, Gordon D., and Douglas Stuart. *How to Read the Bible for All Its Worth: A Guide to Understanding the Bible*. 2nd ed. Grand Rapids: Zondervan, 1981.

France, R. T. *Women in the Church's Ministry: A Test Case for Biblical Interpretation*. Grand Rapids: Eerdmans, 1995.

Fuller, Daniel P. "Paul and Galatians 3:28." *TSF Bulletin* (November-December 1985): 9-13.

Gagnon, Robert J. *The Bible and Homosexual Practice: Texts and Hermeneutics*. Nashville: Abingdon, 2002.

Garland, Diane R., and David Garland. *Beyond Companionship: Christians in Marriage*. Philadelphia: Westminster Press, 1986.

Grenz, Stanley. *Welcoming but Not Affirming: An Evangelical Response to Homosexuality*. Louiseville, Ky.: Westminster John Knox Press, 1998.

Grudem, Wayne. "Does κεφαλη ('Head') Mean 'Source' or 'Authority Over' in Greek Literature? A Survey of 2336 Examples." *Trinity Journal* 6 (1985): 38-59.

—————. "Scripture's Self-Attestation and the Problem of Formulating a Doctrine of Scripture." In *Scripture and Truth*, edited by D. A. Carson and John D. Woodbridge. Grand Rapids: Zondervan, 1983.

Gundry, Patricia. *Women Be Free: The Clear Message of Scripture*. Grand Rapids: Zondervan, 1977.

Gundry, Robert H. *Matthew: A Commentary on His Literary and Theological Art*. Grand Rapids: Eerdmans, 1982.

—————. *Sōma in Biblical Theology with Emphasis on Pauline Anthropology*. Cambridge: Cambridge University Press, 1976.

Gushee, David P. *The Future of Faith in American Politics: The Public Witness of the Evangelical Center.* Waco, Tex.: Baylor University Press, 2008.

———, ed. *Toward a Just and Caring Society: Christian Responses to Poverty in America.* Grand Rapids: Baker Books, 1999.

Hagin, Kenneth. *Seven Things You Should Know About Divine Healing.* Tulsa, Okla.: Faith Library Publications, 1979.

Harrison, Everett. "The Phenomena of Scripture." In *Carl F. H. Henry, Revelation and the Bible.* Grand Rapids: Baker, 1958.

Hauerwas, Stanley. *The Peaceable Kingdom: A Primer in Christian Ethics.* 2nd rev. ed. London: SCM Press, 2003.

Hawthorne, Gerald F. *Philippians.* Word Biblical Commentary 43. Dallas: Word Books, 1983.

Hays, Richard B. *The Moral Vision of the New Testament: A Contemporary Approach to New Testament Ethics.* San Francisco: HarperSanFrancisco, 1996.

Hennecke, Edgar, Wilhelm Schneelmelcher and Robert McLachlan Wilson. *New Testament Apocrypha.* London: Lutterworth, 1963.

Henry, Carl F. H. *A Plea for Evangelical Demonstration.* Grand Rapids: Eerdmans, 1971.

———. *The Uneasy Conscience of Modern Fundamentalism.* Grand Rapids: Eerdmans, 1947.

Hill, Alexander. *Just Business: Christian Ethics for the Marketplace.* Downers Grove, Ill.: InterVarsity Press, 2008.

Holben, L. R. *What Christians Think About Homosexuality: Six Representative Views.* North Richland Hills, Tex.: Bibal Press, 1999.

Hubbard, David. "The Current Tensions: Is There a Way Out?" In *Biblical Authority,* edited by J. Rogers. Dallas: Word Books, 1977.

Jeremias, Joachim. *Jerusalem in the Time of Jesus: An Investigation into Economic and Social Conditions During the New Testament Period.* Philadelphia: Augsburg Fortress, 1979.

Jewett, Robert. *Paul's Anthropological Terms.* Leiden: E. J. Brill, 1971.

Jones, David C. *Biblical Christian Ethics.* Grand Rapids: Baker Academic, 1994.

Kaiser, Walter. *Toward an Old Testament Theology.* Grand Rapids: Zondervan, 1978.

Keener, Craig S. *A Commentary on the Gospel of Matthew.* Grand Rapids: Eerdmans, 1999.

———. *The IVP Bible Background Commentary: New Testament.* Downers Grove, Ill.: InterVarsity Press, 1993.

———. *Paul, Women and Wives: Marriage and Women's Ministry in the Letters of Paul.* Peabody, Mass.: Hendrickson, 1992.

————. *Revelation.* NIV Application Commentary. Grand Rapids: Zondervan, 2000.

Kelly, J. N. D. *A Commentary on the Pastoral Epistles.* New York: Harper & Row, 1964.

————. *Early Christian Doctrines.* San Francisco: Harper & Row, 1978.

Kinnaman, David, and Gabe Lyons. *Unchristian: What a New Generation Really Thinks About Christianity . . . and Why It Matters.* Grand Rapids: Baker Books, 2007.

Köstenberger, Andreas, ed. *Whatever Happened to Truth?* Wheaton, Ill.: Crossway, 2005.

Kraus, Hans-Joachim. *Worship in Israel: A Cultic History of the Old Testament.* Richmond, Va.: John Knox Press, 1966.

Kraybill, Donald B. *The Upside-Down Kingdom.* Scottdale, Penn.: Herald Press, 1978.

Kroeger, Catherine C. "The Classical Concept of 'Head' as 'Source.'" In *Equal to Serve: Women and Men in the Church and Home,* edited by Gretchen Gaebelein Hull. Old Tappan, N.J.: Fleming H. Revell, 1987.

Kümmel, Werner G. *Man in the New Testament.* London: Epworth, 1963.

La Sor, William S., David Allan Hubbard, and Frederic W. Bush. *Old Testament Survey: The Message, Form and Background of the Old Testament.* 2nd ed. Grand Rapids: Eerdmans, 1996.

Ladd, George Eldon. *A Theology of the New Testament.* Rev. ed. Grand Rapids: Eerdmans, 1993.

Lampe, G. W. *A Patristic Greek Lexicon.* London: Oxford University Press, 1968.

Larkin, William J., Jr. *Acts.* IVP New Testament Commentary. Downers Grove, Ill.: InterVarsity Press, 1995.

Leith, John H., ed. *Creeds of the Churches: A Reader in Christian Doctrine from the Bible to the Present.* Rev. ed. Richmond, Va.: John Knox Press, 1973.

Liddell, Henry G., and Robert Scott. *Greek-English Lexicon.* New York: American Book Company, 1897.

————, comp. *A Greek-English Lexicon.* Revised and augmented by Sir Henry Stuart Jones and Roderick McKenzie. New York: Oxford University Press, 1996.

Lohmeyer, Ernst. *Kyrios Jesus.* Heidelberg: Carl Winter, 1928.

Louth, Andrew, ed. *Genesis1-11.* Ancient Christian Commentary on Scripture, Old Testament, vol. 1. Downers Grove, Ill.: InterVarsity Press, 2001.

Lucado, Max. *Grace for the Moment.* Nashville: Thomas Nelson, 2000.

Maahs, Kenneth H. *Of Angels, Beasts and Plagues: The Message of Revelation for a New Millennium.* Valley Forge, Penn.: Judson Press, 1999.

MacGregor, G. H. C., and Andrew C. Purdy. *Jew and Greek: Tutors unto Christ.* New York: Charles Scribner's, 1936.

Marsden, George M. *Fundamentalism and American Culture: The Shaping of Twentieth-Century Evangelicalism, 1870-1925.* New York: Oxford University Press, 1980.

Marshall, I. Howard. *Biblical Inspiration.* Grand Rapids: Eerdmans, 1982.

———. *The Gospel of Luke: A Commentary on the Greek Text.* New International Greek Testament and Commentary. Grand Rapids: Eerdmans, 1978.

Martin, Ralph P. *Carmen Christi: Philippians 2:5-11 in Recent Interpretation and in the Setting of Early Christian Worship.* Cambridge: Cambridge University Press, 1967.

May, Rollo. *Power and Innocence: A Search for the Sources of Violence.* Scranton, Penn.: W. W. Norton, 1972.

McConnell, Dan R. *A Different Gospel.* Peabody, Mass.: Hendrickson, 1995.

McMillan, Samuel I. *None of These Diseases.* Old Tappan, N.J.: Fleming H. Revell, 1979.

McQuilkin, Robertson. *An Introduction to Biblical Ethics.* 2nd ed. Wheaton, Ill.: Tyndale House, 1995.

Megoran, Nick Solly. *The War on Terror: How Should Christians Respond?* Downers Grove, Ill.: InterVarsity Press, 2007.

Metzger, Bruce M. *A Textual Commentary on the Greek New Testament.* New York: United Bible Societies, 1971.

Michaels, J. Ramsey. *1 Peter.* Word Biblical Commentary 49. Waco, Tex.: Word Books, 1988.

Mickelsen, Berkeley, and Alvera. "What Does *Kephalē* Mean in the New Testament?" In *Women, Authority and the Bible,* edited by Alvera Mickelsen. Downers Grove, Ill.: InterVarsity Press, 1986.

Moberg, David O. *Wholistic Christianity.* Elgin, Ill.: Brethren Press, 1985.

Morris, Leon. *Galatians: Paul's Charter of Christian Freedom.* Downers Grove, Ill.: InterVarsity Press, 1996.

———. *I Believe in Revelation.* Grand Rapids: Eerdmans, 1976.

Mott, Stephen C. *Biblical Ethics and Social Change.* New York: Oxford University Press, 1982.

Moule, C. F. D. "Paul and Dualism: The Pauline Conception of Resurrection." In *Essays in New Testament Interpretation.* Cambridge: Cambridge University Press, 1982.

Mounce, Robert H. *The Book of Revelation.* Rev. ed. New International Commentary on the New Testament. Grand Rapids: Eerdmans, 1998.

Mouw, Richard. *Politics and the Biblical Drama.* Grand Rapids: Eerdmans, 1976.

Murphy, Roland. "The Interpretation of Old Testament Wisdom Literature." *Interpretation* 23 (1969): 289-301.

Murphy-O'Connor, J. *1 Corinthians.* The New Testament Message. Wilmington, Del.: Michael Glazier, 1979.

———. "Sex and Logic in I Corinthians 11:2-16." *Catholic Biblical Quarterly* 42 (1980): 482-500.

O'Brien, Peter T. *Colossians, Philemon.* Word Biblical Commentary 44. Waco, Tex.: Word Books, 1982.

Olson, Roger E. *The Mosaic of Christian Belief: Twenty Centuries of Unity and Diversity.* Downers Grove, Ill.: InterVarsity Press, 2002.

Orr, James. *Revelation and Inspiration.* Grand Rapids: Eerdmans, 1952.

Oswalt, John. *The Book of Isaiah: Chapters 1-39.* Grand Rapids: Eerdmans, 1986.

Packer, J. I. *"Fundamentalism" and the Word of God.* London: Inter-Varsity Fellowship, 1958.

———. *God Has Spoken.* London: Hodder and Staughton, 1985.

Pagelow, Mildred. *Woman-Battering: Victims and Their Experiences.* Thousand Oaks, Calif.: Sage, 1981.

Rad, Gerhard von. *Wisdom in Israel.* Nashville: Abingdon, 1972.

Ramm, Bernard. *Special Revelation and the Word of God.* Grand Rapids: Eerdmans, 1961.

Rauschenbusch, Walter. *A Theology of the Social Gospel.* New York: Macmillan, 1922.

Ridderbos, Hans N. *Paul: An Outline of His Theology.* Grand Rapids: Eerdmans, 1975.

———. *Studies in Scripture and Its Authority.* Grand Rapids: Eerdmans, 1978.

Robinson, H. Wheeler. *Corporate Personality in Ancient Israel.* Philadelphia: Fortress, 1973.

Rogers, Jack B., and Donald K. McKim. *Authority and Interpretation.* New York: Harper & Row, 1979.

Rogers, Jack B., ed. *Biblical Authority.* Dallas: Word Publishers, 1977.

Rutenber, Culbert. *The Reconciling Gospel.* Valley Forge, Penn.: Judson Press, 1960.

Samuel, Vinay, and Chris Sugden, eds. *The Church in Response to Human Need.* Grand Rapids: Eerdmans, 1987.

Sanders, E.P. *Paul and Palestinian Judaism.* Philadelphia: Fortress, 1977.

Schaeffer, Francis A. *Pollution and the Death of Man: The Christian View of Ecology.* Wheaton, Ill.: Tyndale House, 1970.

Schechter, Solomon. *Aspects of Rabbinic Theology.* New York: Schocken, 1961.

Schlier, Heinrich. "κεφαλή, ἀνακεφαλαιόομαι." In *Theological Dictionary of the New Testament,* 3:673-82. Edited by Gerhard Kittel. Grand Rapids: Eerdmans, 1965.

———. *Principalities and Powers in the New Testament.* Freiburg: Herder, 1961.

Schmidt, Thomas E. *Straight and Narrow? Compassion and Clarity in the Homosexuality Debate.* Downers Grove, Ill.: InterVarsity Press, 1995.

Scholer, David. "1 Timothy 2:9-15 and the Place of Women in the Church's Ministry." In *Women, Authority and the Bible,* edited by Alvera Mickelsen. Downers Grove, Ill.: InterVarsity Press, 1986.

Scorgie, Glen. *The Journey Back to Eden: Restoring the Creator's Design for Women and Men.* Grand Rapids: Zondervan, 2005.

Scott, R. B. Y. *The Way of Wisdom.* New York: Macmillan, 1971.

Sider, Ronald J. *Christ and Violence.* Scottdale, Penn.: Herald Press, 1979.

———. *Completely Pro-Life: Building a Consistent Stance.* Downers Grove, Ill.: InterVarsity Press, 1987.

———. *Cup of Water, Bread of Life.* Grand Rapids: Zondervan, 1994.

———. *Good News and Good Works: A Theology for the Whole Gospel.* Grand Rapids: Baker Books, 1999.

———. *Just Generosity: A New Vision for Overcoming Poverty in America.* Grand Rapids: Baker Books, 1999.

———. *One-Sided Christianity? Uniting the Church to Heal a Lost and Broken World.* Grand Rapids: Zondervan, 1993.

———. "The Religious Right Has Lost the Evangelical Center." *Prism* 14, no. 4 (2007): 40.

———. *Rich Christians in an Age of Hunger: Moving from Affluence to Generosity.* Dallas: Word Publishing, 1997.

———. *The Scandal of the Evangelical Conscience: Why Are Christians Living Just Like the Rest of the World?* Grand Rapids: Baker Books, 2005.

Sine, Tom. "Celebrating the Demise of America's Culture Wars." *Prism* 14, no. 4 (2007): 4-5.

Smart, James. *The Inspiration of Scripture.* Philadelphia: Westminster Press, 1961.

Smedes, Lewis B. *Mere Morality: What God Expects from Ordinary People.* Grand Rapids: Eerdmans, 1987.

Smith, Timothy L. *Revivalism and Social Reform in Mid-Nineteenth Century America.* New York, Abingdon, 1957.

Spencer, Aída Besançon *Beyond the Curse: Women Called to Ministry.* Peabody, Mass.: Hendrickson, 1989.

Stacey, W. D. *The Pauline View of Man in Relation to Its Judaic and Hellenistic Background.* London: Macmillan, 1956.

Stagg, Frank, and Evelyn. *Women in the World of Jesus.* Philadelphia: Westminster Press, 1978.

Stassen, Glen H., and David P. Gushee. *Kingdom Ethics: Following Jesus in Contemporary Context.* Downers Grove, Ill.: InterVarsity Press, 2003.

Stuhlmacher, Peter. *Paul's Letter to the Romans: A Commentary.* Louisville, Ky.: Westminster John Knox Press, 1994.

Swartley, Willard M. *Homosexuality: Biblical Interpretation and Moral Discernment.* Scottdale, Penn.: Herald Press, 2003.

————. *Slaves, Sabbath, War and Women: Case Studies in Biblical Interpretation.* Scottdale, Penn.: Herald Press, 1983.

Terrien, Samuel. *Till the Heart Sings: A Biblical Theology of Manhood and Womanhood.* Philadelphia: Fortress, 1985.

Thielicke, Helmut. *How the World Began: Man in the First Chapters of the Bible.* Philadelphia: Muhlenberg Press, 1961.

Thielmann, Frank. *Paul and the Law: A Contextual Approach.* Downers Grove, Ill.: InterVarsity Press, 1994.

Tiede, D. L. *Luke.* Augsburg Commentary on the New Testament. Minneapolis: Augsburg, 1988.

Tower, Wayne S. "The Renewed Authority of Old Testament Wisdom for Contemporary Faith." In *Canon and Authority,* edited by George W. Coats and Burke O. Long. Philadelphia: Fortress, 1977.

Van Biema, David. "Does God Want You to be Rich?" *Time,* September 2006.

Van der Kooij, Arie. "The Old Greek of Isaiah 19:16-25: Translation and Interpretation." In *LXX: VI Congress of the International Organization for Septuagint and Other Cognate Studies, Jerusalem 1986,* edited by C. E. Cox. Missoula, Mont.: Scholars Press, 1987.

Van Leuwen, Mary Stewart. *Gender and Grace.* Downers Grove, Ill.: InterVarsity Press, 1990.

VanDyke, Fred, David C. Mahan, Josepg K. Sheldon and Raymond H. Brand. *Redeeming Creation: The Biblical Basis for Environmental Stewardship.* Downers Grove, Ill.: InterVarsity Press, 1996.

VanGemeren, Willem A., ed. *New International Dictionary of Old Testament Theology and Exegesis,* vol 1. Grand Rapids: Zondervan, 1997.

Volf, Miroslav. *Exclusion and Embrace: A Theological Exploration of Identity, Otherness and Reconciliation.* Nashville: Abingdon, 1966.

Wall, Robert W. "The Acts of the Apostles." In *The New Interpreter's Bible,* Vol. 10. Nashville: Abingdon, 2002.

Wallis, Jim. *Agenda for Biblical People.* New York: Harper, 1976.

————. *Faith Works: How to Live Your Beliefs and Ignite Positive Social Change.* New York: Random House, 2005.

————. *God's Politics: Why the Right Gets It Wrong and the Left Doesn't Get It.* San Francisco: HarperSanFrancisco, 2005.

Watts, John D. *Isaiah 1-33.* Word Biblical Commentary 24. Waco, Tex.: Word Books, 1985.

Webb, William J. *Slaves, Women and Homosexuals: Exploring the Hermeneutics of*

Cultural Analysis. Downers Grove, Ill.: InterVarsity Press, 2001.

Wells, David F. *No Place for Truth, or, Whatever Happened to Evangelical Theology?* Grand Rapids: Eerdmans, 1993.

Wolterstorff, Nicholas. *Until Justice and Peace Embrace.* Grand Rapids: Eerdmans, 1983.

Work, Telford. *Living and Active: Scripture in the Economy of Salvation.* Grand Rapids: Eerdmans, 2002.

Wright, G. Ernest. *The Old Testament Against Its Environment.* Studies in Biblical Theology 2. London: SCM Press, 1957.

Wright, N. T. *The Last Word: Scripture and the Authority of God—Getting Beyond the Bible Wars.* San Francisco: HarperSanFrancisco, 2005.

————. "The Letter to the Romans." In *The New Interpreter's Bible*, Vol. 10. Nashville: Abingdon, 2002.

Yoder, Howard. *The Politics of Jesus.* Grand Rapids: Eerdmans, 1972.

Scripture Index